Sex and Gender

SECOND EDITION

Sex and Gender is a substantially revised edition of a classic text. Adopting a balanced and straightforward approach to the often controversial study of sex differences, the authors aim to introduce the reader to the fundamental questions relating to sex and gender in an accessible way, at the same time as drawing on the very latest research in this and related areas. New developments which are explored in this edition include the rise of evolutionary psychology and the influence of social role theory, as well as new psychoanalytic and ethnomethodological approaches which have all contributed to a greater understanding of the complex nature of masculinity and femininity.

John Archer is Professor of Psychology at the University of Central Lancashire, Preston, UK. His research interests are aggression, violence, sex and gender, and grief. He is the author of a number of books, including *The Nature of Grief* (1999), *Ethology and Human Development* (1992) and *The Behavioural Biology of Aggression* (1988). He is a Fellow of the British Psychological Society and President-Elect of the International Society for Research on Aggression.

Barbara Lloyd is a Senior Research Fellow in the School of Social Sciences at the University of Sussex where she was previously Reader in Social Psychology. She has an active psychoanalytic psychotherapy practice and was a founding member and Chair of the Brighton Association of Analytic Psychotherapists. Barbara is the author of a number of books, including *Social Representations and the Development of Knowledge* (1990) and *Gender Identities and Education: The Impact of Starting School* (1992) with Gerard Duveen. Recently she and Kevin Lucas published *Smoking in Adolescence: Images and Identities* (1998) which describes her current research. She is a Fellow of the British Psychological Society and a Full Member of the British Association of Psychotherapists.

Sex and Gender

SECOND EDITION

JOHN ARCHER

BARBARA LLOYD

CAMBRIDGE
UNIVERSITY PRESS

PUBLISHED BY THE PRESS SYNDICATE OF THE UNIVERSITY OF CAMBRIDGE
The Pitt Building, Trumpington Street, Cambridge, United Kingdom

CAMBRIDGE UNIVERSITY PRESS
The Edinburgh Building, Cambridge CB2 2RU, UK
40 West 20th Street, New York, NY 10011-4211, USA
477 Williamstown Road, Port Melbourne, VIC 3207, Australia
Ruiz de Alarcón 13, 28014 Madrid, Spain
Dock House, The Waterfront, Cape Town 8001, South Africa

http://www.cambridge.org

First published by Penguin Books in 1982
Revised edition published by Cambridge University Press 1985
Second edition published by Cambridge University Press 2002

Printed in the United Kingdom at the University Press, Cambridge

Typefaces Times 10/13 pt and Formata   *System* LaTeX 2_ε [TB]

A catalogue record for this book is available from the British Library

Library of Congress Cataloguing in Publication data

Archer, John, 1944–   .
Sex and Gender / John Archer and Barbara Lloyd. – 2nd edn.
   p.   cm.
Includes bibliographical references and index.
ISBN 0 521 63230 7 (hardback) – ISBN 0 521 63533 0 (paperback)
1. Sex differences (Psychology)   2. Sex differences.   3. Sex role.
I. Lloyd, Barbara, 1933–   II. Title.
BF692.2 .A72   2002
155.3'3 – dc21   2001052482

ISBN 0 521 63230 7 hardback
ISBN 0 521 63533 0 paperback

Contents

Figures

Tables

Preface

This new edition of *Sex and Gender* builds upon an intellectual collaboration that began a quarter of a century ago. We have seen major changes in the area described as sex differences. The pace of change has been particularly rapid in the past seventeen years since our 1985 American edition of the original 1982 book and has prompted us to radically revise our earlier texts.

Piecemeal, almost opportunistic research on sex differences has given way to theoretically driven studies summarised through the use of coherent statistical models. Perhaps the most striking change is the influence of evolutionary psychology. It has gained many adherents but does not hold complete sway. In seeking to be heard, social scientists of other persuasions have sharpened their arguments. Social role theory has become a serious contender, while a variety of psychoanalytic accounts and ethnomethodological approaches have contributed to a deeper understanding of the nature of masculinity and femininity. We hope that this volume goes some way to produce clarity in a complex and changing field.

Readers of the earlier work will recognise the familiar structure of ten chapters. The first sets the scene. Each of the eight that follows focuses on a broad theme: stereotypes, origins, developmental influences, sexuality, aggression–violence–power, fear–anxiety–mental health, the domestic sphere, and, finally, work–education and occupational achievement. In chapter 10 we consider changes and suggest the direction studies of sex differences may take in the future.

This new edition has been some time in the making and we wish to thank the individuals who helped us along the way. Catherine Max originally encouraged us to consider a new edition and Sarah Caro, at Cambridge University Press, has seen the project to fruition. A number of academic colleagues have contributed valuable advice both in reading chapters and in offering us their to-be-published material. They include Anne Campbell, Michelle Davies, Niki Graham-Kevan, David Hitchin, Barbara Krahé, Kevin Lucas, Felicio Pratto, and John E. Williams. We are particularly grateful to Alice Eagly who read the complete manuscript and provided many thoughtful comments. Once again special thanks are due to Peter Lloyd.

1 Commonsense beliefs and psychological research strategies

Commonsense beliefs

Everyone has ideas about the nature of men and women and knows in a commonsense way what they are like. For most people throughout most of human history that was the whole story. Beliefs handed down through the generations provided a way of understanding first-hand experience so that the nature of men and women, and their place in wider society, became matters that were taken for granted. Today, those of us who live in liberal Western nations have become used to traditional beliefs about the natures of men and women being contested. No longer is there an unquestioned consensus about what is the natural order regarding women and men.

Nevertheless, many of our current commonsense beliefs derive from a time before public consciousness was challenged by modern feminist thinking. Admittedly, obviously sexist statements are easier to locate before this time, when they were more or less taken for granted by everyone. Such statements reflect a limited number of general principles about men and women.

The first principle is that women and men are fundamentally different. Consider the following lines from *A Hymn to Him* in *My Fair Lady* (© 1962 A. J. Lerner and F. Loewe), the musical version of Bernard Shaw's *Pygmalion*. The context is that Henry Higgins is puzzled because, after achieving a social triumph at the ball, Eliza Doolittle has disappeared. Henry laments about the nature of women:

> Women are irrational, that's all there is to that!
> Their heads are full of cotton, hay and rags!
> They're nothing but exasperating, irritating, vacillating, calculating,
> agitating, maddening and infuriating hags!
> Why can't a woman be more like a man?
> Men are so honest, so thoroughly square;
> Eternally noble, historically fair;
> Who, when you win, will always give your back a pat!
> Why can't a woman be like that?

Such comparisons as this deliberately ignore our common humanity in favour of doggedly pursuing the differences between women and men. They are generalisations emphasising the fundamental difference between the sexes. Lest this be seen as of no relevance to today's world, since it is admittedly old-fashioned, there are many examples of more contemporary discourses that echo the same principle. In David Lynch's early 1990s cult TV series, *Twin Peaks*, Agent Cooper remarked: 'In the grand design, women were drawn from a different set of blueprints.'

The second principle is that men are superior and women their inferiors. Henry Higgins is sure of this. These lines leave us in no doubt that women are not a patch on men. He contrasts women's emotionality with men's steadfastness. In other verses he comments adversely on women's intelligence, conformity, vanity, and sensitivity to slights. The reader may think that this is just one man's outmoded opinion of the opposite sex when one of them has upset his plans. Nevertheless, with the exception of some feminist writing, it is difficult to find comparisons which err in the opposite direction by presenting women in overwhelmingly positive light with regard to characteristics that are seen to matter in the world. Higgins' view is commonly found in writings from previous centuries where it is often given a religious backing. In Genesis for instance woman is presented as an afterthought, made with man in mind. As Tennyson wrote: 'God made the woman for the man.'

One paradoxical aspect of the belief that women are inferior is that they are often seen as nicer, more morally upright, human beings. This is reflected in modern studies of attitudes towards women and men described in chapter 2, and nursery rhymes such as little girls being made of 'sugar and spice and all things nice'. It is also reflected in contemporary discourse about masculinity, which excuses the thoughtless behaviour of young men in terms of the cult of laddishness, portrayed as entertainment in the British 1990s TV series *Men Behaving Badly*. In many ways, the distinction between men being effective in the world but not necessarily nice and considerate, and women being ineffective but nicer people, follows a distinction that lies at the heart of gender stereotypes (chapter 2), the attributes people ascribe to the two sexes. This distinction has been described as agency (or instrumentality) versus communion (or expressiveness). The first involves action in the world, which is seen as the province of men, and the second as nurturance and caring about other people, which is seen as the province of women.

A third principle reflected in Henry Higgins' lines is that women are seen as illogical and irrational. This is viewed as the negative side of being nurturant and caring about people, in that it involves being swept away by emotion. Men by contrast are viewed as being sensible and level-headed and therefore not so prone to be swept away by their emotions. One influential contemporary commonsense belief is that women's supposed emotional lability is the result of hormonal changes associated with reproductive events, such as menstruation, pregnancy, childbirth, and the menopause. Paralleling this belief is a strand of medical thinking which has sought to link mood changes among women to the hormonal changes underlying reproductive events. Research evidence does not support these commonsense generalisations, as we show in chapter 7. An interesting modern theme in media reports about young men is a tendency to attribute some of their inconsiderate and anti-social behaviour to high levels of the male hormone testosterone. Again, the research evidence (chapter 6) provides a more complex picture.

The view that women are emotional and men stoic conveniently omits the emotion of anger, which, although little different in the two sexes in terms of its ease of arousal, leads to far more damaging consequences when experienced by men (chapter 6). The situation of a trivial dispute which escalates into violence out of all proportion to the original incident is one that is depressingly common in the pages of our newspapers, and almost always involves two men, who are certainly not behaving rationally.

Commonsense beliefs about men and women are not arbitrary. They are associated with coherent ways of understanding the world in which we live, which for many centuries have been presented to each succeeding generation in the form of religious truths. From Charles Darwin's time onwards, science has replaced religion in providing a credible account of human origins, and of the impact of physical events on behaviour. In the Western world, commonsense beliefs have come to be derived from science rather than religious sources in media-led discussions of issues such as the attributes of men and women. As the previous example of hormones and the emotions shows, scientific findings have not necessarily been portrayed accurately in such discussions.

One common theme that can be found in traditional commonsense beliefs about the nature of women's and men's characteristics is that they stem from the societal roles the two sexes occupy, and that these in turn are based on their roles in reproduction. For example, women are seen as more caring and nurturant because they are the ones who bear and suckle the infants. Because men are freed from this constraint, their role is as protectors and providers for wives and children. Men therefore have both physical characteristics such as greater musculature, and mental ones such as greater aggression and striving for status in competition with other men.

Until recently, there was little need to seek explanations for beliefs about the different natures of men and women. In the Judaeo-Christian tradition, God created woman as the helpmate of man but not his equal. This was the natural order of things, and it is one that can be found in the teachings of other major religions. In modern secular states, as we have indicated, biological research and theories have been used to support the same supposed natural order. Biological knowledge was used to counter some of the claims of the first wave of modern feminist writings in the late 1960s and early 1970s (Archer and Lloyd, 1985). Similar views can be found in newspaper columns in the late 1990s, as this extract from a polemical column by Richard Ingrams in the London newspaper *The Observer* illustrates:

> It is an indisputable fact about good music that almost all of it has been written by men. If you made a list of the top 50 composers – of popular as well as classical music – there would not be a single female name on the list. This has nothing to do with male subordination of women or anything like that. It is something to do with chromosomes or genes and nothing can be done to alter it. (Ingrams, 1999)

Ingrams goes on to castigate the British Arts Council for awarding £30k to an organisation that campaigns against the imbalance between the sexes in music by encouraging female musicians. These aims reflect a different and very widespread view about the causes of the psychological attributes of men and women, one that emphasises the social environment.

This view has also been applied to physical sex differences, in that boys and men have traditionally been encouraged to take part in sports and body-building activities whereas girls and women were restricted to less demanding physical pursuits (Lowe, 1982). From the modern perspective of women running marathons, engaging in kick-boxing, and playing soccer, we may forget that women were excluded from most sports during the first half of the twentieth century (Cashmore, 1999). This exclusion arose from assumptions held about women's bodies, in the form of commonsense beliefs which received emphatic backing from medical opinion of the time. One example is middle- and long-distance running, which were regarded as too exhausting and dangerous for women until comparatively recently. Another is the case of women's soccer in the UK. In 1917, a successful team (The Dick Kerr Ladies Football Club) was formed in Preston, Lancashire, playing teams from all over the country over the next four years, in famous stadiums and in front of crowds in the tens of thousands (Newsham, 1994). By 1921, there was a growing lobby against women's football, enlisting the support of medical practitioners, whose 'expert' opinion was that soccer was a dangerous pursuit for women. The British Football Association announced at the end of 1921 that soccer was unsuitable for women and should be discouraged. This they did by requesting clubs belonging to the association to refuse use of their grounds to women's teams. Cashmore (1999) argued that medical opinion that women's bodies were unsuitable for engaging in sports and athletics arose from a view of the human body, prevalent in medical texts over the last 300 years,[1] that emphasises sex differences at the expense of common features. Later in this section, we return to the issue of emphasising differences between men and women rather than their common humanity in relation to psychological differences.

The process whereby social values are transmitted to the next generation is colloquially known as conditioning (a different usage from that in psychology, where the term denotes the technical procedures first outlined by Pavlov). When it involves a narrow agenda concentrating on a specific set of values, the term indoctrination is used to denote disapproval. According to the conditioning view, sex differences in temperament and ability are seen in terms of societal pressures that have in most societies resulted in women's subservience and underachievement. They are the consequence of patriarchal values being learned by each succeeding generation as a result of men being in positions of power and influence in all human societies. Men's power is not viewed as God-given or the inevitable consequence of the biological roles of men and women. This view of the potential malleability of men and women is similar to that associated with feminist writers who emphasise the potential for similarity in men and women ('liberal feminists' or 'liberal equity feminists'), and it has had a widespread general influence on educated opinion in Western Europe and North America.

---

[1] A more accurate reading of Laqueur (chapter 5) would place this at 200 years.

In the first wave of public debates about the role of women that followed feminist writings of the 1960s and 1970s, the contrasting views of sex differences as arising from conditioning or from the natural order were associated with different opinions about the desirability – and the ease – of change. To believe that men's and women's temperament and abilities were different as a result of patriarchal conditioning meant that they could be amenable to change through a different non-patriarchal upbringing. This view focused on the conventional upbringing of boys and girls that thrust dolls into girls' arms and encouraged competitiveness in boys from an early age (chapter 4). The challenge was to devise a way of bringing up children that avoided this overt indoctrination into patriarchal values. This egalitarian view of men and women emphasised the inequity of current social arrangements, and sought to rectify it through social change, in the form of non-sexist rearing of children, egalitarian education, and also legislation that challenged patriarchal practices.

The view of the malleability of men's and women's nature produced counter-arguments from those who believed in the natural order and saw attempts to change existing arrangements as potentially disastrous. One bastion of conservative thinking about gender, the prolific romantic novelist Barbara Cartland, put it thus: 'All this striving and clawing into a man's world will eventually end in tears.' The implication here is that, since it is not natural for women to compete in a man's world, for them to try to do so will be so against the natural order of things that it will lead to personal unhappiness and non-fulfilment.

An interesting parallel to the conservative viewpoint that emphasises differences between men and women are two strands of feminist opinion. Cultural feminism (Henley et al., 1998) emphasises the undesirability of male characteristics and the positive nature of women's values, and is similar to psychological accounts that emphasise the different values of men and women (e.g., Gilligan, 1982). Radical feminism (Beasley, 1999; Henley et al., 1998) views the oppression of women as the most deep-rooted, widespread, and fundamental form of oppression of any social group. Although there is generally a reluctance by most feminist writers to seek the origins of these differences in biology, some of the arguments parallel those derived from modern evolutionary thinking (Wright, 1996).

A related issue that has been debated among feminist psychologists is whether we should be looking for differences between the sexes or whether we should be emphasising the overlap in many psychological characteristics, i.e. our common humanity. Feminist psychologists who have studied sex differences in social behaviour, notably Eagly (1987, 1995a), and those who have studied such undesirable male features as violence towards their sexual partners and rape, such as Koss et al. (1987), and Walker (1989) have – for different reasons – defended the strategy of looking for differences between men and women. Others have viewed the emphasis on differences as turning attention from what women and men have in common. This division loosely follows a fundamental split between liberal and radical feminists (Beasley, 1999; Henley et al., 1998), between those who emphasise equality (the assimilationists), and those committed to more fundamental social change, including the assertion of women-associated values (integrative or transformative feminists: Miles, 1996).

Commonsense influences on psychological research

Scientific research and commonsense beliefs

Unlike many other belief systems, such as those in the religious or political sphere, scientific research does not (or should not) involve a set of dogmas, but instead provides a way of deciding between competing explanations of the natural world. It therefore seeks to be objective, open, public, and accountable. Yet, at the same time, science is an enterprise as located in society as any other, and is therefore subject to political and religious pressures. There are many well-known examples of this, from religious opposition to the ideas of Galileo, to the suppression of Mendelian genetics in the Soviet Union.

These examples involve obvious and overt pressures on the development of scientific knowledge. It is only fairly recently that women have made up more than a tiny minority of those researching in the human sciences. In many ways, the development of the various disciplines within this umbrella term was constrained by masculine viewpoints and interests. Topics such as animal sexuality and aggression, both of interest to human psychologists, were researched from a viewpoint that tended to neglect the part played by females. Accounts of human evolution neglected the female side of human life until around 25 years ago, when women anthropologists became active in this field (e.g., Hrdy, 1981; Slocum, 1975).

This male-centred, or androcentric, view of the human sciences has now been exhaustively discussed and analysed by feminist writers on science. It is perhaps worth mentioning that it did not arise from a specific and conscious conspiracy on the part of male scientists, but from the impact of their commonsense views of the world on the way that science was carried out. Although the scientific method itself is a neutral process, in that it provides an objective way of deciding between alternatives that scientists set up, the generation of these alternatives (hypotheses) in the first place, and the way that findings are interpreted, are strongly influenced by the conventional thinking of the day. It is here that commonsense explanations – including those about men and women – come into play.

Perhaps the most pervasive way that commonsense views of the world impact on scientific research is in terms of agenda-setting. Certain topics are deemed worthy of investigation, whereas others are not, or more commonly not even entertained as possibilities. Thus it would be fair to say that investigating women's issues was largely out of bounds in the earlier part of the twentieth century, whereas it became fashionable in Western social sciences from the 1970s onwards. Certain other ideas about human social behaviour, that it can be influenced by bodily symmetry, or by bodily secretions, or by sperm competition, were only introduced into the realms of empirical debate as a result of the evolutionary ideas that were generated since the 1960s (see chapter 3). There would have been no reason for a conventionally trained social psychologist to have even entertained the idea that people's degree of bodily symmetry has an impact on their sexual attractiveness. It was not part of an agenda set by the commonsense view of the world that informed conventional social psychology. In contrast, many of the ideas derived from modern evolutionary thinking seem counter to everyday commonsense. Tooby (1999) has argued that in this sense Darwinian thinking is similar to quantum theory, which also generated counter-intuitive hypotheses. He wrote:

> The world Darwin and Wallace led us into is every bit as strange as quantum mechanics: A world of chemical replicators, billion-year-old cellular symbiosis, intrauterine siblicide, intragenomic conflict, kin-selected self-sacrifice, chemical computers, fish that change sex in response to social status, parasite-driven sexual recombination, brood parasites mimicking host offspring appearance . . . No novel, no film, no philosophy, no deliberate dissident attempt to rebel against everything orthodox is remotely as outlandish as these discoveries . . . The strange Darwinism that is transforming the scientific world is simply beyond the conceptual horizon of any existing lay culture, nonbiological scientific community, or even most biologists. (Tooby, 1999:1–2)

Certain forms of research have been constrained by considerations of morals and taste rather than by the consensus of commonsense beliefs about the world. Research on sexuality is of course a prime example. It is well known that Kinsey only came to the study of human sexuality after many years spent establishing a reputation in a conventional area of zoological research (Lloyd, 1976). In recent times, the socio-political climate is much more accepting of research that inquires about people's sexual activities. Nevertheless, there is still resistance when a scientist goes beyond collecting accounts. Research by Robin Baker and Mark Bellis (Baker and Bellis, 1995) on sperm competition not only went out on a limb in terms of the conventional ideas held in reproductive physiology at the time, but also involved techniques that some people regarded as intrusive of people's privacy and dignity. The research was based on ideas from evolutionary biology about subtle psychological influences on reproductive physiology. It was only possible at all because of the willingness of male staff in a large university biology department to collect, in condoms, samples of their own sperm that were ejaculated during intercourse, and the willingness of female staff to collect samples of their partners' sperm that flowed out of their vaginas after intercourse.

The available research evidence on which we base our account of sex and gender has therefore been framed by both commonsense views about men and women, and also – with a few exceptions – by what is regarded as acceptable and sensible to investigate. Both of these vary greatly depending on the socio-political context, that is, the time and place of the research, and they both influence and constrain what is available on any specific topic. Nevertheless, we should note that the social climate in the USA and other Western nations has been very accepting of research on topics connected with sex and gender over the last few decades of the twentieth century. Had we still been operating in the socio-political and scientific climate of the 1950s, there would have been no feminist[2]-inspired

---

[2] This term is here used in its broadest sense: see Beasley (1999) for a detailed discussion of the variety of feminist thinking.

research, i.e. little research on issues important to women but not men; very little sex research (certainly nothing involving intrusive techniques); and no research on issues highlighted by evolutionary analyses. This would have added up to an impoverished agenda that would have hardly merited a book at all. In many parts of the world today, women are even less publicly visible and politically effective than they were in America and Britain in the 1950s. In Iran, for example, when Khomeini's revolutionary Islamic regime was established in 1979, women were forced to stay in the home and to wear the chador (Moin, 1994). In more recent times, even more stringent restrictions on women's lives were forced upon them during the Taliban's control of Afghanistan. There is understandably little or no research evidence on gender issues available from such countries.

Similarities and differences

Within Western culture where most of the research is located, commonsense beliefs have influenced the way scientists have approached the study of men and women. In particular, a belief in the fundamental difference between women and men is paralleled by an influential scientific approach, one seeking differences rather than emphasising our common humanity. The search for differences is not necessarily associated with a belief in fundamental differences between the sexes. Once differences have been established, a matter of further dispute is whether they are rooted in cultural or evolutionary history, explanations that correspond to commonsense views involving, respectively, 'conditioning', and 'the natural order'.

There has been considerable debate between feminist psychologists about whether emphasising sex differences is detrimental to the aim of creating a climate of equality between the sexes (e.g., Eagly, 1995a; Hyde and Plant, 1995; Marecek, 1995). The issue of whether there are intellectual differences between men and women has been debated since the nineteenth century (e.g., Woolley, 1910). Pre-feminist research on individual differences (e.g., Anastasi, 1958; Garai and Scheinfeld, 1968) contains accounts of how men and women differ in specific intellectual domains and personality characteristics, although these generally arose from incidental findings rather than a deliberate intention to look for differences. The modern feminist movement that began in the 1960s stimulated renewed interest in whether men and women differed psychologically, and, if so, why they did. It was these concerns that led Maccoby and Jacklin (1974) to assemble an encyclopaedic summary of the evidence that was available at the time. They concluded that there was only good evidence for sex differences in three intellectual domains: linguistic, visual–spatial, and mathematical. Women were better at the first, and men were better at the other two. Men were also more aggressive than women. Their conclusions were reached as a result of examining studies comparing men and women for a wide range of psychological attributes.

To evaluate these and other claims about ways in which men and women differ, we need to examine what lies behind the term 'sex difference'. It usually refers to a statistically significant difference in the mean values (or average performances) of men and women on a particular measure. However, these can range from cases where there is no overlap in the two means – for example in physical attributes such as possessing a penis or a womb – to those where there is considerable overlap – for example in height. Most psychological sex differences exhibit overlapping differences.

The criterion Maccoby and Jacklin used to identify differences was statistical significance, in other words, that the differences were unlikely to have arisen by chance. They examined each study and recorded whether there was a significant difference in one or the other direction, or no statistically significant difference. A vote-counting procedure was used to add the total number of significant findings in the same direction. There is, however, a fundamental problem with this method. Statistical significance is a measure of the reliability of a particular finding. When it is used to count the cumulative impact of individual studies it considerably underestimates differences that are small in magnitude. This, and the omission of a number of characteristics that later turned out to show large differences, has led Maccoby and Jacklin's synthesis to be viewed as unduly conservative, erring on the side of no differences. Their conclusion supported a dominant strand of feminist thinking at the time; it emphasised the similarities between men and women, rather than their differences, as part of a campaign for widening women's educational and occupational opportunities (chapter 9).

The idea that we should be emphasising our common humanity rather than seeking to find differences between men and women is one that has been maintained up to the present day (e.g., Archer, 1987; Beaumeister, 1988; Marecek, 1995). Eagly (1995b) identified it as resulting from the feminist movement's influence on the emerging consensus surrounding the study of sex differences. However, the extent to which there was or still is such agreement can be questioned, since there has always been a strong tradition within North American psychology that has emphasised the study of differences. The tradition, of which Eagly is a leading contemporary exponent, is now associated with several methodological and theoretical innovations in psychology. One of these is the introduction of a new set of statistical procedures called meta-analysis, and another is a shift in interest to examining sex differences in *social* behaviour.

Meta-analysis refers to a set of statistical techniques that allow researchers to combine findings from many different studies, and to compare subsets of findings within a collection of studies (e.g., Eagly, 1987; Rosenthal, 1984; Willingham and Cole, 1997). As long as the comparisons are made between standard categories (such as male and female), and involve comparable measures (e.g., mathematical ability), the procedure is extremely valuable for assessing and making sense of an entire area of research. We referred to reservations about Maccoby and Jacklin's synthesis of the available research, because it was based on numbers and direction of significant differences across studies. Statistical significance is a measure that is dependent on the size of the samples used in particular studies. The basic measure of meta-analysis is not dependent on the sample size, and does not have an arbitrary cut-off point as does statistical significance. It is a measure of the magnitude of a particular effect, or the average difference between individuals in the two categories in a study, rather than the reliability of the difference.

This measure is the 'effect size', which is the difference between two mean scores, expressed in terms of the common standard deviation of the sample, which is a measure of the dispersal of the values around the mean. By using this standard measure, it is possible to summarise and compare the size of differences between categories across a variety of psychological attributes. It is a particularly appropriate statistic for sex differences because the categories being compared – male and female – are the same from study to study.

An early conclusion drawn from examining the magnitude of sex differences, rather than their statistical significance, was that these differences were small, even 'trivially small' (Deaux, 1984; Jacklin, 1979). Hyde (1981) reanalysed Maccoby and Jacklin's data on intellectual test performance, and found effect sizes of 0.24 (of a standard deviation) in the female direction for verbal ability, and of 0.43 and 0.49 in the male direction for numerical ability and spatial ability respectively. She characterised these as small in practical terms, because they could not readily explain the much larger differences in occupational roles associated with these abilities, for example in science and engineering.

Hyde's inference would seem to be straightforward. However, a number of other considerations have been raised since that complicate it. These are considered in more detail in chapter 9, but two are outlined here. The first is that effect size provides us with only a summary statistic for the difference between typical individuals taken from two contrasting populations. As Feingold (1995) explained, at the highest and lowest ends of the distribution, there will be considerably more individuals from one population than from the other, even if the effect size is small. Therefore, there will be considerably more of the group with the higher mean score among the higher levels of ability (and correspondingly, more of the group with the lower mean score among the lower levels of ability). The practical implications of this again run counter to the conclusion that 'small' effect sizes are unimportant. Feingold (1995) also showed that, if one of two groups had a wider distribution than the other, this would result in more of this group being found at one of the two ends of the distribution. Which end this is depends on whether the group has the larger or smaller mean score: if it has the larger score, it will be overrepresented at the high end, if it has the smaller, it will be overrepresented at the lower end (Fig. 1.1). These considerations have practical implications because it is men who have wider distributions than women for certain intellectual abilities, which when combined with higher average ability, can produce considerably more men than women in the higher ability range (Feingold, 1992b). The implications of this are discussed further in chapter 9.

A second point about Hyde's characterisation of effect sizes in specific abilities as small is that, if we take findings within the social sciences generally as the reference point (Cohen, 1988), the differences range from small (verbal ability) to medium (quantitative and spatial abilities). Subsequent meta-analyses have shown much larger sex differences for certain subcategories of mental abilities

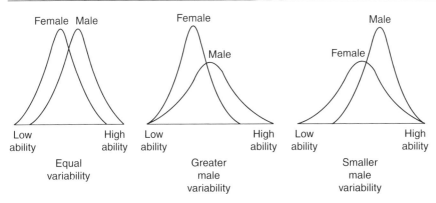

Fig. 1.1 Hypothetical distributions of values for men and women on a task for which men
show higher mean scores, showing equal variability, greater male variability,
and smaller male variability (from Feingold, 1992b).

(chapter 9). For example, when those spatial tasks involving mental rotation in
three-dimensional space are considered, the sex difference is in the region characterised as 'large' by Cohen (Willingham and Cole, 1997). Sex differences in
verbal fluency are larger in the female direction than are those for other verbal
tests (Halpern, 2000; Kimura, 1999). These findings, together with the considerations outlined above, have led some researchers to view cognitive sex differences as
substantial and of practical importance, contrary to the earlier views emphasising
similarities in cognitive abilities between the sexes.

The application of meta-analysis to sex differences in social behaviour paralleled
its application to sex differences in intellectual abilities. Hall's (1978) analysis of
the decoding of non-verbal cues was, in fact, the first substantial meta-analysis of
psychological sex differences. It was closely followed by Cooper's (1979) analysis of conformity. Hall (1984) found comparatively large differences (in the male
direction) in measures such as interrupting conversations, and using extensive body
movements, contrasting with the view around at that time (Hyde, 1981) that sex
differences in cognitive abilities were trivially small. It is now known that there are
both large and small differences in the cognitive and social domains (Eagly, 1995a).
A number of North American psychologists have since undertaken extensive meta-
analyses of sex differences in social behaviour, showing a variety of magnitudes
of difference in characteristics such as helping behaviour, influenceability, conformity, leadership, aggression, sexual behaviour and attitudes, and qualities preferred
in a mate (e.g., Eagly, 1987, 1995a; Eagly and Wood, 1991; Feingold, 1992a; Oliver
and Hyde, 1993).

Feingold's (1994a) meta-analysis of sex differences in personality illustrates
the scope and usefulness of the meta-analytic method. He employed evidence collected over a number of years (1940 to 1992), and analysed it in relation to the
popular 'big-five' model of personality. The higher-level factors are neuroticism,
extraversion, openness, agreeableness, and conscientiousness. There are a number of lower-level facets which make up each of the factors. Feingold's analysis

concentrated on the facets. He found that there were sex differences on 5 out of 9 of these. In descending order of magnitude of effect size, women were (very much) more tenderminded than men; men were (considerably) more assertive; women were (slightly) more trustworthy and anxious than men; and women were (very slightly) more gregarious than men. An interesting aspect of these findings is that men's and women's descriptions of their own personalities corresponded to the beliefs or stereotypes people hold about men and women, the commonsense beliefs we discussed earlier.

The widespread application of evolutionary principles to social psychology that has occurred over the last 10 to 15 years (Archer, 1996, 2001b, 2001c; Buss, 1994, 1999) is a further development that relates to the issue of whether to emphasise differences or similarities. The basic premise underlying an evolutionary approach to sex differences is that the sexes will differ as a consequence of different selection pressures during evolutionary history (chapter 3). These selection pressures have resulted in men and women differing in a range of characteristics, such as mate selection criteria, sexuality, aggression and dominance, jealousy, and sexual aggression. In contrast to theories that emphasise environmental influences, the differences are viewed as arising from the different inherited dispositions of women and men. This emphasis has led in some cases to parallels with the views of radical feminists, for example in the identification of men as the perpetrators of nearly all domestic violence (chapter 6). Nevertheless, there are some dissenting voices from an evolutionary view that emphasises *differences* between men and women. Gangestad and Simpson (2000) set out an evolutionarily based argument that differences between individuals of the same sex are as important as overall differences between the sexes. Just as males and females are different ways of achieving reproductive goals, some individuals within each sex will adopt reproductive strategies that differ from those of other individuals within those categories, and such strategies will be associated with different psychological characteristics. At present, this theory requires further testing. It is interesting in the present context because it represents a shift away from the emphasis on sex differences that has so far characterised the writings of most evolutionary psychologists.

The nature of explanations

The sorts of explanations favoured by psychologists also provide parallels with commonsense accounts. One dominant strand of thinking throughout the history of psychology is that nurture has a profound influence on psychological development. Nowhere is this more apparent than in the different rearing experienced by boys and girls. The way that children are treated by parents and the adult world generally, differs as soon as their sex is identified (chapter 4). The broad view that the manner in which a child is reared has profound influences on adulthood can be found in many dominant approaches throughout psychology and the social sciences. It is held by psychoanalysts and behaviourists alike, and corresponds to the commonsense belief identified earlier in this chapter as the 'conditioning' view, and, as indicated before, it has been adopted by liberal feminists, including many feminist psychologists.

One particularly influential environmental approach to sex differences in social behaviour is the social role theory, which had its origins in the classic role theory of George Herbert Read and others, later developed in psychology by Sarbin (1954). Parsons and Bales' (1955) analysis of the role differentiation of husbands and wives is particularly important for the modern application of role theory to gender roles by Alice Eagly and her colleagues. They view sex differences in social behaviour as arising from the widespread division of labour between men and women in most societies, as a consequence of differences in socialisation patterns and through situational influences during adulthood (Eagly, 1987, 1997; Eagly, et al., 2000). Their explanation has recently been developed to take account of biological constraints that shaped the formation of the division of labour, and of male power (Wood and Eagly, in press). We return to the social role theory in subsequent chapters.

Although the dominant influence in North American psychology was, and probably still is, broadly environmental, there have always been those who have sought to explain the behaviour of men and women in terms of their different biological heritage. Earlier writings emphasising an evolutionary background or the influence of hormones have always commanded attention from commentators in the media, and from those arguing against earlier feminist accounts (Archer, 1976; Archer and Lloyd, 1985). Within psychology, their influence tended to be weaker, and their impact on the prevailing environmental consensus was minimal in areas concerned with sex and gender. However, there were some notable exceptions to this generalisation among the most prominent researchers in the area. Eleanor Maccoby, whose work is described in chapters 4 and 10, has always acknowledged the possibility that biological differences may play an important part in the social development of boys and girls.

There are now two main challenges to the environmentalist account of the development of psychological sex differences. They both correspond broadly to the commonsense notion that differences in men's and women's behaviour are rooted in the natural order. One emphasises ultimate origins, and the other physiological mechanisms. One is associated with the resurgence of evolutionary thinking in psychology, and the other is derived from research in neuroscience.

The implications of evolutionary psychology are broader than its emphasis on fundamental differences between men and women, discussed in the previous section. Its starting point is a view of human nature based on principles derived from natural selection. The defining statements of the evolutionary psychological approach refer to the environmental consensus within psychology as the 'standard social science model' or SSSM (Tooby and Cosmides, 1992), a phrase which is not accepted by conventional social scientists (e.g., Eagly, 1997) because it implies that they have more in common than they perceive to be the case. It is a phrase that is used provocatively by evolutionary psychologists to distinguish the fundamentally different approach they adopt from all those in conventional psychology whose starting point is cultural influences on behaviour rather than evolved dispositions. Evolutionary psychologists argue that it is only through considering evolved dispositions, including those that distinguish men and women, that we can understand why culture takes the forms it does. We discuss this further in chapter 3.

Research in neuroscience focuses upon the mechanisms through which evolved dispositions to act are reliably developed in each individual. Findings from the 1960s and 1970s were applied to the development of psychological sex differences such as those in intellectual abilities and in aggression. Many of these applications and the findings that lay behind them were in the past considered to be doubtful or speculative (Archer and Lloyd, 1985), but the intervening years have resulted in a far firmer research base being established for some of the claims; for example, it is now thought more likely that male hormones (androgens) secreted before birth do influence the play preferences of boys (chapter 4), and that performance on tests of spatial and verbal skills are subject to the influence of both the male and female hormones (Geary, 1999; see chapter 9).

Research strategies

Nomothetic versus ideographic approaches

Throughout the history of psychology there has been a contrast between those who sought to establish general or *nomothetic* laws that apply to all individuals (or all individuals of a particular class), and those who adopted an *ideographic* approach, one that is concerned with the individual (Lerner, 1976). This distinction can be seen in studies of sex and gender. Most research has been nomothetic in character, in that it has sought to establish generalisations about the categories 'men' and 'women', with individual variation within each category being relegated to a minor role. Both social role and evolutionary explanations are of this type. The meta-analytic method, which synthesises whole research areas, and draws general conclusions from these syntheses, is also nomothetic in approach.

In contrast, some feminist psychologists seek to study the experiences of particular women, and to interpret these from a feminist perspective. This form of ideographic approach involves the application of qualitative methods to the study of small numbers of individuals, rather than seeking to make generalisations from a large quantitative database. This approach became particularly popular among British feminist psychologists (e.g., Wilkinson, 1986) where it was associated with a rejection of the scientific method in favour of the construction of accounts reflecting the experiences of people who were participants in the studies. The very nature of this endeavour makes it difficult to derive generalisations and to generate the sorts of broad theories characteristic of nomothetic research (Morgan, 1996).

As many North American feminist psychologists (e.g., Eagly, 1995a; Matlin, 1987; Peplau and Conrad, 1989) have pointed out, there is no logical link between researching issues of interest to feminists and using qualitative methods. Hyde (1994) has argued instead that the nomothetic meta-analytic approach is better equipped for making what she referred to as 'feminist transformations', for example by challenging long-held but incorrect generalisations about women and sex differences. In other areas, such as sexual aggression and rape, quantitative research has been successful in pursuing a broadly feminist research agenda (Koss et al., 1987; see chapter 6).

Levels of explanation

Research strategies can differ in the type or level of explanation they involve as well as differing in terms of their degree of generality. Social behaviour, the main subject matter of most contemporary sex and gender research, can be considered at a variety of levels, from that of the social structure in which the person lives, to the social interactions of individuals. Doise (1986) identified four levels of analysis at which social psychology can operate: the *intrapersonal*, which is concerned with the processes whereby individuals organise their perception and evaluation of the social world; the *interpersonal and situational*, which concerns the immediate context, but not the individual's different social positions outside the immediate context; the *positional*, which does take account of different social positions of the people concerned; and the *ideological* or *societal*, which concerns the beliefs shared by large numbers of people in a society.

Our consideration of research on sex and gender involves all four levels. For example, research on individuals' thought processes associated with gender (chapter 2), which are manifest in commonsense views, involves the intrapersonal level. The shared beliefs that individuals hold about gender arise from their interactions with others at the interpersonal level, in particular people with whom they have close relationships.

Feminist analyses are concerned with the positional and ideological levels. In fact they are based on the premise that the positional level is of overriding importance when considering social interactions between men and women. From this perspective, whatever the particular topic, whether the social development of boys and girls, or how men and women behave in their families, it is crucial to acknowledge that the sexes have different – and unequal – social positions. It is from this standpoint that feminist social scientists have criticised those who approach the topic of marital violence as a general problem of conflict resolution, without acknowledging the different societal positions of the people involved in the conflict (chapter 6).

What Doise termed the ideological or societal level concerns the ways that the unequal power relations between men and women operate as structural constraints on women's actions, for example barring them from certain occupations,

or restricting their financial opportunities (chapters 8 and 9). Explanations of phenomena at a positional level, for example of how husbands and wives interact, are
seen as reflecting processes operating at a societal level, through either legal frameworks or consensual beliefs about appropriate behaviour (chapter 8). For most of
the topics discussed in the following chapters, higher-level societal analyses have
been used to explain lower-level, intrapersonal, phenomena. Marital violence can
again be used as an example. The history of a legal framework that enabled and
encouraged husbands to control 'their' wives' actions, by force if necessary, is
viewed as determining how individual men and women behave when they live
together as man and wife (e.g., Dobash and Dobash, 1980).

It is fair to say that such explanations, which are sometimes referred to as top-
down, have dominated much of the writing in this area until fairly recently. They
have been favoured both by those who adopt an explicitly feminist agenda (as in
the example just given) and also by those who view social processes in terms of
environmental influences. Since this involves the inculcation of widespread values
from one generation to the next (chapter 4), it lends itself to a framework that
views societal-wide processes being transmitted down to the individual.

Evolutionary psychology marks a radical departure from this 'top-down' form
of explanation. When combined with neuroscience research on hormones and
brain mechanisms, the explanatory direction becomes reversed. Instead of the
individual's behaviour being determined by the societal position of men and
women, and by gendered culture, it is instead seen as being determined from the
bottom-up by biologically derived dispositions influencing how people behave.
Ultimately, the shape taken by human societies will reflect these dispositions. For
example, the striving for dominance and eminence that is held to be characteristic of men's social behaviour is seen as underpinning the nature of all societies
that have men in the positions of power (Campbell, 1999). The ubiquitous double
standard of sexual morality is viewed as arising from a selection pressure associated with internal fertilisation and paternity (paternity uncertainty): cultural rules
surrounding it reflect the ways in which different cultures handle this potentially
disruptive human disposition (Daly et al., 1982).

The co-evolutionary approach (e.g., Durham, 1991) is an attempt to examine
how biological evolution and cultural evolution interact. Although culture may in
some cases reflect biological dispositions, as in the case of the double standard,
in others it may work in the opposite direction. Indeed, many moral prohibitions
and restrictions are efforts to stop some of the more socially disruptive aspects of
human behaviour. Prohibitions against adultery can be seen in this light, as can
monogamy. In chapter 3, we outline the view (Wright, 1994) that, in the human
species, monogamy was imposed on an original tendency towards mild polygyny in order to reduce the numbers of disaffected and unattached young men that
occur when more powerful men are allowed several wives. Again, this is a viewpoint that regards culture as a way of dealing with problems arising from natural
dispositions.

Sex or gender?

Finally, we turn to the potentially confusing issue of terminology. The term 'gender' was first used by Greek Sophists in the fifth century BC to describe the threefold classification of the names of things as masculine, feminine, and intermediate. The category 'neuter' with which we are familiar from French or German, derives from later Latin usage that described the third category as 'neither' (Lyons, 1968).

Although older dictionaries show that 'gender' was only used as equivalent to 'sex' in a jocular manner, it has now entirely replaced 'sex' in politically correct speech, except when sexuality is meant (as in 'the sex act'). Thus, when a form asks whether a person is a man or woman, it is now customary to use 'gender' rather than 'sex'. Many psychologists habitually use the term 'gender differences' rather than 'sex differences'.

The purpose of this change of usage was to emphasise that distinctions between men and women arise largely from cultural rather than biological sources, which might be implied by the term 'sex difference'. Gender was seen as the cultural part of what it is to be a man or a woman. Words such as 'womanly' or 'manly' and 'masculine' or 'feminine' were viewed as not being connected with a person's biological sex, but as describing culturally variable characteristics. Gender was therefore cultural (Maggio, 1988).

Unlike many other non-sexist[3] terms, such as 'chair' (or 'chairperson'), 'fire-fighter', 'humankind', and 'homemaker', there would appear to be no firm logical foundation for replacing 'sex' with 'gender'. First, it is doubtful whether the term 'sex difference' ever did imply a biological origin for the character under consideration, and, even if this were the case, replacing it by 'gender' to signify that all such differences are cultural in origin replaces one set of dubious assumptions with another. In practice, as we show in this book, psychological and behavioural differences between men and women arise from a variety of sources involving both the biological and the cultural.

There is reason to maintain a distinction between the terms 'sex' and 'gender' when discussing findings from social psychology. Following Maccoby (1988), Bem (1989), and Eagly (1995a), sex refers to the binary categories 'male' and 'female', and gender to the attributes associated to a greater or lesser extent with the two sexes, i.e. 'masculine' and 'feminine' features rather than 'male' and 'female'. This usage, which has been adopted by a number of influential researchers in the area (e.g., Eagly and Karau, in press; Halpern and LaMay, 2000; Konrad et al., 2000), enables us to distinguish reasonably clearly between sex differences, i.e. differences between the categories male and female, and gender roles and gender stereotypes, i.e. characteristics generally associated with one or the other category. This is the convention we have adopted in this book. It differs from that used before

---

[3] It is ironic that people who insist on 'gender' rather than 'sex' also use the term 'sexism' rather than 'genderism'.

(Archer and Lloyd, 1985), which was based on an ethnomethodological standpoint. We consider it to be clearer for our subject matter, and hope that readers will appreciate our clarity, even if their own preference is for the modern colloquial usage.

Further reading

Eagly, A. H. (1995). The science and politics of comparing women and men. *American Psychologist*, 50: 145–58.

An argument put forward by those who seek to emphasise our common humanity at the expense of sex differences is that such differences are small, inconsistent across studies, often artifactual and counter to the stereotypes. Alice Eagly shows that there is clear evidence for a range of differences across the cognitive and social domains, which she interprets in terms of social roles.

Hyde, J. S. (1994). Can meta-analysis make feminist transformations in psychology? *Psychology of Women Quarterly*, 18: 451–62.

Janet Hyde puts the case for the use of quantitative statistical methods to summarise the evidence on sex differences. She argues that this sort of empirical evidence is better placed to aid feminist causes than is the alternative approach of using qualitative methods.

2   Stereotypes, attitudes, and personal attributes

Introduction

Stereotypes are the shared beliefs that people hold about a group of people such as an ethnic group, or people in a particular occupation. Gender stereotypes refer to the beliefs people hold about members of the categories man or woman. They can be viewed as elaborations of the commonsense notions we considered in chapter 1. In this chapter, we examine first the content of gender stereotypes – which attributes people commonly associate with men or women. We then discuss explanations of the stereotypes, principally whether they are exaggerations of reality, or whether they serve to justify social positions and prejudice.

We also consider attitudes to women and men. Attitudes are broader than stereotypes, in that they encompass feelings and intentions to act, as well as beliefs and thoughts, and they can apply not only to categories of people but to issues and events. Attitudes are identified when the three interrelated components are formed around particular persons, such as rock stars, or ethnic groups, or to a type of food, or to a political issue such as capital punishment. When people hold attitudes about a social group, the belief or cognitive component of their attitudes is equivalent to their stereotypic beliefs about that group. Attitudes about men and women also include feelings about them, whether they are liked or disliked. We examine measures of attitudes towards women and men, which generally indicate that people have a more positive view of women than of men. We contrast these measures with attitudes towards equal rights for women, to show that people can like women as a category, yet form attitudes about issues relating to women that are sexist or discriminatory.

The later parts of the chapter are concerned with self-descriptions: the extent to which individuals of both sexes describe themselves in terms of personality traits that make up the stereotypes for their own and the other sex. Here we move from generalisations about men and women as a group to how individual men and women see themselves in relation to these generalisations. The reason this has attracted the attention of researchers is that gendered personal attributes were first linked with well-being and mental health, through the influential *androgyny theory*. This held that people who had both masculine and feminine personalities – those who were androgynous – would feel better about themselves and be better adjusted.

A second influential theory, *gender schema theory*, regarded people who viewed themselves in terms of gendered attributes as using gender as a selective filter through which to view the social world. They interpreted the world in terms of gender, and they used gender-related concepts to judge other people. Although the evidence is not supportive of the theory as a whole, it does reveal some interesting links between holding stereotypic beliefs and the way social judgements are made.

In the final section, we consider the extent to which gender-linked personal attributes are related. If they are closely associated, global descriptions such as masculinity and femininity would be appropriate generalisations to make about people's psychological make-up. If not, the extent to which such descriptions were useful would be limited, especially when based on one type of measure, such as personality traits.

The content of gender stereotypes

In everyday conversations, people make all sorts of generalisations about men and women. Consider the following examples:

FIRST MALE TEENAGER: You know what women are like?
SECOND MALE TEENAGER: They're always talking.
FIRST MALE TEENAGER: Yes, they're all the same.
                                        (overheard by first author)

WOMAN TO HER DAUGHTER: Men are selfish bastards and there's nowt you can do about it.
                                        (from a cartoon in Quillin, 1984)

In both cases, a particular attribute is generalised to all members of the category 'women' or 'men', who are viewed as more homogeneous than they really are. Stereotypes minimise individual differences. In these two examples, the characteristics are not seen as particularly desirable ones, and can therefore form the basis of prejudice and discrimination against the group concerned. In other instances, stereotypes may be normative, i.e. viewed as desirable for a particular category of people: for example, it may be seen as desirable for women to be nurturant. In this case, stereotypic beliefs will overlap with social norms or the perceived social role of the stereotyped group. In this example, it would be the role of women as child carers.

Here we concentrate on the attributes that make up the stereotypes, or consensual beliefs, about men and women. Most research has involved beliefs about personality traits, as opposed to other aspects of stereotypes such as interests, occupations, and appearance. The first social psychological research on stereotypes explored racial or ethnic stereotypes, an important issue in the ethnically diverse North American culture. It used a method called the Adjective Checklist, which involved presenting people with a long list of adjectives and asking them

Table 2.1 Adjectives associated with women, with evaluative classification

Affected	−	Feminine	0	Prudish	−
Affectionate	+	Fickle	−	Rattlebrained	−
Appreciative	+	Flirtatious	0	Sensitive	0
Attractive	+	Frivolous	−	Sentimental	0
Charming	+	Fussy	−	Soft-hearted	0
Complaining	−	Gentle	+	Sophisticated	0
Dependent	0	High-strung	0	Submissive	0
Dreamy	0	Meek	0	Talkative	0
Emotional	0	Mild	0	Weak	−
Excitable	0	Nagging	−	Whiny	−

Source: Based on Williams and Bennett (1975) and Gough and Heilbrun (1965).
+ = positive; − = negative; 0 = neutral.

Table 2.2 Adjectives associated with men, with evaluative classification

Adventurous	+	Disorderly	−	Realistic	+
Aggressive	0	Dominant	0	Robust	0
Ambitious	+	Enterprising	+	Self-confident	0
Assertive	0	Forceful	0	Severe	0
Autocratic	0	Handsome	0	Stable	+
Boastful	−	Independent	+	Steady	0
Coarse	−	Jolly	0	Stern	0
Confident	+	Logical	+	Strong	0
Courageous	+	Loud	−	Tough	0
Cruel	0	Masculine	0	Unemotional	0
Daring	−	Rational	+	Unexcitable	0

Source: Based on Williams and Bennett (1975) and Gough and Heilbrun (1965).

to identify the particular racial or ethnic groups to which the words applied (Katz and Braly, 1935).

The same technique was later applied to gender stereotypes in the USA by Williams and Bennett (1975). They asked university students to indicate which adjectives from a list of 300 were typically associated with either women or men. The students were able to categorise over 90 per cent (272) of adjectives as belonging to either women or men. There was considerable agreement about this assignment among female and male students. Tables 2.1 and 2.2 show those adjectives that were agreed upon by 75 per cent of all students (both sexes combined). This produced 30 adjectives describing women and 33 describing men. These were each assigned an evaluative classification of positive, negative, or neutral, developed in an earlier study (Gough and Heilbrun, 1965).

Williams and Bennett's results are similar to those from other investigations of gender stereotypes carried out at various times (Ellis and Bentler, 1973; Komarovsky, 1950; Rosenkrantz et al., 1968; Williams and Best, 1982, 1990). It is often found that raters ascribe greater value to male than to female attributes. In Williams and Bennett's study, 15 adjectives in each list (Tables 2.1 and 2.2) had a positive or negative evaluation: for women, 5 were positively valued and 10 negatively valued. The values for men were the opposite, 10 positive and 5 negative. These findings suggest that the greater societal power of men is reflected in the affective meaning of the words used to describe the traits most associated with them. It takes us back to the commonsense beliefs discussed in chapter 1, one of which was that women were viewed as inferior to men.

The specific words shown in Tables 2.1 and 2.2 generally reflect commonsense views of men and women, as they should, because it is common sense that is used to make the judgements. There are also a few surprises. Words such as coarse, disorderly, jolly, and severe are not the first to come to mind when describing men in general; nor are appreciative, complaining, and sophisticated obvious choices for women.

It is important to note the exact instructions used by Williams and Bennett. They asked students to choose from a predetermined list of adjectives those *typically associated* with a woman or a man. Spence et al. (1974, 1975) used two different sets of instructions, asking which traits were *typical* of men and women (as did Williams and Bennett) and which were *ideal* for each sex (also introducing the notion of evaluation). The traits were presented as bipolar scales (e.g., active–passive; timid–not timid). Those that were viewed as typical of one sex but not the other, yet were seen as desirable for both sexes, were termed *female-valued* or *male-valued* items. They are listed in Table 2.3. For example, it was found that women are more likely than men to be gentle (or tactful), yet it is still desirable for a man to be gentle. Raters are in effect saying that they believe most men are not gentle (or tactful) but that ideally they ought to be. Likewise, it is widely believed that men are more ambitious than women, yet it is seen as desirable for both sexes to be ambitious.

Traits that were viewed as typical of one sex but not the other, and were only desirable for this sex, are listed separately in Table 2.3, classified as female and male *sex-specific* items. Thus 'aggressive' is seen as typical of men rather than women, and is moreover seen as desirable for a man but not for a woman. The notion that some personality attributes are evaluated differently when possessed by a man or a woman is shown in the following comment attributed to the former British Prime Minister, Margaret Thatcher, no doubt in response to remarks made about her: 'When a woman is strong, she is strident. If a man is strong, gosh he's a good guy' (November 1990).

Overall, the traits used to describe men and women in these and other studies can be summarised by the adjectives Janet Spence applied to them: traits assigned to men form part of an overall characteristic of instrumentality, acting upon the world and getting things done; traits assigned to women form part of an overall characteristic of expressiveness, expressing emotions and caring for others. This distinction is very similar to that made by the sociologists Parsons and Bales (1955)

Table 2.3 Items from the Personal Attributes Questionnaire

18 Female-valued items	23 Male-valued items	12 Sex-specific items
Aware of others' feelings	Active	*Female*
Considerate	Acts as leader	Cries easily
Creative	Adventurous	Excitable in major crisis
Devotes self to others	Ambitious	Feelings hurt
Does not hide emotions	Competitive	Home-oriented
Emotional	Does not give up easily	Needs approval
Enjoys music and arts	Feels superior	Need for security
Expresses tender feelings	Forward	Religious
Gentle	Good at sports	*Male*
Grateful	Independent	Aggressive
Helpful to others	Intellectual	Dominant
Kind	Interested in sex	Likes maths and science
Likes children	Knows ways of the world	Loud
Neat	Makes descisions easily	Mechanical aptitude
Strong conscience	Not easily influenced	
Tactful	Not excitable in minor crisis	
Understanding	Not timid	
Warm to others	Outgoing	
	Outspoken	
	Self-confident	
	Skilled in business	
	Stands up under pressure	
	Takes a stand	

Source: Based on Spence et al. (1975).

when describing the family roles of men and women. They argued that instrumental properties were important for effective performance of behaviour enacted in roles usually (at that time) occupied by men; similarly, expressive traits were seen as important for behaviour in roles usually occupied by women. The argument that stereotypic traits follow from the traditional societal roles of men and women – the worlds of paid work and homemaking – has more recently been extended by other researchers, as social role theory (Eagly, 1987; Eagly et al., 2000; Yount, 1986). This is explored in the following section.

Stereotypes and roles

Williams and Best (1982, 1990) reported a cross-national study of the gender stereotypic traits held by people in a range of modern societies, and found a large measure of agreement between them. Eagly (1987) explained the consistency in terms of the traits being prescriptions for gender roles. She added:

> Gender roles and stereotypes held in a society at any one point in time are
> rooted, not primarily in the society's cultural tradition, but more importantly
> in the society's contemporaneous division of labor between the sexes. Women
> are viewed as suited for the specific social roles that women typically occupy, and
> men are viewed as suited for the specific social roles that men typically occupy.
> (Eagly, 1987:21–2)

This view of gender stereotypic traits is known as the social role theory, because it
links the traits to the societal roles of men and women. It predicts that if the roles
change, the stereotypes will also change. Lueptow et al. (1995) identified large
changes in the social roles of men and women over the last 20–25 years in the USA,
in the form of new opportunities for women in the workforce (chapter 9). They
have been paralleled by changes in attitudes towards the roles of women (Twenge,
1997a). An analysis of the gender stereotyping of traits over this period (Lueptow
et al., 1995) showed that these had hardly changed. Lueptow at al. interpreted these
findings, along with Williams and Best's (1982, 1990) evidence of consistency
across cultures in gender stereotyping of traits, as evidence for the universality of
the traits despite differences in women's roles. They argued that this supports an
evolutionary rather than a social role interpretation (chapter 3). However, Cejka and
Eagly (1999) have noted that there is still considerable occupational segregation
according to sex, and most predominantly female occupations are similar to the
earlier domestic role. In addition, women still do most of the housework and child
care, so that the domestic role has not changed substantially over this time period
(Eagly, personal communication). We should also note that self-descriptions do
show that women have become more instrumental over the last 25 years (Feingold,
1994a; Twenge, 1997b).

A study by Eagly and Steffen (1984) found more direct evidence that gender
stereotypic traits were linked in people's thinking with men's and women's traditional societal roles. Participants were asked to rate the traits associated with
women and men whose occupations were not specified, and of women and men
when they were labelled as either homemakers or full-time employees. Irrespective of their sex, homemakers were rated higher in expressive traits and lower in
instrumental ones than were full-time employees. Women whose occupation was
unspecified were rated as higher in expressive traits and lower in instrumental ones
than were men whose occupation was unspecified. However, homemakers of both
sexes were viewed as higher in expressive traits and lower in instrumental ones
than a woman whose occupation was specified. Thus, the important feature for
assigning traits seems to be occupational role, rather than assumptions about the
basic natures of men and women, which is what we would have expected from
Lueptow et al.'s findings. Additional support for a link between stereotypic traits
and the role of homemaker or full-time employee comes from an earlier study by
Locksley and Colten (1979), who found that trait descriptions of 'woman' and
'housewife' were similar, but differed from those for 'career woman', which were
more instrumental. Further support comes from a more recent study (Diekman and
Eagly, 2000) in which people were asked to imagine the average man and woman at

the present time, 50 years ago, and 50 years hence. Their assumed characteristics changed according to estimated changes in their roles, and in particular the assumed characteristics of women became more instrumental across the three time periods. In fact, women were seen as becoming more masculine in several ways, in their thinking and physical attributes, as well as their personalities. This change in masculine but not feminine attributes fits the pattern of role changes over time, that women have entered paid labour, but men have not taken on domestic roles to any significant extent.

Eagly and Steffen (1984) also examined the importance of status, finding that high-status people were seen as more instrumental than were lower-status people. This included the belief that they would be more likely to influence others and would be less likely to be influenced. However, status did not affect expressive traits, although it did in a later study where it was separated from the requirements associated with particular occupations (Conway et al., 1996). Status is, of course, important because men are more likely to occupy higher-status occupations, to exert power over women in domestic situations, and are more likely to be assigned higher-status positions in informal groups.

To summarise Eagly's argument, it is not sex per se to which expressive and instrumental traits are attached, but the roles usually filled by women and men, and the status differences attached to these roles. Studies directly manipulating the occupational role and sex of a target person show convincingly that traits do follow the roles, even though there is no evidence that gender-stereotypic traits have changed during the time when women's occupational roles have changed.

The two studies just described investigated the implied characteristics associated with the general categories 'man' and 'woman', by using subtypes such as 'housewife' to examine the similarities between these and the general gender stereotype. Other studies of such subtypes have taken a different track. They have been concerned with the cognitive structure of gender stereotypes, which is viewed as having multiple components. Clifton et al. (1976) found five subtypes of woman: 'housewife', 'career woman', 'woman athlete', 'bunny woman' (i.e. sex object), and 'clubwoman' (i.e. country club woman). The aim of their study was to explore the stereotypic attributes associated with these subtypes. England (1988) narrowed the subtypes down to 'housewife', 'professional woman', and 'sex object', and Noseworthy and Lott (1984) added 'woman athlete' to this list. Deaux et al. (1985b) reported four subtypes for the masculine stereotype: 'athletic man', 'blue-collar working man', 'business man', and 'macho man'. England and Hyland (1987) found three categories: 'family man', 'business man', and 'macho man'. Edwards (1992) reported 'family man' and 'business man', but also 'loser', and 'womaniser' ('ladies' man') – regarded as equivalent to 'macho man' in other studies.

To some extent, the different subtypes reported in these studies reflect differences in the methodology and samples used. It is questionable whether they address the general issue of the link between gender stereotypes and roles, since in some studies (e.g., Eckes, 1994) the typical man does not correspond to any of the subtypes.

Instead they address the cognitive structure of stereotypes, the subcategories (and micro-categories) of the global categories men and women. They show that the generalisations that form the basis of gender stereotypes begin to break down when further group membership is specified.

Do stereotypes reflect prejudice or reality?

An issue which is more central to our understanding of the nature of stereotypes is how they relate to reality. Originally, stereotypes were viewed as being primarily prejudicial. They were rationalisations, illogically derived from the social world, and incorrect in content (Lippman, 1922). This view informed important early research on stereotypes (e.g., Allport, 1954; Katz and Braly, 1935). Beginning with the papers by McCauley and Stitt (1978) and McCauley et al. (1980), a different way of viewing stereotypes emerged. They argued that stereotypes are formed as a result of experiences with the groups concerned and hence are based on reality. Stereotypes can therefore be understood in terms of the probability that a member of a particular group will behave in a particular way. These probabilities are then used as predictions, which are useful because they simplify the complex social world we inhabit. Their drawbacks involve possible inaccuracies or exaggerations in forming the predictions, and if they are used in preference to personal information when dealing with a particular individual.

The hypothesis that stereotypes are generalisations, but not necessarily incorrect ones, was applied to gender stereotypes by Martin (1987). She asked college students to estimate the percentage of men and women in North America who possessed each of a set of stereotypic traits like those discussed earlier. For each trait, the mean percentage of men ascribed the trait was divided by the mean percentage of women ascribed the trait. Martin named this value the diagnostic ratio. It would be 1.0 if the sexes were rated as equally likely to possess the trait, greater than 1.0 if more men than women were believed to have the trait, and less than 1.0 if more women than men were viewed as having it.

Martin asked a different sample of women and men (the parents of students going to university) to rate themselves on these traits, and then compared these ratings with the stereotypes. Self-ratings were in the same order as the diagnostic ratios, but were less extreme, a finding that was later replicated by Allen (1995). Martin concluded that people generally exaggerate existing sex differences when they form stereotypes. For example, on average, men do tend to be more assertive than women, and women are more nurturant than men. The stereotype makes these sex differences larger than is really the case, and ignores the overlap between men and women in these traits.

Judd and Park (1993) identified some problems with Martin's study. The sample used for the stereotype ratings was very different from that used for the self-reports. It is known that there are differences between young and middle-aged samples in their self-ratings of gender-stereotypic traits (Spence and Helmreich, 1979). There is also a problem with the accuracy of self-ratings of traits, in that it is difficult to tell the extent to which individuals present themselves in a good light. However, there is evidence for a good measure of agreement between self-reports and those of outside observers (such as spouses) for measures of personality (McCrae and Costa, 1990) and aggression (O'Connor et al., 2001b).

Judd and Park viewed the problem of comparing stereotypes with reality as one of deciding on an accurate measure of reality. All measures, whether self-reports, official statistics, or peer reports of others, have their particular reporting biases. Hall and Carter (1999) addressed this problem by using the findings from the numerous meta-analyses of sex differences as their standard. They found that ratings of sex differences in various traits and activities made by young adults were highly correlated with the actual differences revealed by the various meta-analyses. The implication of studies such as this is that common sense may after all be a useful overall guide to sex differences and similarities.

There is, however, a compelling alternative to the emphasis on stereotypes as predictive devices based on experience with the group concerned. This alternative view takes us back to Eagly's social role theory, which links stereotypic traits with the roles of men and women. It implies that stereotypes are not based on detailed experience with the groups concerned but with their societal roles. We have already seen that there is compelling evidence for a link between stereotypes and roles from studies that manipulate the implied roles of men and women.

Hoffman and Hurst (1990) developed this view further, and proposed that stereotypes are *rationalisations* of the general roles of men and women, ways of locating them in the natural order of things (chapter 1). The reasoning behind the stereotypes goes like this: it is understandable that women look after children because they are more nurturant; it is understandable that men run businesses because they are more logical and independent. Hoffman and Hurst's view of stereotypes cuts the necessary link with reality. Instead, stereotypes can be exaggerations, accurate reflections, or fictions – to which Jost and Banaji (1994) applied the Marxist term 'false consciousness'. The important point is that they justify existing social arrangements. We are back to the view of stereotypes found in the earlier work of Allport on prejudice and in Williams and Best's (1982, 1990) cross-cultural analysis of gender stereotypes.

Hoffman and Hurst reported a complex study in which they asked participants to complete ratings of the traits possessed by two fictional groups on another planet, the Orinthians and the Ackmians. Their occupations were presented as, in the first case, 80 per cent child raisers and, in the second, 80 per cent city workers. Examples of each group were given, and each example was linked with equal numbers of instrumental, expressive, and neutral traits. Despite this, raters spontaneously ascribed traits to the groups as a whole, that justified their predominant roles. The Orinthians, the child raisers, were viewed as generally more patient, kind, and understanding than were the Ackmians, the city workers, who were viewed as more confident and forceful than were the Orinthians. A second study replicated these findings using two other labels for groups with different roles, in this case ones that did not correspond to the roles of women and men. These were business persons and academics, who were stereotyped as extraverted and ambitious on the one hand and introverted and intellectual on the other.

These findings take us some way back to the view of stereotypes as rationalisations, rather than accurate descriptions of group characteristics. Although the finding that people view traits as changing with social roles is compelling evidence for this view, it does not account for other evidence, notably how similar stereotypic traits are to the personality traits that really do differ between men and women (Eagly et al., 2000; Feingold, 1994a; Hall and Carter, 1999). One way of reconciling the two views is to regard stereotypic features as needing to be both true, *and* regarded as useful for the particular role (Schaller and Latané, 1996).

Attitudes towards women and men

People hold an attitude about a wide range of abstract concepts, including political opinions (Eagly and Chaiken, 1993). When attitudes concern groups of people, the cognitive components are the same as the stereotypes about these people (Eagly and Mladinic, 1989), and, like attitudes, stereotypes have evaluative aspects. The earliest rating scale measure of gender attitudes concerned whether women should have equal rights with men, although the naming of the questionnaire ('Attitudes Toward Women Scale' or AWS) implied that it measured attitudes towards the category 'women'[1] (Spence and Helmreich, 1972; Spence et al., 1973). The scale has been used in many studies, in the US and the UK (Parry, 1983). Similar measures include The Sex Role Egalitarianism Scale (SRES: Beere et al., 1984), and the Sexist Attitudes Toward Women Scale (SATWS: Benson and Vincent, 1980). Items from the second of these are illustrated in Table 2.4.

Some of the items shown in Table 2.4, and those on the AWS, have a dated and ridiculous feel to them when viewed from a contemporary more egalitarian perspective. This raises two issues. The first is that in many cultures and subcultures attitudes to gender issues are radically different than those held by college-educated Westerners. What would seem to be blatant sexism may be defended as part of an ancient culture and religion by those who practise it. Here issues of gender, race, and religion become entwined in a way that makes addressing what might appear to be the most blatantly sexist acts a politically sensitive issue. In the UK, the issue of forced marriages between British Muslim women and men from Pakistan aroused considerable media comment in the late 1990s (e.g., Watt, 1999), which was followed by government measures designed to aid its victims (Perry, 2000).

A second issue is that, in a culture where sexism is recognised and officially disapproved, it is more likely to emerge in covert or subtle forms. Samples of Western college students are unlikely to endorse the more blatant items on scales such as the AWS and the SATWS. Swim and Cohen (1997) devised a rating scale

[1] The subtitle was 'attitudes towards the rights and roles of women' in Spence and Helmreich (1972), but this seems to have been lost in most subsequent research.

Table 2.4 Examples of items from the Sexist Attitudes Toward Women Scale (SATWS)

1   Women should be handled gently by men because they are so delicate.
2   Men will always be the dominant sex.
3   Women shop more than men because they can't decide what to buy.
4   A woman's place is in the home.
5   It would make me feel awkward to address a woman as 'Ms'.

Source: Benson and Vincent (1980).

that measured more subtle forms of sexism, terming it the Modern Sexism scale (MS). They also devised a scale containing more blatant items, and referred to this is as Old-Fashioned Sexism (OFS). They showed that the subtle forms of sexism were distinguishable from the old-fashioned items , which were closely related to the AWS. However, people's scores on either the AWS or the MS scale were negatively associated with their attitudes to the categories 'women' and 'feminist', and positively with their attitudes to the categories 'traditional man' and 'chauvinist'. Furthermore, the measure of subtle sexist attitudes, the MS, was a better discriminator of reactions to a sexual harassment episode, predicting a lesser willingness to define it as such, less sympathy for the victim, and more leniency to the perpetrator. These findings illustrate the way that attitudes have moved among the more educated and visible members of society[2] so that blatant sexism – like overt racism – is no longer acceptable, and therefore sexism emerges in more covert ways. Swim and Cohen's study shows that covert sexist attitudes can be reliably measured and used to predict reactions to issues such as sexual harassment which are important in the modern mixed-sex workplace.

Scales that measure attitudes towards equal rights for women, such as the AWS, can be contrasted with measures of attitudes to women and men in general. Eagly and Mladinic (1989) compared people's ratings on the two types of scale, and found no correlation between their evaluative ratings of the general categories men and women, and the AWS scale, which measures equal rights towards women.[3] However, AWS ratings were positively correlated with attitudes to equal rights for women.

Another interesting aspect of Eagly and Mladinic's study was that women as a general category were viewed more positively than were men, a finding which replicates earlier findings using a range of descriptive adjectives (Heise, 1965). This occurs despite men having more societal power than women. In chapter 1, in reference to this aspect of commonsense beliefs about women, we noted that, although they may be seen as nicer, more morally upright, human beings, they are viewed as less powerful and effective in the world than are men.

---

[2] A meta-analysis by Twenge (1997a) showed very large changes away from conservative attitudes to women (measured by the AWS) for college students of both sexes from 1970 to 1995.

[3] We should note that, in contrast to this finding, Swim and Cohen (1997) found that both the AWS and the Modern Sexism scale were (slightly) associated with negative evaluations of the category 'women'.

Table 2.5 Examples of items from Benevolent (B) and Hostile (H) sexism scales of the Ambivalent Sexism Inventory (ASI)

1	Women seek to gain power by getting control over men (H)
2	Men are incomplete without women (B)
3	Women, compared to men, tend to have a superior moral sensibility (B)
4	Women exaggerate problems they have at work (H)
5	Women are too easily offended (H)
6	Women should be cherished and protected by men (B)
5	A good woman should be put on a pedestal by her man (B)

Source: Glick and Fiske (2001).

In a follow-up study, Eagly et al. (1991) found that people evaluated women more favourably than men, on a number of measures (but not on a list of emotions), whether using pre-determined lists of traits, or free-responses involving beliefs. They concluded that the more favourable evaluation of women comes from ascribing to them positive expressive qualities, which at the same time are those characteristics that fit them less well for the world of work, particularly high-status positions. This conclusion is supported by the finding from an older attitude study (Heise, 1965) in which women received much lower ratings than men on another attitudinal dimension, 'potency', which corresponds to instrumentality rather than expressiveness. In chapter 9, we explore the way in which assumed possession of expressive traits increases bias against a person in the context of occupational selection.

One implication of these findings is that it is possible for someone to like women in general, i.e. have positive attitudes towards them, and at the same time hold very traditional views about what is appropriate and allowable for them to do. This theme was taken up by Glick and Fiske (1996, 1997, 2001) who devised 'The Ambivalent Sexism Inventory' (ASI). They measured two forms of sexist attitudes. The first was benevolent sexism, which was associated with positive attitudes towards women and positive stereotypes about them, but also included a paternalistic attitude which involved a belief in restricting women's sphere of activities. Hostile sexism was associated with negative attitudes towards women, and negative stereotypes about them, and, of course, also included a belief in restricting them. Both aspects of the ASI (Table 2.5) were associated with general measures of sexist attitudes, such as the AWS and the OFS and MS scales (Swim and Cohen, 1997), but the association was much stronger and more consistent for the hostile aspect (Glick and Fiske, 1996, 1997). Hostile sexism is associated with a range of different manifestations of hostility to women, principally that relations with them are viewed as adversarial in nature. Such attitudes are associated with proneness to physical aggression to partners and to sexual coercion (chapter 6).

Glick et al. (1997) examined attitudes to subcategories of women, such as those described in the section on stereotypes and roles, in relation to hostile and benevolent sexism. Certain categories of women that were spontaneously generated by college men had well-known negative labels, such as 'slut', and these were generated more often by sexist men (i.e. those with high overall ASI scores). Men with higher hostile sexism scores were more likely to evaluate negatively the subclass 'career woman'. Men with higher benevolent sexism scores were more likely to evaluate positively the subclass 'homemaker'. Glick et al. (1997) suggested that men with overall high scores on both these scales hold compartmentalised attitudes to women, enabling them to view women as a general category both positively and negatively. This has parallels with the findings of Buss and Schmitt (1993) that men evaluate certain attributes of women differently according to whether they are contemplating a long- or short-term relationship with them (chapter 3). Having had many previous partners would be a positive characteristic for a short-term relationship, but a negative one in a prospective long-term partner.

Individual differences in stereotypic traits

We now turn from consideration of generalisations made about people on the basis of their sex, to the way in which gender stereotypic attributes are used to describe individuals. It is a commonsense observation that people are viewed as masculine or feminine in terms of their personality. In 1991, a British Member of Parliament compared the new Prime Minister with the previous one, Margaret Thatcher, in the following way: 'Despite being a man, Mr. Major has a much more feminine personality' (*The Guardian*, London, 27 March 1991, p. 23).

Bem (1974), and Spence et al. (1974, 1975) set out to measure such intuitive judgements made by people about themselves. Most earlier researchers had assumed that psychological femininity and masculinity were opposite ends of a single dimension (Constantinople, 1973). The innovative aspect of the scales developed by Bem and Spence was that they assessed these dimensions separately. A person could be said to possess varying degrees of masculine and feminine traits. We should, however, note that, whereas Bem viewed gender-linked traits as general measures of a person's masculinity and femininity, Spence regarded them only as indications of the more limited personality dimensions, instrumentality and expressiveness, and referred to them as personal attributes. The point in making this distinction was that we cannot be sure that a person having an instrumental personality will be masculine in other respects, such as their interests.

People who describe themselves as possessing masculine (instrumental) and feminine (expressive) traits to an equal extent, were termed *androgynous* (Bem, 1974; Spence et al., 1974, 1975). Bem argued that androgynous people are better adjusted psychologically, in that they have high self-esteem, and are able to behave instrumentally or expressively as the situation demands (Bem, 1975). Spence was more cautious in making general claims about the link between androgyny and adjustment. Bem's viewpoint became very influential, and the concept of androgyny was later transferred to other areas of psychology such as counselling (Cook, 1985). Androgyny was seen as a goal towards which people should strive.

We should note that this coincides with the aims of liberal equity feminists who emphasise similarities between the sexes (chapter 1).

There are, however, a number of controversies surrounding the research on which the concept of androgyny is based, and these may undermine the supposed link with adjustment. Bem (1974) constructed the BSRI (Bem Sex Role Inventory) from 20 adjectives viewed as desirable for men, such as assertive, 'independent', and 'analytical', 20 viewed as desirable for women, such as 'loyal', 'warm', and 'shy', and 20 neutral ones, such as 'happy', 'tactful', and 'jealous'. People rated each one along a 7-point scale, in terms of how much it applied to them. Bem originally defined someone as androgynous if they scored similarly on the masculine and feminine scales. If their score was significantly different on the two scales, they were labelled as 'sex-typed'. The initial definition of androgyny did not last long. Spence et al. (1975) defined an androgynous person as someone who had high scores on both the instrumental (masculine) and the expressive (feminine) scales of their scale, the *Personal Attributes Questionnaire* (PAQ). Whereas such a person had high self-esteem, someone with low scores on both scales had low self-esteem. The term 'undifferentiated' was later used for such a person. Bem (1977) adopted the four-way classification into androgynous, undifferentiated, masculine 'sex-typed', and feminine 'sex-typed', and that was used extensively in subsequent research (Cook, 1985), and up to the present day (e.g., Milovchevich et al., 2001).

Two subsequent critics of Bem's research on androgyny (Locksley and Colten, 1979; Taylor and Hall, 1982) concluded that there was clear evidence for the association of masculine traits with mental health measures of adjustment, but no specific link with androgyny: androgynous people tend to be well adjusted because they have masculine traits. The link between self-esteem and androgyny also comes about primarily because of the association with masculine traits (March et al., 1987; Spence and Helmreich, 1978; Spence et al., 1975), a link which is partly spurious, since many masculine traits are similar to items used to measure self-esteem (Archer, 1986; Baldwin et al., 1986). Perhaps more interestingly, a subsequent study demonstrated that men and women appear to derive their self-esteem from different sources, men from a belief in their abilities and women from their attachments to and connections with significant others (Josephs et al., 1992).

The essence of Taylor and Hall's critique of androgyny was that it involved no new properties other than those that can be predicted from separate effects of the instrumental and expressive scales. Although the evidence supports this view (Helmreich et al., 1979; Lubinski et al., 1981, 1983) it could still be the case that people possessing both masculine and feminine traits are more flexible, as Bem suggested. This line of reasoning led Marsh and Byrne (1991) to assess whether the two sets of traits were related to different aspects of the self-concept. Traditional measures of self-esteem were found to relate to masculine traits, such as assertiveness and achievement. Other aspects of the self-concept, such as honesty and relations with significant others, were more closely related to feminine traits.

Using a measure of well-being that included both positive and negative aspects, Hunt (1993) found that both expressive and instrumental traits independently predicted most aspects of well-being equally well, but expressive traits were much more closely related to feelings and expression of positive emotions. Aube et al. (1995) used a wider range of measures, including behaviour and interests as well as traits. They also assessed people's relationships, from the person's perspective and those of their partners and friends. Their findings supported a much more complex view of the relationship between these measures and adjustment than would be predicted from the view that only instrumental traits are linked to psychological well-being. Expressive traits, and both masculine and feminine behaviour and interests, contributed to adjustment. Expressive traits predicted pleasant interpersonal emotions and good functioning in one-to-one relations for men.

Such findings show that, when a wider-ranging concept of well-being is used, some aspects of it are related to masculine traits and others to feminine traits. When a wider definition of masculinity and femininity is used , there are specific ways in which different features are related to adjustment. This takes us away from the simple assessment of masculinity and femininity through stereotypic traits, and echoes Spence's reservations about labelling the trait measures in this way.

Gender schema

Bem (1981) developed a further theory from the BSRI scales. She suggested that the position on her scales of masculine (instrumental) and feminine (expressive) traits represented a person's 'readiness to use gender as a lens to the world', i.e. the degree to which gender was a salient variable in their interactions. She articulated this view as *gender schema theory*. The term 'schema' has been widely used in other areas of psychology to refer to hypothetical mental structures which organise, select, and act on information from the outside world. Bem argued that people differ in the extent to which their mental schema incorporate gender as an organising principle. Although this may seem intuitively reasonable, the empirical basis of the theory has proved controversial. Whereas the BSRI was originally used to distinguish sex-typed and androgynous people, these categories became, in terms of the new theory, gender schematic and gender aschematic people. A schematic person will be more aware than an aschematic one of someone who deviates from the gender stereotype, and their behaviour towards others will be more dependent on that person's sex.

Spence and Helmreich (1981) expressed reservations about using BSRI trait self-ratings to indicate this more fundamental distinction. There seemed to be a logical objection, in that the BSRI was designed to measure the two dimensions, masculine and feminine traits: how could it then be used to indicate a single dimension, the degree of schematic processing? No clear answer to this question was forthcoming.

A variety of studies have tested predictions from Bem's gender schema theory. Usually these take the form of classifying people on the BSRI or the PAQ, and then assessing their schematic processing in some way. In several studies, the assessments have used words or concepts similar to those on the trait scales, and are therefore not independent of them (Archer, 1991).

One procedure that is independent of trait self-rating involves the extent to which people use the masculine or feminine connotations of words when trying to recall them from a list. It involves counting the numbers of sequential masculine or feminine words remembered before switching to the other gender category. Bem (1981) used this method, and found that sex-typed individuals (classified on the BSRI) showed more clustering by gender connotations than any of the other three gender categories. However, this difference was small, and five subsequent studies (mostly involving larger sample sizes), failed to replicate the findings (Archer et al., 1995; Deaux et al., 1985a; Edwards and Spence, 1987; Payne et al., 1987). These failures to replicate Bem's results strongly suggest that her original findings were subject to type 1 error, a false positive that occurs occasionally when statistical significance is relied upon as the criterion (chapter 1). We should note that there is nothing wrong with the method itself, since it has been used successfully in other contexts to measure the way in which certain words are grouped together in people's thinking. Cairns (1980), for example, found that Protestant and Catholic Northern Irish schoolchildren grouped together names with a similar religious connotation (such as Patrick and Mary) when recalling them.

A second method derived from cognitive psychology relies upon the well-known finding that, when people recall a series of lists containing a similar category of words, they improve whenever the category is changed. Mills and Tyrell (1983) assessed whether the extent of the improvement when gender was the category was related to the person's gender trait classification. They found that it was not. Yet the method itself is again a sound one, having been used to measure ethnic and religious discrimination, among children from Northern Ireland (Houston et al., 1990).

These studies indicate that there is no link between endorsing gender trait self-descriptions and using gender as a category for processing information. Yet there is clear evidence that gender traits are associated with the sort of social judgements that form the basis for prejudice and discrimination. Based on a method used to study racial discrimination, Frable and Bem (1985) asked participants to listen to a taped conversation between men and women, and then answer questions about who said what. Both cross-sex-typed (and to a lesser extent sex-typed) individuals confused members of the opposite sex with one another proportionately more than androgynous or undifferentiated raters did. In the racial discrimination studies, people who were more racially prejudiced tended to mix up people within a racial category (especially the one they discriminated against), but they could very easily identify from which group an individual came.

Other studies demonstrate a link between being sex-typed and making discriminatory judgements. Bem (1981) found that sex-typed people showed more animation, enthusiasm, and interest than androgynous individuals to those of the opposite sex they found more attractive. Susser and Keating (1990) asked people to observe a videotape of a mixed-sex pair of children in which one of them behaved aggressively. Sex-typed people judged the boy's aggression to be more intentional than the girl's, and proposed that the boy receive more severe reprimands. It would seem from such studies that sex-typed people are using stereotypes to a greater extent than androgynous people when they evaluate others. Thus we can conclude that, although there is little evidence to link Bem's trait classification to memory tasks involving gender, these classifications are related to the greater or lesser use of stereotypes when making social judgements. Because Bem viewed all sorts of evidence in terms of its support for gender schema theory, she blurred the distinction between the memory (where there is no link) and social judgements (where there is).

Masculinity and femininity

Most of the existing research on gender stereotypes, and in individual differences, has focused on personality traits. However, both gender stereotypes and gender-related personal attributes involve other components, such as behaviour, occupations, and physical appearance. Deaux and Lewis (1984) suggested that people link the different components of gender stereotypes together in their minds. For example, if we know that someone likes cooking, we may think that they will also like sewing, as both of these are feminine activities. There may be links from one component to another, for example from liking sewing, a feminine activity, to being nurturant, a feminine trait. Indeed, we would expect such links from the social role theory that stereotypic traits are derived from roles, i.e. activities.

Orlofsky and his colleagues designed an individual difference measure of stereotypic activities, the Sex-Role Behavior Scale, SRBS (Orlofsky et al., 1982; Orlofsky et al., 1985; Orlofsky and O'Heron, 1987a,b). In doing so they provided information about the content of role behaviour and occupations. Using the method designed by Spence to study stereotypic traits, Orlofsky (1981) asked people about the behaviour and occupations that were *typically* undertaken by women or men, and those that were *desirable* for each sex. An extensive list of activities that were viewed as desirable for both sexes, but typical of only one, was produced. These were called *male-valued* or *female-valued* activities, following Spence's terms (Table 2.6). Sailing is an example of a male-valued activity, and playing bridge an example of a female-valued activity, because they were viewed as leisure pursuits typical of men, or of women, yet they were viewed as no more desirable for that sex than the other.

Some of the activities that were viewed as typical of one sex were also viewed as more desirable for that sex than for the other. Orlofsky called these *sex-specific* items, again using Spence's term. Knitting and playing football are examples of sex-specific activities, the first being female-valued and the second male-valued. Table 2.6 shows some examples of male-valued, female-valued, and sex-specific activities from Orlofsky's list. They are associated with recreational activities, marital behaviour, and vocational interests, which, along with interpersonal activities (social and dating behaviour), are the four areas covered. Marital behaviour involves three more specific components, associated with domestic, childcare, and sexual activities.

Table 2.6 Examples of male-valued, female-valued, and sex-specific stereotyped activities (from the Sex Role Behavior Scale)

Domain	Gender classification	Examples
recreational activity	male-valued	sailing
		playing chess
	female-valued	disco dancing
		playing bridge
	sex-specific	playing football (m)
		knitting (f)
marital behaviour	male-valued	preparing tax returns
		initiating sexual relations
	female-valued	buying groceries
		being sexually faithful to spouse
	sex-specific	driving when going out with spouse (m)
		buying children's clothing (f)
occupations	male-valued	accountant
		lawyer
	female-valued	social worker
		bank teller
	sex-specific	truck driver (m)
		hairdresser (f)

Source: Based on Orlofsky, 1981.

There are two opposing ways of viewing the individual attributes derived from the components of gender stereotypes. One regards them as part of a global entity, so that traits are linked with behaviour and occupations. Someone rating themselves as masculine on Orlofsky's SRBS would also be expected to rate themselves as masculine on the BSRI which contains personality traits. If this were the case, it would make sense to invoke general concepts, such as masculinity and femininity, to distinguish between people who have more or less masculinity and/or femininity on a range of attributes. This was the view advocated by Bem (1974, 1985) and Frable (1989), known as the *unidimensional* view of gender. However, many researchers took the opposite, *multidimensional*, view that the components of gender stereotypes, and their associated individual differences, can vary independently of one another (e.g., Archer, 1989a; Deaux, 1984; Orlofsky, 1981; Spence, 1984, 1985, 1993; Spence and Buckner, 2000). Thus, a man may have a nurturant (feminine or expressive) personality, and have masculine interests such as football and cars.

Across a number of studies, people's scores on gender-trait tests did show some modest associations with those on the respective measures of gendered activities (Archer, 1989a). Correlations between egalitarian views about the rights of women and both personality and activities measures were lower. The low association between trait self-reports and gender attitudes was confirmed in a more recent study using the modern attitude measures of Glick and Fiske, and of Swim and Cohen, described above (Spence and Buckner, 2000). Although these findings tend to support the multidimensional view of gender attributes, it is possible that there is some degree of commonality between the attributes and also a degree of specificity. However, most of the evidence considered in relation to androgyny and gender schema theory did indicate considerable independence when the different components that go to make up a person's self-concept were examined as separate measures.

Conclusions

At the beginning of the chapter we described the content and structure of gender stereotypes, the commonsense views introduced in chapter 1. We also showed that stereotypic traits associated with men and women follow from their traditional roles, and could be manipulated by qualifying the general category 'man' or 'woman' to indicate a different role. At the same time, these traits did have a basis in reality, in that they coincided with measured differences between the sexes. One influential view of stereotypes is that they are derived from simplified versions of reality: on this view, a parallel with sex differences in personality would be expected. An alternative position is more compatible with the link between stereotypes and roles, that stereotypes provide rationalisations for the roles into which people are placed, irrespective of their real individual characteristics. It was possible to reconcile these two views by suggesting that, although stereotypes do justify social positions, they must contain a measure of truth in order to do so effectively.

While women as a category were likely to be evaluated more positively than men, attitudes to equal rights and opportunities for women were not related to these positive evaluations. These findings paralleled a commonsense view identified in chapter 1, that women may be seen as 'nice' or 'good' and yet be discriminated against. This paradox formed the basis of the Ambivalent Sexism Inventory (Glick and Fiske, 1997) which was designed to measure two forms of sexism, hostile and benevolent. In doing so, the researchers identified a particularly important feature of sex as a social category. Although men or women can be said to form separate groups in terms of their societal roles and behaviour, most people have repeated and intimate contact with members of the opposite category, a feature that is very different from people's experience of other social categories. The Ambivalent Sexism Inventory acknowledges this special feature when measuring attitudes about the opposite sex, in particular, men's attitudes to women.

Research on individual differences in gender traits is more closely linked with that on stereotypes than with studies of gender attitudes, although both have the goal of creating self-report measures that can predict prejudicial and discriminatory behaviour. Attitude research has been more successful in doing so, since measures of attitudes involve an evaluative component.

Trait-based individual difference measures were linked to two influential, but in the end not entirely satisfactory, theories, androgyny and gender schema. They both supposed that all types of gender attributes were closely linked, but this was not supported by the evidence. Masculinity and femininity turn out to be more complex than is often supposed, and most people have masculine and feminine aspects to their personality, interests, appearance, and behaviour.

Further reading

Glick, P. and Fiske, S. T. (2001). An ambivalent alliance: hostile and benevolent sexism as complementary justifications for gender inequality. *American Psychologist*, 56: 109–18.

This article provides a summary of research on the measurement and implications of two sorts of sexism. One involves benevolent and paternalistic attitudes towards women, and is associated with restricting their activities. The other is a more hostile set of attitudes that is associated with physical aggression towards partners and with sexual coercion.

Hall, J. A. and Carter, J. D. (1999). Gender-stereotype accuracy as an individual difference. *Journal of Personality and Social Psychology*, 77: 350–9.

This is a contemporary study of whether stereotypes accurately reflect reality. The authors used evidence from meta-analyses of sex differences in personality and behaviour as their standard, and found that young adults rated men's and women's traits and activities in similar way, suggesting that common sense is a useful guide to the actual behaviour of men and women.

3   Origins

Introduction

The way men and women behave is the end-result of a long historical process and a much longer evolutionary one. Many of the sex differences we observe today, such as those in mating and reproductive behaviour, and in aggression, are similar to those found in other animals, and fit the pattern expected from evolutionary principles. Some differences between men and women are less obviously connected to their different reproductive roles, but none the less have attracted evolutionary explanations. Findings indicating the superiority of women in certain memory tasks involving widespread scattered objects have been attributed to women's specialisation for gathering widely scattered plant foods in the human ancestral environment. This explanation is specific to the human species, as the division of labour into male hunters and female gatherers of plant food is found only in humans.

Other sex differences may be associated with the historically more recent division of labour into work outside the home and in the domestic sphere. This is one of the major implications of the social role theory introduced in the previous chapter (Eagly, 1987; Eagly et al., 2000). Men and women typically show a range of differences in their social behaviour that correspond to instrumental and expressive traits. For example, women show greater emotional sensitivity and responsiveness than men (Grossman and Wood, 1993), and men are more likely than women to take charge in groups that are engaged in a specific task (Eagly and Karau, 1991). These differences are viewed as arising from the position of men and women in the domestic and public spheres of work (chapters 8 and 9). A more recent development of this analysis (Wood and Eagly, in press) has concentrated on the origins of sex differences through an interaction between evolved physical sex differences, notably those directly involved in reproduction, and the economic and stuctural demands of social life.

As Wood and Eagly note, there are different emphases in accounts of the origins of sex differences. Their analysis contrasts with both that of evolutionary psychologists, who emphasise evolved psychological dispositions, and of social constructivists, who emphasise the meanings that culture constructs from biological sex differences. In this chapter we try to evaluate whether some sex differences in behaviour are better explained in evolutionary terms, whereas others may be better explained as a result of historically more recent cultural processes.

Analyses of the social roles of men and women also involve the issue of male power. In addition to occupying *different* social roles according to the nature of their work, men and women – and boys and girls – occupy roles of unequal status. In most societies men exert power over women. Recognition of this fact does not deny that many men are in low-status or powerless positions relative to other men: indeed the world of men is typically hierarchical. Likewise, it does not deny that many women exert power within their sphere of influence. It does mean that, typically, throughout history men have collectively sought to control the activities and choices of women. For example, there is a long legal and cultural tradition in the West that a man's wife is his possession (e.g., Dobash and Dobash, 1980), although this view has gradually changed, leading to the relative equality of women in many industrialised countries.

Feminist analyses typically concentrate on the legacy of male domination, and explain aspects of male behaviour such as wife battering, rape, and sexual harassment, as direct consequences of male power (e.g., Dobash and Dobash, 1980; Walker, 1989). More subtle differences between the sexes have also been identified as a direct consequence of male power over women. For example, Eagly (1983) explained the finding that, when interacting with each other, men tended to be more influential and women more easily influenced, as being a consequence of the wider societal inequalities in the status of men and women.

Although feminist analyses highlight the historical legacy of male domination, they seldom address the issue of its origins, but there is usually an assumption that it has arisen more recently than in evolutionary time. This assumption was challenged by Hrdy (1981), and by Smuts (1992, 1995), who regarded patriarchy as having arisen out of power relations between the sexes that can be identified in our primate relatives. Smuts suggested that subsequent cultural elaborations have built on the consequences of biological evolution. Wood and Eagly (in press) presented a contrasting account of the origin of patriarchy, viewing it not as a universal feature, but as something that emerges (or not, as the case may be) from an interaction between physical sex differences, ecological conditions, and cultural values.

Before exploring these accounts of the origins of behavioural differences between men and women in more detail, we first consider why the division into two sexes occurred in the first place. This is such a widespread feature of the natural world that it is clearly rooted in evolutionary biology. There are three related questions to consider. First, why did sexual reproduction evolve? Second, why does sex usually involve only two sorts of germ cells, eggs and sperm? Third, why are there separate sexes in some species, while in others the same individual produces both eggs and sperm?

The origins of sexual reproduction

Asexual reproduction involves budding off a part of the parent's body. This is an exact genetic copy, equivalent to an identical twin or a clone. Sexual reproduction involves parents exchanging genetic material. Since this halves the genetic material that each partner passes to the next generation, it would seem to be less efficient than the asexual method. The simple logic is that two asexually reproducing virgins can produce twice as many offspring as a heterosexual couple, and without the added cost of having to find a suitable mate (Maynard Smith, 1978; Ridley, 1993). Yet sexual reproduction is widespread throughout the living world, in plants as well as animals. The difficult question, that evolutionary biologists have been wrestling with for 30 years, is what additional advantages of sexual reproduction are there that have led to its evolution and maintenance despite the obvious disadvantage. Among a variety of suggestions, the most plausible one is the 'Red Queen' theory (Hamilton et al., 1990; Ridley, 1993).

In Lewis Carroll's *Alice Through the Looking Glass*, the Red Queen had to run fast just to stay still. Applied to evolutionary change, the Red Queen refers to two species competing with one another: one makes a change to counter the malevolent influence of the other, which in turn evolves something to block this, and so on, a situation also known as an evolutionary 'arms race'. Each species continually has to come up with something new just to fend off the other's latest adaptation. This way of looking at evolution emphasises dynamic competition with many other organisms, rather than an animal pitted against its physical environment and a few obvious competitors. The Red Queen view applies particularly to evolutionary competition between the countless bacteria and other parasites that swarm through the bodies of all large animals that act as their hosts. The important point about these minute parasites is that their lifetime is very short and they produce generation after generation of offspring during one lifetime of their host. This enables them to evolve much more quickly than the host species, and to produce new ways of counteracting the host's defences. The immune system found in humans and many other vertebrates plays an important role in managing their side of this 'arms race'.

Microscopic parasites produce protein molecules that bind on the surface of the host cells that they subsequently destroy. Each protein molecule must fit that particular cell surface, a situation that readily lends itself to the analogy of a key fitting a lock (Ridley, 1993). The exchange of genetic material involved in sexual reproduction provides endless variations in the 'locks', the types of cell surface, so that the 'keys', the protein molecules evolved by a micro-organism for one generation of host, are unlikely to fit the locks present in the cells of the next generation. In contrast, asexually reproducing lines will have the same locks for generations, so that they will be vulnerable to their cells being invaded once the micro-organism has the appropriate key. Parasites provide a strong selection pressure favouring genes that exist in many different forms (polymorphic genes), and are therefore able to produce a variety of different locks. Sexual reproduction provides a readily available way of achieving this, through the mixing of genes from two separate individuals.

Why two sexes?

Human beings are one of many species whose members are divided in roughly equal proportions into males and females. All mammals are so divided, sex determination being fixed at conception, by the possession of XX (female) or XY (male) chromosomes. This arrangement is not universal among animals, or even among vertebrates. In birds, it is the male that possesses two longer chromosomes (termed ZZ) and the female that has the shorter sex-specific chromosome (ZW). In some shrimps, fish, and reptiles, sex is determined by environmental conditions, such as temperature, and not by sex chromosomes. In other cases, sex is influenced by social conditions. In the coral fish, *Anthias squamipinnis*, the presence of a male provides a signal that keeps any nearby females from transforming into a male (Shapiro, 1979). In his absence, the largest nearby female changes sex.

The feature that biologists use to define an animal's sex is which of two types of *gametes* or germ cells the individual produces. If these are large, contain food, and are immobile, that individual is defined as female. If they are small, without food stores, and are mobile, that individual is defined as male. This raises the question of why there are only two sorts of gametes (leading to two sexes). Why not more than two?

Some simpler organisms engage in a form of sexual reproduction known as conjugation – the transfer of the cell nucleus (containing the genes) down a narrow tube from one individual to another. When this occurs, as in one-celled Protozoan animals such as *Paramecia*, and in mushrooms, there are many different types of individuals, roughly corresponding to the different sexes in complex forms. However, when reproduction involves the fusion of two cells that we generally associate with sex, there are invariably only two sexes. The reason we presented for this in the previous edition of *Sex and Gender* involved selection for specialisation either for storing food for the next generation or for seeking out other gametes. Contemporary evolutionary explanations for the occurrence of only two sexes require us to enter the often counter-intuitive world of modern evolutionary thinking (Tooby, 1999; see chapter 1).

Over the past 20 years, evolutionary biologists have explored the implications of competition between genes within the same individual. There are two sets of genes in each cell, one on the chromosomes in the cell nucleus, and the other outside the nucleus in the cytoplasm (cytoplasmic or mitrochondrial DNA). One convincing explanation for the evolution of two sexes is based on the finding that in nearly all plants and animals only the mother passes on cytoplasmic DNA. Cosmides and Tooby (1981) proposed that the exclusion of the males' cytoplasmic DNA prevents the damaging competition which would occur between genes from the two sources and would be likely to destroy most of the cytoplasmic DNA (and hence the offspring so produced). This does happen in the green alga *Chlamydomonas*, which lacks any measures to prevent it (Cosmides and Tooby, 1981). In organisms that reproduce by conjugation, it is prevented by the narrow tube, the cytoplasmic bridge, enabling only genes from the cell nucleus to be exchanged between individuals. In the vast majority of other cases, the solution is to have two sexes, one of which leaves its cytoplasmic DNA behind.

Cosmides and Tooby (1981) argued that competition between cytoplasmic genes from two individuals would set in train selection pressure for larger and larger gametes, containing enough cytoplasm to ensure survival without the potential danger of having to supplement it from another gamete. Once gamete size had reached a particular point, it would open the way for the evolution of an alternative strategy, to produce many smaller gametes with the minimum structure necessary to deliver the nuclear genes to the egg. These two alternatives represent specialised strategies which could not be improved upon. In this analysis, the male sex becomes defined as the one that does not contribute cytoplasmic genes to the next generation. One practical consequence is that all an individual's cytoplasmic DNA is inherited through the female line of the family, and that this has occurred through countless generations.

This theory explains the occurrence of two types of gametes, their existence as large and small forms. A further question is why the two forms are located in different individuals, males and females, as in humans and most other vertebrates. These species are *dioecious*, in contrast to hermaphrodites, where each individual produces both male and female germ cells, as is the case in most plants, and many invertebrates. The answer to why there is this variation is again a difficult and perplexing one. Suggested explanations have concentrated on evolved responses to competition between the different sets of genes involved in the process of sexual reproduction. To simplify a complex argument, separation into two sexes provides one way of preventing potentially harmful competition between genes in the male and female germ cells within one organism (Cosmides and Tooby, 1981). As Ridley (1993) put it, separation of the sexes counteracts the tendency towards 'genetic mutiny' in germ cells.

Sexual dimorphism and sexual selection

The term *sexual dimorphism* refers to differences in the bodily features and behaviour of males and females of the same species. It is widespread throughout the animal kingdom, including humans. If there is only one essential difference between males and females – their specialisation for producing different-sized gametes – why are there all the other differences that are found between the sexes? Why are males often larger than females, why do they tend to fight more, and why are many male birds more brightly coloured than their female counterparts? And why do men but not women have beards and women but not men have breasts? One influential evolutionary explanation is that all these are a consequence of one essential difference between the sexes, gamete size.

Darwin (1871) noticed that, in animals, sexual dimorphism usually follows a particular pattern: males are larger, and more likely to fight over resources or access to females; females are likely to be more discriminating than males in their choice of mates. He suggested that these differences arose from *sexual selection*, selection of features fitting the individual for success in mating, and that it takes these different forms in males and females. From these two selective forces arise many of the sex differences in form and behaviour found in the animal kingdom. For example, female choice leads to the evolution of elaborate bodily adornments and displays in males such as the peacock.

It was not until 100 years later that a plausible theory of why sexual selection took different forms in males and females was published. Trivers (1972) realised that male competition and female choice arose not from anything inherent in being a male or a female, but from a consequence of the initial specialisation of males and females in gamete production. Typically, the production of egg cells and their associated food sources requires more time and energy than does the production of sperm which contain no food stores. The female's contribution is more costly. If she mates with a male producing non-viable or poor quality offspring, the time and energy required to abandon this effort and start again will be much more than in the case of the male, who only has to produce his relatively low-cost sperm.

Trivers referred to this imbalance as a difference in *parental investment*. The term refers to the time and effort spent producing germ cells, and in incubating and protecting eggs and young. The initial parental investment of females is greater than that of the male as a consequence of the type of germ cell they produce. This often puts them in the position of 'holding the baby'. If the offspring can be reared by one parent only, the male will have less to lose by abandoning his mate soon after fertilisation, and seeking another female to fertilise. The female, on the other hand, will have to expend more time and energy in starting again, so that she may as well stay with the existing offspring. This analysis (developed by Maynard Smith, 1977, and Lazarus, 1990) indicates why parental care is usually undertaken by the female when one parent will suffice. It also explains why specialisations for nurturing the young, such as placental and lactational feeding in mammals, are typically found among females.

The degree of imbalance in parental investment is associated with the degree of competition among males for access to fertile females, and with the degree of polygyny (one male mating with several females) typically found in the mating system. An extreme case in the animal world is that of the elephant seal where 1 male can guard around 40 females (Le Boeuf, 1974). Competition has led to the evolution of a very large size difference between the sexes in this animal. Of course, for every successful male bull seal there will be 39 others deprived of a mate. The variation in reproductive success among males in this species is very high. Typically, it is higher in males than females in most species, but in the elephant seal it is particularly high.

In some societies, very powerful men have been able artificially to raise this limit, either by keeping their wives and concubines in captivity, or by sexual access to many women. The maximum possible numbers of children that can be fathered under these circumstances remains a matter of controversy. The Guinness Book of Records lists Emperor Moulay of Morocco, as having the record for fathering the most offspring, at 888 (Daly and Wilson, 1988), although Miller (1998) has argued that the first emperor of China is likely to have exceeded that number. On the other hand, Einon (1998) has argued that a figure of nearly 900 offspring would have been unobtainable for a number of reasons, in particular problems arising from women's low fertility, and the mistaken attribution of biological paternity. Whatever the exact figure, it is still almost certain to be far more than the numbers of children that any woman could produce.

In the animal world, there are circumstances under which the consequence of male desertion is that the offspring are unlikely to survive. These conditions lead to the evolution of paternal care and to *monogamy*, relatively enduring relationships between one male and one female, found in the majority of bird species. This mating system is associated with less pronounced male competition, and less pronounced size and other differences between the sexes. Trivers' theory identified the greater degree of parental investment by the male as the reason for the relatively low degree of sexual dimorphism in these cases. He also noted that, even in these cases, female parental investment was probably greater than that of the male and that males of such species would seek additional matings from other females if the opportunity arose. This has been confirmed by many studies since then (e.g., Birkhead and Moller, 1992; Gowaty and Bridges, 1991; Riley et al., 1995). In addition, as Miller (1998, 2000) argued, sexual selection will still be a driving force for evolutionary change, even under conditions of strict monogamy, where it will lead to evolutionary changes in both sexes.

The crucial test of Trivers' theory was whether there would be a reversal of the usual pattern of sex differences when there was a reversal of the usual pattern of parental investment. The answer is provided from studies of species of birds where the male performs all the incubation of the eggs and provides the parental behaviour for the chicks. In these species, such as phalaropes and the wading birds (Jenni, 1974), the females are larger and more aggressive than the males, supporting Trivers' theory.

Trivers also noted that when fertilisation is internal and there is substantial paternal care, the male always runs the risk of raising another male's offspring, of being cuckolded. He argued that adaptations would evolve to decrease the chances of this happening, and he noted the violent emotions aroused by human adulterers in this context (chapter 6). Subsequent studies have revealed a variety of mechanisms in animals which would counter cuckoldry, ranging from widespread mate-guarding (Berrill and Arsenault, 1982; Parker, 1974) to the killing of another male's offspring prior to mating with a female (Bertram, 1975; Hrdy, 1981).

Trivers' theory provides a comprehensive and convincing account of the origins of commonly observed sex differences and their variation across species. Its influence has, however, lead to a relative neglect of other evolutionary reasons why the sexes may come to differ in form and behaviour. For example, the emphasis on female choice and male competition has perhaps led to a neglect of mate choice by males, and competition among females (Cunningham and Birkhead, 1998). Studies of primates (Hrdy, 1981; Wrangham, 1980) show that females tend to compete for resources and the opportunity to raise their offspring without interference. In a range of animals, females compete for feeding territories, and in other cases competition can result in the reproductive systems of subordinate females being suppressed (Breed and Bell, 1983; Hrdy, 1981).

Another evolutionary reason for sex differences is niche specialisation, mainly in the form of different feeding habits by males and females. In several groups of predatory birds, the sexes are adapted for different sizes and types of prey (Selander, 1972), and a similar explanation has been advanced for the case of elongated carnivores such as the weasel (Brown and Lasiewski, 1972). Although such cases are far less common than the circumstances underlying sexual selection, they may be relevant to the human case, as it would seem that humans specialised for different methods of food collection (hunting and gathering) from early in hominid history. As indicated earlier, some human sex differences have been attributed to this division of labour.

The sexual natures of men and women

Trivers' analysis concerns broad principles underlying the evolution of sex differences and we would expect them to apply to humans no less than to other species. In the animal world, the size difference between males and females tends to correspond to the degree of male competition and the degree of polygyny. The small but consistent difference in size between men and women suggests that there was a slight tendency towards polygyny in evolving humans (Short, 1980; Miller, 1998; Plavcan and van Schaik, 1997). This pattern would have pre-dated the historical examples of exaggerated polygyny by despotic rulers, and before human societies had laws permitting only monogamy.

The ancestral tendency towards mild polygyny survives today. Ethnographic surveys indicate that in most societies high-status men are allowed more than one wife. It also survives in the form that even when a nation officially permits only one legal marriage, wealthy and powerful men establish sexual liaisons with other women. In cases where divorce is available, serial monogamy is widely engaged in by men who can afford to acquire a younger wife at the expense of an existing older one. In countries such as the USA, this is likely to have the same effect on the variation in male reproductive success as polygyny, as each new wife of an older man deprives a younger man of a possible mate (Wright, 1994:101).

Wright (1994) argued that there is a good reason for society to impose monogamy, because 'leaving lots of men without wives and children is not just inegalitarian; it is dangerous' (p. 100). The reason it is dangerous arises from sexual selection among males. Where there is free competition between men, they will be more likely to incur risks and commit crimes to obtain resources to attract women or to fight over women. Consider the following natural experiment, which occurred after the famous mutiny on the *Bounty* (Brown and Hotra, 1988). Fifteen men (9 mutineers and 6 Polynesians) and 13 women Polynesians formed a colony on the uninhabited Pitcairn island in the Pacific Ocean. When they were found 18 years later, 10 of the women but only 1 of the men were alive. Twelve of the men had been killed by other men and 1 committed suicide. Most of the murders resulted from sexual jealousy.

Both the identification of mild polygny as the basic mating system of our hominid ancestors and the recognition of the widespread existence of institution-alised monogamy hide differences between the sexual natures of men and women. What is observed as the overall pattern of sexual relationships may not be what both sexes want. The evidence is consistent with what we should expect from Trivers' analysis, that men would prefer greater sexual variety than they settle for in a monogamous marriage, whereas women are far more discriminating in their mate choice. Of course, these are overall generalisations, and we note various departures from them.

One source of evidence on the different sexual natures of men and women is their behaviour when they are unaffected by what the other sex usually wants. Symons (1979) argued that the sexual activities of male and female homosexuals in the pre-AIDS communities of the USA can provide us with this information. Whereas gay men typically had vast numbers of sexual partners, the relationships formed by lesbians were very similar to those of stable heterosexual couples. Symons argued that this analysis showed how men would behave if they were not normally subject to female choice and the possibility of an extra-pair sexual liaison leading to loss of the current partner. Accounts of the behaviour of powerful rulers throughout history support this view (Betzig, 1992), as do the biographies of male rock and film stars, and some national leaders, today. They all suggest that men would – if they could – indulge a taste for variety in their sexual partners.[1] As Symons indicated, what stops them is that women are generally not interested. Only the rich and famous, and gay men, have the option of casual sex open to them to any degree, unless of course they pay for it, and there are plenty of men who take this route. Many others fantasise about it.

While most of the social psychological studies on this topic have tended to confirm these conclusions, they have generally been concerned with what men say they would *like* to do if they could get away with it because – as we have seen – most men do not get the opportunity. One study (Clark and Hatfield, 1989) set up a situation which went beyond this. A moderately attractive member of the opposite sex went up to a male or female student on an American campus and said: 'I've been noticing you around campus. I find you to be very attractive', followed by one of three questions. These were: 'Would you go out with me tonight?'; 'Would you come over to my apartment tonight?'; or 'Would you go to bed with me tonight?' Around half of the students approached agreed to the date, and this proportion was

---

[1] It may be said that there are also examples of women in positions of power who have had many sexual partners. The point is that many women *could* have many partners, but choose not to, whereas many men *would like to*, but cannot.

the same for men and women. However, even more of the men – three-quarters – agreed to have sex, whereas none of the women did. Around two-thirds of the men but only 6 per cent of the women agreed to go to the apartment. These findings again suggest that men but not women are receptive to offers of casual sex.

Sexual selection and psychological sex differences

Trivers' analysis predicts that the psychological differences between men and women will be more widespread than their attitudes to casual sex. There will be differences in criteria for choosing a mate, and in sexual jealousy, aggression, risk-taking, and dominance. Sexual selection theory highlights the importance of female choice, and Trivers' analysis indicates some of the criteria that females use in choosing between males. Because the survival of human infants is greatly increased by care from both parents, women will value features indicating the ability to provide resources and protection for the woman and the offspring. Consequently, Buss (1989, 1994) studied the desirability of various characteristics possessed by a potential mate, involving over 10,000 respondents from 37 cultures in 6 continents. Women consistently preferred men with higher earning potential, and they tended to rate industriousness and ambition higher than men did. The attraction of rich and powerful men for women throughout history and through to the present day illustrates this finding, summed up by the famous phrase 'power is the ultimate aphrodisiac', attributed to Henry Kissinger. We should, however, note that such findings do not necessarily mean that women have an innate disposition to prefer rich and powerful men. We only know that it is a consistent preference under many cultural conditions today. It may be of ancient origin, as Buss (1994) argued, or it may only be found where women can only gain access to essential resources through a relationship with a man, as others have argued (Eagly and Wood, 1999; Hrdy, 1997; Kasser and Sharma, 1999; Wood and Eagly, in press). Miller (1998) has argued that the coming of agriculture distorted ancient mate choice patterns, and that during hominid evolution men were never the great providers they are often made out to be today, a view supported by Wood and Eagly's (in press) detailed cross-cultural analysis. This issue is still being debated (e.g., Kenrick and Li, 2000), and it is unlikely that the last word has been written on it.

Even for a contemporary man, money and status are not everything for attracting women. Several studies have shown that women respond preferentially to physical cues which reliably indicate health and fitness, i.e. that the man possesses 'good genes'. Again, this is what we should expect from Trivers' sexual selection theory, and we should expect it to be especially the case when the man is unlikely to be a long-term partner. In other words, when the woman is having a sexual liaison with a man who is not a regular partner, looks should be a major consideration (Buss and Schmidt, 1993). The evidence comes from studies of two bodily features. The first is body build, or more specifically waist-to-hip ratio, which shows little overlap between the sexes and reflects the influence of sex hormones on subcutaneous fat distribution. Young women found line drawings of male physiques with a normal weight and a ratio of around 0.9 to be more appealing than other body shapes (Singh, 1995). This ratio is associated with optimum health for men. A further study showed that physique interacted with financial status, so that when both were optimal the man was perceived as especially attractive.

The second bodily feature is a more subtle one: the extent to which the body deviates from perfect bilateral symmetry. In animals, this has been shown to indicate developmental instability: the extent to which development is subject to the impact of environmental agents such as parasites and toxins. Symmetry is associated with signs of fitness such as growth, survival, and reproductive health (Gangestad and Thornhill, 1997). Women find symmetrical men more attractive than asymmetrical men. Bodily symmetry predicts how many partners a man has had, in particular those that are in addition to a current relationship. Men's symmetry was also found to predict a greater frequency of orgasms among their partners (Thornhill et al., 1995). Women were more likely to choose symmetrical men for a short-term sexual relationship which is again consistent with symmetry being a cue for good genes (Gangestad and Thornhill, 1997).

The cross-national study of Buss (1989) found that men consistently rated a woman's looks as important when choosing a mate, in agreement with more extensive findings from the USA (Buss and Schmidt, 1993). Symons (1995) argued that men find cues associated with women in their teenage years (15 to 18 years) most attractive. This is when women marry in traditional societies. In modern Western societies, these cues are found among women of older ages, through a combination of delaying reproduction and the use of cosmetics, diet, and exercise.

Men of different ages and different ethnic groups were found to prefer line drawings or photographs of a female form with a waist-to-hip ratio of 0.67 to 0.80, which coincides with reproductive health, hormonal status, and longer-term health (Henss, 2000; Singh, 1993; Singh and Luis, 1995). The optimum ratio was around 0.70, which is the value that Marilyn Munroe shares with other women famous for their beauty. However, more recent studies have challenged the universality of the male preference for this body shape, finding preferences for a larger body build and higher ratios among Hazda hunter–gatherer men (Marlowe and Wetsman, 2001) and among men from an indigenous Peruvian people who had little contact with the Western world (Yu and Shepard, 1998). Other studies using Western samples have found that these preferences are relegated to a minor role when facial attractiveness is available as an alternative cue (Furnham et al., 2001), and that they only operate within a restricted weight range (Tassinary and Hansen, 1988). Outside this range, body mass index is a much better predictor of attractiveness (Tovee et al., 1998). Singh (2001) has argued that such studies involve a very wide range of body builds, and that the waist-to-hip ratio preference is restricted to the normal range. His recent data indicate that this preference is present among tribal peoples from southern India.

As indicated in the previous section, Trivers identified paternity uncertainty as an important selection pressure on males when there is internal fertilisation and paternal care. In the animal world, there are widespread tactics for males to discourage other males from being interested in their mates, and their mates from being interested in other males. Evolutionary psychologists have viewed men's sexual jealousy in this light, and interest has focused on sex differences in sexual jealousy. Symons (1979) argued that men's jealousy would be concerned with sexual interest in view of the importance of paternity certainty, whereas women's jealousy would centre on the diversion of attention and resources to a rival. This hypothesis has now been tested in several countries (Buunk et al., 1996; Buss et al., 1992, 1999; Wiederman and Kendall, 1999), by measuring the degree of reported distress (and in one case physiological arousal) generated by participants thinking about their partners forming either an emotional attachment to someone else or having sexual intercourse with them. As predicted, men were more upset than women by thinking about sexual infidelity and women more upset than men by the emotional infidelity.

A related issue is whether this concern with paternity certainty underlies men's attempts to control women's reproductive lives, which has been viewed as the basis for the sexual double standard and for men's violence to their partners (e.g., Wilson and Daly, 1992b, 1993b; see chapter 6). Wood and Eagly (in press) have challenged this interpretation. First, they argue that the extramarital double standard is not uniform cross-culturally. Second, where it does occur, it is associated with indices of men's patriarchal control over women, and in particular with the patrilineal inheritance of wealth. They therefore argue that men's control of women's sexuality arises from their greater political power rather than paternity uncertainty.

Sexual selection also predicts that competition will be more pronounced among men than women, and most pronounced among men of peak reproductive age. Evidence that this is the case comes from young men's greater willingness to take risks associated with status and competition, compared with other age and sex categories, their higher levels of violence, and the greater importance of dominance and status relations for men than for women. Figures for violent crimes and homicides illustrate this pattern dramatically, and it is found across different cultures and among nations with very different absolute rates of violent crime (e.g., Campbell, 1999; Courtwright, 1996; Daly and Wilson, 1988; Wilson and Daly, 1993a). Again, there are alternative interpretations of these findings, and the topic is considered further in chapter 6.

It is also possible that sexual selection has produced other psychological sex differences that are more widely attributed to the societal roles of men and women. One of these is different views about social inequalities (Pratto, 1996), which may play an important part in occupational sex differences (chapter 9). Intermale competition may have led to male emotional inexpressiveness as a by-product of the importance of dominance relations among male groups (Archer, 1996). Geary (1999) argued that women's superiority over men in non-verbal skills and in language abilities (chapter 1) forms part of a series of related adaptations for competing with other women, and that sexual selection also accounts for male superiority in spatial and mathematical ability (chapter 9).

Miller (1998, 2000) proposed an innovative theory, based on sexual selection, that is radically different from those discussed so far in that its main concern is the evolution of traits that do not differ substantially between the two sexes, in particular the intellectual expansion that has occurred during the last 2 million years of human evolution. He argued that mate choice by both sexes, together with the substantial genetic linkage that occurs between male and female traits, could account for sexual selection operating to produce human rather than sex-differentiated features. The driving force would be the utility of social intellect, language, and artistic displays in mate choice, and the ability of such features to form a positive feedback loop, referred to as runaway sexual selection in the animal world.

The hunter–gatherer way of life

The ancestral way of life of the human species involved obtaining food by hunting animals and gathering plant food. With the exception of societies living in harsh environments with little plant food, there is a division of labour in nearly[2] every known society of hunter–gatherers so that men hunt and women gather (Martin and Voorhies, 1975). The various artefacts associated with human and pre-human remains indicate that hunting animals pre-dates *Homo sapiens*. In contrast, the nearest living primate ancestors do not regularly hunt animals in the way that humans do. Chimpanzees do supplement their mainly plant diet by co-operating to catch and kill animals of another species that come their way. However, they do not form the organised hunting bands that are characteristic of the traditional human way of life.

Food foraging specialisation by the two sexes is the likely reason for the evolution of some forms of sexual dimorphism in a few animal species (see above). There has been no shortage of suggestions that this has also been the case for humans. In particular, a range of male characteristics has been attributed to selection pressures for more effective big-game hunting by hominid ancestors. At one time, the 'hunting hypothesis' was a popular explanation of both men's characteristics, such as dominance and male bonding (Tiger, 1970) and for characteristics such as intelligence shown by both sexes (e.g., Alcock, 1975; Washburn and Lancaster, 1968). This view was soon criticised for omitting selection pressures operating on women (e.g., Hrdy, 1981; Leakey and Lewin, 1979; Slocum, 1975). The gathering way of life poses more of a problem for attempts to reconstruct the past than hunting does because it has left fewer artefacts in the fossil record.

Although both physical features, such as greater size, strength, and musculature, and psychological ones such as aggression and dominance relations, have been attributed to the hunting way of life, these are all characteristics found in males of species that do not hunt. They are more plausibly attributed to male competition. Earlier versions of the hunting hypothesis also included suggestions that male characteristics such as superiority in spatial ability might be the result of selection pressures for attributes adaptive for a hunting way of life (e.g., Kolakowski and

---

[2] See Wood and Eagly (in press) for a discussion of the small minority of societies where women hunters have been reported.

Malina, 1974; Harper and Sanders, 1978). This hypothesis can be found in more recent accounts which link it with the influence of brain lateralisation and prenatal hormones on spatial ability (Wynn et al., 1996).

Several considerations cast doubt on the hunting way of life as the origin of the abstract abilities (such as mental rotation) found to differ between men and women (chapters 1 and 9). The first is that sex differences in the spatial abilities underlying navigational skills have been found in other species of mammals (meadow voles) where they coincide with the size of the male's home range, which in turn coincides with the degree of polygyny in that species (Gaulin and Fitzgerald, 1989). This at least raises the question of whether men's spatial ability is attributable to a similar origin, given the evidence for mild polygynous tendencies in the human species. However, detailed examination of archaeological evidence suggests that the brain lateralisation associated with human spatial ability is of a more recent origin, dating from archaic *Homo sapiens*, rather than further back in evolutionary history (Wynn et al., 1996).

Another more recent qualification to the hunting hypothesis highlights its male-centred nature. A complete theory based on the hunter–gatherer way of life would include female as well as male adaptations for specialisation in finding food. Such a theory has been advanced by Silverman and Eals (1992). They identified male skills – required for hunting – as being able to perform mental transformations to maintain accurate orientations while moving, orientation in relation to places or objects in a landscape, and accurate aiming of projectiles. Female skills required for finding and relocating food sources involved peripheral attention and the inci- dental learning of the placement of objects. While the first of these corresponds to known sex differences in tests of spatial ability (chapter 9), the second had not been investigated before. Silverman and his colleagues found that women were consis- tently better than men at locating the spatial configuration of arrays of objects, especially when the learning of such an array was incidental to ongoing activities (Silverman and Phillips, 1998). Although Silverman and Eals' theory seems more complete than the older one-sided hunting hypotheses, it is still by no means clear that the archaeological evidence showing the advent of lateralisation of the brain does coincide with evidence of a change in the way of life of evolving hominids (Wynn et al., 1996).

Gender roles

A division of labour between men and women would seem to occur in nearly all known societies, from the ancestral hunter–gatherer pattern, to agricul- tural and herding societies, through to the industrialised world. The form it takes is variable, although there are certain common themes (Wood and Eagly, 2001). In the social sciences there is a long tradition of explanations for the origin of gender roles that have concentrated on patriarchy, male domination of women. Nineteenth-century anthropologists such as Lewis H. Morgan constructed a series of changes through which human society was supposed to have passed, from promiscuity to matrilineal descent to patriarchy. Engels based his *Origin of the Family* on this view, and it, in turn, influenced later feminist speculations. Both de Beauvoir (1953) and Mitchell (1966) followed Engels in attaching importance to the advent of private property for women's subjugation by men. In these accounts the origins of gender roles are bound up with the origins of male domination, since the division into the public and domestic spheres of work is seen as the source of men's power over women. We return to the issue of patriarchy in the next section.

Cancian (1987) identified the origin of public and private division of labour in fairly recent history as becoming distinct in American and British society in the early nineteenth century. She viewed this as producing expressive traits in women, and instrumental traits in men, referred to as the feminisation of love and the masculinisation of work. She also identified a similar polarisation of men's and women's roles in other parts of the world over the previous two centuries. According to this view, as the workplace became separated from the home and family, it became more impersonal and instrumental, distinguishing it from the warm personal private sphere. Thus the personality traits of men and women, and the stereotypes associated with them, arose from the social structure that divided men's and women's spheres of activity.

Eagly's social role theory (chapter 2) also emphasised the derivation of sex differences in personality and behaviour from the division of labour (Eagly, 1987, 1995a, 1995b; Eagly et al., 2000). These sex differences were viewed as a consequence of a social structure that involved dividing the labour of men and women into full-time paid work outside the home and unpaid work in the home. Since these roles involve different expectancies, different psychological characteristics are developed or adopted by individuals who occupy them. Again, these characteristics are summarised as instrumental for the masculine role and expressive for the feminine role. The higher status of men is an additional feature, arising from the connection between higher power and instrumental characteristics (Eagly, 1987; Eagly et al., 2000). It is clear that Eagly's social role theory views the origins of the division of labour as going much further back in history than the view advocated by Cancian. Wood and Eagly (in press) viewed women's work as arising from the practical considerations that it had to be fitted in with child care, and that men could more easily perform certain tasks that required physical strength. Where the social and physical environment is such that these constraints on efficiency are minimised, the contrast between men's and women's roles and behaviour will be reduced. In this explanation, the emphasis is less on a particular time in history when the division of labour originated, and more on how it emerged to different degrees under different conditions.

Social role theory can potentially explain the origin of a wide range of differences between the social behaviour of men and women (Eagly, 1987; Eagly et al., 2000). It has also been extended to explain sex differences in mate choice, one of the main areas researched by evolutionary psychologists. Eagly and Wood (1999) reanalysed

Buss' (1989) cross-cultural data on mate selection criteria, and found that the extent to which a society valued women's domestic skills predicted the extent to which women preferred older men and those with a high earning power. These findings are consistent with the view that women's choices are the consequence of the degree of division of labour in a particular society. Both these preferences (but not men's preference for physical attractiveness in a potential mate) decreased as women's societal power increased. Another reanalysis of Buss' cross-cultural data (Kasser and Sharma, 1999) showed that women's preferences for resource-rich men followed the extent of educational inequality and lack of reproductive freedom, again supporting the social role position.

Social role theory has also been invoked to account for sex differences in aggression (Eagly, 1987; Eagly and Steffen, 1986). In this case, it would seem to provide a less convincing explanation for the origin of sex differences than evolutionary theory (Archer, 1996, 1997). As indicated earlier, the pattern of age and sex differences follows those predicted by sexual selection, and they parallel sex differences observed in other species. Similarly, aspects of sex differences in sexuality and mate choice preferences, such as liking for impersonal sex and jealousy patterns, fit better into an evolutionary account of their origins.[3] It is also possible to argue (Archer, 1996) that many of the features attributed to the social roles of men and women could have an older origin in evolutionary history. For example, male inexpressiveness might have originated from intermale competition and the greater emphasis on status and dominance among male than female groups; female deference may have its origins in male domination, which could predate the relatively recent division of labour highlighted by social role explanations.

If the major differences between men's and women's social behaviour directly result from expectations associated with their social roles, we might expect that a change in roles should produce a change in their behaviour. The last two decades have seen many women occupying vocational roles which entail power and influence, and which were in earlier times the province of men. We might ask whether women have become more instrumental over this time. Current analyses have provided a mixed answer to this question (Feingold, 1994a; Twenge, 1997b).

The origin of patriarchy

We have already noted earlier theories linking patriarchy with the advent of private property. A number of twentieth-century anthropologists identified the change from the hunter–gatherer way of life to a settled agricultural life as coinciding with men becoming the dominant group (e.g., Draper, 1975; Martin and Voorhies, 1975). The role of primary producer changed, with men herding animals and ploughing the land. A crucial change was in the ability to store surpluses of food and to accrue wealth through trading. This made it all the more worthwhile for men to dominate not only women but also other men.

---

[3] See Wood and Eagly (in press) for a criticism of the evolutionary position on sex differences in jealousy.

These accounts locate the origin of male domination at some time in history. In contrast, Smuts (1995) located it in men's control of women's sexuality, something that can be traced back to the evolutionary history of the species. She argued that, while feminist theory identifies how men have come to exercise power, evolutionary theory informs us why they wanted such power in the first place. It is because men and women have different reproductive interests, which often conflict in the natural world. In non-human primates, males often employ coercion: it is this way around because males are larger and it is females that are choosy. Female primates show ways of countering the coercive tendencies of males, for example through alliances based on kin and friendships with males. Smuts argued that, in humans, men show more extreme patterns of dominance, controlling the movement of females and their access to resources. This was initially possible because of the pattern of female dispersal from the natal group (patrilocal residence) which is associated with weaker female bonds. It was also accentuated by the occurrence of male alliances in humans. In other species of mammals, males in alliance with one another coerce females both in sexual and non-sexual terms (Clutton-Brock and Parker, 1995).

Smuts followed earlier anthropologists in identifying the coming of a settled agricultural way of life as enabling men to gain further control over the resources necessary to survive and reproduce. Once it was possible for a few men to hoard resources, there existed the potential for more extreme forms of male domination, both over other men, and over women. Smuts further suggested that women's competitive strategies have aided the perpetuation of patriarchy, for example in their preference for rich men and in their support of customs designed to control women's sexuality. Her view of gender ideologies is that they go back to the beginnings of language, and reflect a pre-existing pattern of behaviour that is as old as – or older than – humankind itself. Thus, the ideologies of male domination and subordination of women are viewed as having arisen out of ancient evolved patterns of behaviour, rather than beginning at some time in human history.

The view that male domination of women is a legacy of human evolution rather than human history has been challenged from both an evolutionary and a social role position. Miller (1998) has argued that human life in the Pleistocene period (from 2 million years ago) involved neither brutal male domination nor monogamy (both being of relatively recent invention). Instead, social life centred around matrilineal groups of females and their offspring, with males being rather peripheral figures in their social life. It is interesting that this situation has re-emerged in the modern world where men have few economic resources to offer women (e.g., Scheper-Hughes, 1992; Tiger, 1999). Turning the old emphasis on man the hunter on its head, Miller wrote: 'Male scientists have been reluctant to recognise that, for the most part, adult male hominids must have been rather peripheral characters in human evolution, except as bearers of traits sexually selected by females for their amusement value or utility' (1998:109–10).

Also in agreement with the emphasis on the change in subsistence activities is Wood and Eagly's (in press) biosocial view of the origin of patriarchy. They reviewed evidence to show that male domination is not universal, and is variable according to different criteria that can be used. For example, men's dominance over their wives was reported in two-thirds of a representative sample of 93 non-industrial societies. They viewed patriarchy as emerging from the interaction between the biological differences between men and women (notably their re-productive roles and differences in size and strength), culture, and the economic demands of the way of life. They regarded the last of these as having a partic-ularly strong impact, notably in the form of the coming of intensive agriculture, which increased the proportion of women's work that was domestic, and took them away from higher-status public positions. Conversely, it put men at the centre of economic activity via access to transportation, trading, and commerce, leading to other specialised roles away from the domestic sphere. Wood and Eagly also iden-tified the development of warfare, patrilocal residency, and complex economies as important influences on the establishment of male domination.

Smuts' position differs from that of Wood and Eagly mainly in terms of its emphasis on evolved dispositions as laying the foundations for patriarchy. In other respects, there are similarities. Both emphasise the transition to settled societies and agriculture, and the impact of patrilocal residence. Smuts is more impressed by accounts of male domination of females in the animal world, whereas Wood and Eagly view the association between sex differences attributed to evolution (such as control of women's reproduction) and patriarchal societies as telling evidence that they are the consequence not the cause of male domination. As Wood and Eagly acknowledged, the cross-cultural evidence they reviewed concerns overt behaviour, rather than psychological states or dispositions, which are the main concern of evolutionary psychologists. We leave the reader to ponder the difference between the following two positions: (1) that men have the potential to domi-nate women, but that this occurs to a greater or lesser extent depending on the culture and the costs and benefits of doing so; and (2) that male domination arises from the interaction of biology, culture, and economic contingencies.

Conclusions

Trying to trace the origins of sex and sex differences necessarily involves making inferences from indirect evidence. Evolutionary biology has progressed remarkably over the last 30 years, both in terms of theory and of evidence. Evidence has been driven by technical advances and new discoveries in a range of fields, notably biochemistry and genetics, physical anthropology, and animal behaviour. All these have fed into disciplines more directly concerned with human behaviour, psychology, and anthropology, so that discussions that are not informed by the new evolutionary knowledge may sometimes appear dated. At the same time, we must temper enthusiasm for the new ways of looking at human origins with the caution that we are only making plausible interpretations in the light of available evidence.

This applies to questions concerning both the origins of sex and the origins of sex differences in human behaviour.

On the basis of current evidence, the Red Queen theory seems the most plausible explanation for the origin of sexual reproduction. An adaptation to overcome competition between cytoplasmic genes from two individuals is the most plausible current explanation for the origin of two rather than more types of sex cells. Trivers' version of Darwin's theory of sexual selection provides the most likely account of the origins of features that differ between men and women, such as size, many aspects of sexuality, and aggression. These can be understood in terms of principles applying to most sexually reproducing animals, and they are similar to sex differences in other animals. Nevertheless, we should emphasise that an origin in evolutionary history does not mean that such a characteristic is fixed today. It can be influenced, and in some cases greatly altered, by present-day environments.

Sexual selection can explain why, in most societies, men are more physically aggressive with one another than women are with one another. It can also help to appreciate the conditions under which these differences are accentuated or attenuated. For example, male competition tends to be accentuated when there are many young men and few women (Courtwright, 1996). Similarly, scarcity of resource-rich men tends to be associated with more physical aggression between young women (Campbell, 1995).

It is likely that some of the circumstances to which these dispositions respond have changed drastically during the course of history and pre-history. One example we encountered earlier was the coming of agriculture, which may have shifted the nature of resources available, and hence enabled certain men to become much more powerful than had been the case before. Many aspects of the behaviour of men and women may have changed accordingly. The currently available evidence provides scope for emphasising either history or evolution to a greater extent in accounting for patriarchy. Social role theory has been developed considerably to account for the origins of male domination and women's relegation to the lower-status domestic sphere. It also provides a coherent account of many of the sex differences in social behaviour apparent today, and in its latest form provides an informed challenge to a number of evolutionary explanations of the behaviour of women and men.

Further reading

Buss, D. M. (1994). *The Evolution of Desire: Strategies of Human Mating*. New York: Basic Books.
 A fascinating summary of research on sex differences associated with mate choice and mate attraction, including much of David Buss' own research.
Eagly, A. H., Wood, W., and Diekman, A. B. (2000). Social role theory of sex differences and similarities: a current appraisal. In T. Eckes and H. M. Trautner (eds.), *The Developmental Social Psychology of Gender* (pp. 123–74). Mahwah, NJ: Erlbaum.

Social role theory places the origins of men's and women's behaviour in the different social roles adopted since pre-historical times, as a consequence of constraints placed upon each sex by their role in reproduction and their physical differences. In so doing, it provides the main challenge to the view that men and women show different evolved dispositions.

Mealey, L. (2000). *Sex Differences: Developmental and Evolutionary Strategies.* New York: Academic Press.

A clear and incisive coverage of human sex differences from an evolutionary strategic perspective. Linda Mealey views men and women as having different strategies and tactics in their behaviour, as a result of the different roles of the sexes in reproduction. She applies this approach to sex differences in biology, emotional expression, cognition, and behaviour.

Ridley, M. (1993). *The Red Queen: Sex and the Evolution of Human Nature.* London: Viking.

A well-written and accessible book that covers evolutionary biological theories of the origins of sexual reproduction, and of evolutionary accounts of sex differences in behaviour and mental processes.

4   Developmental influences

Introduction

There are two sources of influence on psychological development, heredity and the environment. Although they can be separated conceptually, from the viewpoint of the developing child they form a continuous interaction throughout life. We tend to think of environmental influences beginning at birth, but they also exert their influence before this, in the womb. We also tend to think of heredity as having its impact early in life, but it can operate throughout life.

Many commonsense explanations, and psychological theories, have emphasised either the environment or heredity as the dominant influence in development. Arguments over their relative importance are known as the nature–nurture issue, and are apparent in the writings of the earliest Western philosophers and throughout the history of modern psychology. Utopian political systems have been built around the notion that, if only humans were given the appropriate environment, they would live in peace and harmony. American behaviourist psychology emphasized learning as the route to human perfectibility, and the legacy of this influence can be seen in social and developmental psychology today. Others writing about the human condition, notably Sigmund Freud and the ethologist Konrad Lorenz, have countered the notion of human malleability by arguing that the human species possesses innate destructive impulses.

The pervasive influence of the nature–nurture issue is evident in accounts of the development of psychological characteristics associated with the sexes. The debate is bound up with views about whether it is possible, by means of an appropriate upbringing, to rear boys who are non-sexist in outlook and peaceful in behaviour, or girls who are assertive as well as nurturant. Those who think that it is possible, view the environment as the dominant influence on the development of these characteristics. Those who see such aspirations as going against nature view hereditary make-up as having a major impact on the development of psychological sex differences.

A major concern of developmental psychologists has been to chart the changes involved in a person's journey through life, either through the entire lifespan or until a time in young adulthood that is regarded as maturity. The concept of developmental stages through which everyone passes has had less impact on everyday thinking than the nature–nurture issue, but it is reflected in the expectation that children will outgrow undesirable patterns of behaviour. In this chapter, we consider this perspective in relation to changes in the ways that boys and girls understand concepts connected with sex and gender, and also in examining the overall pathways of development of boys and girls.

Socialisation: the information potentially transmitted to boys and girls

Routes of cultural transmission

We begin our discussion of the nature–nurture issue by outlining research on the influence of nurture. The *socialisation* approach is based upon the assumption that the interpersonal and cultural environment provides the dominant source of influence on psychological development. The process of socialisation can be studied at various levels. We can begin – as many accounts do – by examining the values and attributes that are widespread in society, in other words the cultural messages that are potentially available to the child. These messages are influenced strongly by the available stereotypes and attitudes held about gender (chapter 2). Here we are concerned with their availability as potential influences on the next generation. Throughout our discussion, the reader should bear in mind that in most studies it is assumed – but not demonstrated – that these potential influences have an impact on the child, and that this is long-lasting.

Cultural transmission involves a number of different routes (Cavalli-Sforza and Feldman, 1981). The parent to child route, the source of cultural transmission most often studied by psychologists, is only one of several. Others include transmission by peers, and by teachers to pupils. These are based on personal, one-to-one transmission, which contrasts with the impact of the mass media, which involves one-to-many transmission, and has become so important in many parts of the world over the last few decades. This route has the potential to induce rapid cultural change and has produced similar youth cultures in modern industrial societies. Group identity is also of crucial importance for deciding whether or not a particular individual takes up a specific message. Thus a video may provide the *opportunity* for a one-to-many transmission, but if its message conflicts with the viewer's value-system, the video will exert no influence. As indicated later, this is particularly important for the impact of sexist or counter-sexist messages.

Parents' responses to infants

As there are several possible routes for the transmission of gendered messages, an initial question is whether parents react differently to babies on the basis of their perceived sex. Rubin et al. (1974) interviewed a sample of first-time parents, half of whom had sons and half had daughters. Parents were likely to describe their daughters with feminine words such as 'little', 'cute', and 'pretty' and as resembling their mothers. To assess whether parents apply these stereotypic labels

to their infants early in life, or whether they derived them from the infants' behaviour, researchers carried out experimental manipulations of babies' perceived
sex, to separate this from the actual sex of the baby. In these 'baby X studies', a
baby is presented to recent parents as a boy or a girl – in reality half of the 'boys'
are really girls, and half of the 'girls' are really boys.

In one of the first of these studies, Smith and Lloyd (1978) invited mothers of
first-born infants, aged 5 to 10 months, to play with a 6-month-old baby, who would
be presented as, and dressed as, either a boy or a girl. Toys viewed as appropriate
for one or other sex, or both, were present in the room. The mothers were found
to pick up and show the infants gender-stereotyped toys, and to encourage those
they thought were boys to engage more in large bodily movements. They also
responded to the large bodily movements of supposed boys by making similar
movements back. These findings suggested that parental responses to an infant's
perceived sex were to some extent gender-stereotyped.

Stern and Karraker (1989) summarised 23 similar studies published in the
following decade, and drew the following conclusions. Labelling the sex of the
infant generally produced similar results to those of Smith and Lloyd, but not
always. The effects are not strong ones, and may be qualified in various ways.
However, when found, they are in accordance with stereotypic beliefs about boys'
and girls' behaviour: for example male infants are perceived as louder or noisier
than females. Stern and Karraker's overall conclusion was cautious: that we should
be careful in assuming that there is strong evidence for differential parental treatment of infants according to their sex. Again, we should note that these studies do
not tell us whether the differential treatment influences the infants' behaviour.

Parents' treatment of boys and girls

If we look beyond infancy, at how parents treat boys and girls, we find conflicting
opinions among developmental psychologists. In their classic summary of the
evidence on sex differences up to the early 1970s, Maccoby and Jacklin (1974) concluded that the evidence then available revealed relatively few differences in treatment by parents according to the child's sex. They inferred from this conclusion
that psychologists should look more closely for possible biological differences.
While this remains a possibility, it is not the only one. Parental influences may
be relatively subtle, and have escaped the measuring devices of psychologists.
Alternatively, the main environmental influences may have arisen from sources
other than parents (Harris, 1995, 1998).

After the publication of *The Psychology of Sex Differences*, a large-scale US
study (Block, 1978) found considerable differences in the ways parents treated
boys and girls. For example, parents of sons were more concerned with punishment and negative sanctions and with making sure that boys conformed to gender
expectations than were those of daughters. As we show later, gender conformity
is an important theme in the social development of boys. Fathers and mothers
also differed in their treatment of boys and girls. Fathers were more accepting of

aggression towards themselves by daughters than by sons, and they provided more comfort to daughters than sons. They also accepted competitiveness by sons but not by daughters.

Block criticised Maccoby and Jacklin's conclusions in two ways. The first was that they had used global concepts, such as aggression, independence, and restrictiveness, which may mean different things when applied to sons and daughters. The second concerned the role of the father. Block noted that Maccoby and Jacklin had often combined evidence for both mothers and fathers, or used evidence that was only available from mothers. Importantly, Block showed that mothers and fathers responded differently to the sex of the child.

Block's point about the role of fathers was taken up by Siegal (1987), who used the term *reciprocal role theory*, to describe the view that fathers make greater distinctions than mothers do between sons and daughters, and it is fathers who transmit norms and expectations derived from outside the family. In evaluating the evidence for this view, Siegal found some support: half of 39 published studies that were examined showed that fathers' treatment of sons differed significantly from that of daughters. In contrast, few studies found that mothers treated girls and boys differently. Again, we should note that we are not considering how effective the parents' behaviour is in changing the child's behaviour. Discipline and physical involvement were the areas in which fathers' behaviour showed the most marked differences towards sons and daughters. They were firmer, stricter, less affectionate, and more directive with boys. They were more physically affectionate to girls. These differences were smaller among parents of infants and toddlers.

In chapter 1, we described the technique of meta-analysis which enables large numbers of studies of a similar kind to be combined, and for those with different characteristics to be compared. Lytton and Romney (1991) carried out a meta-analysis of parental treatment of boys and girls. From 172 studies, they found that the overall difference in parental treatment according to the child's sex was small. However, in the more numerous North American studies, there was clear indication that both parents encouraged gender-typed activities, such as play and household chores. This analysis confirmed that fathers made a greater distinction between sons and daughters than mothers did, particularly in relation to encouraging masculine activities and traits for boys. This review is important because it included a large number of studies and used quantitative analyses. The overall message is one that runs through the earlier reviews: that the evidence for pronounced and wide-ranging socialisation influences by parents is not strong, but that there are some consistent differences in the ways parents – particularly fathers – treat sons and daughters.

Another source of parental influence is the physical environment provided for the child, for example the type of decor and available playthings. Rheingold and Cook (1975) found that gender-stereotypes were reflected in the contents of 1- to 6-year-old children's rooms. Girls' rooms had more floral wallpaper, fabrics, and lace. Boys' rooms contained more toy animals, vehicles, and live animals, whereas those of girls contained dolls and dolls' houses. However, when they were tested in a laboratory playroom, the play preferences of 18-month-old infants, were not consistent with the types of toys found in their own rooms.

In a similar study involving children aged 5, 13, and 25 months, Pomerleau et al. (1990) found that boys were provided with more sports' equipment, tools, and vehicles and girls were given more dolls, fictional characters, child's furniture, and drawing, cutting, and pasting toys. Girls were more often dressed in pink or multicoloured clothes, and were given jewellery and pink dummies; boys were dressed in red, white, or blue clothing, and were supplied with blue dummies. Blue bedding was more common in boys' rooms, yellow being preferred for girls. Again, these young children's rooms were full of gender-stereotypic information. Again, we should note that the assumption that these exert an important impact on the development of sex-typed behaviour was accepted but not tested.

The social environment outside the family

We have already seen that parents are only one of several possible avenues of cultural transmission. Extended families, teachers, and peer groups may also influence children. Several studies (e.g., Fagot, 1977; Serbin et al., 1973) have shown that nursery-school teachers treat boys and girls in a gender-stereotypic way, and that peers ostracise and criticise children for behaving in gender-inappropriate ways. Peer groups are a particularly important source of ideas for pre-school age children. Pitcher and Schultz (1983) reported that the gendered ideas found in young children's playgroups tend to be caricatures of adult stereotypes, simplified in form and content. Other researchers who have tested individual children under more controlled conditions have also noted this reliance on simplified representations at younger ages (e.g., Levy and Fivush, 1993; Martin et al., 1990). A very important channel of cultural transmission is the mass media, which provides transmission from one to many on a grand scale. Earlier studies of the content of television programmes for young children in the USA (e.g., Sternglanz and Serbin, 1974) showed that gender-stereotypic images were portrayed. There were more male than female characters, and males were more likely to be shown as aggressive, constructive, and protective. They were more likely to be actively engaged, and to be rewarded for their actions. Females were more likely to be deferent, or to be punished for engaging in activities.

There are now many studies which document the existence of gender-stereotyped messages in television programmes watched by children (e.g., Durkin, 1985a; Thompson and Zerbinos, 1995), and also in the advertisements that accompany these programmes (Browne, 1998). One point which emerges from this research is the difficulty of constructing effective counter-stereotypic images (e.g., Durkin, 1985b,c). For example, Drabman et al. (1981) showed young children televised scenes in which the role of physician was played by a woman and that of a nurse by a man. After viewing the tape, the children were asked to identify photographs or names of the physician or nurse. The younger children (about 5 years, and about 9 years) selected names on the basis of gender stereotypes; i.e. a man would be identified as the doctor and a woman as the nurse, rather than on the basis of what they had seen. Older children (about 12 years) gave the correct identification. The results from the younger children were consistent with other research showing a general bias in the direction of gender stereotypes when younger children recall information involving gendered activities (e.g., Liben and Signorella, 1993; Ruble and Stangor, 1987).

These findings illustrate the importance of considering the way that children process and recall the information available to them, and they also have important implications for any attempts to reverse rigid gender stereotypes. More recently, Durkin and Nugent (1998) have investigated the stereotyped beliefs and expectations that young children themselves bring to their television viewing. This research takes us some way from considering television influences only in terms of the content of programmes. In the next section we consider how the developing child acquires information about gender.

Socialisation: transmission through social learning

Social learning theory addresses the question of how cultural information is transmitted to children (Bandura and Walters, 1963; Dollard and Miller, 1950; Miller and Dollard, 1941). It emphasises the processes of learning that are involved. Its first systematic application to gender development was by Mischel (1966, 1970), who viewed the principles of positive and negative reinforcement, punishment, and imitation as processes enabling the transfer of gender-stereotypic messages from one individual to another. Punishment occurs, for example, in the form of parental disapproval of cross-gender behaviour, particularly when it is shown by boys. Peer-group pressure and teachers' reactions provide other sources of reward and punishment for appropriate and inappropriate gender behaviour (Fagot, 1977; Serbin et al., 1973).

Imitation of role models

Social learning theory (Bandura and Walters, 1963) highlights the process of imitation, rather than the 'carrot-and-stick' mechanisms described in earlier behaviourist psychology. Boys and girls are held to acquire different patterns of behaviour through imitating the behaviour of adults and children of their own sex. Someone who is imitated is referred to as a *role model*. It is clear that boys and girls have access to different role models, although this is not really a concern of social learning theory, which concentrates on the way that imitation occurs. Nevertheless, the widespread phenomenon of boys and girls playing in single-sex groups throughout most of their childhood is particularly important for placing imitation in context. Opposite-sex role models will be less available than same-sex ones, and have to be sought out.

Mischel (1970) raised the possibility that children would selectively imitate their own sex when both sexes were present. He based this on a finding that children watching a film showed more eye movements when looking at major characters of their own sex than when looking at those of the opposite sex. Since then, other studies have found same-sex preferences (Bussey and Bandura, 1999), and studies of infants have investigated such preferences early in life. Some have located them as early as the first year of life (Bower, 1989; Kujawski and Bower, 1993; Lewis and Brooks-Gunn, 1979). In a longitudinal study of infants aged 3, 6, and 18 months, Shirley (2000) found that overall both sexes attended significantly more to photos of male than female infants. At 3 months, only boys showed a preference for pictures of boy babies.

Under circumstances where both sexes are available as models, children may learn behaviour associated with both sexes, but only perform that associated with their own sex. The greater contact between children of the same sex will restrict the opportunities to learn the opposite-gender activities, and lack of motivation will restrict its performance when it is learned (Bussey and Bandura, 1999). Further, it is likely that many gender-typed tasks will require practice for their effective performance. Nevertheless, there is evidence that children can, under some circumstances, behave like the opposite sex. Hargreaves (1976, 1977) analysed the contents of children's drawings made to the instructions to complete circles by drawing objects. He found that the content followed gender-stereotyped lines, boys drawing more mechanical and scientific themes and girls drawing more domestic themes. When children were given a similar test but asked to supply drawings that the opposite sex would make, boys' and girls' responses were reversed.

The children in Hargreaves' study were 10 to 11 years old. Studies examining the development of gender-stereotyped knowledge (e.g., Martin et al., 1990) show that younger children first learn about the characteristics associated with their own sex, and only later (by about 8 years) acquire extensive knowledge about the opposite sex. Investigations of sequences of events with masculine or feminine connotations (Levy and Fivush, 1993) also show that knowledge of same-sex activities predominates at younger ages .

The learning of gender-appropriate behaviour

There are several studies demonstrating that a child's performance is influenced by whether a task is viewed as appropriate for their own or for the opposite sex. Montemayor (1974) demonstrated that describing a game as 'like basketball' (masculine) or 'like jacks' (feminine) influenced the performance of 5- to 6-year-old US children. Where the task was gender-consistent, performance was higher than in the neutral condition (where no gender label was provided), and where it was gender-inconsistent, performance was lower than in the neutral condition.

Davies (1982, 1986) followed up this study with three groups of older British children (11, 13, and 16 years of age). The task involved trying to thread a metal loop through a bent wire without touching it. Whenever they touched the wire, a sound gave the participants feedback, and these occasions were scored as errors. This task was labelled as showing how good people are either at needlework or at electronics. Both sexes made fewer errors when the task label was gender-consistent than when it was inconsistent. One puzzling aspect of this study was that these findings occurred despite each child undertaking the same task under the two labelling conditions. It would seem to stretch the bounds of credibility to say to children 'here's a task that measures needlework ability' and then to present them with the same task as a measure of ability in electronics. Nevertheless, the findings were replicated in another study using the same task for the two labelling conditions (Hargreaves et al., 1985).

These studies show that the gender-appropriateness of a task affects a child's performance on it, and hence that the gender-appropriateness of a task may also influence whether a child imitates a person who is carrying it out. Barkley et al. (1977) drew this conclusion from studies of imitation by boys and girls. Children imitated behaviour they viewed as gender-appropriate, irrespective of the sex of the person performing it. This finding runs counter to the widespread belief that imitation is necessarily based on the individual identifying with a role model. The importance of the gender-appropriateness of an activity is shown in a more recent study. Using an interview measure of play preferences, Alexander and Hines (1994) found that 4- to 8-year-old boys preferred a girl playmate with a masculine style to a boy playmate with a feminine play style. Similarly, 8-year-old girls also chose on the basis of the gender of play rather than the sex of playmate. However, 4-year-old girls chose on the basis of sex rather than play style.

Social cognitive theory (Bandura, 1989; Bussey and Bandura, 1999), an important subsequent formulation of social learning theory, highlights the more explicit role of mental structures in guiding action. It is concerned, as was the earlier social learning theory, with how the social environment influences the cognitive structures that regulate gender development. Processes such as imitation, tuition, and feedback from one's own behaviour all guide the self-regulatory mental processes. Studies informed by this perspective are concerned with investigating the shift in the control of gender-typed behaviour from sources in the outside world to those within the child's mind, and they have found that such a shift occurs between 3 and 4 years of age (Bussey and Bandura, 1992).

Socialisation: acquisition through cognitive processes

Gender identity

In a seminal paper, Kohlberg (1966) applied Piaget's framework for understanding the development of thinking to gender. Like Piaget, Kohlberg viewed children as active agents seeking to make sense of the world outside. Children's own beliefs about gender were seen as guiding their interaction with the social world. Awareness early in life that there are two sexes, and that the child belongs to one of these, was held to be crucial for starting this process. Kohlberg (confusingly[1]) termed this *gender identity*. It enabled children to select those parts of the social world that applied to their sex, and to ignore those that applied to the opposite sex. Thus, the process of identification with one's own sex was seen as the beginning of a guiding force of socialisation. However, in the same article Kohlberg (1966) also stated that gender identity could not provide a stable organising principle until the child was certain of the stability of gender as a category, which he called *gender constancy*,[2] and this he placed later in development (see below).

Kohlberg (1966) suggested that a sense of gender identity appeared between 2 and 3 years of age, although Leinbach and Fagot (1986) have since demonstrated that children as young as 19 months can use the labels 'mummy' or 'daddy' to discriminate the sex of adults. Use of the labels 'boy' and 'girl' to discriminate between children occurs a little later (only 8 per cent of their sample could do this at 26 months of age). Correct labelling, however, is not the same as gender identity in the sense that Kohlberg used the term. Another study (Fagot et al., 1986) did find that a child's ability to label its sex accurately was associated with a preference for playing with a same-sex child, but not with gender-stereotyped toy choice. Other studies (e.g., Bussey and Bandura, 1992; Fagot and Leinbach, 1993) have reported mixed findings on the association between gender labelling and gender-linked behaviour. Kohlberg (1966) viewed these processes as connected, in that preference for, and the identification with, one's own sex was seen as driving subsequent imitation and reinforcement (processes which are primary in social learning theory). Kohlberg offered no suggestion as to why children should prefer their own sex in this way. We return to this issue in a later section.

Several studies have shown that children possess considerable knowledge about gender-typed activities at ages as young as 2 to 3 years (Huston, 1985), and that this increases to around 5 years (Martin, 1993). Kuhn et al. (1978), presented children with two paper dolls, one called Michael and the other called Lisa, and asked questions in the form of a game, about the dolls' likes and dislikes. They also asked what Michael and Lisa would do when they grew up. It was apparent that children of 2 to 3 years of age have an extensive, if stereotyped, knowledge about gender-typed activities. For example, they believed that girls would clean the house when they grew up and that boys would be the boss and would mow the lawn.

Gender constancy and stability

One issue that has proved controversial over the years since Kohlberg's influential article is gender constancy: the understanding that the two sexes are fixed categories and cannot normally be changed. Kohlberg claimed that before

---

[1] It would be more appropriate to call it sex identity since it concerns sex as a category.
[2] Again it would have been more appropriate to use the term sex constancy, as Bem (1989) subsequently did.

the age of 6 years children know relatively little of the essential differences between men and women, and concentrate on superficial markers of a person's sex, such as hair length and clothing. Using this way of thinking, a 3- or 4-year-old child believes that a girl can be changed into a boy by cutting her hair and wearing boy's clothing. Piaget identified this level of thinking as pre-operational thought. The child focuses only on the immediate properties of an object, and cannot reverse in thought a transformation that has occurred in real life so as to conserve the identity of that object.

At about 6 to 7 years of age, this way of thinking changes, so that conservation of the properties of objects, such as their volume or mass, is established, as is the understanding that categories such as sex are constant. Children come to realise that sex remains constant despite superficial changes such as hair length and clothing. The implication of this way of thinking, according to Kohlberg, is that it enables gender identity to act as a stable organising principle for gender knowledge and behaviour, something that is uncertain before this time (although Kohlberg noted that gender stability – knowing that one stays the same sex throughout development – occurred at younger ages, from 3.5 to 4.5 years). Later analyses (Martin, 1993; Martin and Halverson, 1981) proposed that gender identity is a sufficient organising principle, rather than requiring constancy, and evidence supports this view (e.g., Marcus and Overton, 1978; Martin, 1993; Martin and Little, 1990). The approach of Martin and her colleagues is often referred to as *gender schema theory*, to highlight the difference from Kohlberg's.

Stangor and Ruble (1987) proposed the compromise position that gender constancy increases the child's responsiveness to information about gender rather than initiating it. A study by Frey and Ruble (1992) supported this prediction for boys but not for girls, in that gender-constant boys played with a gender-typed toy despite it being uninteresting, whereas boys who lacked gender constancy did not. However, Lobel and Menashri (1993) found no association between gender-typed toy choice and gender constancy despite also varying the attractiveness of the toy.

One of the earliest empirical investigations of the nature of gender constancy was by DeVries (1969). She studied 64 intelligent 3- to 6-year-old US children, with the aim of testing whether they had achieved *generic constancy* (the stability of categories such as animals), which included gender constancy. To examine the stability of animal categories, she used the bizarre procedure of training a cat to wear a dog or a rabbit mask. Interviews with the children indicated an increasing understanding of generic constancy with age, that is, the child was more likely to say that a cat could not be changed into a dog or rabbit. Gender constancy was assessed using pictorial transformations of one sex (a girl or a boy) into the other by changing hairstyle and clothing. The children were asked whether the girl or boy in the picture had remained the same sex or changed as a result of the transformations. Again, a gradual increase in the understanding of constancy was found with age.

Subsequent studies involving pictorial transformations (Emmerich et al., 1977; Gouze and Nadelman, 1980; Marcus and Overton, 1978) found broadly similar results. However, Slaby and Frey (1975) found that if you simply ask children questions such as 'When you were a baby, were you a little boy or a little girl? or 'When you grow up are you going to be a mummy or a daddy?', 4-year-olds do answer correctly (as indeed Kohlberg had noted). This poses the question of how knowledge about one's own developmental stability, which is understood by a pre-operational stage child, differs from knowledge evoked by pictorial transformations. Bem (1989) answered this question by arguing that knowledge about oneself does not involve a Piagetian transformation, whereas a test involving an outside object undergoing a superficial does. We can recognise the distinction by naming them *gender* (i.e. sex) *stability* and *gender* (i.e. sex) *constancy*, respectively (Kohlberg, 1966; Smith, 1986).

Shields and Duveen (1982, 1986) found that few 3-year-old children believed that their own sex could be changed by a change of clothes, whereas 80 per cent of the same children believed that the sex of a figure could be changed in this way. These findings clearly demonstrate that there are two processes, one applying to the self and the second to other children. When these children were questioned about the nature of the transformations, they clearly distinguished real and hypothetical ('pretend') ones. Martin and her colleagues (Martin and Halverson, 1983; Martin and Little, 1990) also recognised the importance of this distinction.

Leonard and Archer (1989) questioned 3- to 4-year-olds about transformations involving real children and themselves. Again, stability over time was found for the self at this age, and also for another child, although to a lesser degree. When asked about transformations involving clothing, there were fewer correct answers for both others and the self. However, supplementary questions indicated that these transformations were seen as 'pretend' rather than 'real', supporting suggestions that this is an important distinction. It may simply be the case that younger children more readily operate a pretend way of thinking when attending to pictorial and fictional characters (which in the world of television, computer games and children's books can undergo magical transformations).

Cues for identifying sex

The issue of what cues young children use to distinguish male and female is related to that of whether they view sex as a fixed category. Thompson and Bentler (1971) showed 4- to 6-year-olds naked dolls on which the hair, upper torso, and genitals were either male or female in form. In each case the child was asked to choose a name, to decide whether boys' or girls' clothing was more appropriate, and to predict whether the child would grow up to be a 'mummy or daddy'. The usual cue the children used in making these decisions was hair length. Most children ignored the upper body and the genitals when these conflicted with the hairstyle.

These findings may not be surprising when we consider that, under most conditions, adults construe a person's sex from superficial cues such as dress and hairstyle. Kessler and McKenna (1978), who examined how people decide whether another individual is male or female, highlighted this. They do not do so as a biologist would, by inspection of their chromosomes or genitals. Instead, sex is mentally constructed from a variety of cues, such as dress, ways of moving, length of hair, facial hair, and breast development. The decision process is rapid and unconscious, and only comes to conscious awareness when someone has to search for the relevant cues, when a person such as a transsexual shows cues associated with both sexes.

Bem (1989) argued that children have picked up from adults a message about what sex is from this process of deciding on the basis of superficial cues. Bem stated:

> We dress males and females separately, and give them different hairstyles so that their sex will always be apparent even when their genitalia are hidden. In supermarkets, on playgrounds, and in every other social context, we also readily identify people as male or female for our children while giving no specific information about those people's genitalia. In doing these things, we adults are not only relying on visually salient cultural cues ourselves. We are also unwittingly communicating to our children that these are defining attributes of male and female. (p. 661)

Bem found that some children from a sample of 3- to 5-year-olds did show *both* knowledge about genital differences *and* that these differences took priority over other cues to define sex. Furthermore, she found that this was strongly associated with demonstrating gender constancy in a task involving pictorial transformations. Bem obtained these results by testing whether the children could correctly identify sex by means of genital cues, using a variety of photographs of children partially dressed or undressed where the genitals were the only salient feature. The pictorial transformations were in the form of photographs of similarly aged children, without clothes, or dressed up as the opposite sex, or dressed as the same sex. They were told that it was the same child in each case, and that the child was 'playing a silly game' (since the children would presumably be puzzled as to *why* the children had dressed up in this way). Bem then asked in each case whether the child was a boy or a girl. We should note that in this version of the pictorial transformations, the child concerned was identified as a real person – which should have made it easier to understand that essential features remained constant despite their wearing different clothes. Bem's conclusion was that genital knowledge enabled the younger child to appreciate the essential nature of a person's sex despite superficial transformations. Genital knowledge was one way of identifying an invariant feature of sex at a time when this would otherwise have been more difficult to understand. Bem's test of young children's genital knowledge has been replicated with a sample of British children (Lloyd and Stroyan, 1994).

Socialisation from a cognitive developmental perspective

This discussion of research on the development of knowledge about sex and gender has taken us some way from the topic of socialisation. Nevertheless, cognitive approaches to gender development do involve the underlying premise that whatever information there is in the social world can only have an impact on behaviour if there is a certain level of understanding present. At earlier ages, preferences and choices made along gender lines are viewed as being driven by the person's gender identity; later, gender constancy provides the first in a series of changes that eventually enable gender roles to be understood as a social arrangement rather than as something that is fixed (Ullian, 1976).

Underlying cognitive approaches is the assumption that understanding about gender comes first, and behaviour in the form of preferences and choices follow. There would be no place in the theory for gender-typed behaviour and preferences that by-passed the cognitive route. Researchers adopting a social cognitive approach (Bussey and Bandura, 1992) have questioned this assumption, and so have those who have investigated very early sex-linked social preferences (Kujawski and Bower, 1993; Shirley, 2000; Shirley and Campbell, 2000). We explore the implications of these and other findings that might suggest a direct biological influence on the behaviour of boys and girls in the next section.

Does biological development influence behaviour?

General issues

The suggestion that important aspects of the psychological dispositions of men and women can be attributed to their biological make-up has a long history, and was closely associated with the view that men and women are not only different, but that men are – by nature – superior. Of course, in ancient times such views were associated with religious beliefs, but with the development of the human sciences in nineteenth-century Europe and the USA, biological and anthropological writings were used to buttress the same view (chapter 1).

Whilst the view that women are men's intellectual equals is seldom challenged in the educated Western world today, biological research has over the past 30 years been used in debates over sex equality in other fields. In the early 1970s, the argument that women's social position is a consequence of their natural psychological dispositions was advanced to challenge the feminist position that it is a consequence of patriarchal values (e.g., Gray 1971; Gray and Buffery, 1971; Hutt, 1972). These biological arguments relied on the increasing amount of apparently relevant endocrinological and neurological research that was available. Most of this evidence was derived from experimental studies of non-human mammals and from reports of clinical conditions involving the presence or absence of the usual sex hormones. Because this evidence is necessarily indirect, it had a number of problems, in particular the problems of generality from studies of rodents to human development, and of alternative cultural explanations for effects found in the clinical conditions (Archer, 1971, 1975, 1976; Archer and Lloyd, 1985).

There is now a large body of research suggesting possible biological influences on the psychological characteristics of men and women (e.g., Berenbaum, 1998; Collaer and Hines, 1995). Before considering some selected examples, it is important to comment upon biological explanations more generally. Most are concerned with an event that occurs at a particular time in development, for example a sex hormone secreted at a particular developmental stage. They therefore focus upon a specific process rather than the developmental sequence as a whole. In this respect, they are similar to the sorts of influence considered by social learning theory. Cognitive developmental theory does take more account of the sequence of development, but it is still rather restricted, concentrating on certain important developmental transformations. In a later section, we argue that a fuller appreciation of the influences on gender development requires consideration of both socialisation and biological influences on the sequence of development. It should therefore be borne in mind that the aim of this section, to outline some of the more important biological research findings, is limited to documenting these effects rather than placing them in a developmental context.

The role of sex hormones in development

An early biological difference that could have consequences for the psychological dispositions and behaviour of boys and girls is the different pattern of sex hormone secretion that occurs in the prenatal and early postnatal phase. At about six weeks after conception, the presence of the SRY gene on the Y chromosome of the male activates particular genes in the embryonic gonad (Arnold, 1996). This leads to the development of the testes. In the absence of the SRY gene, the gonad develops into an ovary at about 12 weeks after conception. This mechanism of sex determination is the same in all mammals.

Beginning 8 to 10 weeks after conception, the embryonic testes secrete testosterone, which induces development of the male internal ducts. A second substance, Mullerian-inhibiting substance, leads to degeneration of the female internal ducts (Goy and McEwan, 1980), which are also initially present. Male and female external genitals develop from the same type of embryonic tissue. The presence of the androgen,[3] dihydrotestosterone, during the third and fourth months of pregnancy is responsible for differentiation as a male (Goy and McEwan, 1980).

In 1947, Jost first demonstrated the crucial role played by testicular androgens in the differentiation of the male and female reproductive organs in experiments on rodents (Jost, 1972). Another landmark discovery was that of Phoenix et al. (1959). They demonstrated that androgens secreted during early development influence the developing brain of rodents so as to affect sexual behaviour during adulthood. It is now known that androgens secreted during the period before and after birth, known as the perinatal phase, influence physiology and behaviour during both juvenile and adult stages of life. Only some of these influences generalise to primates, and here we concentrate on one particular type of behaviour, rough-and-tumble play, where the evidence is more consistent than for other possible influences (Collaer and Hines, 1995; Wallen, 1996). It should also be noted in passing that

---

[3] Androgen is the general name for hormones with biological actions like those of the main testicular hormone, which is referred to by its chemical name, testosterone. Other androgens have slightly different biological actions to testosterone.

there is rapidly accumulating human evidence for the influence of early androgens on a wide range of psychological attributes (Berenbaum, 1998, 1999), and for the continuing influence of lower levels of ovarian hormones on the brain and behaviour of women (Fitch, Cowell and Denenberg, 1998; Fitch and Denenberg, 1998). This research has led to ambitious theories that high levels of prenatal androgens are responsible for a wide range of traits more commonly found in males, and which have negative consequences for biological fitness (chapter 3). These include autism, dyslexia, homosexuality, and auto-immune diseases (Baron-Cohen and Hammer, 1997; Manning et al., 2001; Robinson and Manning, 2000).

Rough-and-tumble play

Rough-and-tumble play involves energetic activity with bodily contact, and behaviour associated with fighting in adults, but it is carried out in a relaxed and playful way (Archer, 1992a). It has been studied in a variety of mammals, largely from the viewpoint of its function. Males, paticularly those from polygynous species where there is more adult male competition, engage in more rough-and-tumble play than do females (Smith, 1982). Studies of rats have shown that prenatal androgens are responsible for the higher levels of rough-and-tumble play in males (Olioff and Stewart, 1978). Similarly, prenatal androgens administered to female rhesus monkeys increases their rough-and-tumble play (Goy, 1968; Phoenix, 1974; Wallen, 1996).

Rough-and-tumble play occurs in most human cultures, with boys showing higher levels than girls in both industrial and hunter–gatherer societies (Blurton et al., 1973; DiPietro, 1981). Evidence for the involvement of early hormones in producing these higher levels of rough-and-tumble play among boys is necessarily indirect. It relies on studies of the behaviour of girls who have been exposed to prenatal androgens, usually as a consequence of a clinical condition associated with the secretion of excessive androgens by the adrenal glands (congenital adrenal hyperplasia, or CAH). Earlier studies (Money and Ehrhardt, 1972) found that these girls played more energetically than girls without CAH, that they were more athletic and interested in sports, and that they preferred playing with boys. They were known as 'tomboys'. They also showed less interest in dolls and infant caregiving, and had fewer daydreams about pregnancy and motherhood.

Although the findings have been explained in terms of androgens having a masculinising and a defeminising influence on the developing brain, there are possible alternatives (Archer and Lloyd, 1985). The girls might have been treated differently by their parents, who already knew that they had been exposed to a masculinising hormone. In many cases, they had had to undergo corrective surgery to their masculinised genitals (Quadagno et al., 1977), which may have identified them as different. Ehrhardt and Baker (1974) interviewed the girls' parents, and concluded that there were no obvious influences via parental beliefs and treatment. Nevertheless, subtle differences in parental treatment remained a possibility. Some of the reported effects may have involved inaccurate perceptions of the girls' behaviour, since the information was derived from interviews and questionnaires to the mothers and the girls.

Studies of the impact on the foetus of progesterone – which has an anti-androgen effect – indicate that this is associated with a lessening of masculine interests among boys and a decrease in tomboyish behaviour among girls (Baker, 1980; Ehrhardt et al., 1981). In these studies, there was no confounding influence of genital appearance, and therefore less obvious differences on which to base labelling effects or reporting biases.

Hines and Kaufman (1994) studied CAH children, aged 3 to 8 years. Their observers did not know which children were CAH and which were matched controls, relatives of the CAH girls. Although no difference in their rough-and-tumble play was found, the CAH girls did show a stronger preference for playing with boys. Using the same sample, Berenbaum and Hines (1992) found that CAH girls played more with boys' toys and less with girls' toys than did the controls. Again, these findings were obtained from interviews by people who did not know which children were the CAH girls and who were the controls. These researchers also administered a questionnaire to the girls' parents to ascertain whether they were treated in a more masculine way. The results indicated that they had not been, and hence the researchers argued against the possibility of an indirect, socially mediated, effect.

Activity levels

The precise way in which early androgens might influence later behaviour has seldom been considered. It could operate through an influence on activity level, since most boys' toys facilitate active play (Berenbaum and Hines, 1992). In support of this hypothesis, there is evidence that early in life (from 13 months onwards) boys prefer more active play than girls do (Goldberg and Lewis, 1969; Jacklin et al., 1973; Lloyd and Smith, 1985; O'Brien and Huston, 1985; Smith and Daglish, 1977). There is also an intriguing study showing that young rhesus macaques choose human toys they have not seen before along gender-typed lines (Hines, personal communication).

A meta-analysis of sex differences in activity levels (Eaton and Enns, 1986) found that, across all ages, males were generally more active than females.[4] Pre-school and older children showed clear sex differences,[5] and the mean difference during the first postnatal year was also statistically significant.[6] There were 6 studies of activity levels before birth, which showed an overall effect size comparable to those during the first year afterwards.[7] A subsequent meta-analysis of 46 studies involving infants in their first postnatal year (Campbell and Eaton, 1999) again found that boys were more active than girls. This was more pronounced when the findings were based on substantial periods of observation and least when

---

[4] The effect size (d) was 0.49.   [5] The effect sizes (d) were 0.44 and 0.64.
[6] The effect size (d) was 0.29 ($p < 0.001$).
[7] The effect size (d) for the prenatal phase was 0.33, but this difference was not statistically significant.

parents' ratings were used. This finding suggests that the sex differences are not the product of different parental treatment of the infants along gender-stereotypic lines; a conclusion also supported by the consistency of the effect size with age. These findings indicate that boys show higher activity than girls from a very early age, so that the proposed mechanism for prenatal androgens influencing toy choice is plausible. At present the direct evidence supporting it (from a study of CAH girls: Dittmann, 1992) is suggestive rather than conclusive.

There is also evidence that infants can use body-movement differences to discriminate boys and girls early in life (Kujawski and Bower, 1993), and that propulsive or explosive movement is more characteristic of infant boys than girls (Benenson et al., 1997). In a more extensive longitudinal study, Shirley (2000) found, at 3 and 9 months of age, that boys strongly preferred looking at masculine rather than feminine sex-typed activities (e.g., chasing, climbing, and wrestling, compared with whispering, drawing, and dressing up). Girls also preferred masculine activities, but to a lesser degree. At 18 months of age the results were very similar to those found at 3 and 9 months.

Although the implications of early activity differences associated with the play styles of boys and girls for the development of later sex differences are not yet clear, there is one important implication of evidence for recognisable behavioural differences between boys and girls. This may enable boys and girls to discriminate the two sexes at an early age, before 'gender' (i.e. sex) identity, or even the ability to use any form of gender label, had developed (Leinbach and Fagot, 1986; Lewis and Brooks-Gunn, 1979; Shirley and Campbell, 2000). To be able to discriminate between two categories and to prefer one rather than the other is a low-level cognitive ability that is found in non-human mammals, and in birds such as pigeons. It does not require self-recognition or the understanding of the categories involved, and would lie outside the processes identified by either the social cognitive or cognitive developmental frameworks (Campbell et al., 1998; Kujawski and Bower, 1993).

A biosocial approach to gender development

The research we have considered so far highlights either environmental or biological influences on development. Of course, no one really thinks that such influences operate in isolation. Development is a complex process that must ultimately involve the interplay of both. But, for the purposes of identifying specific influences that really make a difference, researchers have tended to forget this wider picture. For example, the social learning tradition involves concentrating on the process of imitation and ignoring the impact of prenatal androgens because these are regarded as unimportant in explaining what is imitated and under what circumstances. Biological approaches concentrating on the influence of prenatal androgens would tend to ignore details of the social environment, since these are regarded as unimportant compared with the hormonal influence. What is implicit in both research strategies is a belief that the variable under investigation is the main controlling influence on the behavioural outcome being investigated. This can be termed a *main effects model* (Archer, 1992a; Archer and Lloyd, 1985) in that the main control resides either in biological processes or in the external environment. Although there is a continuing interplay of both sorts of process throughout development, the main effects model assumes that only one or other of these exerts overall control for the character in question.

A main effects model may provide a simplified account of those cases where there is a predictable outcome of the behavioural process that can be attributed to one or other source of influence. But, as soon as we are dealing with any of the variety of instances where both biological and environmental variables contribute substantially to the outcome of development, it will not be adequate. The two sources of influence may interact with one another in a wide variety of ways. Approaches that seek to identify the nature of these interactions are generally described as *biosocial* (e.g., Raine et al., 1997) to highlight their recognition of both sources of influence, or as *interactionist* (Archer, 1992a) to identify their recognition that the two sources of influence do not operate independently.

Wallen (1996) set out a biosocial approach to the development of behavioural sex differences in rhesus monkeys. While prenatal androgens masculinise various aspects of behaviour, many of the typical sex differences in behaviour can also be markedly altered by different early rearing conditions. In humans, a biosocial approach has been applied to the developmental origins of violent crime (Raine et al., 1997) and to personality development (Harris, 1995). Harris argued that personality is influenced by a combination of inherited temperament interacting with peer group influences. The controversial aspect of her theory is the claim that direct parental influences on personality development are minimal – a position that flies in the face of the assumptions inherent in psychological theory from psychoanalysis to behaviourism.[8] However, a framework that emphasises peer group socialisation operating on earlier biological influences would seem to apply to gender development. The ability to distinguish categories of other people, and to show a preference for one such category, is crucial for group socialisation to occur. As we noted earlier, the ability to discriminate between two categories and to prefer one over the other are simple processes that have been demonstrated during the first year of life in humans, and occur widely in other mammals.

Sex is perhaps the first social category distinguished by developing humans and involves a same-sex preference. In the next section, we show that the segregation of children's playgroups by sex and age is likely to be the consequence of children's initial preferences rather than the imposition of adults. The important feature of sex-segregated groups is that they involve different patterns of social behaviour and values – different subcultures – that provide the context for a major source of socialisation influences.

---

[8] For a balanced critique of Harris' position as advocated in her later book (Harris, 1998), see Rutter (1999). See also Sulloway (1995) for the influence of birth order on personality.

Sex-segregation in childhood

Single-sex groups are found throughout childhood in widely different cultures, for example in Kalahari hunter–gatherers, in China, Japan, India, Mexico, and Zaire (Freedman et al., 1988). This begins in the early pre-school years, becoming more pronounced throughout middle childhood (Maccoby, 1986, 1988, 1990, 1998; Maccoby and Jacklin, 1987). There are some exceptions to this pattern. Harkness and Super (1985), studying children in rural Kenya, found that, despite considerable segregation of the sexes in adulthood, younger children played in mixed-sex groups, and sex-segregation was still incomplete at 6 to 9 years of age. Thorne (1986, 1993), who observed children in two elementary schools in the USA, found a number of contexts in which sex-segregation was lessened: when children were engaged in an absorbing activity that involved co-operation; in games not involving teams; and when adults organised mixed-sex encounters.

These findings have provoked different interpretations. The authors of the two studies viewed them as evidence that sex-segregation is a consequence of the particular school arrangements imposed on Western children. Others (e.g., Archer, 1992b; Maccoby, 1998; Maccoby and Jacklin, 1987) have viewed them as deviations from the basic pattern of sex-segregation caused by situations that either limit the children's available playmates or impose restraints on their natural preferences. This view is supported by the findings that when active preferences and friendship patterns of young children are measured, they show a stronger pattern of segregation than when the measures simply involve who associates with whom. Pre-school children show a clear preference for interacting with their own sex (Maccoby, 1986, 1998; Maccoby and Jacklin, 1974, 1987). Exceptions occur when children have formed enduring friendships with the opposite sex early in life (Howes and Phillipsen, 1992).

Same-sex preferences have been found as early as 2 years of age in an observational study of social play among children at a Canadian urban day-centre (LaFreniere et al., 1984). In this study, girls were observed to show these preferences earlier than boys did, although studies of slightly older ages indicate that it is boys who are more likely to refuse girls' invitations to play (Howes and Phillipsen, 1992). As we noted in the previous section, there is also some (conflicting) evidence for selective attention to, and preference for looking at, same-sex individuals in the first year of life. Maccoby and Jacklin (1987) argued that early same-sex preferences do not show the within-sex variations found for other early sex differences, for example in temperament (Freedman, 1980), where there is considerable overlap between the sexes. In terms of the magnitude of sex differences (chapter 1), same-sex preferences are much larger.

Maccoby and Jacklin (1987) also argued that same-sex preferences and gender-stereotyped play preferences develop independently of one another. The degree of gender-stereotyping in a child's play at around 4 years of age was unrelated to their preferences for playing with same or opposite-sex children, at this age or a year later. When the same play equipment was provided for boys and girls of this age, the sexes still played separately. Other studies support the view that early preferences for individuals of the same sex develop independently of preferences for gender-stereotyped play activities and toys (Alexander and Hines, 1994; Fagot et al., 1986).

Maccoby and Jacklin (1987) argued that the origin of sex-segregation has to be understood as a process of group membership. It is members of their own sex in general that boys and girls prefer: which specific individuals are chosen may differ from week to week, whereas gender stereotyping in play is more consistent for any particular child. Two features are necessary for individuals to make group membership distinctions. The first is the ability to distinguish between the groups (distinctiveness), and the second is the importance of belonging (membership must be salient). Maccoby (1986, 1998) suggested that the interaction style of most young girls is ineffective in influencing the majority of male play partners, and hence girls find interacting with this category of individual aversive. Powlishta and Maccoby (1990) found that the techniques used in dominance disputes by pre-school-age girls are mainly verbal, and that, although they are effective with other girls, they tend to be ignored by boys of these ages. This is consistent with the finding that it is girls who initially avoid interacting with the opposite sex (LaFreniere et al., 1984) .

It would therefore take only a few adverse experiences of playing with boys for a girl to notice the distinguishing features of the two sexes (outward appear-ance or play style), and to be motivated to avoid boys. Alternatively, it would take only a few good experiences of playing with girls for girls to discover that associating with girls was more rewarding. This would involve only a simple form of discrimination learning, and would not require the cognitive elabora-tion that cognitive developmental theorists view as essential. Although Maccoby's theory is plausible, we still do not know how the sexes come to differ in inter-action style early in life. One clue provided by research described earlier is a difference in activity levels, which begins prenatally, and which is clearly noticed by infants of both sexes from early in postnatal life (Shirley, 2000; Shirley and Campbell, 2000).

Maccoby's (1986) account implied that early sex differences in behaviour may be a consequence of prenatal androgens. There is now firmer evidence for hor-monal involvement (described above). It is also interesting to note that boys show elevated testosterone levels during the first 3 months following birth (Forest et al., 1974; Winter et al., 1976). At present there is no evidence on whether this has any influence on the developing brain. Although early androgenic influ-ences occur exclusively in the prenatal phase among other primates, the human infant is much more immature at birth, so that it would not be surprising for some sexual differentiation of brain areas to occur during postnatal life as well (Archer, 1992a).

A biosocial view of gender development involves several components. In this section, we have concentrated on the origins of the initial preferences of boys and girls and how these might be transformed into sex-segregation. But this is only the beginning of a continuous process of development. In the next section, we outline the different social worlds inhabited by boys and girls once they enter sex-segregated groups.

Sex-segregated groups as the context for socialisation influences

Once they have formed same-sex groups, there are social processes that cause boys and girls to maintain the boundaries between them. These are known from experimental research on artificially formed adult groups (Brown, 1988), and involve group favouritism, exaggeration of the differences between the sexes, exaggeration of similarities within each sex, and the belief that one's own sex is more varied than the opposite sex. Powlishta (1995) found that most applied to 8- to 10-year-old children's perceptions of boys and girls.

The importance of maintaining sex-segregation is that it provides the context for boys and girls to experience different social worlds, or different subcultures (Archer, 1992b). Girls tend to play intensely with one or two close friends, and to show more stable friendships than boys, who typically play in larger groups. This applies to a wide age-range of children, from early childhood (e.g., Benenson, 1993, 1994) through to adolescence and adulthood (e.g., Rubin, 1985).

Boys' groups involve more fighting and rougher games, and there is more overt concern with who is tough and who is the boss, i.e. dominance and status relations (Weisfeld, 1994). Boys play more in public places, whereas girls play more in private situations. Girls' play tends to involve more turn taking and to emphasise co-operation more than boys' play does (e.g., Neppl and Murray, 1997). For girls, self-disclosure and sharing secrets is important, and break-up of friendships can be emotional, with new ones occurring at the expense of old ones. It is within the context of these closer personal relationships that girls' main style of aggression can be understood. It involves features such as disclosing secrets about another individual, or seeking their social exclusion, or spreading malicious gossip about them (chapter 6). Maltz and Borker (1982) summarised the ways in which speech is used differently in boys' and girls' groups. Girls tend to use it to maintain friendly interactions, and to facilitate close relationships, based on appeals to equity and fairness. Boys tend to use speech to assert their status, to attract and maintain an audience, and to assert themselves when others are speaking, patterns that fit their larger, more hierarchically arranged groups.

These different patterns are maintained into adolescence and young adulthood. Young women tend to have one best friend or a small number of closer friends, and these friendships are generally more intimate than those of men (Griffin, 1986; Rubin, 1985; Wright, 1988). Men are less likely to have these sorts of close friendships, and, if they do, they are less likely to disclose personal matters to their friends. Men's friendships are more likely to be based on shared activities such as sport or work, and involve an element of competition, as well as co-operation over a shared task. These features are accentuated in violent subcultures such as gangs (e.g., Anderson, 1994).

Historical analyses indicate even more pronounced female friendships in former times, for example among the middle classes in eighteenth- and nineteenth-century North America (Smith-Rosenberg, 1975), when there was pronounced separation of the social worlds of men and women, even within the family, and relations between the sexes was formal. Women's reproductive life bound them together in physical and emotional intimacy. This pattern of female friendships is likely to be found whenever the worlds of male and female are rigidly separated, as they are in many cultures today. The contemporary Western pattern of closer association between the sexes seems to be a historically recent development, superimposed on an older pattern. The different friendship patterns of men and women still provide partial continuity with traditional social relations.

The boundaries of childhood gender roles

A striking aspect of gender roles in childhood is the different extent to which boys and girls can cross gender boundaries. The masculine role involves greater rigidity: deviations from the expected forms of behaviour occur less often among boys, and incur greater disapproval when they do. Effeminate boys, or 'sissies', are discouraged or ridiculed, whereas masculine girls, or 'tomboys', are tolerated. The evidence for these generalisations is extensive (Archer, 1984, 1989b, 1992b; Lobel and Menashri, 1993), and can be briefly summarised as follows. There is early awareness by both sexes that it is important for boys to avoid gender-inappropriate activities, and most cases of gender reversals in play are girls playing with boys. Boys experience strong peer-group pressure to conform to their gender role. Adults also show disapproval of cross-gender activities in children, and these views are brought to bear on children from 12 months onwards.

Boys displaying feminine behaviour are not only teased and shunned by other boys (e.g., Thorne, 1986), but they also attract parental concern and alarm. In the USA, from the 1970s onwards, feminine boys were viewed as requiring treatment. Rekers and Yates (1976) described the UCLA Gender Clinic Program, to which boys who showed 'childhood gender disturbances' were referred. The boys preferred girls' clothing, girls' games, and girls as their friends. They tended to avoid rough-and-tumble play and sports.

Parents' major concern was that these boys would grow up to be homosexual. A follow-up of a sample originally referred when they were under 12 years of age, was made when they were between 13 and 23 years of age. This did indeed show that they were much more likely than a matched control sample to be homosexual or bisexual (Green et al., 1987). It was found that doll play and feminine role playing in childhood were most closely associated with later homosexual orientation. Other features, such as cross-dressing and the absence of rough-and-tumble play, were not. Bem (1996) stated that there is now overwhelming evidence that cross-gender role behaviour is the strongest predictor of adult homosexual orientation. Whilst the evidence that this is the case for women is doubtful, it remains a powerful association for males (e.g., van Wyk and Geist, 1984).

The concern over feminine boys can be contrasted with the partial legitimisation of the masculine girl or 'tomboy'. Studies of young women show that a substantial proportion (half or more) described themselves as being tomboys during childhood (Burn et al., 1996; Hyde et al., 1977). Playground observations (Thorne, 1986, 1993) indicate that there are usually several girls classed as tomboys and that they enjoy enhanced status with other girls as a result of mixing with boys. We should, however, note that in some senses the comparison between tomboys and feminine boys is misleading, since tomboys are involved in both masculine and feminine activities (Plumb and Cowan, 1984) whereas feminine boys tend to substitute feminine for masculine interests (Green et al., 1987). The different attitudes to crossing gender boundaries persists into adulthood, and historical sources (e.g., Bullough, 1974; Wheelwright, 1989) indicate greater acceptability of women adopting the masculine role and passing as men, than of men behaving in a feminine manner in Western societies (chapter 5).

The more rigid boundaries of the masculine role have been explained in terms of the relative status of men and women in society (Archer, 1989b, 1992b; Feinman, 1981, 1984). Boys soon learn that males are more valued than females, that the masculine role is more important than the feminine one. Hence feminine behaviour represents a loss of status for a boy, whereas masculine behaviour represents an increase in status for a girl. This was expressed aptly by characters in Ian McEwan's novel, *The Cement Garden*. Tom, the youngest of a group of children, has been dressed as a girl by his sister, after their parents' death. The older brother objects, and his sister replies:

> Girls can wear jeans and cut their hair short and wear shirts and boots because it's OK to be a boy – for girls it's like promotion. For a boy to look like a girl is degrading . . . because you secretly believe that being a girl is degrading. Why else would you think it humiliating for Tom to wear a frock? (McEwan, 1978:44)

Consequently, tomboys show enhanced status within their peer group and girls may seek to enter the world of boys, but are not often granted entry. This fits the pattern of intergroup behaviour identified in social psychological research on experimentally formed social groups (Archer, 1992b). Members of low-status groups identify less with their own group than with a higher-status group. If members of a lower-status group see themselves as possessing abilities relevant for a higher-status group (e.g., football in the case of girls), their identification with their own group will be even less. Under these circumstances, they will seek to gain entry to the higher-status group, as tomboys do.

Conclusions: why socialisation and biology are not independent of one another

We have outlined several different accounts of the development of gender roles and psychological sex differences. We began with explanations rooted in the traditional nature–nurture issue, particularly the nurture side of this in the form of socialisation influences. It is widely assumed that parental treatment provides the major route of cultural transmission. However, evidence for substantial differences in parental treatment of boys and girls was weaker than is generally believed, although it was clearer for fathers and for the encouragement of masculine behaviour in boys. There are several other potential routes for the cultural transmission of gender-stereotyped messages, peer groups and the mass media being two that may be particularly important.

Social learning theory provided explanations of the ways in which gendered messages could be learned, and showed that it is particularly important for the child to perceive an activity as being gender-appropriate before it will be imitated. The cognitive developmental perspective viewed knowledge of one's own gender identity as the driving force behind preference for and identification with one's own sex. Studies indicating early preferences in the absence of such knowledge have cast doubt over this premise, although the available evidence is not entirely consistent.

There has been an accumulation of evidence for early biological influences, principally focused on the action of prenatal androgens on the developing brain, and differences in activity levels or play styles of boys and girls. We suggested that the operation and development of such biological processes are best understood in terms of a biosocial or interactionist model. This involves a recognition that both biological and environmental influences are important and that they are likely to interact in one of a number of ways in development. We considered one biosocial model, which proposed that early biological differences between boys and girls initiate a pattern of preferences that would lead to sex-segregated groups and also to different patterns of social behaviour within these groups. Two distinct socialisation patterns become elaborated in the social worlds of boys and girls, and these eventually turn into something that is very different from the initial biological influence that initiated them. The type of behaviour shown in boys' and girls' groups reflects their biological differences, and hence the socialisation they experience reflects biological differences. In other respects, the social settings can develop independent features, which reflect their historical and cultural settings, for example in the case of different masculine subcultures (e.g., Gilmore, 1990). We also suggested that the impact of the higher status of males in human society exerts an early and enduring impact on the nature of boys' and girls' groups, and especially on the boundaries between them and the acceptability of crossing them.

This biosocial model places socialisation influences in a different light. Parental socialisation is seen as only one source of influence on the developing child, and may indeed be secondary to that of peers. Thus initial learning in the home may be superseded by peer group influences where these are substantially different from those of parents. The degree to which peer group and parental influences exert their effects depends on the subsequent developmental pathway. Where fathers are absent, peer rearing is likely to be more important, whereas, where two parents are available, the impact of peer groups may be lessened and access to particular sorts of peers more controlled by parents (Draper and Harpending, 1982, 1987). Some messages are likely to be consistent across several sources of influence: for example, both peers and parents, particularly fathers, strongly discourage boys from engaging in stereotypically feminine activities. Throughout social development, any gendered message in the outside world will be understood and acted upon in the light of already established gender preferences, including those that arise from biological influences. Such early preferences will influence the sort of environment that is sought – thus controlling the sources of socialisation influences that will be experienced.

The particular biosocial model we outlined is based on currently available research evidence. It is inevitable that it will be modified or replaced in the light of further findings. A biosocial model will be needed to accommodate the realities of a developmental sequence involving socialisation both operating on, and partly arising from, early biological influences whatever the future modifications.

Further reading

Collaer, M. L. and Hines, M. (1995). Human behavioral sex differences: A role for gonadal hormones during early development. *Psychological Bulletin,* 118: 55–107.
    A comprehensive review of evidence from studies on non-humans and humans on the influences of reproductive hormones on brain and behaviour.
Maccoby, E. E. (1998). *The Two Sexes: Growing Up Apart, Coming Together.* Cambridge, MA and London: Belknap Press of Harvard University Press.
    A summary of Eleanor Maccoby's influential research on the different social worlds of boys and girls, including the possible origins of these and their conseqences for how men and women relate to one another in adult life.

5 Sexuality: psychophysiology, psychoanalysis, and social construction

Introduction

We began our detailed examination of reproduction in chapter 3 by asking how and why sex evolved. In this chapter we explore human sexuality from three different perspectives: those of psychophysiology, psychoanalysis, and history–sociology.

Using the term *psychophysiology*, we review the classic studies of Masters and Johnson and of Kinsey. Their research provides antiseptic, empirical descriptions of adult sexual behaviour and offers answers to questions such as 'What are the measurable physiological correlates of orgasm?' and 'In what circumstances do people find sexual satisfaction?'

In examining the psychoanalytic approach, we move from the readily observable world of physiological function and conscious experience to explore the meaning of sexual experience in our inner worlds. Here we seek answers to different sorts of questions and pursue the origins of adult sexual satisfaction in early childhood experiences. We ask how the child's recognition of anatomical sex differences influences adult personality and how erotic excitement serves social life.

In the final section we consider the social construction of the concepts of sex, gender, and sexuality, and the influence of social values on the creation of gender roles and identities. Historical research suggests that our current binary representation of gender only emerged in the late eighteenth century (Laqueur, 1990). First we examine the classical, hierarchical view of sex and then consider critiques of binary roles, heterosexuality, and homosexuality. From these analyses we gain a perspective on our own society's definitions of the roles of men and women, and explore the limitations of framing sexuality in terms of reproductive success. In stepping beyond the reproductive paradigm we encounter a range of solutions that include the possibilities of third and fourth genders (Herdt, 1994; Roscoe, 1998; Wikan, 1977).

The three approaches differ in their modes of study and in the data they seek to explain. The objective methods of Masters and Johnson provide precise physiological descriptions of sexuality, but they ignore the deeper levels of meaning pursued by psychoanalysis. Although the unconscious bears the marks of an ordinary understanding of anatomical sex differences, it interprets them in ways that are not available to common sense. Whatever its elaborations and complexities, the unconscious is influenced by culture. Recent historical and sociological studies have challenged the paradigm of reproductive sexuality. In contemporary Western societies, sex is viewed as an arena of recreation. Examination of gender roles in Omani society or Native American cultures raises issues that force us to re-examine binary gender roles and to think about alternatives beyond those of adult heterosexuality.

The physiological measurement of sexual behaviour

The studies of Masters and Johnson attracted considerable publicity when they appeared in the 1960s, but staid public attitudes towards the study of human sexuality had already begun to change with publication of the Kinsey reports more than a decade earlier. Scholarly interest in sexuality existed before the twentieth century, but our inheritance of a Victorian morality shaped twentieth-century study of human sexuality (Weeks, 2000). Ancient Chinese physicians writing within the Taoist tradition carried out careful observations and offered advice that enabled both women and men to achieve great sexual satisfaction (Chang, 1977). The Talmud, one of the major repositories of the Jewish tradition, contains detailed instructions concerning not only sexual satisfaction but also contraception, love, and procreation, which, like food, were considered important aspects of life. The rise of Christianity introduced a profound duality of body and soul that included a hatred of the body and suspicion of sexuality (Horrocks, 1997). Neither the physiology nor behavioural aspects of human sexuality were considered suitable for open discussion or for study (see chapter 1).

Here we only highlight specific aspects of Masters and Johnson's research. Interested readers may pursue further details in their three major works, *Human Sexual Response* (1966), *Human Sexual Inadequacy* (1970) and *Homosexuality in Perspective* (1979), or in comprehensive textbooks on sexuality (e.g., Hyde and DeLamater, 1996; Katchadourian, 1985; Masters et al., 1992).

The human orgasm

Masters and Johnson presented a four-stage description of the sexual response that emphasised similarities rather than differences between men and women. Their 1966 study was based on observations of 10,000 orgasms, or *sexual response cycles*, as they described them. Of these, three-quarters were orgasms of heterosexual women, and the remaining 2,500 were those of heterosexual men. In their 1979 work they reported observations of 1,200 orgasms of 82 lesbian women and 94 gay men. Their aim has been to provide sound physiological information about sexuality in order to dispel myths maintained through ignorance. They studied masturbation as well as the orgasms of heterosexual and homosexual couples, and employed a plastic phallus containing photographic equipment to record the internal changes in women which accompany arousal and gratification.

Masters and Johnson applied their four-stage description of sexual response cycles to both women and men. They reported that the structure of orgasms was not modified by sexual orientation (Masters and Johnson, 1979) and was independent of the nature of sexual activity – heterosexual, homosexual, or autoerotic. It was also independent of the source of stimulation, tactile or psychological. The activities of the sex organs differed according to their anatomical structures, but the mechanisms of arousal were similar: vasocongestion and myotonia, engorgement of blood vessels with increased blood flow into tissues, and muscle tension.

The first or *excitement phase* of the sexual response is the filling of the pelvic region with an increased supply of blood and other fluids, and the second or *plateau phase* is a general and widespread increase in muscle tension. The excitement phase varies in terms of the sources of stimulation that trigger it, its length, and whether tension will increase to reach the plateau phase or dissipate. The vagina rapidly produces a lubricant, the clitoris swells, the cervix and uterus move upward. One feminist writer and physician (Sherfey, 1973) compared the production of the vaginal fluid in the excitement phase to the rapid appearance of penile erection and elevation of testes. Viewed in this way, observable evidence of sexual arousal is available to both men and women.

In the *plateau phase* there are further changes in both sexes due to vasocongestion. The tip of the penis may increase in size and deepen in colour, and the outer passageway of the vagina narrows. These changes are specific to the structure of each sex. Unlike the erect penis, the erect clitoris tends to disappear into its hood.

The contractions of the third or *orgasmic phase* initially occur with a frequency of one every 0.8 seconds in both sexes, although only males experience ejaculation. The rate slows down after 5 to 12 contractions in women, but after only 3 to 4 in men. Once the orgasmic phase is reached, these responses become involuntary. Orgasm is a total body experience that has been shown to involve the brain too (Cohen et al., 1976).

In the fourth, or *resolution phase* congestion gradually disappears and muscles relax. While women in the resolution phase may react to further stimulation and experience additional orgasms, men experience a refractory period of at least some minutes during which another erection cannot be achieved whatever the nature of the stimulation. Although women described multiple orgasms as feeling more intense, Masters and Johnson recorded them as being identical to earlier ones.

Technical criticism about Masters and Johnson's description – for example, that it is difficult to separate the excitation and plateau stages – throws no doubt on their major conclusion. Functionally, men and women achieve sexual satisfaction in a similar manner even though anatomically they differ, and these general similarities are found regardless of sexual orientation or mode of stimulation.

Masters and Johnson's systematic observations dispelled three widely held beliefs. These were:

• that women experience different sorts of orgasms
• that only men seek sexual satisfaction
• that homosexual and heterosexual satisfaction are fundamentally different.

Masters and Johnson demonstrated that the clitoris not only receives stimulation but is also crucial in transmitting feelings of arousal, while the vagina is relatively lacking in nerve endings and thus relatively insensitive. The Freudian view of mature female sexuality, as we shall see in the next section, places considerable emphasis on the vagina as distinct from the clitoris, as a source of satisfaction.

O'Connell et al. (1998) have challenged the accepted description of the clitoris provided in standard anatomy textbooks (Williamson and Nowak, 1998). Using photography to map the structure of nerves in the clitoris, they found that the visible tip of the clitoris is connected to a sizeable internal mass of tissue that is pyramidal in shape and capable of erection. As these findings questioned accepted anatomical knowledge, O'Connell and her colleagues sought an explanation for this long-delayed discovery. Alongside issues relating to a Victorian heritage of prudery about female sexuality, and the internal position of the tissue mass, they described a further surprising aspect of this research. Anatomical dissection is usually undertaken on bodies of the elderly. O'Connell et al. examined the bodies of two women under 40 and their anatomy was startlingly different! Their findings illustrate the distortion which data from a limited age cohort can produce (a theme to which we return in chapter 10).

The second myth Masters and Johnson dispelled was the notion that 'nice', morally correct women, 'endured' sexual relations whereas only 'fallen' women enjoyed them. Initially Masters and Johnson employed female prostitutes but found that they rarely experienced orgasms. Instead, it was women having intercourse with their regular partners who provided the bulk of their evidence of orgasmic behaviour. Is it surprising that Waterman and Chiauzzi (1982) have also reported a statistically significant relationship between orgasm consistency and sexual satisfaction in women, but not for men?

Masters and Johnson's assertion that physiologically there were no differences in the sexual response cycles of heterosexual and gay and lesbian individuals was based upon the observation of 1,200 gay sexual response cycles. Orgasmic frequency was comparable, although modes of stimulation varied.

Masters and Johnson also reported sex differences. Although there was considerable overlap in the orgasmic behaviour of women and men, men were generally more variable than women in achieving orgasm but women were more variable in frequency of orgasm. If we think of this dimension as running from never at one end, to a very great number during one sexual incident at the other end, we find women spread evenly along it. Many women, though perhaps not as many as was thought 50 years ago, never experienced orgasm. At the other end there were a number of women who experienced multiple orgasms, and their high rate could not be matched even by very young men (Masters et al., 1992).

The men observed by Masters and Johnson achieved fewer orgasms at any one time and experienced more failures than women. Although three times as many female cycles were observed, only 118 failures to achieve orgasms were recorded for women. In 2,500 male cycles there were 220 failures. Before rushing to conclusions about the sexual natures of women and men, we should note that all participants were volunteers capable of achieving orgasm. Perhaps only women who were particularly sure of their performance offered to participate in the study.

Sources of sexual satisfaction

Kinsey began his studies of human sexual behaviour several decades before Masters and Johnson carried out their observational research. The moral climate was more restrictive and he depended upon interviews and self-report. Kinsey and his colleagues investigated the array of arousing events and behaviour that lead to orgasm and the conscious factors that affect the experience of sexual satisfaction.

Their first book, *Sexual Behavior in the Human Male* (1948), reported interviews with 5,300 American men, mostly white. A similar report based on interviews with 5,940 American women was published in 1953. The description of male orgasms as 'sexual outlets' has a quaint ring today, but Kinsey's findings belong to the contemporary scene more than to Victorian notions of sexual behaviour, which they explicitly challenged. Although the Kinsey reports described men as sexually more active than women, they present no major challenge to the conclusions drawn by Masters and Johnson. Indeed, Masters and Johnson validated Kinsey's data on multiple orgasms among women.

Kinsey divided the array of activities that lead to orgasm into six major categories, roughly equivalent for women and men. These are masturbation, nocturnal sex dreams (or emission for men), heterosexual petting, heterosexual intercourse, homosexual relations, and intercourse with other species. Although slightly more women than men were interviewed, it was men who reported more orgasms. None the less, Kinsey maintained, as did Masters and Johnson later, that physiologically the orgasmic potential and response of the sexes was similar.

Kinsey reported that age and social class influenced the sexual behaviour of men. An older commonsense view recognised that men experienced fewer orgasms as they got older, but it was generally assumed that men reached their peak of orgasmic frequency somewhere in their twenties and only began to experience a decline in their forties. A very different picture emerged in terms of the number of sexual outlets per week recorded by Kinsey. On average, men were shown to reach a peak in adolescence, and by the late twenties a decline from this early peak was reported; none the less, Kinsey revealed that men's sexual behaviour often continued into their seventies and eighties.

Kinsey used education as a major indicator of social class. Although he sometimes employed a tripartite system, separating those who had attended primary school only, secondary school, and finally college or university, he often grouped together those of primary and secondary education and compared them with people who had had higher education. Men with less education reported the majority of their outlets in genital intercourse, regardless of whether these were premarital, marital, or extramarital, with prostitutes, or in homosexual relations. More educated men reported far more masturbation, petting to orgasm, or nocturnal emissions. Educated men grew less faithful the longer they were married, whereas men with less education showed the opposite pattern, growing more faithful with age.

One of the most widely discussed findings of the report on male sexual behaviour was the statistic showing that 37 per cent of men had at one time or another engaged in homosexual behaviour. The form in which this result was reported reflects Kinsey's views on the nature of homosexuality. He believed that it was incorrect to describe an individual as either homosexual or not, in an all-or-nothing fashion. His definition of homosexuality challenged the absolute categories of straight and gay. Kinsey constructed a 7-point scale that ran from 0 to 6. Individuals who reported never having achieved sexual satisfaction with persons of their own sex scored zero, and those of exclusively homosexual experience scored 6. Empirically many individuals scored at points in between 0 and 6. We consider the social definition of gender and its relation to sexuality in the final section of this chapter.

Kinsey reported less clear-cut evidence of the influence of age and social class on the sexual behaviour of women. Women built to a peak of orgasmic frequency slowly; generally it occurred in their late twenties and early thirties and was maintained until their fifties. Only then did it show a gradual decline. Extramarital intercourse was the only activity affected by social class and echoed the patterns of infidelity first described for men. More educated women also reported a greater incidence of homosexual relations than less-educated women.

Religion, which had had a negligible effect on men's sexual behaviour, emerged as the most important factor influencing sexual satisfaction for women. Women who described themselves as religious achieved fewer orgasms in any circumstances; in particular, they were less likely to achieve orgasm in heterosexual intercourse. Historical factors, such as date of birth and cultural attitudes influencing socialisation, also affected female sexuality. Women born after 1900 reported more orgasms in all contexts. Perhaps these women were breaking free of the constraints of Victorian values.

We can only sample the differences between women and men reported by Kinsey extensively in the 1953 volume. There are fascinating behavioural differences, such as the female peak of outlets through nocturnal dreams in their forties compared to the male peak in the late teens and the more pronounced decline in masturbation as a source of satisfaction after marriage for men than for women.

One of the most interesting contrasts is Kinsey's own formulation of the differing natures of female and male sexuality. He believed that female sexuality was based on physical stimulation, while he ascribed the frequency and regularity of male gratification to men's susceptibility to psychological stimulation. Kinsey believed that men were more easily conditioned and thus became susceptible to a variety of psychological stimuli. This view of the differential effects of learning, which presumably also accounted for the sharp class differences in male behaviour, overlooked the equally plausible hypothesis that women, too, were conditionable, but that they had been conditioned not to respond with sexual arousal in the same situations that allowed male excitement.

Baumeister's (2000) suggestion that it is women who are more malleable and that their sexuality is more easily influenced by cultural and social factors is the contemporary twist on differences in erotic plasticity. His proposal, that this difference reflects evolutionary, biological forces, has been challenged both for overlooking important aspects of evolutionary theory (Anderson et al., 2000) and for neglecting aspects of a socio-cultural explanation (Hyde and Durik, 2000). In reply, he and his colleagues noted that his critics have not challenged the gender difference he described, only its explanation (Baumeister et al., 2000).

Recording and reporting physiological arousal

Kinsey's hypothesis concerning sex differences in sexual arousal was investigated among students who would be described as sophisticated in terms of Kinsey's data. Almost 80 per cent of them had had sexual intercourse and 84 per cent of the women reported experiencing orgasm. While these students were listening to four different kinds of stories, Heiman (1975) recorded vaginal and penile pulse and blood pressure to measure the students' physiological arousal.

One group of students heard romantic stories and another erotic tales. In addition to a control group, who heard neither erotic nor romantic stories, a fourth group listened to a mixture of the two. Each student participated in two sessions. With few exceptions, only students listening to erotic or mixed erotic and romantic stories showed evidence of arousal. Women found the stories in which women were the initiators and the main focus the most arousing. Men showed a similar but less-marked preference for this type of story. Stories that featured a male initiator but focused on a female were the next most arousing story for both sexes. In physiological terms – that is, pulse rate and blood pressure – there appeared to be little difference in women's and men's physiological arousal reactions.

Heiman also examined the conscious recognition of their physiological arousal by the two sexes. Students were asked to report any general arousal, specific genital arousal such as erection or lubrication, or more diffuse genital arousal. These self-reports were then compared with the physiological measures. By and large, women were not as accurate as men in reporting their own arousal. Women made more errors in reporting arousal to non-erotic stimuli, that is, to romantic or control stories, than did men. Sophisticated women may experience and recognise physiological arousal in exciting circumstances, but they are less willing, perhaps even unable, to report arousal when the context of the stimulus fails to provide socially acceptable support for their erotic feelings. These results suggest that Kinsey's findings may reflect the influence of social factors on women's and men's self-reports of their sexual arousal rather than in their physiological responses to particular types of stimuli.

Steinman and colleagues also found similarities and differences in men's and women's arousal using both physiological and subjective measures (Steinman et al., 1981). When shown various erotic and neutral films, university men and women exhibited greater physiological arousal to the erotic material. Both found films of male homosexual encounters the least physiologically arousing and group heterosexual behaviour the most physiologically stimulating. Although men found both female homosexual and heterosexual films highly arousing, among the women, high levels were recorded only for heterosexual films.

Although Steinman et al. treated the physiological measures as equivalent for men and women in much of their analysis, differences in the magnitude of response were reported along with differences in the pattern of responses. Alongside their measure of physiological arousal they had employed three subjective measures:

- a verbal rating of arousal
- a written assessment of pleasantness after each stimulus presentation
- an overall assessment of arousal during the post-experimental debriefing session.

These subjective measures were found to produce roughly equivalent results and to correlate with the physiological measure. The pattern of interrelations between the physiological and subjective measures differed for men and women; a relationship between pleasantness and subjective arousal was reported only for men. The intricate patterns of arousal reported in this study are governed by rules of social acceptability, but the precise grammar of this domain remains to be described.

A meta-analysis of self-reports of sexual arousal avoided the issue of the relationship of physiological and psychological measures (Murnen and Stockton, 1997). Physiological measures of arousal were specifically ruled out as the authors claimed 'an inability to compare males and females on the measure' (p. 142.). A moderate overall effect size (d = 0.31) was reported with men describing more arousal than women, but there was considerable variation across the 62 studies. Larger effects were reported in studies using samples of college-aged people than from those employing older individuals. Pornographic as opposed to erotic stimuli increased effect sizes in comparisons of men and women. Data collected in large group settings reduced effect sizes. The authors concluded that their pattern of results lends greater support to social influence theories than to evolutionary explanations, but their report leaves questions concerning the nature of the relationship of physiological and psychological variables unanswered.

Questionnaire reports of sexual experience

Kinsey's studies were based upon interviews and reflected the social attitudes of the 1940s. *The Hite Report* (1976) and *The Hite Report on Male Sexuality* (1981) were also products of their time. The first book, based upon questionnaire responses provided by 3,000 American women volunteers, contained vivid verbatim accounts of women's masturbation, their feelings at orgasm, and their evaluation of various aspects of their sexuality. A unifying theme of the *Hite Report* was the author's assertion that the female potential for sexual satisfaction is equal to, if not actually greater than, that of the male. Although Hite's account of female potential follows those of Masters and Johnson and of Sherfey (1973) her respondents did not share their views. Hite reports: 'Most women in this study did not seem acquainted with these facts, the great majority reporting a desire for only one orgasm and being unaware of how many they might be capable of' (p. 165).

Hite's redefinition of the term *sexuality* emerged clearly in her second book wherein heterosexual genital intercourse was considered to be only one specific source of sexual pleasure and satisfaction. A focus on heterosexual genitality has been identified as a masculine bias in research on sexual behaviour by a number of feminist writers (e.g., Rossi, 1973; Tiefer, 1978). In the context of this criticism it is surprising that the older men who took part in Hite's study reported a greater variety of ways to gain sexual satisfaction than did younger man, and focused less on genital intercourse than did younger men.

Sex differences in 21 aspects of sexual behaviour and attitudes were examined in a meta-analysis reported by Oliver and Hyde (1993). Only two large differences, both favouring men were found – incidence of masturbation (d = 0.96) and permissiveness of casual sex (d = 0.81). Analysis of changes over time using dates of publication showed sex differences becoming smaller. Great similarity in men's and women's attitudes was reported for attitudes towards homosexuality, incidence of masturbation, number of sexual partners, frequency of intercourse, and acceptance of engaged couples' premarital sex. This evidence is congruent with changes in marriage and the family reviewed in chapter 8.

A major survey of the sexual behaviour of almost 19,000 British 16- to 59-year-olds by Johnson et al. (1994) also reflected changes. An individual's sex was not a strong predictor of differences in sexual experiences, such as age at first intercourse and sources of orgasm, but, when analysed by ethnic identity, sex did have significant effects. This is seen in age at first intercourse. For both white men and women the average age was 18 years. However, the average of 18 years for black women contrasted with an average of 17 years for black men. For Asians, here defined as people coming from the Indian subcontinent, average age of first intercourse was comparatively late, but again there was a sex difference. It was 20 years for Asian men and 21 years for Asian women.

Johnson et al. reported that 62.4 per cent of women viewed one-night stands as always wrong, but only 35.8 per cent of men held this opinion. These sex differences in attitudes towards casual sex may provide a partial explanation for the greater number of sexual partners reported by men. These findings echo the results of the meta-analysis reported above (Oliver and Hyde, 1993). Yet again, men and women are generally similar in terms of sexual performance, but even conscious choices are influenced by attitudes, beliefs, and distinctive gender scripts.

Psychoanalytic explanations of sexuality

Psychoanalytic theory encompasses a variety of explanations of the patterning of sexuality and of the relationships between men and women. These accounts are virtually unique among psychological theories, as they reflect a deep concern with irrational aspects of human behaviour. In considering psychoanalytic explanations of sexuality, we begin by moving back in time, but, before doing so, it is worth asking whether psychoanalysis has relevance today when smart drugs and newer psychotherapies are replacing the traditional talking cure. In the book *Freud 2000*, Elliott (1998) argues that, even today, Freud provides us with the best theoretical framework within which to understand human nature. Since many attack Freud's theory without coming to terms with it, we will go back to basics and examine the fundamental concepts relating to human sexuality.

By 1905, when Freud first published his classic *Three Essays on the Theory of Sexuality*, he had developed a revolutionary view of the nature of human sexuality. His theories derived primarily from his clinical experience with psychologically distressed, mainly neurotic, patients, and not from physiological measurements nor from interview or questionnaire self-reports of normal sexual behaviour. Freud was concerned with psychosexuality and the pursuit of pleasure or unpleasure. To understand Freud's view of the inner world it is necessary to begin by examining his approach to mental functioning and the unconscious. We then move on to examine Freud's discovery of the sources of sexual pleasure in infant experience.

The unconscious

In order to understand the *Three Essays* and psychosexuality it is essential to appreciate Freud's theory of mental functioning and the role of the unconscious. The academic psychology of Freud's day was a psychology of conscious experience, that which was accessible to trained, introspective reflection. Normal individuals were viewed as rational and their thought was believed to obey the rules of logic. The wheel has come full circle. Cognitive psychologists today accept the importance of unconscious processing and see a need to provide 'an adequate account of the nature and function of consciousness' (Williams et al., 1997:260). Freud found his way to the unconscious through attempting to understand the symptoms, fantasies, and dreams of his patients.

Most of us would not quarrel with Freud's view of our conscious thought as obeying the laws of logic, or *secondary process*. *Primary process*, or unconscious mental functioning, which obeys different rules, is not readily accessible or acceptable. A couple of concrete examples will help to bring the unconscious into focus. First, let us imagine a hypnotist telling a person he has put into a trance that when the person wakes up he will feel thirsty and ask for a cup of tea. Although the suggestion subsequently appeared to have been forgotten, the individual felt thirsty and asked for a drink. Conscious thought had been modified by hypnotic suggestion. A more familiar example is the common experience when our own unconscious plays tricks on us – say when we wish to introduce someone we know to another friend but for the moment the name is gone, lost in our unconscious, or, more technically correct, in our preconscious.

In order to understand the meaning of symptoms and fantasies, Freud set about studying the mental functions of the unconscious, which he believed were unconstrained by reality, time, order, morality, or the rules of logic. Initially, Freud regarded dreams as providing special access to these processes; later, the inter-personal relationship established during therapy, the *transference*, was used to understand the unconscious meaning of thought and action.

This discussion began with consideration of the unconscious because of its crucial role in all mental functioning. Those who attack the psychoanalytic inter-pretation of sexuality often overlook unconscious influences. Juliet Mitchell (1974) argued that feminist critics first distorted psychoanalytic theory and then, by apply-ing only the rules of logic rather than those of the unconscious, found it wanting.

Unless we believe that the infant is born rational, with knowledge of the world, the unconscious and its functions must be seen as primary in the infant. Essentially, Freud viewed an infant as hedonistic, seeking pleasure or satisfaction and with-drawing from 'unpleasure'. He postulated that when an infant feels hungry it hallucinates the experience of feeding if its feed fails to arrive. This primary process activity, hallucination, does not satisfy the biological hunger, and so slowly, out of such failures to find pleasure or escape unpleasure, the infant begins to recognise the outer world or reality. In his structural theory, Freud (1923) described the agency that deals with reality as the *ego*, and that arising from the instincts or drives as the *id*. Even after the reality principle and the ego are well established, they do not replace the pleasure principle and the id. Feelings and thoughts that were unacceptable to the world of reality, to the ego, do not disappear but are pushed into the unconscious, or repressed, and seek expression disguised by unconscious thought processes. The dynamic or conflicted quality of mental life reflects the tension between the ego and repressed feelings and thoughts. It is with this inner world of the unconscious and the id that Freud's explanation of sexuality begins.

Psychosexual development

Freud sought an understanding of adult sexuality in the earliest experiences of the infant. This does not imply that he believed interpersonal, object-oriented (that is, person-oriented), genital sexuality was present in infancy. Rather he considered that the mature heterosexual response, measurement of which we examined in the first section, had motivational origins in early sensual experiences. Although his view of infantile sexuality was unconventional and led to censure by his medical colleagues, Freud persisted in relying on his work with his patients, and his under-standing of their emotional problems continued to guide his theorising. He heard tales of childhood seduction and rape by their fathers from his neurotic female patients and initially believed these accounts to be true. Gradually he came to view them as fantasies expressing repressed sexual wishes. Just as neuroses reflect re-pressed infantile sexual wishes, so Freud believed, he could detect the expression of infantile sexuality in the 'perversions' – sado-masochistic practices, fetishism, and homosexuality. In order to understand these far-reaching conclusions to which Freud was led by his clinical experience, we need to examine the nature of this 'polymorphously perverse' infantile sexuality that Freud postulated and follow the developmental path that results in adult heterosexuality.

We begin by considering the classic Freudian theory of infantile sexuality and its development, noting in particular similarities and differences in the routes taken by women and men. The theory itself has a developmental history, and we consider some of the changes that have been introduced throughout the twentieth century as the result both of further clinical investigations and of researchers' observations of children.

Our account of Freud's use of the term *instinct* is as concise and incomplete as our statements about mental functioning and the structures of personality. Freud viewed instinct as a concept on the borderline between biology and psychology. Unlike external stimuli, which release reflexes, instincts have their source in the human body, and this makes withdrawal an impractical method for a person to use in dealing with them. The component sexual instincts have sources of excitation in the erogenous zones of the lips, mouth, and anus as well as in the genitals. Initially, they function independently, only becoming organised as adult libido in the course of development. The sexual instincts are the mental representations or symbols of these bodily excitations. The strength of the instinct is determined both by its bodily origins and by its role in the individual's psychological system. The aim of an instinct is satisfaction and, in Freud's system, the reduction of tension. A moment's reflection on the number of ways in which human beings gain sexual satisfaction tells us that sexual aims are achieved through a great variety of objects, both interpersonal and material. Freud believed that he had found an explanation for this diversity of sexual aims and objects in infantile sexuality.

Freud noted that human sexuality is different from that of other animals in important ways. Not only are we flexible in terms of aims and objects, but human females lack the extreme periodicity of most other mammals. Women are sexually receptive continuously throughout most of their adult lives, although recent studies indicate subtle changes across the menstrual cycle, e.g., in preference for novel partners, style of dress, and responsiveness to men's smells. Freud (1940) drew attention to another difference that he held to be of major significance for psychological development – the latency period. He believed that our species experiences a unique sexual moratorium that even the most closely related primates lack – our closest animal relations, chimpanzees, reach sexual maturity at about 5 years of age.

Freud's earliest descriptions of infantile sexuality reflected his preoccupation with the essentially bisexual nature of human beings. His study of embryology made him aware of the early parallel development of male and female internal organs. In the first edition of the *Three Essays*, Freud (1905) drew no distinctions between the oral, anal, and phallic stage of development of girls and boys. The acts of feeding, defecating, and urinating, from which each of the component sexual instincts arise, were, he believed, undifferentiated. In both girls and boys the aim of the oral instinct is sucking, and later biting, and the normal object is the breast. In the anal stage the aim is either expulsion or retention, and the appropriate object is the stool or faeces. Even the phallic stage was seen as similar: girls, Freud believed, have not yet discovered the vagina, and both girls and boys view the mother as phallic. The clitoris was held to function as a small penis and to be the source of erotic feelings. The aim of phallic fantasies for both boys and girls Freud held, was penetration. He wrote: 'So far as the autoerotic and masturbatory manifestations of sexuality are concerned, we might lay it down that the sexuality of little girls is of a wholly masculine character . . . The leading erotogenic zone in female children is located at the clitoris, and is thus homologous to the masculine genital zone of the glans penis' (1905:219–20). The phallocentric character of Freud's view, evident in such passages as this one, became the focus of much feminist criticism of Freud (e.g., Stockard and Johnson, 1979).

At this point it is useful to return to the interpersonal relationships of the developing child. Focus on the sexual instincts as they originate in the erogenous zones makes it easy to overlook the social psychological aspects of development. In the first edition of the *Three Essays*, Freud expressed his view that separate female and male sexuality develops only at puberty, but attention to the parent–child relationship led to a reformulation of the account of psychological differentiation. Freud based this upon the child's recognition of the anatomical differences between men and women, and he believed that both boys and girls interpret these differences as a lack in the female. In this way, the boy's love for his mother leads to fear of his father's jealousy and retaliation through castration. The girl feels disappointment at not having a penis; she abandons her mother who had made her this way and turns to her father, hoping to make up for her loss. The sexual instincts and love relationships within the family come together in penis envy, fear of castration, and the Oedipus complex.

Freud modified his theory of the Oedipus complex as it had been presented in the *Three Essays* after his final reformulation of his theory of instinct (1920, 1923, 1924, 1925, 1931). The life instincts, or Eros, were seen in opposition to the destructive instincts, or Thanatos. This meant not only that each individual struggles with masculine and feminine trends in the Oedipal conflict, but that for each there is both a positive, erotic element and a negative, destructive factor. Before we consider this additional complexity, we need to examine Freud's views of masculinity and femininity in greater detail. Freud considered the concepts of *masculinity* and *femininity* difficult and confusing. He identified three different senses in which these terms were used. We have described one of these, the biological sense, in chapter 3. In our discussion of stereotypes in chapter 2, we examined social psychological attempts to quantify a commonsense understanding of masculinity and femininity. The meaning of masculinity and femininity, crucial in psychoanalytic theory, refers to activity and passivity, but it is only with the development of adult sexuality that this distinction can be made and become meaningful for the individual.

Freud viewed phallic sexuality as active and penetrating and saw both boys and girls as essentially masculine. For boys, the active aim in the Oedipus complex remains the active penetration of the mother, but passive penetration by the father is also a possibility. To further complicate the picture, there are passive aims directed towards the unrelinquished phallic mother, or fantasy mother, and active aims directed towards the father. But, typically, male development continues the active aim of the phallic stage and is directed towards the female. The other possibilities are repressed and lost in the unconscious. They may return as symptoms or, when repression fails, as those adult practices that Freud labelled 'perversions'.

For the boy, threat of castration leads to the resolution of the Oedipal conflict and the establishment of the *superego*, or moral agency. Freud saw the beginnings of sexual differentiation for the girl in her recognition of her own and her mother's imagined loss of the penis. Freud was precise in describing the consequences of the girl's discovery of anatomical difference. In 1925 he wrote: 'Thus the little girl's recognition of the anatomical distinction between the sexes forces her away from masculinity and masculine masturbation on to new lines which lead to the development of femininity' (p. 256). For the girl, the castration complex leads to feelings of inferiority and penis envy. It is in order to regain the lost penis that the little girl turns to her father and to fantasies of replacing her mother.

The Oedipus complex for the girl is a secondary development dependent on phallic sexuality, recognition of the anatomical differences between the sexes, castration anxiety, and penis envy; but it, too, gives rise to the superego, though in a weaker form. Given all these conditions, it may be difficult to appreciate that Freud believed that the Oedipus complex was simpler for the girl to resolve than for the boy (1924). Its resolution leaves the girl with a passive aim – to be penetrated – and, at puberty, with a new source of sexual excitation, the vagina. We have already noted that Masters and Johnson demonstrated that at a physiological level the clitoris and not the vagina is the main source of pleasure. Their research has been used to attack psychoanalytic views of female sexuality. Freud, we need note, was describing the psychological experience and not just its bodily source. In addition, studies of the musculature of the vagina suggest that there is, in fact, more than one physiological source of the female's experience of orgasm (Graber, 1982); plainly, the last salvo has yet to be fired in this controversy.

The paths leading to the resolution of the Oedipus complex are different for girls and boys, but the resolution is a major developmental landmark for all children. The incorporation of parental standards in the superego results in the development of internal constraints on action. The post-Oedipal child is believed to repress the component sexual instincts – oral, anal, and phallic. At an unconscious level, the post-Oedipal child is prepared for sex-appropriate aims and object choices in adulthood, as the earlier component instincts are now fused in a mature structure. Repression during latency frees sexual energy for other activities, and the sublimated energy can find fulfilment in intellectual and artistic pursuits. Indeed, a certain amount of such repression is considered essential for development in the early school years.

Freud's phallocentric theory of infantile sexuality was the target of criticism almost from its inception. Hostility arose not only from those who condemned the very idea of childhood sexuality, but also from within the psychoanalytic group. Karen Horney (1924) challenged the notion of penis envy as an inevitable consequence of the girl's discovery of her genitals. She suggested that girls are jealous of boys' achievements in being able to urinate a greater distance, see their genitals, and more easily manipulate them. Horney was one of the earliest critics to consider the issues of control and power and the influence of the male position in society on the formulations offered by Freud and other male psychoanalysts. Melanie Klein's clinical work with very young children resulted in detailed descriptions of the first year of life and led to greater awareness of the mother's role in psychosexual development. From the work of Horney, Klein, and Ernest Jones a second, *gynocentric* position developed within psychoanalytic theory (Stockard and Johnson, 1979). Among theorists of an explicitly psychoanalytic orientation, both views, the phallocentric and the gynocentric, can still be found.

Freud (1931) himself was aware of many shortcomings in his account of infantile sexuality. In 1905 he acknowledged in the *Three Essays* that he knew more about the sexuality of boys than of girls. While he always retained the firm conviction that full female sexuality only develops from the castration complex, he urged his psychoanalytic colleagues to examine the pre-Oedipal period more closely. He recognised the special importance of the girl's relationship to her mother and the sources of her psychosexual identity in it. A contemporary psychoanalyst has suggested that the term Oedipus complex be restricted to male psychosexual development and has reintroduced the myth of Electra to describe female development (Halberstadt-Freud, 1998). From her analysis of mother–daughter relationships in the first year of life, she concludes that girls do not abandon their attachment to their mothers and that there is an undercurrent of strong homosexuality in female heterosexuality.

Critics who basically accept the psychoanalytic view of psychosexual development have revised the theory as the result of systematic observation of infants. Typical of this approach is the work of Galenson and Roiphe (1977). From their observations of 70 infants, with equal numbers of boys and girls, they reported differences in genital play and the age, within the first year of life, that it occurs. They described a distinctly female infant masturbation, preoccupation, and emotional love, along with elements of fantasy. This evidence, together with their clinical work with children, led them to propose a differentiated sense of gender identity as early as 18 months (see chapter 4 for other views of gender identities). Galenson and Roiphe also observed an awareness of anatomical sex differences in the second year. While accepting Freud's views about penis envy and the feminine castration complex, they saw these in relation to the 2-year-olds' fear of loss of love objects and his or her anal concerns. According to Galenson and Roiphe, by 2 years of age girls and boys follow very different paths in the psychological development of their inner worlds.

The work of Galenson and Roiphe can be linked to another trend within psychoanalytic thinking, represented, for example, by Sayers (1982), who sees the gynocentric view of Horney, Klein, and Jones as rooted in a biological essentialism. Just as the phallocentric approach might be construed as deriving from male anatomy, so a distinctive female psyche is alleged to arise from the female infant's interaction with her body. This view is most clearly expressed in the writings of the French feminist psychoanalyst Luce Irigaray. She identifies a uniquely female desire, the representation of bodily excitations arising from female genitalia (1977).

Criticisms of Freud's theory are legion. However, psychoanalysts who accept the basic tenets continue to develop and to modify it. An examination of Roy Schafer's (1977) position allows us to return to the evolution of sex, while a summary of Michael Parsons' (2000) views on 'perversion' illustrates the nature of change.

In a paper examining problems with Freud's psychology of women, Schafer asserted that in a most curious way Freud turned on his own discovery of the psychological plasticity of human sexuality, in terms of its aims and objects. He eventually espoused the values of nineteenth- and early twentieth-century evolutionary biology. Hence Freud posited procreation and heterosexual genital intercourse as the normal outcomes of development and crafted an explanation for it in terms of the diverse currents of infantile sexuality. Thus, he considered pleasure of an exclusively oral or anal nature immature and perverse, while non-procreative (e.g., homosexual) intercourse he characterised as an inversion.

Using the insights of his clinical experiences, Freud expanded our understanding of biological sexuality, yet his deep personal commitment to the procreative values of Western society led him to consider the outcome of psychosexual development in terms of biological necessity. His theory rests upon a drive towards species propagation at the same time as it points to an explanation in terms of the psychological representations of diverse sensual experiences. The structure of Freud's argument encourages neglect of questions of cultural learning and social values and instead focuses attention upon the anatomy of sex differences and hypothesised imperatives of species survival. At the very time that Freud was able to account psychologically for the allegedly natural revulsion and anxieties that the perversions arouse, he himself was trapped by the prevailing scientific and commonsense theories of his day. Contemporary theorists recognise that: 'The Western model of sexuality can no longer be regarded as unique or the norm' (Green, 1997:350). Indeed, Michael Parsons (2000) has proposed a very different view of 'perversion'. He argues that the sex of partners is not the primary criterion in identifying perverse activity. Rather, Parsons suggests perversion occurs when anything is placed between the person and their partner so that the relationship between them is not based upon 'respect for and pleasure in the otherness and personhood of the other' (p. 46) and the occasion is one of sexual excitement alone. This shift in thinking about perversion is related to a shift in the way psychoanalysts currently think about sexuality.

The decision to examine criticism only from within the psychoanalytic movement reflects our recognition of the impact of Freud's thinking on the understanding of sexuality in the twentieth century. In order to give full attention to its complexity, we have ignored many other critics. Those who disagree fundamentally with concepts such as the repressed unconscious and infantile sexuality attack psychoanalytic theory, but they often fail to illuminate the nature of this influential theory. Rather than examine sociological critiques of psychoanalytic theories of sexuality, we next consider the use of sexuality in defining people's positions in society.

The social construction of sexuality

At the beginning of this chapter we approached the question of the similarities and differences in women's and men's sexual experiences from the viewpoint of positivist physiological or psychological investigators. Our examination of psychoanalytic explanations sought to describe the meaning of sexuality and desire and introduced the inner world of feelings and fantasies, but largely ignored the biological or the broader social and cultural world. We considered theories about the effects of infantile experiences in shaping men's and women's unconscious attitudes – the aims and objects of their sexual pleasure. Here we examine the influence of recent accounts of cultural diversity on the construction of the concepts of sex, gender, and sexuality. These analyses allow us to explore the limits of our own binary representations of gender in terms of male and female, and of sexuality as defined by hetero- and homo-sexuality.

In the beginning there was man

Readers familiar with the Old Testament will remember that we are told that God created Eve from Adam's rib. Laqueur (1990) has shown that our current binary representation of the sexes only emerged in the late eighteenth century. He wrote:

> Thus the old model, in which men and women were arrayed according to their degree of metaphysical perfection, their vital heat, along an axis whose telos (end or purpose) was male, gave way in the late eighteenth century to a new model of radical dimorphism, or biological divergence. An anatomy and physiology of incommensurability replaced a metaphysics of hierarchy in the representation of woman in relation to man. (pp. 5–6)

Laqueur asserted that this fundamental, epistemological change in understanding was *not* the result of the discovery of a new set of facts. Rather, it reflected a profound shift in Western beliefs about science and knowledge, and fundamental changes in meaning and causal explanation.

Our modern scientific view is so pervasive that it is difficult to think in Neoplatonic, pre-Newtonian, modes. The notion that the world we experience is only an approximation, a degraded version of ideal types or forms, is alien. The telos, in the quotation from Laqueur, refers to such a perfect form, that of humanity. Man and woman were recognised as being different versions of this single ideal and they were viewed hierarchically, in terms of their approximation to the perfect form. Men were viewed as closer to the ideal because they were hotter. Women, who were cooler, were viewed as less perfect than men, but both were measured against the ideal; there was one ideal form or One-sex. Maintaining the One-sex view, anatomists described the female body as inverted. The uterus was equated to the male scrotum; the ovaries seen as testicles, and the vagina as an inverted penis. So widely accepted was this view that models of female anatomy were not necessary. When the German anatomist von Soemmerring published his folio in 1796, he claimed that it contained the very first illustrations of a female skeleton.

Just as the Two-sex model is a comparatively recent construction, so, too, is the concept of sexuality. Horrocks (1997) has described its relatively short developmental history. He has argued that the very term sexuality is a modern one, and that its history may be traced to Enlightenment discourse. Horrocks acknowledged that creators of the One-sex model, the Greeks and Romans, considered sexual behaviour and desire. However, he asserted that it has only been in modern times that sexuality as an entity, and, more particularly, the notion that it is the defining aspect of individual identities, has come to the fore. For just this reason Halperin (1990) warned that it is inappropriate to describe ancient Greek men's sexual behaviour as homosexual. The concept of a homosexual sexual identity is a very modern one.

Although of recent creation, the concept of sexuality is of sufficient significance that the French philosopher Foucault (1979) produced a three-volume history of its role in modern society. He attacked both rationalist and Marxist analyses of sexuality. In the first volume, he asserted that the bourgeois culture that developed with the rise of capitalism exploited sexuality rather than, as widely believed, repressed it. The effects of repression, he suggested, are not undifferentiated but are linked to social power. The exercise of power had influence on at least four aspects of sexual knowledge. These objects of sexual knowledge are:

- the hysterical woman
- the masturbating child
- the Malthusian (procreative) couple
- the perverse adult.

All four of them have a place in psychoanalytic theories and, indeed, it is the Malthusian couple that frames the perverse adult. We turn here to sociological research to broaden our understanding of that fourth object, the perverse individual. Alongside the binary concept of male and female there is the other significant binary contrast which defines identity, that of heterosexual and homosexual.

From two to many

The Malthusian couple, the heterosexual man and heterosexual woman engaged in procreative sex, have defined male and female gender roles and also delimited perverse sexuality. But the negative valuing of other forms of sexual behaviour and the modern definition of other social identities as consequently deficient, perverse, or illegal, is an aspect of recent Western civilization. Research undertaken in other societies highlights the limits of our two-gender view of human sexuality and the constraints of our gender-polarizing culture (Bem, 1993, 1995).

The *xanith* of Oman: a third gender role?

Wikan (1977) studied the gender system of the Omani, an Arab sultanate on the eastern side of the Arabian peninsula, and in particular the role of the *xanith*. She has argued that the Omani do not have the two-gender system with which we are most familiar, and that the *xanith* constitute a third gender.

Wikan reported that the *xanith* are biologically men who sell themselves in passive homosexual relationships, but these transactions are not their main source of income. They also work as skilled domestic servants and are in demand. Their dress is distinctive, cut like the long tunic worn by men but made of the pastel-colored cloth used in women's dress. Although they retain men's names, *xanith* violate all the restrictions that *purdah*, the system of female seclusion, imposes on men. They speak intimately with women in the street without bringing the reputations of the women into question; they sit with the segregated women at a wedding and are permitted to see a bride's unveiled face. *Xanith* do not sit or eat with men in public nor play the musical instruments reserved for men. Their manners, perfumed bodies, and high-pitched voices appeared effeminate to Wikan. She described the *xanith* as transsexuals in the sense that their essential gender identity was that of a woman rather than a man.

In our own society, transsexuals do not attempt to violate the two-gender/sex system and are no longer a great rarity. Twenty-eight years ago, Jan Morris (1974) recounted her own journey from boyhood, through the army, marriage, fatherhood, and a successful career in journalism to her long-sought identity as a woman. In her case, and that of many less well-known transsexuals, the path to achieving their desired identity is an arduous one involving hormone treatments, deliberate study of the habits in dress, movement, and speech of the desired gender, and, finally, surgery. In a more recent account, Griggs (1998) described his/her reluctant journey from a male gender identity to a female one detailing sociological, economic, and psychological criteria for successfully living as the other gender and being viewed by others as the desired gender. S/he does not celebrate the experience and would rather not have undertaken it. Her personal account is enriched with material from interviews with 100 individuals who have had similar experiences, some male to female (MTF) and other female to male (FTM) transsexuals. The experiences of individuals in the two groups are different and reflect the different statuses of women and men in American society. For example, MTFs reported being comfortable in men's clothes, but they said that they wished for, and dreamed about, wearing women's clothes. FTM individuals, on the other hand, said that they felt like drag queens when wearing dresses. FTMs generally reported being pleased and relaxed when they began living as men, while MTFs replied that the pressures to conform to standards of womanly behaviour or dress proved irksome. It is important to note that these were comments about feminine-role requirements, not about their inner sense of identity as women. The higher status of male attributes and behaviour has an impact even in the realm of transgender experience whether the origins of patriarchy lie in evolution or in history (see chapter 3).

The Omani situation is illuminating because *xanith* is a social phenomenon and can be construed as a space between the roles of men and women. There are three quite different possibilities open to the *xanith*. Should they wish to become men again, they need only marry and prove themselves able to perform heterosexual intercourse with their brides. Some *xanith* never choose this path and remain as women until they grow old, when, having given up prostitution and homosexual intercourse, their anatomical sex again places them – though perhaps only tenuously – in the category of old men. In addition, Wikan reported that some *xanith* become women, then men, and then women again. This comparative ease of passage, based as it is on behaviour rather than anatomy, is part of the evidence Wikan presented in arguing that Omani *xanith* represent a gender role – a third one – intermediate between Omani male and female gender roles. She has also claimed that *xanith* function to maintain the sharply differentiated roles of men and women.

If *xanith* is indeed a socially constructed role, this may explain the relative ease with which men pass from the male category into *xanith* and back again to male. The fact that in old age, when they are no longer sexually active, *xanith* are again classed with men suggests that these transitions are of a different order from those that transsexuals in our own society experience. In our own society, the passage becomes irreversible with sex-reassignment surgery involving genital reconstruction. Even then some MTFs go on to facial surgery, breast implants, and tracheal shaves to reduce their Adam's apple (Grigg, 1998). All of these procedures suggest the widespread acceptance of only two gender roles in our own society and of a need to ensure congruence between biological sex and gender attribution.

Native North American genders

In recent years, the ethnography of North American societies has been re-examined and efforts made to understand sex, gender, and sexuality without imposing the binary categories of male–female and heterosexual–homosexual dominant in Euro-American culture. In 1975, Martin and Voorhies asserted that: 'It seems possible that human reproductive bisexuality establishes a minimal number of socially recognised physical sexes but these need not be limited to two' (p. 86). An extensive scholarly reanalysis of reports of *berdache* has led Roscoe (1994, 1998) to propose that berdache roles filled by men and women constitute third and fourth gender categories in Native American societies.

Europeans have written about berdache since contact with Native North American societies in the sixteenth century and sought to understand the roles in terms of contemporary theories of sex, gender, and sexuality. Male berdache have been reported in almost 150 North American societies and accounts of women filling such roles have been provided in almost 75. Roscoe (1998) has also surveyed other parts of the world and found extensive evidence of similarly complex gender systems. In the past, a bewildering and changing array of concepts such as hermaphrodite, sodomite, homosexual, and transsexual has been invoked to describe these other gender categories. Roscoe notes that these terms usually connote either the gender role or the sexual orientation of these individuals. Most importantly, Roscoe believes that Euro-American culture has lacked the conceptual tools to describe them appropriately; the terms employed have been those current in the contemporary discourse concerning sex, gender, and sexuality.

Although anthropologists are generally sensitive to cultural differences in perception, they have retained their binary model of sexuality and the telos of reproductive sexuality when analysing sex, gender, and sexuality in the cultures of the world. In recent years, feminism, gay and lesbian studies, and the rise of literary theories of alternative sexualities, Queer theory, have provided tools for the reanalysis of berdache and research has flourished.

Roscoe has summarised the findings of this new wave of research on berdache. The dimensions which he lists in order of importance when describing both female and male berdache are their:

- engagement in productive specialisation
- endowment with supernatural sanctions.

Male berdache were unusually skilled in crafts and domestic activities, while female berdache displayed outstanding skills in warfare, hunting, and leadership. Both male and female berdache had experienced a supernatural, spiritual call to their role. Their economic and religious contributions ensured that they were respected and accepted members of their communities.

The attributes that we have observed to define transsexual identity were more variable and of lesser importance. Cross-dressing was common and often visible as a sign of berdache status, but was not always present. Some male berdache dressed in a manner than could not be described as either masculine or feminine, while female berdache usually wore men's clothes only for hunting or in warfare. Although the non-berdache partners of both male and female berdache were often of their own sex, sexual behaviour was also variable. Some berdache were described as bisexual or heterosexual.

Roscoe proposed that acceptance of his argument, that male and female berdache constitute third and fourth genders, requires closer analysis of the concept of gender. In the two-sex model, gender was held to follow sex, but gender diversity breaks this link. Roscoe (1994) viewed gender as 'a multidimensional category of personhood encompassing a distinct pattern of social and cultural differences' (p. 341). Using this definition, Roscoe examined a great deal of anthropological evidence and concluded that it was not individual variation in gender identity or sexual orientation, nor societal contradictions that led individuals to become berdache. Attempting to represent the view of Native Americans, he proposed that these individuals occupy a patterned social and cultural position in their societies. He asserted that Native North Americans interpreted physical differences according to a variety of codes that differed from those of Euro-Americans, but collectively accorded physical attributes less weight than we do. Moving beyond a view of physical sex differences as necessarily binary creates a space within which a society can construct other genders.

At this point, we might wish to return to the inner world of psychoanalysis in seeking an explanation of *xanith* and berdache behaviour and character. The Omani accepted that certain people's natures are different, and their social stance in these cases is one of non-involvement; concern is confined to closest kin. A husband may feel shamed by his faithless wife, or parents may be saddened and grieved by their son's passive homosexual tendencies, but social concern is strictly limited. In Native North American societies, berdache were usually respected and indeed honored, although their supernatural powers may have occasionally provoked fear as well.

Our own society provides a sharp contrast. A question we can ask is the degree to which social recognition and the drawing of boundaries – for example, in designating people transvestites, transsexuals, or homosexuals – influence our own view of them and their own views of themselves. Foucault (1979) believed that Western society sought to classify everything, even things that, he believed, are essentially unclassifiable. He held that the aim of this classification was power, as it allowed differential status and hence value to be attached to categories of people.

The problem of classification and of the ease with which it can be imposed is a useful principle in reconsidering the gender-role system in Oman. Omani women wear their hair long, carrying it forward from a central parting, and are clothed in tight-waisted, brightly patterned tunics. Their heads are covered, as are those of men. But men wear loose-fitting white tunics and have short hair. The *xanith*'s hair is of medium length, and they never cover their heads; their solid-coloured tunics are close fitting, and they wear make-up. Wikan believed that these distinctions are essential and reflect *xanith* status not as biological women but as another category, as a third gender. She argued that, given Omani patterns of dress, were *xanith* to assume the full women's costume, their anatomic status as males would be ambiguous. Dress serves to define three distinct social categories.

Beyond two gender roles

Accounts of alternative sexual identities have been growing at a great pace since the emergence of feminism, lesbian and gay studies, and Queer theory. The thesis we present below, though not representative of this literature, is provocative. It not only draws heavily on Freud's views on sexuality, but is also concerned with the impact of society in moulding sexual desire. Deleuze, a French philosopher, and Guattari, a Marxist psychoanalyst (1977), presented an early anti-Oedipus argument attacking the procreative family. We draw on Hocquenghem's (1978) analysis of their work.

To describe a particular kind of sexual desire as homosexual, Hocquenghem asserted, is to make an arbitrary division along the continuum of desire, a division that, he and many others (e.g., Foucault, 1979) have claimed, is imposed on sexuality by Western society to achieve its capitalist ends. Brief examination of Omani and Native North American beliefs and practices provides evidence that the attempt to classify sexual desire as either heterosexual or homosexual is arbitrary and a product of our gender-polarising society.

In Oman, efforts are made to avoid condemning an individual on the basis of isolated behavioural acts. In contrast, in our own society we seem ever ready to make new classifications. The term *homosexual* evolved only a hundred years ago as a means of connoting a category of people – those who participate in particular kinds of sexual acts (Weeks, 1978). Their behaviour was deemed criminal and men who were thus identified were placed at the risk of both the law and blackmail. The repressive consequences of the categorization are still in evidence. The age of consent for homosexual acts became the same as that for heterosexual behaviour in Britain only in the year 2000. Kinsey's evidence, now 50 years old, that homosexual behaviour occurs along a continuum, has largely been ignored.

Hocquenghem argued that any repressed deviant tendency within those who identify themselves as heterosexual only leads them to persecute and condemn those openly identified as deviant. An empirical psychological study has provided evidence to support Hocquenghem's hypothesis. Sixty-four Caucasian, heterosexual men completed an Index of Homophobia scale which allowed the identification of 29 men as non-homophobic and 35 as being homophobic (Adams et al., 1996). Arousal to explicitly erotic heterosexual, gay, and lesbian stimuli was measured using a penile circumference strain gauge. Although both groups of men underestimated their measured arousal to male homosexual activity, the underestimation was considerably greater for the homophobic group, men who held explicitly negative attitudes about homosexuality.

Hocquenghem's argument echoes Freud's concern with unconscious motives. Recognition of the polymorphously perverse nature of all human sexuality makes even those most interested in repression suspect. The language of anti-Oedipus discourse is altered in the reformulation of Freud offered by Lacan (1966). Lacan sought to rid psychoanalysis of its biological language and to explore the unconscious in terms that he believed to be more appropriate, those of linguistics and of symbolism. In keeping with this project, instinct becomes desire, the penis gives way to the symbolic phallus, but the Oedipus complex remains at the core. For Lacan, as for Freud, the resolution of the Oedipus complex is the turning point in the child's development. It marks the child's recognition of authority and his or her loss of omnipotence, for the phallus symbolises the patriarchal order. It is our society's patriarchal order that demands repression and renunciation of a polymorphous sexuality. No longer can the child obtain just what he or she desires; the authority of the father stands between the child and the child's desire for the mother. It is not the biological father, but language and the symbolic order that gain ascendancy in the child's unconscious mental functioning. The phallus symbolises the authority of the social order.

We concluded the discussion of psychoanalytic explanations of sexuality with Schafer's criticisms of Freud's return to evolutionary biology in his efforts to understand adult genital sexuality – masculinity/femininity, activity/passivity. Lacan described a similar course of development, but in his account the unconscious bears the imprint of society through the social definition of masculinity and femininity. It is the core definition of sexuality derived through the dynamics of the Oedipal conflict that Hocquenghem and that Deleuze and Guattari attack. Hocquenghem's argument is relevant here in that he was concerned with the impact of society on the unconscious mind, but he presented an oversimplified view of society and of mental functioning. A problem arises in trying to compare men and women: nowhere in Hocquenghem's text is there mention of female homosexuals, so we do not know the extent to which his analysis fits female homosexuality. In addition, social class is unspecified. We have seen, in the Kinsey reports, that sexual behaviour varies with social class. Weeks (1978) reported that men's consciousness of themselves as homosexuals also varied with class. In Hocquenghem's analysis, the social system is undifferentiated and the economic system – that is, capitalism – is invoked instead.

In this discussion of some French theoretical approaches to homosexuality, and more generally of the impact of society in determining sexuality, we have come a long way from descriptions of *xanith* and berdache. The discussion has allowed us to link the social and the unconscious, but it has lost track of the comparison between women's and men's sexuality. Two have become many.

Conclusions

In this chapter we began by seeking clear observable differences and conscious explanations of men's and women's sexual experience. Our explorations of basic psychoanalytic accounts of sexuality led to an encounter with deeper motivations and the now widely used concept of gender identity. In the final section, we examined social influences explicitly and recounted examples of social constructions that have challenged the allegedly 'natural' division of human beings into the dimorphic categories of male and female. In each section, the challenge of society in terms of gender scripts, repressed desire, and social categories was significant. It is only by returning to considerations of reproductive success as the ultimate criterion that binary notions of sexuality can be upheld.

Further reading

Benjamin, J. (1998). *Shadow of the Other: Intersubjectivity and Gender in Psychoanalysis*. New York and London: Routledge.
    Benjamin offers a technical but creative synthesis of contemporary psychoanalytic positions concerning sexuality and gender categories.
Elliott, A. (ed.) (1999). *Freud 2001*. Cambridge: Polity Press
    A wide range of theorists are brought together in a single volume. Each illustrates the contemporary relevance of psychoanalytic theory for their discipline.
Herdt, G. (ed.) (1994). *Third Sex, Third Gender: Beyond Sexual Dimorphism in Culture and History*. New York: Zone Books.

In this edited collection the categories encompassing sexuality are considered from historical and anthropological perspectives.

Laqueur, T. W. (1990). *Making Sex: Body and Gender from the Greeks to Freud*. Cambridge, MA: Harvard University Press.

Laqueur's historical account challenges contemporary views about the naturalness of our concepts of sex and gender.

Potts, M. and Short, R. (1999). *Ever Since Eve: The Evolution of Human Sexuality*. Cambridge University Press.

This book, by two eminent reproductive biologists, discusses issues about human reproduction, and their social and political impact. Extensively illustrated, and packed with interesting and bizarre facts, it can be flicked though like a coffee table book, or read as clear and well-informed popular science.

6   Aggression, violence, and power

Introduction

The problem of human violence is often viewed as a *male* problem. Most violent crime and homicides are carried out by men, usually young men (Figs. 6.1 and 6.2). Organised groups who use violence in the name of a larger body of people, whether official, such as the armed services, or unofficial, such as vigilante or paramilitary groups, are usually made up of men. Violence is seen as the masculine way of reacting to the difficulties and frustrations of life. This emphasis on the maleness of human violence can be found in the writings of both feminists (e.g., Dobash and Dobash, 1977–8; Walker, 1989, 1990) and evolutionary psychologists (e.g., Buss, 1994, 1999; Daly and Wilson, 1988, 1990; Wilson and Daly, 1999).

Those who claim that violence is a *male* rather than a human problem are correct in the sense that most overt acts of violence towards other adults now and in the past were committed by men. This view may, however, underestimate the extent to which women are directly and indirectly involved. Under circumstances where resources are scarce, or there is pronounced competition for men who have access to such resources, women's aggression may be more like that of men and involve direct physical conflict. When women from countries such as the USA come into conflict with their male partners, they engage in physical aggression to a greater extent than was formerly realised, and a substantial minority of those injured in such disputes are men.

Women's indirect involvement in aggression takes two forms. First, throughout human history, a great deal of female encouragement has fanned the flames of male violence. The primeval scene of two men fighting over a woman still exists today; the masculine characteristics of toughness and aggression are admired by many women; and women have often played an important part in encouraging soldiers going to war. There is also increasing evidence that girls and women engage in covert expressions of aggressiveness, such as spreading malicious rumours about the person.

In this chapter, we examine the evidence for differences in aggression and violence between the sexes. In order to do so more productively, it is important to distinguish between aggression involving members of the same sex and that involving partners in a sexual relationship. Research into these two topics has been pursued independently, and different explanations have been applied. We also

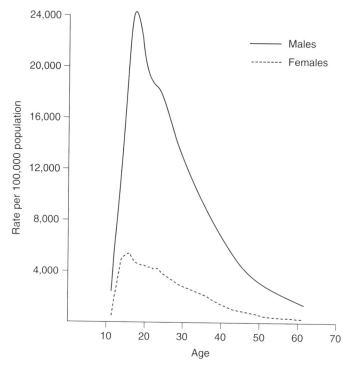

Fig. 6.1 Male and female criminal offenders, by age, for England and Wales 1842–1844 (from Courtwright, 1996).

need to distinguish between different forms of aggression, and, indeed, between aggression and violence. *Violence* is a term that is often used loosely, and generally refers to acts involving great physical force, often in the inanimate as well as the animate world. When applied to humans, it may be useful to restrict the term *violent* to those physically aggressive actions that cause physical or psychological damage to the recipient (Archer, 1994a). In this way, violence, the consequence, can be distinguished from aggression, the intentions, actions, and emotions of the actor (Archer and Browne, 1989).

Aggression and violence between members of the same sex

Are men really more aggressive than women?

Violent exchanges between people of the same sex generally involve young men who are either acquaintances or strangers, and tend to occur in public places, such as a street or a bar or nightclub. The most extreme outcome is for one protagonist to kill the other. Daly and Wilson (1988) regarded homicide figures as the most reliable source of evidence on human violence because homicide has 'a resultant validity that all self-report lacks' (p. 12), i.e. there is a body (or a missing person),

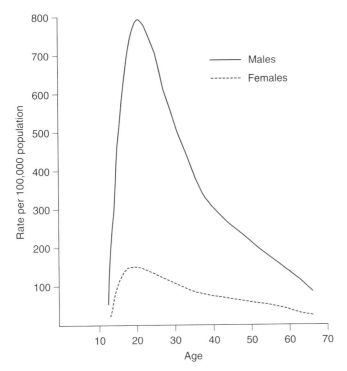

Fig. 6.2 Arrested offenders by age and sex, for the United States,1990 (from
Courtwright, 1996).

and also because homicide is viewed more seriously by the police than is sub-lethal
violence.

Daly and Wilson listed 35 studies of homicides across cultures and historical
times, ranging from 10 individuals to over 10,000. In all but one, both victim and
killer were male in over 91 per cent of cases. The exception contained 15 killings of
dependent children by women. These researchers subsequently examined figures
for unrelated same-sex individuals, in order to exclude cases of infanticide. Across
all 20 studies they reviewed (Daly and Wilson, 1990), 97.2 per cent of nearly
14,000 homicides involved men as both victim and assailant.[1] From the limited
information for other times and other places, this pattern seems to apply to a wide
range of cultures and throughout recorded history. Many fights of the sort that end
in sub-lethal injuries in one culture become homicides in cultures where guns or
knives are readily available. The loser of a fight may leave the scene, and return
soon after with a gun or knife.

Although homicides are perhaps the most reliable source of data on violence
between men, examining violent-crime statistics is also instructive. Studies of the
assault rates for men and women taken from crime figures in various times
and places show that men are the offenders in the large majority of cases
(Campbell, 1995, Figure 1; Dobash and Dobash, 1977–8; Harries, 1974). Where

[1] Figures calculated by John Archer.

same-sex assaults have been analysed, most of these are between men. Crime surveys use interviews to assess the prevalence of a range of crimes, both reported and unreported. They generally support the view that the majority of offenders are male, and in the case of non-domestic assaults most victims and assailants are male (e.g., British Crime Survey, 2000).

These studies concentrate on violence as a criminal act. There are many others that involve self-reports of fights, or questionnaires assessing the frequency of physical aggression. A meta-analysis of these (Archer, 2001a) showed that men engage in more frequent physical aggression with one another than do women, and that this difference is fairly large. We can use one particular study as an example. Gergen (1990) reported a survey of the use of physical aggression and playful fighting among US students. Over the previous 2 years, more than twice as many males showed physical aggression to one another than females did to other females. For specific acts, there was a greater disparity. For example, punching, shoving, hitting with an object, and having a physical fight were all much more common among men than women. However, women showed more scratching, kicking, and pinching one another than men did (Archer, 2000b).

Although they tend to be restricted to US students in terms of the participants, social psychological laboratory studies provide another source of evidence on sex differences in same-sex aggression. A meta-analytic review of these studies, by Eagly and Steffen (1986), again found that men were overall more aggressive than women, but that the difference was relatively small.[2] When physical aggression was involved, the sex difference was larger, but still in the moderate rather than large range.

Overall, we can see a pattern of descending magnitude of sex differences for acts of physical aggression to a same-sex person, from the most damaging consequences (homicide), to criminal acts of violence, to lesser acts of physical aggression, and, finally, to the somewhat artificial world of the social psychological laboratory.

Which men are likely to be violent?

It is not simply men in general who are more likely to use physical aggression to one another than are women in general. It is young men who are particularly prone to escalate disputes from the verbal to the physical. Figs. 6.1 and 6.2 show this pattern for crime figures for England and Wales in the 1840s and in the USA today. Similar figures were reported for France in the 1820s (Quetelet, 1833). Daly and Wilson (1990) showed four separate graphs of homicide rates against age for men and women, for the UK, Canada, Chicago, and Detroit. These places had (and have) very different absolute homicide rates, and yet if the graphs are re-scaled so as to show homicides for each age as a proportion of the total, the graphs are remarkably similar (Fig. 6.3).

---

[2] The mean weighted d value was 0.29, i.e. less than a third of a standard deviation between the values for the two sexes.

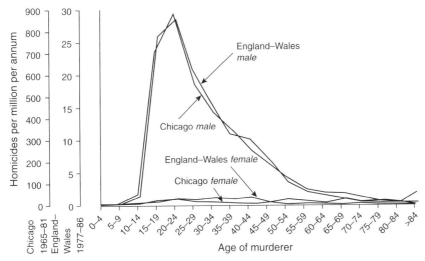

Fig. 6.3 Homicides by age and sex, for Chicago, 1965–1981, and England and Wales, 1977–1986. The absolute values have been rescaled to show the similarity of the age–sex curves (from Cronin, 1991).

So far we have identified being young and male as risk factors for same-sex violence. Violence is also much more likely among those young males who are outside the mainstream institutions of paid employment and marriage. Homicide figures for Detroit in 1972 indicated that men were overrepresented by about four times among victims and offenders if they were unemployed (Daly and Wilson, 1988). Courtwright's (1996) historical analysis of violence in North America, *Violent Land*, is subtitled *Single Men and Social Disorder, From the Frontier to the Inner City*. In frontier times, it was the single man who was most likely to take risks and to get into fights. A married man would be much more likely to stop and think of his wife and children before venturing into a violent confrontation.

In the frontier days, the imbalanced sex ratio exacerbated male violence. Single men went out west to find work, whereas single women tended to stay back in the east. Dodge City, Kansas, made famous through cowboy films, provides an extreme example of what Courtwright (1996) called the 'geography of gender'. In 1870, there were 768 men for every 100 women, and most of these men were young and single. Furthermore, they were generally armed and came into town to get drunk. They were also sensitive about their honour. As we show below, the combination of being drunk and sensitive to what others say is a particularly lethal one, especially when combined with the possession of guns. The American tradition of allowing citizens to carry guns has had a damaging impact in terms of deaths through homicide, from the frontier to the inner cities of today where children as young as 10 or 12 years run around the streets with firearms and drugs (Courtwright, 1996).[3]

---

[3] According to one estimate (Kettle, 1999), a million US teenagers carried guns to school in 1998. The source of this is obscure, but the homicide trends for the 15 to 19 age group in the USA from

The context of most violence between men is a public place, typically in a street in a low-income urban neighbourhood. A large proportion of these assaults arise from arguments or disputes between casual acquaintances. As Campbell (1986) noted, the streets of poor urban areas are male territories, particularly in US Afro-American and Latino cultures, which involve a high level of segregation and antagonism between the sexes. Men spend a lot of time outside the home in a masculine subculture where they seek to make a living in various ways, often outside the law. Machismo, the cult of toughness, is prevalent: this involves a man being able to defend or take care of himself, using violence if challenged.

The stereotype of the bar-room brawl is drawn from frontier times when it was certainly a true reflection of real life (Courtwright, 1996). In a contemporary British study (Archer et al., 1995) of fights among young men, around 14–15 per cent occurred in a bar or pub, and a further 30–40 per cent in a nightclub or disco. These figures are large compared to the relatively small amount of time people spend in these locations. They also mask very large differences between individual bars (Felson et al., 1986; Marsh, 1980), and do not reflect those arguments that begin in a bar and continue as violent exchanges in nearby streets and car parks.

The connection between bars and intermale violence is mediated by two aspects: the masculine tradition of the bar and the cognitive effects of alcohol. Bars provide an opportunity for conflict, by bringing together in one place a violence-prone section of the community, that is young males. Social control is likely to be an issue in bars since rights and obligations may not be clear-cut, giving rise to disputes over who gets served, over a spilled drink, or whose turn it is on the pool table.

According to Gibbs (1986), alcohol has a number of influences that may make violence more likely. It narrows the perceptual field, so that specific actions are not seen in a wider context; it influences the ability to understand fully, and provide accounts for, actions; and, it produces an accentuated feeling of power and self-importance, which makes rule-violation more likely to be perceived in others, and the person's own sense of identity to seem threatened by the actions of others. The importance of threatened identity in causing all sorts of violent behaviour has been emphasised in a general theory of the causes of violence (Baumeister et al., 1996).

Women's aggression

There have been numerous recent media reports highlighting instances of violence by women in Western nations. These reports include America's first woman

1985 to 1991 showed a 50% increase, and in 1994 nearly 90% of homicide victims of these ages were killed by firearms (MMWR Weekly, 1994; National Center for Injury Prevention and Control, 1998).

serial killer (Halasa, 1991), girl gangs and robbers (e.g., Carroll, 1998; Fowler, 1999; Johnson, 1994), and a long-standing controversy over women boxers (Archer and Lloyd, 1985; Duncan, 1998). Such reports usually highlight the discrepancy between the physically violent woman and the traditional feminine stereotype (chapter 2). Violent women are frequently seen as particularly deviant for this reason, and alarm is often expressed at the apparent increase in instances of female violence, blame for which is typically placed at the door of feminism or the associated greater independence of young women, described in the British media as 'girl power'.

Whilst we may question the ability of isolated and newsworthy incidents of women's violence to provide an accurate picture of overall trends, it is certainly the case that the stereotype of the non-aggressive woman is misleading. White and Kowalski (1994) have, from a feminist perspective, questioned the portrayal of women as non-aggressive in several strands of the academic literature, arguing that this serves to accentuate men's power over women. A major part of this argument is that, when women show instances of 'masculine' forms of aggression involving direct physical and verbal confrontation, these are seen as pathological or due to hormonal imbalance, or their actions are unreported, or viewed as insignificant. Campbell (1999) has also suggested that patriarchal cultures stigmatise women's aggression, and seek to offer excuses for it.

A related issue is whether there is a distinct form of aggression preferred by girls and women that has not been acknowledged because it does not fit the stereotypic masculine form. Indirect aggression among children was first described by Feshbach (1969), and later studied by Bjorkqvist et al. (1992a). They found that girls used forms of aggression such as spreading untrue stories and ostracising another person substantially more than boys did. This finding has since been replicated in other studies in Finland (e.g., Bjorkqvist et al., 1992a), the USA (Galen and Underwood, 1997), the UK (Tapper and Boulton, 1998), and Australia (Owens, 1996).

Whether there is a similar sex difference in indirect aggression beyond 18 years of age (Bjorkqvist et al., 1992b) is not clear. People are generally reluctant to admit using such devious ways of hurting another person, and for this reason most studies involving children have used reports by peers. Bjorkqvist et al. (1994) did devise a comparable scale to measure harassment at work, and found two forms of covert aggression among university employees. One, which was termed social manipulation, was used more by women than men. The other, described as rational-appearing aggression, was used more by men. It would seem that in organisations such as universities, where direct aggression is likely to be counterproductive, men learn to disguise their methods of inflicting harm so that they can be presented as justifiable criticism. However, subsequent studies involving an adult version of the measures originally used to study schoolchildren (Bjorkqvist et al., 1992a), did not find sex differences among British undergraduates (Archer et al., 1997; Campbell et al., 1997).

Why is there a sex difference in same-sex violence?

Masculine values and their evolutionary underpinning

One way of beginning to answer the question of why men are more often violent to one another than women are, is by examining the supposed reasons for homicides involving male victims and protagonists. A classic study of the motives for murder by Wolfgang (1958) involved examination of the files of the Philadelphia police force from 1948 to 1952. The most frequent motive was 'an altercation of relatively trivial origin; insult, curse, jostling etc.' Subsequent studies have confirmed this, and reports of homicides in the contemporary media reveal similar motives. For example, British newspaper reports of intermale homicides in the early 1990s contained the following situations: a conflict over a parking space, an argument over a noisy dog, a disagreement in a game of dominoes, and a dispute between neighbours over barbecue smoke.

Nevertheless, labelling the exchanges leading to these killings as 'trivial' shows a lack of understanding of their meaning for the protagonists (Archer, 1994b; Campbell, 1986; Daly and Wilson, 1988). What is usually at stake is some perceived breach of social rules. A hostile social exchange then begins, and the initial rule violation becomes transformed into a verbal exchange about reputation and social identity (Felson, 1984). Often this occurs in front of an audience of peers, and involves exchanged insults, which have been identified as a common cause of fights among young men (Archer et al., 1995).

Such verbal exchanges assume far greater importance among male groups where the impact of law or moral restraints is absent. Where there is truly little outside restraint – such as in the US frontier towns and modern American prisons – a man's reputation will depend wholly or partly on the extent to which he poses a credible threat of violence to other men (Daly and Wilson, 1988). Autobiographical accounts of men living under such conditions emphasise the need to establish a reputation as a 'hard man' by violence. As Jimmy Boyle, the now reformed Scottish criminal, wrote of his early gang fights: 'The one giving the most stitches got the reputation. It made the others think twice before coming near you' (Boyle, 1977). Under the conditions enjoyed by most of the middle classes in modern Western nations, it is easy to overlook the reality that the rule of law has replaced the rule of violence. As Daly and Wilson (1988) put it:

> The utility of a credible threat of violence has been mitigated and obscured in modern mass society because the state has assumed a monopoly on the legitimate use of force. (p. 128)

They argued that in pre-state societies any man who is not able to protect himself physically will be helpless to stop his possessions – and his female partner – from being taken by any other man who cares to try. Viewed from an evolutionary perspective (chapter 3), a man in such a position would leave few, if any, offspring. From this viewpoint, Wolfgang's supposedly trivial altercations are not really trivial but concern the relative status of the protagonists, which will be a matter of life or death (or at least reproductive death) where there is no effective rule of law.

Nisbett and Cohen (1996) have developed this argument in relation to what they refer to as the 'culture of honour', found in the south of the USA and in many other parts of the world. The notion of honour is an abstract one, but it is precisely appreciated by individuals living in such cultures, and dictates a conduct of respect to those with a reputation for credible retaliation. Insults are crucial in violating this code: they are the verbal equivalent of an attack on the person himself or on his family. If they are not retracted, they must be avenged, or the insulted person will have lost face and therefore reputation. Until fairly recently, it was tacitly accepted in the south of the USA that it was justifiable for a man to kill when his honour was insulted, especially if he had warned the victim and the insult was not retracted or compensated. A conversation between two men in Nicholas Mosley's novel *Hopeful Monsters* expresses the connection between fighting and honour thus:

> I said 'You think men have to fight?'
> He said 'If they are to keep their honour.'
> I said 'Do they have to keep their honour?'
> He said 'They have little else.'
> (Mosley, 1990:110)

Nisbett and Cohen located the emergence of a culture of honour in herding economies throughout the world. Men would have to establish a reputation for a credible threat of violence in order to deter theft of their livelihood where there was no effective rule of law. Nisbett (1998) identified this principle as 'everyman his own sheriff'. The prevailing principle in such a culture is the rule of retaliation, and the perceived threat to a person's honour was treated as the equivalent of a challenge to fight. It is of interest in this connection that game theory analyses of the evolution of animal fighting strategies (Archer and Huntingford, 1994) have identified the principle of retaliation as underlying a stable strategy which evolves under a wide range of conditions in the natural world. In the human case, Daly and Wilson are probably correct in identifying it as the necessary male strategy in the absence of the rule of law. The occurrence of valuable resources that can be taken from one individual within a short space of time merely makes the operation of this strategy more worthwhile in terms of material gain (which from an evolutionary viewpoint can be transmitted into reproductive success).

Nisbett and Cohen (1996) found that, although men coming from the north and south of the USA did not differ in their general attitudes to violence, those from the south were more likely to approve of violence to protect order or in response to an insult. Southern men also saw more justification in a fictitious man reacting violently to being affronted in different ways, such as an insult to him or to his wife. Southern men were also more likely to say that a man who did not respond violently in such circumstances was 'not much of a man'. The link between violence and masculine identity is discussed below.

Nisbett and Cohen also set up experimental tests of the different reactions to a challenge among northern and southern men in the USA. Their basic method was to deceive the participants, who came from the north or the south, into thinking they were carrying out a psychological experiment on another topic, which included walking down a corridor to deliver a questionnaire to a room. On the way, half the participants would have to pass a confederate supposedly getting something from a filing cabinet in the corridor. As the participant passed by, the confederate pulled out the drawer and bumped into the participant, insulting him. There were three separate experiments. In the first, two observers rated how angry or amused the participant looked just after the insult: as predicted, southerners were rated as being more angry than northerners and northerners more amused than southerners. The participants subsequently completed a scenario describing going to a party with their fiancée, where another man whom they knew made sexual advances to her. Respondents were asked how the evening would end; those southerners who had been insulted were more likely than northerners to say that it would end with violence towards the other man. Southerners who were not insulted responded like the northerners.

The second experiment found that insulted southerners showed a greater rise in levels of cortisol (a stress hormone), and testosterone, after being insulted. The third experiment involved a version of the 'chicken' game: participants were asked to walk along a narrow corridor after the insult had occurred, and someone who was large and imposing-looking walked briskly towards them. This person, who was another confederate, had been trained to estimate how close the participant came to them before veering away. The insult drastically affected the behaviour of the southerners but not the northerners. Southerners went much closer before veering away. In a subsequent test where they met a much smaller confederate, insulted southerners acted in a much more domineering way to him than did other participants. There had also been an observer of the insult in this study, and when insulted southerners met this person later, they were much more likely to say that he would rate them lower on dimensions indicative of machismo and dominance, such as weak–strong and manly–not manly.

This last finding is an indication that the connection between violence and the southern culture of honour is part of a wider link with a set of values commonly referred to as *macho* which manifests itself in different ways in different cultures. The term is derived from the Spanish *machismo*, which means to prove one's manhood by courageous action. This aspect is found to be associated with masculinity in traditional cultures throughout the world (Gilmore, 1990). It can be regarded as the cultural manifestation of the need for a man to present a credible threat of violent retaliation.

In modern industrial societies, there is a tension between two conceptions of masculinity. The first is the equivalent of machismo, a physically based emphasis on toughness, physical prowess, and a willingness to engage in violence if necessary. The second emphasises intellect and achievement in areas where physical attributes are not necessary, such as business and politics. These two views of masculinity can be found in rating scale measures of what are called 'male role norms', i.e. stereotypic attributes of masculinity. Three components were identified by Thompson and Pleck (1986). The first involved gaining status and respect from others by achievement in a variety of fields not underpinned by violent means. The second is avoidance of femininity. The third involved self-reliance and toughness, which, as we have seen, assumes importance when the rule of law is absent, and also in modern societies where the code of honour remains from earlier times, and in those parts of modern society where do-it-yourself retribution is encouraged as desirable *macho* behaviour.

The proximate cause of male aggression and violence: is testosterone involved?

So far, we have considered the evolutionary background to male violence, and how this might relate to masculine cultural values surrounding men's willingness to engage in violent acts. The evolutionary principle of sexual selection provides the ultimate reason why males of many animal species are more competitive and combative with one another than are females. In many vertebrates, the immediate or proximate cause of heightened male aggression is the reproductive hormone that controls male reproductive physiology and male sexuality, testosterone.

In chapter 4, we outlined the crucial role of testosterone during prenatal life for determining the development of male genitalia in humans and other mammals. We also referred in passing to evidence from laboratory rodents that male hormones (androgens) act on receptors in the brain at this time, and early in postnatal life, to produce extensive behavioural effects later in life. Among these effects is an influence on aggression that occurs through the early androgens sensitising the developing brain, so that it responds to the testosterone secreted by the testes at puberty by increasing the readiness to fight other males.

In the spotted hyena, there is a dramatic effect of androgens on the female foetal brain and reproductive system (Frank et al., 1991), which causes females to be larger and more aggressive than males, and to be able to dominate them. This probably evolved as an adaptation for better nutrition and offspring survival under circumstances of considerable competition for food (Frank, 1994, 1997; Glickman et al., 1993). Female spotted hyenas are masculinised to such an extent that their genitals look like those of the male. The clitoris is enlarged to the size of the male penis, is fully erectile, and has the urinogenital canal running down its centre, as it does in the male. Birth is, not surprisingly, a difficult and apparently painful process, since the young have to travel down this narrow canal (Frank, 1994, 1997; Glickman et al., 1993). These genital changes are likely to be the costly by-products of the highly adaptive increases in aggression and dominance found in females of this species. The spotted hyena provides an interesting example of what can evolve when there is an adaptive advantage to be gained. It clearly demonstrates that prenatal androgenic action can have a pronounced influence on adult aggressiveness, and, indeed, on aggressiveness throughout life, since spotted hyenas are highly aggressive from birth onwards (Frank et al., 1991).

In the female spotted hyena, aggression and size are in the male range. The effect of prenatal testosterone is large and obvious. In humans, there are cases of girls subjected to the influence of androgens in the uterus (chapter 4). Studies of these girls have produced mixed results regarding measures of aggression, usually taken before puberty (Ehrhardt and Baker, 1974; Ehrhardt et al., 1968; Ehrhardt et al., 1989; Reinsch, 1981). Berenbaum and Resnick (1997) did find evidence for increased physical and overall aggression compared to girls who were relatives, among two samples tested at around 20 years of age. The size of the differences reported in this study were large and were similar to sex differences in aggression found in the same tests.

Most studies have concentrated on the possible effects of testosterone secreted during adult life in the human male, since this is the time of life when the impact of testosterone on aggression is most pronounced in non-human animals (Archer, 1988). Although there seems to be a widespread belief in a causal link between testosterone and young male violence, the research evidence generally does not support it.

A meta-analysis of 22 studies measuring associations between testosterone and measures of aggression (Archer, 1991) showed a small positive correlation where self-report measures of aggressiveness were used, but a significantly larger correlation[4] where the measures came from sources such as criminal records, peer reports, and staff ratings (of institutionalised participants). Individual studies have produced variable results, some finding a significant association and others not finding one. More recent studies have continued to find variable results (e.g., Archer, 1994d; Campbell et al., 1997; Harris et al., 1996), which cannot be attributed to different levels of aggressiveness in the different samples (Archer et al., 1998). Several studies comparing prisoners classified as high or low in aggression on the basis of their crimes indicate higher testosterone in the 'aggressive groups' (Archer, 1991), although there are conflicting findings in two other studies (of young offenders and young male volunteers).

In those cases where there is a positive correlation between testosterone and aggressiveness, it is possible that the causal link is in the direction of the outcome of aggressive behaviour increasing testosterone levels, rather than the reverse. There is evidence that winning or losing aggressive or competitive exchanges increases the testosterone levels of winners, and decreases that of losers (e.g., Archer, 1991, 1994d; McCaul et al., 1992; Mazur and Lamb, 1980). It is therefore possible that people who successfully use aggressive actions to obtain their goals have raised hormone levels compared to those who tend to back away from such exchanges.

There is also a crucial study that suggests that there is no link in the other direction between testosterone and aggression at puberty, the time when a pronounced rise in aggression occurs in males of other species. Halpern et al. (1994a) measured testosterone and aggression in 100 early adolescent boys as they went through

[4] $r = 0.38$.

puberty (from 12.5 to 13 years and at three annual follow-up times). During the pubertal phase, measures of testosterone showed the expected dramatic increase, but measures of aggression did not. Furthermore, measures of testosterone taken at an earlier time did not predict later aggressiveness. Yet testosterone levels at puberty were associated with sexual activity among the same sample, albeit modified by a social influence, the degree of religious observance (Halpern et al., 1994b). This careful longitudinal study of boys going through puberty indicates that the pronounced increase in testosterone levels at puberty is not accompanied by a rise in aggression, as it is in some other mammals. This conclusion is consistent with findings that the neurohormonal mechanisms underlying the hormonal control of behaviour show considerable variations between species. As we observed in the case of the spotted hyena, natural selection acts on existing mechanisms to produce variations that would not have been dreamt of had researchers limited themselves to convenient laboratory rodents such as the mouse (Frank, 1994).

Socialisation explanations of men's aggression

If testosterone is not the causal agent promoting men's greater same-sex direct aggression, what is responsible for it? Studies reviewed above indicated a strong link with masculine values, in particular those associated with reputation and honour. The socialisation approach (chapter 4) explains the greater male direct aggression in terms of the different upbringings of boys and girls. This involves cultural values being transmitted through parents, peers, the educational system, television, and other media (Tieger, 1980). Although there is broad agreement among psychologists that such a process must be operating, there is disagreement over whether early hormonal influences play any part in directing different social choices by boys and girls (chapter 4). There is also disagreement over the importance of different socialisation influences, such as parents, peer groups, or the media.

Cultural stereotypes involve greater disapproval of overt aggression by girls than boys. Although there is disapproval of indiscriminate physical aggression for both sexes, toughness is an important component of social status in boyhood (Archer, 1984, 1992a), and boys learn the important message that being regarded as afraid to fight is unmanly. It is generally believed that parents, peers, and teachers react differently to the aggression of boys and girls, boys receiving more encouragement and fewer restraints than girls. However, there are few studies that have assessed whether this is the case, and the evidence from those that have is mixed, at least for pre-school ages (Maccoby and Jacklin, 1980).

Even the famous laboratory study by Bandura et al. (1961), that appears in most developmental psychology textbooks, is questionable as a demonstration of children's imitation of aggression. Children aged between 3 and 6 years watched an adult 'playing' either aggressively or peacefully with a 'Bobo Doll' – a large inflatable doll anchored to a solid base. The children were taken to another room and given toys with which to play, and it was found that they imitated the aggressive behaviour of the adult. Moreover, the boys imitated aggressive actions more than girls did. However, the interpretation of these findings remains unclear. Ethologists – those whose work has involved detailed observation and analysis of the social behaviour of children – question whether it is aggression that is being imitated. Instead, their view is that most of the children's behaviour in the imitation study involved rough-and-tumble play or play fighting (Archer, 1995; Blurton Jones, 1967, 1972; Smith, 1989), which is motivationally distinct from aggression. The photographs in the original paper support this interpretation (Smith, 1989). Other studies indicate that children as young as 4 years of age make a clear distinction between real aggression and rough-and-tumble play (Boulton, 1991; Smith and Boulton, 1990; Smith and Lewis, 1985).

On the other hand, the remarks made by the children in this study (Bandura et al., 1961) about the appropriateness of the adults' behaviour did indicate aggression rather than play. The man's actions generally met with more approval than the woman's, with comments such as 'He's a good fighter like daddy' and 'I want to sock like Al' (the man's name). The children in the study also indicated that the woman's actions were not appropriate for her sex and that she behaved 'like a man'.

Most of the studies using the socialisation approach to children's aggression have concentrated on learning from adults. There is, as indicated in chapter 4, another social context that is particularly important as a learning influence for boys and girls, and that is their respective peer groups. In these, the cultural rules are different. For boys, they provide a forum to enact a direct physically based form of conflict resolution which is associated with the status-based form of masculinity discussed in an earlier section. For girls, they enable the establishment of closer relationships, which provide the context for the indirect forms of aggression characteristic of girls. The origin of these different peer cultures is still not entirely clear, but research described in chapter 4 suggests that early hormonally induced dispositions could play an important part. If so, we would again be dealing with the interaction between biological and social processes in development, of the sort described in chapter 4.

Women's aggression from an evolutionary perspective

In seeking to explain sex differences in within-sex aggression, we have considered explanations that focus on reasons why the male is more directly aggressive than the female. Most applications of the principle of sexual selection likewise emphasise the reasons why male competition, and hence intermale aggression, is heightened compared with interfemale competition. Campbell (1999) has argued that, while this approach rightly identifies the reasons why men should compete to a greater and more damaging extent than women do, it neglects the evolutionary reasons for the less damaging forms of female competition.

Campbell (1995) outlined some of the reasons why heightened competition – and hence the likelihood of violence – can occur among young women. She identified these as involving reproductive competition in the form of sexual reputation, access to a desirable partner, and the protection of an established partner from the threat of a take-over by another woman. In this context, sexual reputation relates to the male perception of the woman as a potential long-term mate with whom paternity is likely to be certain (chapter 3). A reputation for promiscuity would therefore have an adverse effect on the woman's future reproductive prospects. It contrasts with the sort of reputation important among men, which is concerned with toughness, lack of fear, and fighting ability. Just as a boy does not want to be labelled a chicken or a coward, so a girl does not want to be labelled a slag or a slut.

Campbell (1999) outlined the reasons for expecting women's aggression to be less damaging than that of men. Essentially these concern the need to stay alive to look after the offspring, and the complete certainty of parenthood (in contrast with men's uncertainty). Women's aggression would not therefore be concerned with maintaining status and reputation as someone who should not be challenged. It occurs as a more direct response to competition for scarce resources, and is more likely to take the form of the lower-cost aggressive acts outlined in the earlier section on women's aggression.

Violence in heterosexual relationships

There are few studies comparing aggression by the same people to individuals of their own sex and those of the opposite sex. Two studies that involved such comparisons among samples of young college students found a very different pattern for the two sorts of opponent (Gergen, 1990; Harris, 1992). While there were usually large sex differences in the male direction for acts of within-sex physical aggression, there were less pronounced differences in the female direction for physical aggression to someone of the opposite sex (Archer, 2000b).

This pattern of between-sex physical aggression is also found in studies of aggression between dating partners among young college students in the USA (Archer, 2000a). Similarly, when all acts of physical aggression are considered, large representative surveys of married or cohabiting couples (e.g., Straus, 1990, 1997) typically find little difference between men and women (Archer, 2000a, 2001b). The findings from this research, undertaken by sociologists interested in family interactions, would seem to run counter to the widespread opinion that partner violence consists mainly of men assaulting women. This view is associated with feminist writings (e.g., Dobash and Dobash, 1980; Pagelow, 1984; Walker, 1989; White et al., 2000), and is also shared by evolutionary psychologists (e.g., Wilson and Daly, 1992a, 1993b). In Britain, it has had powerful advocates in the Government's Women's Unit, the British Medical Association, and research initiatives funded by the Economic and Social Research Council.

The research methods and the samples used to support the two views are very different, the feminist position being largely based on studies of women as victims, or male perpetrators on programmes for violent men, or crime surveys. Family researchers use rating scales asking people from community samples to report on specific acts of physical aggression for themselves and their partners regardless of consequence.

There have been two main attempts to reconcile the two positions. Dobash et al. (1992) claimed that the measurement used by the family researchers – which concentrates on specific acts – does not reflect the context and consequences of these acts. They argued that if injuries – the consequences of physical aggression – were considered, nearly all the victims would be women. Johnson (1995) emphasised the samples rather than the measures. He argued that feminist researchers have concentrated on samples selected for their high levels of violence by male partners, such as women in refuges or men on programmes for assaultive husbands. Johnson suggested that in such samples men systematically use violence to control and terrorise their partners. These men are a minority but concentration on selected samples will identify them disproportionately to their frequency in the general population. In contrast, he argued that the physical aggression found in community and student samples is generally mutual and does not involve controlling tactics. It is the result of ordinary people getting angry with one another, hitting out and regretting it afterwards. Johnson dramatically termed his two suggested types of partner violence respectively 'patriarchal terrorism' and 'common couple violence'.

A meta-analysis of around 80 studies measuring acts of physical aggression (Archer, 2000a) confirmed that overall there was little difference between men and women in the proportions showing any act of physical aggression to a partner, or in the frequency of such acts. These findings clearly support the mutual-combat view of partner physical aggression in community samples advocated by Johnson, and by the family conflict researchers. On the other hand, a meta-analysis of injuries across 14 to 16 studies showed that men were more likely than women to inflict injuries on their partners than vice versa, apparently supporting the view of Dobash et al. (1992) that injury and act-based measures would produce different findings. This was confirmed in an analysis of studies which had used both sets of measures: there was indeed a different pattern of results in the two cases. Nevertheless, the effect size for the greater female than male injuries was relatively small: over all the studies analysed, 62 per cent of those injured were women, and 65 per cent of those receiving medical treatment were women. Although women were more likely than men to be injured by a partner, a substantial minority of those injured were men, a finding which does not support the feminist view that nearly all the victims of partner violence are women.

Johnson's suggestion that there would be a different pattern of findings for samples selected for high levels of male violence was supported in that both samples from a refuge, and samples from couples referred to a treatment programme for marital violence showed large effect sizes in the male direction for acts of physical aggression (Archer, 2000a). Two subsequent studies (Graham-Kevan and Archer, 2001a,b; Johnson, 1999) have supported Johnson's distinction between a different pattern of partner aggression in community samples and in those selected for high rates of partner violence. Based on the pattern of physical aggression and other forms of controlling behaviour by both members of a couple, it is possible to accurately predict from which type of sample they are derived. This indicates that the refuge samples are indeed atypical of the general population and involve the equivalent of a prolonged and one-sided use of terror by one individual, almost always the man.

One problem with drawing conclusions from the current evidence is that the current information is largely derived from modern Western nations. What little there is from other countries (e.g., Efoghe, 1989; Kim and Cho, 1992; Kumagai and Straus, 1983) and from ethnic groups in Britain who originating from the Asian subcontinent (Mirrlees-Black et al., 1998) suggests that physical aggression is more clearly in the male direction among non-western cultures.

One interesting question this analysis raises is why in modern Western societies women are as likely or more likely than men to cross the line between verbal and physical aggression when overall it is their sex that is more likely to be injured by a partner's physical aggression. In most cases, the male partner is bigger and stronger, and it is usually the case that people – like their animal counterparts (Archer, 1988) – do not start physical fights with those who are larger than themselves. A possible answer to this question can be obtained by considering the two different attitudes about men's physical aggression towards women. The first, emphasised by feminist writers (e.g., Dobash and Dobash, 1980), arises from the long history of acceptance and encouragement of men assaulting their wives to force compliance with patriarchal values about how wives should behave. A second set of attitudes involves disapproval of men being physically aggressive towards women. A number of studies from the USA have shown that acts of physical aggression towards a partner are viewed more negatively when the aggressor is a man and the recipient is a woman than vice versa (e.g., Arias and Johnson, 1989; Harris, 1994; Harris and Cook, 1994; Koski and Mangold, 1988).

Fiebert and Gonzalez (1997) asked US women students about partner assaults they had initiated, and found that 29 per cent of a sample of around a thousand admitted to one or more acts of this sort. Of these, around 20 per cent said that, since men had been trained not to hit women, they felt no fear of retaliation. About a quarter said that, since men could easily defend themselves, they did not regard their own physical aggression as being a problem. Media reports of men who are abused by their partners (e.g., *The Observer*, 2 November 1997) indicate that women's repeated physical aggression to partners does depend on the man's reluctance to hit back. One woman even taunted her husband as she slammed his head against the wall, shouting 'Hit me, you fucking wimp!' This man said that he was afraid that he might end up killing his wife if he started hitting her. The cases described in this article involved big physically fit men and much smaller wives – far removed from the stereotype of the abused man as considerably older or smaller than his wife (c.f. Steinmetz, 1977).

It is, therefore, likely that disapproving attitudes of men hitting women are an important component in enabling some women to be physically aggressive towards their male partners. In addition, there is evidence of negative social reactions to men who are physically attacked by their wives. This was certainly the case in former times (e.g., George, 1994) although it may have become transformed into disbelief rather than ridicule in current Western societies.

A different set of attitudes are likely to prevail in cultures with pronounced patriarchal values, where it is considered a matter of honour for men to control 'their' women, and the inhibiting impact of disapproval of men hitting women is weaker. In a survey of 45 societies from the Human Relations Area Files, Schlegal (1972) found that 34 showed tolerance of extreme violence by husbands to their wives. In rural New Guinea, Morley (1994) found that over half of the men and women sampled said that it was acceptable for a husband to hit his wife, particularly if she 'fails to fulfil obligations'.

It is difficult to obtain cross-cultural evidence on actual rates of physical aggression between partners that is comparable to that from the USA. Some studies report women's victimisation rates, but not those of men. Between 19 and 38 per cent of a sample of women from Bangladesh said that they had been beaten by their husbands during the past year (Schuler et al., 1996). Studies from east and central Africa (Mushanga, 1977–8) and of Australian Aborigines (Khan, 1980) both found high rates of men hitting and beating their wives. These figures contrast with an average value of around 2 per cent for women from US community and student samples reporting on being beaten up by a partner (Archer, 2001b). In the non-Western cultures, it is likely that the influence of attitudes involving disapproval of men hitting women are much less than in the USA and other Western nations.

Nevertheless, even where the societal status of women is low, some women may wreak a terrible and violent revenge on their husbands. In modern Thailand, there have been reports of women cutting off their husbands' penises, usually in retaliation for infidelity (Larimer, 1997). Reliable figures are difficult to obtain, since many victims try to avoid publicity, but it has been a sufficiently common occurrence for surgeons at Bangkok's Siriraj hospital to have developed an expertise in reattaching penises. Although there have been 31 successes, many victims have not been so lucky, in that their organ was disposed of in a blender, or down the toilet bowl, or even fed to the ducks. The potential for just a few well-known cases of this sort for striking fear into the hearts of philandering husbands is enormous, with the phrase: 'Behave yourself, or I'll feed the ducks', becoming an awesome warning.

Sexual aggression

So far, we have been concerned with aggressive acts that have as their aim harming the other person, either as an end in themselves or as a means to another end. Another category of aggression is sexual aggression, which includes all forms of sexual acts that occur without the other person's consent, including, of course, rape. From an evolutionary perspective (chapter 3), it is not surprising that most sexual assaults are perpetrated by men on women, since the higher parental investment by females leads to them being more restricting than males about sexual access

(Archer and Vaughan, 2001). Rape is a sexual act that overrides female choice, and its equivalent is widespread in the animal kingdom (Clutton-Brock and Parker, 1995). Whether it is characteristic of all human societies is a matter of debate. Sanday (1981) examined ethnographic evidence (from a standard cross-cultural sample of 156 tribal societies) and classified 47 per cent of these as 'rape free'. On this basis, she argued that rape arises under particular cultural contexts, involving male domination, interpersonal violence, and separation of the sexes. However, the evidence that rape did not occur in the other 53 societies was unconvincing: illustrative examples showed that in one supposed rape-free society, rape was considered wrong and men were fined for it. In another, informants stated that 'homosexuality is rare, as is rape. Both . . . are regarded as sins, punishable by God.'

Research on rape in modern Western nations such as the USA over the last 30 years or so has identified the scope of the problem. Early on, it was realised that the commonly held view of the typical rapist as a predatory stranger was statistically incorrect. A larger number of women are raped by a dating partner than by a stranger. In the former case, the victim tends to be viewed as having suffered less (Check and Malamuth, 1983) and to be held more responsible for the rape (Hammock and Richardson, 1997), particularly by male judges (Pollard, 1992). Such information is typically derived from laboratory studies asking the participants to judge people described in various scenarios depicting rape.

It should, however, be emphasised that victim-blaming is generally low in these studies undertaken with North American undergraduates. In modern Western societies, mainstream liberal opinion typically does not blame the victim of a stranger rape. A complete contrast can be found in the reactions to rape victims in cultures where a young woman's virginity is regarded as essential for the honour of her family and village. An extreme example is the tribal form of Islamic law operated by the Pathan people on the borders of Pakistan and Afghanistan, where rape victims are killed for bringing shame on to their village (Burke, 1999). It was only in 1999 that the Egyptian government repealed a law that enabled a rapist to escape punishment if he agreed to marry his victim, who was pressured into complying to save the family's honour. The cultural background to this law involved widespread victim blame.

Estimates of the frequency of rape in North American studies vary (Pollard, 1994). Those undertaken from a criminological perspective tend to find victimization figures of between 6 and 8 per cent of women sampled. Other surveys that typically involve asking whether the respondents had had intercourse when they did not want to and were threatened or physically forced, have found between 12 to 17 per cent. These figures were obtained from samples of North American undergraduates (e.g., Koss et al., 1987), but similar values have been reported in three other surveys carried out in the UK and in New Zealand. The percentage becomes higher when responses to a question asking about unwanted intercourse because of drink or drugs is added to the definition of rape.

The variations in these figures have led to much debate and disagreement. For example, it is known that the frequency of reporting physical aggression is reduced if questions are asked in the context of crime, or if words such as battery or abuse are used (e.g., Mihalic and Elliott, 1997). The same is true of the word rape: Koss et al. (1987) found that only a minority of women reporting unwanted intercourse labelled their experiences as rape. While this finding would seem to provide justification for asking the questions without using this emotive word, it also opened Koss' work, and similar surveys, to having different interpretations put upon them (Fillion, 1997). At one extreme, the numbers of women reporting that they had been raped is about 3 to 5 per cent of those sampled. At the other, the numbers reporting having had unwanted sexual intercourse approaches 20 per cent, a figure which increases further if unsuccessful attempts are included.

Feminist explanations for the occurrence of rape have gone hand in hand with its identification as a hidden societal problem. Burt (1980) outlined what she termed 'rape myths', which are prevalent beliefs tending to blame the victim and excuse the perpetrator (see also Pollard, 1992). These are derived from a set of roles involving action-plans which men and women follow in their sexual relations with one another: for example, women are not expected to indicate their sexual interest directly, whereas men are expected actively to seek sexual access to women. According to most feminist accounts, these roles are derived from socialisation experiences in a patriarchal society, although more recently the ultimate origin of patriarchy in evolutionary history has been explored (chapter 3).

The origin of rape in evolutionary history – rather than as a consequence of socialisation in a patriarchal society – focuses attention on which sex is the gate-keeper in sexual relations, something that is perhaps taken for granted or overlooked in feminist accounts, where the emphasis is on power relations. Evolutionary accounts of rape step outside contemporary concerns with rape as a societal and personal problem, and with its importance for gender politics. Instead, they represent pragmatic analyses of the reasons why it occurs at all (female choice) and the circumstances under which its likelihood is increased or decreased (the costs and benefits associated with it). Thornhill and Thornhill (1992) regarded rape as an adaptive tactic, i.e. one whose occurrence in the evolutionary environment led, under certain circumstances, to the man leaving additional offspring. It therefore remains as a disposition among men today. According to this particular evolutionary hypothesis, rape is a conditional tactic, occurring or not depending on current costs and benefits. The implication of this analysis is that all or most men are capable of rape given the right set of conditions.

This pessimistic prediction, which would seem to fit reports of rape in wartime (outlined below), is not the only one that can be derived from evolutionary principles (Archer, 1992c; Archer and Vaughan, 2001). Rape could instead be viewed as an alternative strategy, one that occurs mainly in certain individuals but not in others. Although the Thornhills examined a number of predictions derived from their hypothesis, most of these could be accounted for by non-evolutionary alternatives (Archer, 1992c).

Malamuth (1996) sought to synthesise the concerns of both evolutionary and feminist accounts in a causal model of sexual aggression (the confluence model) which can be applied at the level of predicting which sorts of men are most likely to rape. Sexual selection provides the background for coercive sexuality in that it involves female choice and has resulted in men's greater capacity for impersonal sex. The importance of this is that men will have the potential to engage in sex with an unwilling partner. The extent to which many men can act like this is shown in the examples of rape by soldiers during wartime, when the usual restraints are lacking. Historical evidence reviewed in Brownmiller's (1975) pioneering book on rape indicates how widespread an occurrence this has been throughout human history. Media reports of wars in Africa and Europe during the 1990s indicate its continued occurrence, and its encouragement in the Balkan wars.

The second main strand to Malamuth's (1996) model involves male domination and the ability to coerce, i.e. the power motive emphasised in feminist accounts. The evolutionary background to this is the reproductive conflict of interests between the sexes, and paternity uncertainty, referred to in relation to physical aggression. As indicated in the next section, male domination can be viewed in terms of men seeking to control the reproductive lives of women. Rape provides one very basic way in which individual or groups of men seek to achieve this.

Malamuth's confluence model predicts that men who have two sorts of characteristics are most likely to become rapists. The first involves seeking and engaging in high levels of impersonal sex, and the second involves a hostile dominating disposition, particularly in relation to women. Malamuth suggests that hostility to women moderates the relationship between impersonal sex and sexual aggression. So far, there is evidence supporting the model, both from earlier studies of the correlates of rape likelihood (Pollard, 1994), and from studies specifically designed to test it (Dean and Malamuth, 1997; Malamuth et al., 1991, 1995; Malamuth and Thornhill, 1994).

Research on the characteristics of rape perpetrators has taken our understanding some way from earlier erroneous beliefs (Pollard, 1994) that rapists either were sexually frustrated men with poor social skills, or were mentally unstable (and hence best left to clinical psychologists and psychiatrists). Malamuth's model also enables a synthesis of once polarised views about the motivation for rape, that it involves either purely sexual motives or the motive to dominate the woman by humiliating her. The confluence model involves both aspects, in the form of seeking impersonal sex, and the domination of women.

Although we have characterised sexual aggression as involving male perpetrators and female victims, this is not always the case. Both assaults by men on other men, and assaults by women on men, have been reported in the media and in research reports. Of course, the evolutionary and feminist theoretical traditions we outlined in this section, do not readily encompass these types of sexual assault.

Rape of men by other men is more readily understood when the perpetrator is of a homosexual orientation, and Krahé et al. (2000) found that about 15 per cent of a sample of homosexual men from Berlin reported sexual victimisation through force or the threat of force. There are, however, indications from other studies that some perpetrators use male rape as a way of humiliating their victims, rather than as a means of sexual gratification (Davies, in press). Ironically some of these attacks seem to be perpetrated on gay men by men hostile to their sexual orientation. The debate about power versus sex as a motive for rape therefore recurs in relation to male rape.

Studies that ask both sexes about their experience of sexual aggression in dating relationships consistently find that a substantial minority of men report being the victim of coercive sex. This is defined differently in different studies, and hence rather different prevalence rates have been reported. The first of these studies (Struckman-Johnson, 1988) found that 16 per cent of men from a student sample said they had been pressured into having sex at some point in their lives. Ryan (1998) found that 9 per cent of 256 male college students reported being victims of sexual coercion from dating partners: in this study coercion was limited to the use of physical aggression, alcohol, or drugs to obtain sexual access. Straus et al. (1996) reported the much higher figure of 30 per cent, but this was based on a scale containing several items including verbal coercion and making a partner have sex without a condom. Davies et al. (in press) found that 14 per cent of men from a British student sample reported experiencing forced sexual contact or intercourse at some time in their lives. In each study, the prevalence rates are lower than those for women, but nevertheless sufficiently widespread for these experiences to be investigated further. Davies (in press) notes the considerable strength of the negative emotions generated by such experiences, and the social pressures that act against male sexual victimisation being taken seriously.

Power, aggression, and violence

Our analysis of sex differences in aggression and violence has largely been from an individual perspective, although we did touch on wider considerations in the form of feminist and evolutionary explanations of relationship violence, and the masculine cultural values underlying violence between men. The concept of power can be used to widen our horizons to include sociological and anthropological explanations (the *ideological* or *societal* level of explanation, outlined in chapter 1). The concept of societal power underlies feminist analyses of topics such as men's violence to women. This is regarded as following from men's greater control of access to resources, force being one of several strategies men use to exercise this power. It is important to emphasise that this explanation involves *societal* power stemming from the position of men and women in society, as opposed to power of the sort which is negotiated between individuals when there are no outside restraints. We encountered this sort of individual-level power in relation to men's status relations when considering men's violence to other men. The feminist analysis of societal power has little to say about intermale violence (Archer, 1994c).

The concept of power is a sociological rather than a psychological concept. It has been used in a variety of ways in the social sciences, and there is considerable disagreement over its definition. Clegg (1989) traced the roots of modern thinking about power to Hobbes, and a rival strand of thought in the earlier writings of Machievelli. Hobbes viewed power in individual and interpersonal terms, involving subordination of others' preferences to one's own. This view was based on the model of the seventeenth-century British monarch, and it led to later political scientists taking an individualistic view of power.

Later critics of this view emphasised the need to consider power exercised at different levels. Power could reside in structures – the state and organisations – as well as in individuals. This sort of power assumes importance in feminist analyses of men's violence towards women, where the patriarchal structure of society is seen as encouraging and legitimising men's violence towards their wives, through an ideological and a legal framework.

The Hobbesian view of power stressed its operation in an active and overt manner. It applies to the crude manifestations of power that are apparent in overtly violent acts, and also where one person is dependent on another. But it omits more subtle uses of power (Lukes, 1974), such as controlling the agenda – keeping certain issues out of the realms of overt discussion and argument. The traditional view of men's authority over their wives, which was seldom challenged before the advent of the Women's Movement, is an example of this sort of power. Another subtle view of power is the creation of beliefs that make those without power happy with their lot, what Marxists refer to as 'false consciousness'. Again, this can be applied to patriarchal values before the impact of feminism in the West, and in the many nations today where beliefs include acceptance of a second-class status for women, an arrangement which is actively promoted and endorsed by many women in these societies.

In contrast to the Hobbesian tradition, Machievelli wrote about strategies of power, ways in which power could be exercised. This is particularly relevant to the relations between power and violence. Machievelli realised that, although violence was central to power, power operates more effectively in the absence of violence. In this sense, violence may be a sign that other more subtle ways of exercising power have been ineffective.

In the case of marital violence, family researchers (e.g., Steinmetz, 1977; Straus et al., 1980) can be characterised as operating an individualist approach – a Hobbesian view. This involves the consideration that the rule of law is weakly enforced in most private settings, including the family, and that where this is the case people are left to work out their own power relations. If the man has few inhibitions about using violence to settle disputes, he will generally be able to dominate his wife by force, since he is likely to be bigger and stronger than her. This explanation is similar to that applied to intermale violence.

It is certainly the case that the imbalance in size and strength is necessary for husbands to be able to strike their wives with little prospect of immediate effective physical retaliation. However, according to feminist analyses, an explanation that is restricted to the immediate power relations in the family misses the socio-political context of marital violence. For example, Dobash and Dobash (1977–8, 1980) argued that traditional belief systems, backed up by centuries of religious support, have led to wives being the main victims of family violence. According to the Dobashes, the beginning of legal marriage in Roman times was associated with the complete subjugation of wives, who held a position equivalent to slaves, with no property rights and completely under the control of their husbands. This included the right – even the duty – to beat a wife who did not adhere to the expected code of behaviour. Murder of a wife for adultery – or other forms of 'misbehaviour' (such as drinking wine and other 'immodest' acts) – was accepted and encouraged. In the West, Christianity incorporated the Roman view of the legitimacy of the power of husbands over their wives, and this was maintained by church and state for many centuries. In several European countries, the law specified the ways in which a husband could legitimately 'chastise' his wife. For example, in seventeenth-century France, a wife could legally have her nose broken by her husband. Adultery was widely viewed as justifying severe violence, even murder.

Gradually in Western Europe, severe assaults became outlawed, thus maintaining the legitimacy of wife-beating, yet marking out the boundaries of what was acceptable. The Dobashes went on to argue that present-day violence by men towards women remains as part of this historical tradition and serves the same function, which is to establish and maintain power over a wife when her behaviour becomes unacceptable to the man. This analysis fits with their own study involving interviews with women at a refuge in Scotland (Dobash and Dobash, 1977–8). It also fits Wilson and Daly's (1992b, 1993b) analysis, based on evolutionary principles and homicide data, of the importance of men's proprietary view of women as a cause of male violence to women. One might argue that, at least in Western nations, times have surely changed. To this, the Dobashes remarked that, although wives are no longer the legitimate victims of spousal violence, they are still viewed as the 'appropriate' victims.

The empirical evidence we summarised in this chapter indicates that this analysis may be broadly correct in historical terms, and may apply to countries where strong patriarchal values persist today. However, it seriously underestimates the influence of another set of values in Western nations, that is the liberal consensus of strong disapproval of men who hit their wives.

The Dobashes concentrated on the Roman–Christian tradition. Other religious traditions still operate laws supporting male authority of the sort represented by Roman law. For example, there are many parallels between the Dobashes' description of wives' subjugation in Roman times and contemporary accounts of the position of wives under Islamic law in Pakistan (Frenkiel, 1999[5]), notably the keeping of women in strict purdah, the widespread occurrence of the so-called honour killings of wives, and the leniency of the law on husbands who have killed their wives.

[5] This statement is based on a number of reports – mainly by concerned women journalists – over the last few years. Olenka Frenkiel's is only one of these. It is, of course, practically impossible to carry out a systematic study of violence towards women in a state where this is condoned by the religious and political establishment.

The Dobashes' feminist power analysis is probably the most cohesive and persuasive version of this type of explanation. There have been a number of attempts to test predictions derived from this type of analysis. One prediction is that there will be more violence towards women where their status is low. Levinson (1989) undertook a cross-cultural survey of 90 small-scale and peasant societies and found that economic inequality between the sexes, combined with male dominance in family decision-making, and restrictions on divorce, were strong predictors of wife-beating. In contrast, surveys within one country, the USA, have not generally found an association between the status of women in a particular state and wife assault. Dutton (1994) has argued from such studies that it is more profitable to look for the characteristics of particular men rather than the overall status of men and women as an explanation of wife-beating. While this may well be the case within a particular society, when considering variations across cultures, differences in the endorsement of patriarchal values could still be of primary importance.

Conclusions

In this chapter, we have shown that explanations for differences in aggression between the sexes, and for physical and sexual aggression between men and women, are complex. They operate at many different levels, from the societal to the biological, and involve the legacy of evolution and of history. There has in the past been a tendency for explanations to be polarised so that one particular aspect is emphasised at the expense of others. It may still not be possible to bring together all the available conflicting perspectives on this subject, but recent analyses of partner violence and of sexual aggression have moved in this direction, synthesising previously disparate views offered by feminists and evolutionary thinkers. Similarly, men's violence to other men can be understood from a view that involves both cultural beliefs about masculinity and an ultimate basis for these in evolutionary principles.

Further reading

Courtwright, D. T. (1996). *Violent Land: Single Men and Social Disorder from the Frontier to the Inner City*. Cambridge, MA: Harvard University Press.
   An historical account of violence between men in the USA. The author argues that young single men, who are 'surplus' in terms of societal and reproductive roles, become involved in subcultures of violence, in particular when they are sensitive about their honour, often intoxicated, and armed, and are separated from the civilising influences of women and religion.

Daly, M. and Wilson, M. (1988). *Homicide*. New York: Aldine de Gruyter.
   This is a classic book, describing the systematic application of evolutionary thinking to research on homicide, using criminological, historical, and anthropological sources. It includes a considerable amount on sex and gender. It is original and provocative, and has dated little.

Malamuth, N. M. (1996). The confluence model of sexual aggression: feminist and evolu-
tionary perspectives. In D. M. Buss and N. M. Malamuth (eds.), *Sex, Power, Conflict:
Evolutionary and Feminist Perspectives* (pp. 269–95). New York and Oxford: Oxford
University Press.

Neil Malamuth describes his confluence model of sexual aggression, which seeks
to integrate feminist and evolutionary approaches. The interaction between a hostile
aggressive attitude to women and promiscuous sexuality is the central tenet of the
theory, which has been well supported by the research evidence so far.

Moffitt, T. E., Caspi, A., Rutter, M., and Silva, P. A. (2001). *Sex Differences in Anti-social
Behaviour*. Cambridge University Press.

This book tackles the issue of why men are more likely than women to show a range of
anti-social behaviour, including violence. Drawing upon their longitudinal studies,
the authors identify two main forms of anti-social behaviour. One results from a
neurodevelopmental disorder, which generally affects males. The other emerges within
relationships, and can affect both sexes.

7 Fear, anxiety, and mental health

Introduction

The emotions of fear and anxiety that we examine in this chapter are closely linked with aggression, the subject of the previous chapter. Similar environmental conditions often produce fear, aggression, or both (Archer, 1988; Berkowitz, 1962). These emotions feature among the stereotypic traits associated with men and women, men being seen as more aggressive and women as more 'emotional' or fearful and anxious. Viewed in this way, 'emotional' excludes anger (chapter 2). Stereotypically, women who are overtly aggressive are seen as lacking femininity. Men who cry, seem afraid, or betray other negative emotions, are viewed as unmanly. Bravery, being able to endure pain and suffering without much overt distress or complaint, has traditionally been viewed as a masculine virtue. Throughout the world, manhood is regarded as something to be achieved by courageous actions – those that disregard the possibility of danger and physical pain (Gilmore, 1990). There are strong social pressures on men not to show the negative emotions of fear and anxiety, but women are permitted to do so, and even encouraged in such expressions, which is consistent with patriarchal notions of femininity. These social prescriptions have a long developmental history – boys are taught to avoid 'feminine' behaviour very early in life (chapter 4).

In the first part of this chapter, we address the issue of the difference between men and women in the expression of fear and anxiety. We then question whether mood swings are greater in women than men, and whether they are associated with fluctuations in women's hormone levels, in particular during the premenstrual phase, postpartum, and following the menopause. In the major part of the chapter, we explore differences in the mental health of men and women.

Do women experience more negative emotions?

In an extensive meta-analysis of studies on sex differences in personality attributes (chapter 1), Feingold (1994a) found that anxiety (sometimes referred to as emotional instability) was slightly higher among women than men. Fearfulness is difficult to identify from standard, self-report, personality questionnaires, but timidity may be similar to fearfulness. Although there are no overall sex differences in extraversion (Costa and McCrae, 1992; Feingold, 1994a), men are higher on measures of assertiveness, one aspect of this factor. As this is measured on a bipolar scale from assertive to timid, women are closer to the timid end of the dimension.

Two researchers have sought to place sex differences in fear and anxiety into an evolutionary perspective. Budaev (1999) has argued that men show greater 'emotional stability', that is less anxiety, because this is part of a set of characteristics that has been selected to aid men in dominance disputes with other men, many of which involve overt aggression (chapter 6). In effect, this view claims that women are generally more anxious and fearful than are men because there has been less selection for them to use overt and escalated aggression towards other women.

Campbell (1999) also related women's greater fearfulness to evolved sex differences in aggression, but in a different way. She argued that it is only those circumstances that pose a direct risk to survival, for example through injury, that are associated with greater fearfulness by women. Many other situations, such as those involving new people and places, do not show sex differences. When we consider phobias about open spaces, closed spaces, animals, blood, injury, and dental procedures, women appear in all these categories more than do men (Marks, 1987; see later section below).

New and potentially dangerous situations may evoke fear, or, alternatively, they may lead to positive feelings such as exhilaration. Although there are many women mountaineers, hang-gliders, and even boxers in the modern world, the attraction of such activities is greater for men, resulting, as Campbell noted, in far more male than female fatalities. The ultimate reason for this, she suggested, is that throughout evolutionary history, women risk-takers would have paid a greater price in terms of their reproductive success than their male counterparts. She supports this with historical and contemporary evidence that maternal death increases child mortality to a considerably greater extent than paternal death does.

Although plausible evolutionary explanations for the origins of men being more adventurous and risk-taking have been advanced, the mechanisms that underlie such differences are not entirely clear. There is some evidence from other species of mammals that testosterone reduces fear (Boissy and Bouissou, 1994; Vandenheede and Bouissou, 1993), but there is at present no evidence that there is a similar connection in humans. In addition, human sex differences in fearfulness begin early in life, before testosterone levels become markedly different in boys and girls. Besides, the usual upbringing of boys (chapter 4) would enhance any predisposition for the sexes to differ in fearfulness. Those boys who become easily afraid are under strong social pressure to hide or suppress their reactions, and those girls who are relatively unafraid and forthright in their actions are under – perhaps more subtle – pressure to conform to a stereotypically feminine pattern of behaviour.

Do women's emotions fluctuate more than those of men?

This is a question that is often asked in relation to the more pronounced and regular fluctuations in reproductive hormones that occur during women's lives. Thus the question is really whether women's hormonal fluctuations, during the menstrual cycle, following childbirth, and at the menopause, make them particularly prone to mood changes and emotional outbursts.

We first consider the menstrual cycle. A variety of psychological changes have been reported during the different phases of the menstrual cycle, but here we concentrate on the negative mood changes reported by many women just before menstruation. These have been considered both in terms of changes supposedly experienced by most women, and as something that is a clinically defined dysfunctional state, the *premenstrual syndrome*. The terms 'premenstrual tension' and the 'premenstrual syndrome' were first used in medical and psychiatric reports in the late 1920s and 1930s (Walker, 1997), and research on women's premenstrual mood changes has largely been dominated by a biomedical approach since this time. The premenstrual syndrome has been the concern of both gynaecology and psychiatry. There is substantial disagreement in the medical literature regarding the criteria for the premenstrual syndrome, and its appropriate treatment (Walker, 1997). Suggested treatments have included the administration of female hormones, either progesterone or oestrogen. However, the first has been shown to be no more effective than a placebo, and the second suppresses the menstrual cycle, potentially introducing other problems. Walker argued that there are a series of interconnected vested interests, including the medical establishment, male-dominated employers, and producers of self-help remedies, and that together these can be viewed as perpetuating the continuation of PMT as a medically defined problem. Analysis of women's accounts, however, indicates substantial variability in premenstrual experiences.

Despite taking a sceptical view of the disease model of the premenstrual syndrome, psychologists often assume that there is a simple relationship between fluctuating hormonal levels and the distress experienced premenstrually. Depression and irritability or anger are the two negative emotions that have been most extensively studied by psychologists (Walker, 1997). It is well known that survey and questionnaire presentation strongly influences findings, and this applies particularly to research that has sought to assess how frequently premenstrual mood changes are experienced. Results vary dramatically. At the lower end, 3 to 5 per cent of women have reported severe depression and irritability. The highest value, 95 per cent, is derived from the earliest study (Pennington, 1957), and was based on a long list of 'symptoms', including both minor ailments and painful periods.

In many of the early studies, women were asked to report on a past menstrual cycle or cycles. Such retrospective accounts introduce the possibility that past events were interpreted in terms of the common belief that negative moods occur premenstrually. This suspicion was confirmed by findings from diary studies in which women kept a daily record of moods over several successive menstrual cycles. Using this method, no mood changes across the cycle were reported in many studies. It is difficult to evaluate a set of conflicting findings such as these without undertaking a meta-analysis (see chapter 1). This would enable an assessment of whether those studies finding null results really represented a zero effect when aggregated, and would indicate whether there was an overall effect and how large it was.

A meta-analysis would also enable an assessment of the proposals that have been made to account for conflicting findings (Walker, 1997). For example, there are several studies from the 1970s (Archer and Lloyd, 1985) suggesting that beliefs about premenstrual changes can have an impact on what is reported, or indeed on what is experienced. Such an influence of beliefs on people's experiences of negative emotions or pain is well known, and has been studied by psychologists who have investigated the labelling of physiological arousal (Melzack and Wall, 1982; Ruble and Brooks-Gunn, 1979; Schachter and Singer, 1962). Nevertheless, some studies have found similar levels of mood change reported by women who knew that the research was about menstrual changes and by those that did not. Clearly, these findings cannot can be accounted for by an expectation of negative moods (Walker, 1997).

A further possible explanation for inconsistent findings is simply that there is considerable variability in women's experiences of mood changes across the menstrual cycle. Indeed, there is evidence that this is the case, and also that the same women may experience different moods premenstrually across successive cycles (Walker, 1997).

In one large-scale epidemiological study (Ramcharan et al., 1992), women were asked to report their emotional state on a single day and afterwards to provide menstrual cycle information. Overall, there was no difference in the proportion reporting high levels of negative moods according to their menstrual phase. However, women in one age group (30 to 39 years) reported higher levels of negative affect premenstrually than at mid-cycle, as did those women who had experienced high levels of stress during the previous year. The differences were more pronounced in the high-stress group (7.4 vs. 20 per cent). Two additional findings from this study help to place the menstrual changes in perspective. First, there was a decline in reported high levels of negative moods with age; the 20- to 24-year age group reported 8 per cent and the 45- to 49-year group 4 per cent. Second, some women (3 to 7 per cent) experienced high levels of negative moods on the sample day irrespective of their menstrual phase. These findings indicate that there are other sources of negative emotions in women's lives that are unconnected with the phase of the menstrual cycle, but also that stressful events may exacerbate negative emotions experienced premenstrually.

The claim that during the premenstrual phase there is an increase in behavioural acts indicative of neurotic or anti-social tendencies, such as shoplifting, attempted suicide, and accident proneness, has also been the focus of considerable research.

These claims were made in papers published in widely read British medical journals in the 1960s, and in a series of books designed for the popular market (Dalton, 1969, 1994). They were based on studies that were methodologically flawed and whose interpretation was biased in terms of the author's long-held beliefs (Parlee, 1982; Sommer, 1982). They have generally not been supported by more carefully controlled studies (Walker, 1997). There is, however, some recent evidence for premenstrual behavioural changes that can be interpreted in terms of women seeking to cope with negative feelings at this time: these include choosing more comedy programmes to watch on television, and withdrawing from conversations with others (Walker, 1997).

There has been an emphasis in menstrual cycle research on the elusive negative mood changes and anti-social behaviour during the premenstrual phase, and the physical experience has received less attention. This includes dysmenorrhoea or painful periods, breast pain or tenderness, headaches, and bloated feelings or swelling. The studies that have included questions about these experiences indicate that they are a widespread source of discomfort for many women, and a serious problem for a minority of women (Walker, 1997). These findings provide a contrast with the emphasis found in research, the media, and popular imagination, on mood changes associated with the commonsense belief in 'the emotional woman', whose mood swings are at the mercy of her raging hormones. As we have seen, this simple picture is not borne out the evidence. It is likely that greater understanding of this issue requires an interactionist perspective that involves not only feelings arising from physical changes associated with the menstrual cycle, but also how these influence the perception of external demands and stressors, and the ability of the woman to cope with them.

While premenstrual mood changes have been the focus of most research and speculation about the possible contributions of hormonal changes to women's emotional lability, hormones have also been implicated in the more pronounced mood changes experienced by some women following childbirth. Transient emotional upset or a minor depressed mood occurs widely in up to 60 per cent of women, and may reach 90 per cent, in the immediate postpartum period of new mothers (Nicolson, 1998). There has been more research on the circumstances that increase the risk of clinical depression at this time, something that occurs in a smaller proportion of mothers, around 13 per cent (Whiffen, 1992). To put this figure in perspective, comparable values for depression among women who are not recent mothers are around 2 per cent for those who are married and around 6 per cent for divorced women. Thus a minority of postnatally depressed women would have been likely to become depressed anyway.

Although there is evidence of an increase in depression following childbirth, a precise biological explanation is not forthcoming. Psychologists have consistently sought to link postnatal depression to changes in reproductive hormones. Another line of research has pursued the role of other hormones, and has found evidence for the involvement of thyroid dysfunction in non-psychotic postnatal depression. Harris (1996a) argued that, despite the robustness of this link, a complete account requires attention to psychological and social factors. The notion that women are at risk as the result of extreme changes in reproductive hormones is called into question further by the lower than average rate of mental illness during pregnancy.

Despite repeated suggestions that the postpartum hormonal state results in these mood changes, the evidence does not support this connection (Hagen, 1999). In a wide-ranging attack on the view that women's mental health reflects their hormonal state, Ussher (1991) presents a social psychological explanation of postpartum depression. Drawing upon the work of Nicolson (1990), she suggests that the depressed new mother is actually grieving for her lost self. As a major life event, the birth of the first child entails loss of freedom, increased responsibility, and considerable domestic work. Furthermore, fathers have also been reported to experience depressed mood postnatally, although the prevalence rate is lower than that for mothers. Nicolson (1998) argued that men may also deal with the stress of a new baby by heavy drinking, carrying on pre-birth social life, or other strategies to avoid involvement with their offspring.

Following a suggestion by Daly and Wilson (1988), Hagen (1999) proposed an evolutionary explanation for postpartum depression, which, if correct, would mean that the disorder would have to be viewed very differently from the way it has been in existing medical and psychological accounts. Instead of being seen as a by-product of fluctuating hormone levels or of changing life circumstances following childbirth, Hagan viewed postpartum depression as an adaptive mechanism for reducing or abandoning a mother's (or father's) commitment to the offspring necessitated by unfavourable circumstances.

Hagen's analysis follows a more general view by evolutionary psychiatrists and psychologists that negative emotions and feelings have evolved to motivate individuals in ways that are ultimately beneficial for survival. Just as physical pain motivates people to avoid physically damaging circumstances, so mental pain is viewed as motivating them to avoid circumstances that threaten their well-being in other ways, and ultimately reduce reproductive fitness (Nesse, 1991). Although we would urge caution in accepting the view that all negative moods have arisen in this way,[1] the evidence provided by Hagen indicates that his view may be worthy of consideration with regard to postpartum depression.

Hagen viewed postpartum depression as nature's way of reducing a mother's desire to care for her infant when the signals from the environment indicate that this would be counterproductive for fitness in the longer term. Hagen pointed out that the energy costs of prolonged lactation would have been considerable and prolonged under human ancestral conditions, leading to a reduction in body fats. If this, together with the time and effort spent caring for the infant, are likely to be beyond the mother's capability, it makes sense to terminate interest in the existing infant, and to delay rearing offspring until more favourable circumstances prevail. However, maternal feelings provide a strong motivating force to continue feeding and caring for a new infant. A mechanism is therefore required to switch off these

---

[1] See for example the first author's argument against such evolutionary analyses of grief (Archer, 1999), and the response by a major exponent of the adaptive view of grief (Nesse, 2000).

feelings under adverse circumstances, and, according to Hagen, this mechanism is postpartum depression. Depression is a mood state that is generally associated with a lack of interest in areas of life that would otherwise provide strong motivations and interest, such as food and sex. In the case of postpartum depression, this lack of interest extends to the infant, and this is the primary reason for the occurrence of depression at this time.

The theory predicts that postpartum depression should not be confined to modern Western societies, and should be restricted to circumstances that would have been reproductively costly in ancestral environments. Since paternal investment is particularly important in humans (Geary, 2000), fathers' availability and willingness to be co-parents should be crucial. So too should be the amount of help available from others, usually close relatives. In addition, any indication that infant viability is likely to be low should increase the chances of postpartum depression: Hagen identified pregnancy and delivery problems as a major predictor of poor viability.

Consistent with these predictions, Hagen found that, in existing studies, lack of support from the male partner, family, and others were all strongly associated with postpartum depression. In particular, paternal investment in the offspring predicted lower rates of postpartum depression, whereas marital dissatisfaction predicted higher rates. Hagen's review also identified increased rates of postpartum depression when there were pregnancy, delivery, and infant problems, which was also consistent with his theory. Levels of depression were also higher in poor environments, and in those with hazards or with low levels of resources (i.e. financial impoverishment).

Two other aspects of Hagen's argument were that postpartum depression affects mother–infant interaction, effectively reducing investment in parenting, and provides an effective social signal that the infant is not going to be looked after by the mother. Whether postpartum depression does also function as a signal to others, such as the father of the child and close kin, to provide greater levels of child care, is speculative at present, since existing research has not examined it from this angle.

Hagen's theory provides an interesting and provocative way of looking at postpartum depression, but there are a number of findings that do not fit it, notably the strong association between postpartum depression and a previous history of emotional problems including depression. We would not necessarily expect this association on the basis of depression being an adaptation specifically concerned with the viability of a new infant.

Negative mood states – anxiety, irritability, and depression – have also been attributed to the hormonal changes following the menopause (Archer and Lloyd, 1985). Again, such mood states have alternatively been attributed to the culmination of life stresses and changes at this time, including responses to bodily signals of the end of reproductive life. One particular phrase that became associated with this stage of life is the 'empty nest' (Bart, 1971), which was applied to a woman whose life had been wholly devoted to homemaking and child care. Subsequent studies challenged the generality of Bart's original findings, which were based on interviews with a relatively small number of women. For example, a study involving a community sample of about 3,000 adults aged 25 to 64 years found slightly lower rates of depression among both mothers and fathers after their children had left home, the opposite to that expected on the basis of Bart's study (Radloff, 1980).

Adelmann et al. (1989) examined well-being in two cohorts of middle-aged women from nationwide surveys, each numbering between 300 and 400 women. They found that women from the first cohort, who were young adults during World War II, reported more positive feelings after their children had left home. Women from the second cohort, who had had little opportunity for paid work when they were young adults, reported a decrease in well-being when their children left home. However, employment did not influence the negative experiences among this cohort. These findings support the view, advanced by Borland (1982), that the 'empty nest' phenomenon only occurs under specific circumstances, for example among white women born around the 1920s and 1930s whose norms in early life were centred around women's role in the family.

Although it is the hormonal changes underlying women's reproductive lives that have been the focus of attention in both the media, and psychosocial and medical research, more recently men's hormones have also attracted some attention. Men undergo fluctuations in testosterone levels and these levels decline appreciably during middle and old age. However, such variations cannot be linked with external physical changes as they can for women. Discussion has generally been restricted to speculative attributions of young men's bad behaviour to their high testosterone levels, although there is no research evidence that justifies such attributions.

Following a book entitled *The Male Menopause* by the British physician Malcolm Carruthers in 1996, there has been some debate over the existence of a condition among middle-aged men comparable to the menopause. Carruthers recommends testosterone replacement therapy (TRT), similar to the HRT taken by many post-menopausal women. In 2000, the *British Medical Journal* published articles arguing for and against the existence of this condition in middle-aged and old men (Gould et al., 2000). Although testosterone levels do gradually decline during the later part of the lifespan, there is nothing comparable with the complete cessation of oestrogen secretion that occurs in women. Nevertheless, it may still be the case that one response to some of the problems experienced by an increasing number of men living to older ages is to provide artificial hormones that simulate the natural levels typically experienced by younger men. This may lead to an increased sense of well-being, along with increased ease of sexual arousal, and generally increased quality of life. The extent to which this is the case, and the possible costs involved, will need to be carefully studied in future research, particularly as the positive benefits of TRT are likely to be emphasised, and possibly exaggerated, by drug company publicity. Jacobs warned against regarding hormonal treatment as a remedy for all the problems of ageing, since this may divert attention from other common disorders of older ages, and because research involving older populations has not demonstrated many of the alleged benefits of testosterone treatment.

Are there sex differences in mental health?

The diagnosis of mental illness has become widely standardised with the advent of the most recent version of the *Diagnostic and Statistical Manual of Mental Disorder* (*DSM-IV*). The system was developed by the American Psychiatric Association but it is also used by clinical psychologists. The standardisation of the diagnostic procedure has not changed the overall picture of the factors that interfere with normal living and are viewed as mental illness. More men are reported to abuse substances such as alcohol and drugs, and are diagnosed as suffering from anti-social behaviour. More women experience extreme states of fear and anxiety.

In chapter 6, we observed that crime statistics reinforced our notions of the aggressive male. Similarly, statistics for psychological disorders support the stereotypical description of women as being more emotional than men. Women outnumber men in many categories of mental illness. With the exception of bipolar conditions (involving both depression and mania), they have a higher prevalence than men of affective disorders, and also of anxiety disorders, and non-affective psychoses (Kessler et al., 1994). However, men have higher rates of suicide than women and, as we have already noted, also display more anti-social personality and substance use disorders. The higher prevalence among women than among men of co-morbidity – suffering three or more mental illnesses over a 1-year period – and of a higher reported lifetime occurrence of mental illness (Kessler et al., 1994) does, however, reinforce gender stereotypes.

We begin an examination of the extent to which various types of disorder occur in the two sexes by considering the diagnostic process, and then look more closely at disorders that have been reported to show clear sex differences. Finally, we review explanations of sex differences in depression. As with many other comparisons of women and men, different types of explanations have been used to account for the same findings. Theories may stress biological differences; they may seek to explain vulnerability by looking at the social world or the world of inner experience; or they may combine these accounts. Almost 40 years ago, Meehl (1962) identified predisposing factors, including biological variables, which he described as diatheses. He argued that it is the interaction of these diatheses with stress that leads to mental disorder.

Diagnosing mental disorders

For nearly half a century, psychiatrists worked on the development of a comprehensive system for the identification and diagnosis of mental illnesses. Problems of psychiatric diagnosis are well known, and the very concept of mental illness was once vigorously attacked (Laing, 1967; Szasz, 1970). However, difficulties in the diagnosis of mental illness are not unique (Kennedy, 1980). The decision to label an individual ill requires that a judgement be made irrespective of whether the illness is physical or mental. The decision that physicians, sufferers, and others who are concerned must make is whether the condition (be it physical or behavioural) is sufficiently different from the norm to be considered an illness. In the field of psychiatry, there are particular problems that relate to the dual focus on mind and body. Defining the norms of mental health is undoubtedly a more hazardous undertaking than estimating the normal range of glucose in the blood or of pulse rates.

The inclusion of mental disorders in the sixth edition of *International Statistical Classification of Diseases, Injuries and Causes of Death* in 1948 was an early attempt by the World Health Organisation to standardise psychiatric diagnosis. The American Psychiatric Association published its first *Diagnostic and Statistical Manual of Mental Disorder* (DSM) in 1952. The reliability and validity of the DSM as a diagnostic tool has improved steadily since then. With the introduction of the third edition, DSM-III, clinical assessment has been undertaken using five dimensions or axes rather than simply identifying the current mental illness. The first axis contains over 200 discrete disorders and the defining criteria used to diagnosis each of them. The second axis is used to identify chronic conditions such as mental retardation and personality disorders. The remaining three are used to assess aspects of current functioning: medical, psychosocial problems such as divorce or unemployment, and a global assessment of individual functioning.

Kaplan (1983) argued that the DSM-III norms used to judge women's behaviour as being indicative of illness were biased according to a stereotype of femininity. To illustrate this she suggested that only those aspects of dependence typical of women's behaviour were classified as symptomatic and that the dependence of men was ignored. Her critics have marshalled evidence to show that there is no overall bias against women – in some categories there were more men – but, in total, more women were reported to suffer as the result of mental illness (Kass et al., 1983; Williams and Spitzer, 1983). In DSM-III homosexuality was removed as a disorder, and reference to neuroses, as clinical entities, was also omitted. The latter constituted a major diagnostic category within which women had previously been overrepresented (Archer and Lloyd, 1985). Later editions of the DSM have been criticised despite efforts to avoid sex bias (Tavris, 1992).

A cross-national epidemiological study undertaken by Weissman and her colleagues (1996) using samples drawn from 10 countries illustrates how improved diagnostic validity can clarify sex differences. They employed the revised categories of affective disorders that separate depression alone from disorders involving depression *and* mania, labelled bipolar affective disorders. The extremes of variation in lifetime rate of major depression occurred in Taiwan and Beirut. In the former it was 1.5 per cent of the population, whereas in the latter the rate was 19 per cent. However, in each of the 10 countries the rates for women were higher than those for men. The lifetime rates for bipolar disorder showed both lower rates of occurrence and less variability, with 0.3 per cent in Taiwan and the highest, 1.5 per cent, in New Zealand. Major depression was much more common, although rates varied considerably by nation. Importantly for our concerns, the sex ratios were almost equal in bipolar samples, even though these disorders occurred much less frequently than did depressive disorders. The behaviour and symptoms that led to the diagnoses of major depression and bipolar disorders were similar across cultures. These data have been interpreted as indicating that the contribution of biological factors is greater in bipolar disorders and that cultural factors may account for the variability in rates of major depression. We return to the issue of cultural values defining women as mentally ill later.

The latest manual, DSM-IV (1994), is based upon thorough research that has included field studies designed to improve the validity and reliability of diagnostic categories. One example of the benefit of this approach is the abandonment of two diagnostic categories that had occasioned considerable controversy when DSM-III-R was constructed (Nolen-Hoeksema, 1998). These were the personality disorders, Self-defeating Personality and Sadistic Personality, chronic conditions located on Axis II. It had been argued that the former, initially labelled Masochistic Personality Disorder, would be used to define the behaviour of women trapped in abusive relationships as pathological. When it was suggested that men might claim to be suffering from Sadistic Personality Disorder as a defence against prosecution for abusive behaviour, both disorders were placed in an appendix of DSM-III-R. Neither appears in DSM-IV. The inclusion of eating disorders, post-traumatic stress disorder, and seasonal affective disorder (SAD) results from the recognition of new conditions. Well-defined criteria are specified for their diagnosis.

Individuals employing diagnostic tools may still fail to apply them objectively, despite every effort to develop an instrument that is reliable and valid for use with men and women, or in different ethnic groups and nations. Lipshitz (1978) claimed that the problems of diagnosis were magnified by the fact that the overwhelming majority of hospital doctors were at that time (and still are) men, who may well expect women to be overemotional. Recent editions of the DSM have been held to reflect the male majority in the American Psychiatric Association. Table 7.1 shows that, in the USA, psychiatrists and clinical psychologists are still predominantly men.

They may well see women as overemotional and prescribe psychotropic drugs accordingly, particularly tranquillisers, sedatives, and stimulants (National Commission on Marijuana and Drug Abuse, 1973).

In a classic study, Broverman and her colleagues (1970) investigated the impact of gender stereotypes on norms of mental health. They asked psychiatrists, clinical

Table 7.1 Numbers of clinically trained mental health personnel (USA)

Professional group	Total Number	Men	Percentage of total	Women	Percentage of total
Psychiatry	28,970	21,651	75	7,319	25
Psychology	69,817	39,098	56	30,719	44
Social work	92,841	21,497	23	71,344	77

Note: Adapted from Sarason and Sarason (1999).
Source: *Mental Health, United States, 1996* (1997).

psychologists, and psychiatric social workers to describe a healthy person, a healthy man, and a healthy woman. The verbal portraits of a healthy person and a healthy man were very similar. However, a healthy woman was seen as more conceited, excitable in a minor crisis, submissive and emotional, and less adventurous, aggressive, competitive, independent, and objective, than either a healthy person or a healthy man. Once again we encounter the patriarchal stereotype of the 'emotional' woman. This study demonstrated that in the late 1960s very different standards were used in judging mental health and illness in men and women.

In recent years, psychologists have sought to understand the processes that resulted in different standards of mental health being applied to men and to women. Heesacker and colleagues demonstrated that, just as the professionals studied by Broverman reflected a widely held stereotypic view of women as hyperemotional, both counsellors and undergraduates viewed men as being under or hypo-emotional (Heesacker et al., 1999). In their series of six studies they also demonstrated that counsellors who rated men as hypo-emotional were biased in that they were more likely to blame men for marital difficulties.

Other researchers have sought to understand gender bias through an examination of the English language (Sankis et al., 1999). When their analysis revealed that English contains more 'female-valued than male-valued terms' they concluded that Broverman and co-workers had not sought to offer their raters a representative sample of the English language.

Although there have been few studies designed to test the reliability of the Broverman findings, Australian research on second-year student nurses provides interesting data (Beckwith, 1993). Initially, the nurses completed the Broverman et al. questionnaire describing a healthy adult, man, or woman. After six hours of teaching, the students completed a second questionnaire, this time describing an adult, a man, or a woman suffering from multiple sclerosis. The nurses' verbal portraits of a healthy man or woman differed on only 6 of the 38 traits provided in the questionnaire. The healthy man was described as being blunter, rougher, more competitive, hiding feelings, not crying easily, and liking maths and science more than a healthy women. Men and women were similar on 32 traits even though the characteristics used to describe a healthy man reflect a specifically masculine stereotype. Moreover, the verbal portrait of a healthy woman was more like that of the healthy adult. Perhaps unsurprisingly, more differences (33 out of the 38 traits) appeared in the comparisons of healthy and ill, adults, men, and women.

The original Broverman study included 79 mental health professionals, 58 per cent of whom were men. By contrast, Beckwith obtained her results from student nurses, and only 11 per cent were men. The opinions of clinicians may vary according to their professional training and their sex-group membership, as well as according to the time and place of the study (see chapter 10). Table 7.1 reveals that psychiatrists in the USA are predominantly men, and that men are in the majority among psychologists. Perhaps Broverman et al.'s results reflected not only the training of psychiatrists and psychologists, but also the higher proportion of men in their sample.

Sex differences in specific disorders

Well over 300 disorders and the specific criteria used to identify them are described in DSM-IV. Although we cannot give full definitions that involve theories of mental illness, it is generally agreed that the most severe disorders are those that involve loss of contact with reality, self, or other people. In the past, such behavioural disturbances, with a recognised biological component such as alcohol poisoning or severe infection, were grouped together and described as *organic psychoses*. The severe disorders with no known pathology of the central nervous system were labelled as *functional psychoses*. The term psychosis no longer appears in the DSM as a diagnostic category; the disorders to which it referred are found within major categories on Axis I. The descriptive term psychotic is currently used to label behaviour that is characterised by loss of contact with reality, self, or other people.

We consider the major disorders on Axes I and II of DSM-IV that have shown sex differences. As noted above, Axis II, which includes personality disorders, has occasioned considerable controversy. Most diagnoses on this axis also involve additional diagnoses on Axis I. Since the introduction of the multi-axis diagnostic procedure, evidence has accumulated that in the USA one sixth of the population have a lifetime history of three or more disorders (Kessler et al., 1994). The problems raised by co-morbidity are beyond our concern, although as we have already noted, co-morbidity is more prevalent among women. We begin by considering mood disorders. Recent research has both supported and refuted earlier beliefs that women are moodier than are men.

Mood disorders

Mood or affective disorders are common and include both severe and mild conditions. The major distinction in mood disorders is between the unipolar and the bipolar disorders. We have already examined rates for severe forms of both unipolar and bipolar disorders and observed that women are more often diagnosed as being depressed, but that there is little evidence of a sex difference in diagnoses of bipolar disorders, those involving depression with mania. Here we consider the symptoms that define these conditions. We also examine sex differences in rates of attempted and completed suicide.

Depression varies in severity and duration. The category of major depression includes psychotic depression with symptoms such as hallucinations and delusions, and seasonal affective disorder (SAD). The milder but persistent form of depression is called a dysthymic disorder. According to DSM-IV, the diagnosis of a major depressive episode is based upon an individual experiencing at least 5 of the following symptoms for 2 weeks or more:

- depressed mood or loss of pleasure in previously enjoyed activities
- major weight change (loss or gain) or change in appetite
- insomnia or too much sleep

- fatigue, loss of energy, or psychomotor changes recognisable by others
- feelings of worthlessness or extreme guilt
- reduced ability to think, concentrate, or take decisions
- thoughts of death or suicide.

Research has shown that the highest rate of major depression occurs in individuals 15 to 24 years of age and the lowest rate in 45- to 54-year-olds (Blazer et al., 1994). Women are consistently reported to be at greater risk of experiencing a depressive illness than are men (Nolen-Hoeksema, 1998) and are more than twice as likely as men to be diagnosed with SAD (Dalgleish et al., 1996). In childhood, girls and boys have similar rates of depression, but between the ages of 14 and 15 the incidence among girls increases sharply (Nolen-Hoeksema and Girgus, 1994) and this difference persists throughout adult life (Piccinelli and Wilkinson, 2000)

Psychiatrists have taken a renewed interest in the premenstrual syndrome and labelled it premenstrual dysphoria. Classified under unipolar mood disorders, they claim that it is only just beginning to be understood (Gold and Severino, 1994). The attention which premenstrual dysphoria has attracted reflects a growing awareness within medicine of a need to take account of sex differences and a need to move away from a model of disease based upon men as the norm. Premenstrual dysphoria poses a challenge as researchers have recognised that an adequate account will require an interactionist model that includes biological, psychological, social, and cultural processes.

Diagnoses of the rarer bipolar mood disorders depend upon evidence of both the depressive symptoms we have considered, and an assessment of mania or manic episodes. The latter diagnosis is based upon the presence of extreme euphoria or irritability that impairs life function for at least a week's duration. In addition, such a diagnosis requires evidence of at least three of the following:

- grandiosity or inflated self-esteem
- decreased need for sleep
- increased talkativeness or needing to talk
- racing thoughts
- distractibility
- increased playful activity
- relentless pursuit of pleasurable activity.

The more severe forms of these disorders are labelled bipolar disorder if mania is present and if depression is accompanied by milder manic episodes. The more persistent but much milder cyclothymic disorders are only diagnosed if milder depressive and euphoric mood swings have persisted continuously for at least 2 years.

We include suicide in our discussion of mood disorders since it frequently occurs when individuals are deeply depressed. A recent mental disorder has been implicated in over 90 per cent of suicides and one study has suggested that 40 to 60 per cent of adults who committed suicide had symptoms that indicated a mood disorder (Clark and Fawsett, 1992).

Suicide rates vary according to sex, age, and culture but one conclusion is unequivocal: men are much more likely than women to kill themselves (Hawton, 2000; Moscicki, 1995). The only widely reported exception to this finding is the high rate of suicide among young women in rural China (Cheng and Lee, 2000). Recent figures have shown that, in England, suicide is the second largest cause of death, after accidents, among young men between the ages of 20 and 30 years (Office for National Statistics, 1999). Although an increase in suicides among men has been reported in a number of countries, and contrasts with either stable or declining rates of suicide among older women, these trends are particularly sharp in the UK (Cantor, 2000; Hawton, 2000). Depression was found in 76 per cent of adolescent suicides (Schaffer et al., 1988). Two disorders which occur more typically in men, substance abuse and anti-social behaviour, were each reported in 70 per cent of adolescent suicides.

Sex differences in deliberate self-harm rates provide the inverse of suicide rates. Throughout Europe, women are more likely to harm themselves than are men. However, rates are rising among men, and once again the trend is particularly marked among young men in the UK (Hawton, 2000). It has been assumed, from the high rate of self-harm among women and the close association of self-harm and suicide among men, that self-harm has different meanings for women than it has for men. When women harm themselves, it is suggested that they intend either to communicate distress or to influence the attitudes and behaviour of other people. Men, on the other hand, use more violent means both in suicide and self-harm. Hawton has proposed that the higher incidence of violent suicide among men is accounted for by their 'greater suicide intent, aggression, knowledge of violent means, and less concern about bodily disfigurement' (2000: 484).

Anxiety disorders

Excessive fear that is intense, enduring, and unwanted, and which is displayed in behaviour, thoughts, and emotion, are all aspects of anxiety disorders. The DSM-IV includes phobias, panic attacks, obsessive–compulsive disorder and post-traumatic distress in this category, along with generalised anxiety (GAD) and acute stress disorder. Rapee (1991) estimated that 4 per cent of Americans suffer from GAD and that twice as many women as men are affected by it. GAD is diagnosed when an individual suffers from at least three of the following symptoms for the majority of the time, for a minimum period of 6 months:

- restless, feeling keyed-up or on edge
- easily fatigued
- difficulty in concentrating or mind going blank
- irritability

- muscle tension
- sleep disturbance as in falling or staying asleep or restless and unsatisfying sleep.

Phobias, on the other hand, are characterised by an intense fear of specific things. Spiders are a well-known object of an irrational fear called arachnophobia. Phobias are the most common of the anxiety disorders. The list of phobias is long, since individuals develop irrational fear of all sorts of animals, objects, and situations. In DSM-IV, phobias are divided into three types, and their prevalence estimated in a general population survey varied by type (Magee et al. 1996). Specific phobias, such as arachnophobia, have an estimated lifetime prevalence of 11.3 per cent. Social phobias, that include intense fear of specific social situations such as talking in seminars or eating in restaurants, have an estimated lifetime prevalence of 13.3 per cent. Finally, agoraphobia, which involves fear of crowds and busy public places, enclosed spaces such as tunnels, and of wide open spaces such as the countryside particularly if a person is alone, had an estimated lifetime prevalence of 6.7 per cent.

In a study published more than 30 years ago, statistics based upon reports from out-patient clinics in the USA showed a higher percentage of women than of men in the psychoneurotic and phobic reaction subcategories (Frazier and Carr, 1967). The diagnostic improvements of DSM-IV reveal a more complex picture. A recent survey of the American general population showed that women were twice as likely as men to exhibit symptoms of simple phobias and agoraphobia, while the sex difference in social phobias was smaller, but patterns of co-morbidity were complex (Magee et al., 1996). Overall, this pattern of sex differences being concentrated in circumstances that could pose a risk to survival, and absent or small in the case of social phobias, is consistent with Campbell's evolutionary analysis outlined at the beginning of this chapter.

Panic attacks occur without warning and without specifiable precipitating events. The unpredictability of panic attacks links them to agoraphobia and to the need to be in a safe place should such an emergency occur. Panic attacks involve phys-iological symptoms such as a pounding heart, sweating, trembling, feelings of nausea, choking or smothering, and thoughts of unreality, going crazy, or dying. In a community survey in the USA, 5.6 per cent of people mentioned panic attacks, but only 3.8 of the reports met DSM-IV criteria for panic disorder (Barlow et al., 1994). Diagnoses of panic disorder were twice as common among women than among men, and a recent study estimated that women were 2 to 3 times more likely than men to suffer panic attacks with agoraphobia (Yonkers and Gurgis, 1995).

Nolen-Hoeksema (1998) suggested that panic attacks with agoraphobia may have a genetic basis since female relatives of sufferers are more likely than male relatives to have the same disorder. She went on to speculate that the underlying genetic vulnerability may be expressed as panic attacks with agoraphobia in women but as alcoholism in men, which as we note below, is much more prevalent in men.

Schizophrenia and other psychotic disorders

Schizophrenia, found under the major category 'Schizophrenia and Other Psychotic Disorders', is both one of the most well-known and one of the most misunderstood mental disorders, as it does not (as is popularly believed) involve split personality. According to the criteria of DSM-IV, diagnosis requires that at least two of the following symptoms be present for a month, or one symptom if either bizarre delusions or auditory hallucinations are present:

- delusions
- hallucinations
- disorganised speech
- grossly disorganised or catatonic behaviour
- negative symptoms such as flat affect
- lack of motivation.

A diagnosis of schizophrenia requires an overall assessment of severely impaired general functioning (Axis V) (Kendall and Hammen, 1998: 265).

It is not clear whether men or women are more likely to develop schizophrenia. Prevalence estimates depend upon the nature of the sample studied. Some community surveys have shown a female majority, although results from an investigation of first hospital admission for schizophrenia in both North America and Europe indicated a higher proportion of men (Iacono and Beiser, 1992). There are also significant sex differences in age of onset. It is usually 14 to 24 years for men and 24 to 34 years for women. In addition, the course of the disorder is more severe in men than in women. Women also tend to be hospitalised for shorter periods and to have fewer hospital readmissions. There has been a suggestion that oestrogen, along with women's social skills and social support, may be protective factors (Szymanski et al., 1995).

Eating disorders

Adolescent girls and women are overrepresented in major eating disorders, both in anorexia nervosa and bulimia nervosa. 'Nervous loss of appetite', or anorexia nervosa, is an inappropriate label. Sufferers do experience hunger but it is combined with a terror of becoming obese; in addition, they have a distorted perception of themselves as fatter than they actually are, and refuse to maintain an adequate body weight. Bulimia nervosa involves out-of-control eating, followed by self-induced disposal of the food through vomiting, laxatives, diuretics, or excessive exercise. Anorexia can lead to serious health problems, and it has been estimated that 5 per cent of sufferers die (Steinhausen, 1994).

Anorexia nervosa starts in childhood, with a peak incidence between 14 and 18 years of age. It is typically a disorder of teenage girls, being somewhere between 8 and 11 times more common in girls than in boys (Steinhausen, 1994). College men may have been reported to share symptoms with young women in so far as they display diagnostic criteria of purging, excess exercise, and dissatisfaction with their bodies (Olivardia et al., 1995). Men and women with eating disorders often suffer from depression and substance abuse as well. Although eating disorders are sometimes thought of as illnesses of youth, they may persist into adulthood.

There is also inconclusive, though intriguing, evidence that the prevalence of eating disorders is similar in heterosexual women and lesbians but that the rate is higher in gay men than in heterosexual men (Nolen-Hoeksema, 1998). A study based upon a small number of university students reported no difference in the nature of eating disorders between gay and heterosexual college men (Olivardiea et al., 1995). However, a random survey of individuals working at all levels in a large corporation found that gay men and heterosexual women were similar in terms of eating disorders, in contrast with lesbians and heterosexual men (Schneider et al., 1995).

Substance-related disorders

Alcohol and nicotine are legal substances but they may damage physical and psychological health. In addition, drug abuse often involves prescribed substances such as barbiturates, tranquillisers, and opiates. Substance misuse and its resulting disorders are much more common among men than among women, and patterns of co-morbidity differ too (Kendall and Hammen, 1998). Many men who abuse substances are violent and may consequently be diagnosed as suffering from anti-social personality disorders. On the other hand, mood or anxiety disorders often accompany substance abuse in women.

Alcohol dependence provides an example that varies both by sex and national–cultural group (Helzer and Canino, 1992). The lifetime prevalence of alcohol dependence for women is consistently lower than that of men across all countries. However, total lifetime prevalence among women varies widely from 0.45 per cent in China to 8 per cent in the USA to 22 per cent in South Korea. Kessler et al. (1994) reported that the prevalence of alcohol dependence within a given year was almost three times as common among US men as among US women, at 11 and 4 per cent respectively.

Personality disorders

The 10 patterns of extreme personality traits that have been identified as Personality Disorders (PDs) are classified on the second axis of DSM-IV. PDs are organised in three clusters. Their nature and prevalence have occasioned considerable controversy, particularly concerning sex biases. Cluster A includes paranoid, schizoid, and schizotypal PDs that are characterised by odd or eccentric behaviour. The histrionic, borderline, narcissistic, and anti-social PDs which form Cluster B are characterised by erratic, impulsive, or overdramatic behaviour. Anti-social PD often involves criminal acts, as people suffering this disorder tend to disregard rules and the rights of others. Cluster C PDs are marked by fear and anxiety and comprise avoidant, dependent, and obsessive–compulsive PDs.

It has been suggested that A cluster PDs are more typical of men, and C of women, except for the obsessive–compulsive PD. In group B, men are much more likely to be diagnosed with anti-social PD and women with histrionic and borderline PDs. Nolen-Hoeksema (1998) has noted that certain personality traits – emotionality, heightened concern with appearance, and dependence – are typical of a negative feminine stereotype. In extreme form they become histrionic, borderline and dependent PDs. Since women are widely assumed to fill these stereotypes, they may also be overdiagnosed in these categories. Men are overrepresented as suffering from anti-social PD and the criteria for diagnosis in this category are similar to a negative masculine stereotype. Nevertheless, survey evidence supports the conclusion that there are more men with anti-social PD in the general population than there are women (Nolen-Hoeksema, 1998).

How are sex differences explained?

Our review of mental illness in men and women has already drawn attention to a link between gender stereotypes and the frequent diagnosis of mental illness in women. This link might point to an explanation in terms of Eagly's social role analysis of sex differences (chapters 2 and 3), which involves patriarchy and the societal roles of men and women. Although other researchers, such as Gove and Tudor (1973), had already advanced very similar explanations in the area of mental health, Eagly (1987) did not extend her theory to encompass mental illness and emotional states such as fear and anxiety. At the beginning of this chapter we outlined another major explanatory framework that has been applied to sex differences in fear: sexual selection theory. In this section we look at a range of explanations that include both sociological and psychological influences, and then at explanations that seek to link these together. Finally, we briefly consider an evolutionary explanation. Much of the theorising about sex differences in mental illness has focused on mood disorders, as they have been researched more extensively than have anxiety disorders. From studies around the world there is little doubt that depression is more frequent among women than in men and requires explanation.

Gove and Tudor (1973) approached the issue of sex differences in mental health from a sociological perspective and attempted to link the greater frequency of mental illness in women to roles in society. In particular, they examined the risks inherent in the role of the housewife. Although their account may have a dated tone for the Western world, since the majority of married women, even those with pre-school-age children, are now at work (chapter 9), they have considered this situation as well. Gove and Tudor summarised the sources of stress for a housewife under five headings:

- confinement of possibilities of gratification to home and family to the exclusion of work satisfaction
- frustration of needs for competent performance and achievement, as childminding and housework appear to require little skill and command little prestige

- lack of demands or structure, allowing time to brood over troubles
- limited satisfaction for working wives whose careers are secondary, who experience discrimination in advancement, and carry a double load, working and keeping house
- lack of specificity of demands in that women are required to adjust to their husband's and children's needs and expected neither to formulate nor to afford priority to their own aspirations.

It is interesting to note that a recent large-scale study of depression in the USA has reported a higher prevalence of depression in homemakers than in individuals in all other categories of employment (Blazer, et al., 1994).

Besides marshalling evidence for the different effects of marriage on men and women, Gove and Tudor (1973) considered historical and cultural influences. They pointed to different rates of mental illness in different communities, and related the cohesiveness of traditional communities to an overall lower incidence of mental illness, with even lower rates for women in cohesive communities. Economic stress and unemployment were reported in communities in which there was more mental illness, and in these men outnumbered women in the ranks of the distressed. The limits of sociological explanations become clear when we attempt to account for social change. Not only have women's roles changed in recent years, but so also have men's, and these changing gender roles undoubtedly influence each other and the incidence of mental illness. The Midtown Manhattan study (Srole and Fisher, 1980) provides an example of the limits of sociological explanations. A comparison of the incidence of mental illness between 1954 and 1974 showed that, for men and women of comparable age, rates for women had declined, while those for men had remained the same.

Psychoanalytic and social learning theories have each been combined with a sociological perspective to explain the higher incidence of depression among women. Psychoanalytic theories of the causes of particular disorders do not elaborate the theme of sex differences. Rather, the issue is considered in the developmental theory of infantile sexuality and is most clearly specified in terms of the Oedipus complex. In chapter 5 we noted that this aspect of the theory has come under considerable attack because it posits that women, as a result of their resolution of the Oedipus complex, are typically more narcissistic, lower in self-esteem, and more dependent than men. We saw that its critics, including psychoanalysts, have sought to emphasise the influence of society on the development of women.

Another line of theorising that has distant roots in psychoanalytic explanations of psychopathology views depression in terms of the feelings of helplessness that characterise it (Bibring, 1953). Seligman (1975) developed this approach within a social learning framework. He showed that individuals who find themselves repeatedly in situations in which their behaviour cannot control unpleasant stimulation later do not attempt to gain control in manageable circumstances. In a laboratory experiment, this effect was heightened when people were told that their problem-solving outcomes were determined by chance and among individuals who believed that luck determined their fate. Seligman argued that depression is characterised by helplessness specific to beliefs about one's ability to influence events, and he demonstrated this in comparisons of people who were depressed and those who were not. In one study he showed the different effects of success and failure on the performance of these two groups in tests involving both skills and chance. His manipulation affected non-depressed people's expectations of success in tests of skill; but depressed people's expectations of performance on tests, both of skill and of chance, were unaffected. The overall picture that emerged from laboratory studies of learned helplessness has led to the characterisation of depression in terms of passivity, lack of observable aggression, and reduced effectiveness in solving problems. It has been suggested that the gender-role socialisation of women leads to a similar outcome and that the adult role of women is one in which there is little opportunity for effective control (Litman, 1978).

Seligman's emphasis on learned helplessness was later incorporated into a theory that laid more emphasis on the attributions people made for their condition, and the feelings of hopelessness that many negative life events (or absence of positive ones) generate. Abramson et al. (1989) viewed negative circumstances as acting as 'occasion setters' for generating feelings of hopelessness, which are an immediate cause of depression. In between the negative circumstances and the feelings of hopelessness lie the person's attempts to make sense of what has happened, their attributions. These comprise people's inferences about why an event occurred, its consequences, and its implications for the person's self-worth. When an important negative life event is attributed to stable and widespread causes and is seen as influencing self-worth, a state of hopelessness will be highly likely. This explanation and the investigations of causal attributions and coping strategies that it generated are particularly important because they identified reasons why some people respond to negative events with depression and others remain relatively unaffected.

Abramson and her colleagues moved the emphasis from expectations about success and failure to the person's inferences about the causes of negative events, and their impact on general expectations about what the world has to offer them. Theirs was a general theory of depression that could be adapted to explain sex differences. Men and women may experience different types of negative events, and may make different attributions about them. Abramson and her colleagues view their theory as similar to earlier approaches to depression, such as that of Brown and Harris (1978), who emphasised the low self-esteem that resulted from the restricted life circumstances of working-class English women.

Brown and Harris' theory of depression arose from their classic study that indicated why particular women may be at risk. It was a methodologically sophisticated and sensitive study reported in a volume as long as this one (Brown and Harris, 1978), and it generated a theory to account for the incidence of both clinical and subclinical depression. The study was not a treatise on sex differences per se, since only women were examined, but it did seek to explain the higher incidence among working-class than middle-class women in Camberwell, a district in London. Brown and Harris were able to show that the differences occurred only during particular stages of life – when working-class women had either one child younger than 6 years of age or three or more children under the age of 14 years at home. Furthermore, they were able to account for class differences in depression in the face of equally stress-provoking life events involving long-term loss or disappointment, such as the death of a parent, grown children moving away, the discovery of a husband's infidelity, or the severe illness of a close friend. True, stressful life events were more common among working-class women with children, but even this did not account for the fact that the rate of clinical depression was four times greater in these women than in middle-class women who experienced the same degrees of stress. Again, we return to the way in which stressful events impact on the individual's view of their lives and their selves.

Role identities and interpersonal and intrapsychic elements are each given a place in Brown and Harris' account of depression. The important intrapsychic elements are the absence of feelings of self-esteem and mastery. These echo notions of learned helplessness and hopelessness in the theories outlined above. Role identities were shown to protect or expose inner feelings of self-worth. Women able to maintain a positive outlook despite a distressing life event would typically have employment outside the home, an intimate relationship with husband or boyfriend, and fewer than three children at home under the age of 14. No outside employment, lack of intimacy, and three children under 14 years of age were vulnerability factors associated with general feelings of hopelessness and clinical depression. The relationship between depression and a fourth vulnerability factor, loss of one's mother before one was 11 years old, has been specified more closely in recent years (Brown et al., 1985). The importance of the experience of loss for enduring personality characteristics is not denied. Evidence also showed that women who experience early loss and who dealt unsuccessfully with premarital pregnancy were more likely to be those who subsequently found themselves in a marriage that located them in the working class. The greater likelihood that one or more of these vulnerability factors figured in the background of working-class women was invoked by Brown and Harris (1978) to explain the class difference in depression. Their studies point the way towards a meaningful integration of some of the factors that may be included in future accounts of the different rates of depression and other mental illness among men and women. Nolen-Hoeksema (1998:204) identified an important additional variable and argued that as more becomes known about the physical abuse of women this may assume a place, not only in accounts of depression, but also in explaining anxiety disorders and substance abuse. In a similar vein, Bifulco and Moran (1998) reported that in their 'loss of mother' study 'lack of care' or neglect was more closely related to depression in adulthood than was the early death of a mother. Needless to say, such neglect was related to loss. Once again, comprehensive explanations will require that the interaction of a number of variables be taken into account.

Brown and Harris' theory adds an extra dimension to the explanations considered so far, in that it goes beyond the psychological analysis of the impact of external events on attributions and feelings of self-worth. It also encompasses how social roles can enable people to have the additional psychological resources to maintain their self-worth in the face of external stress. An influential theory of sex differences in depression has yet another slight difference of emphasis. Nolen-Hoeksema (1987, 1990) suggested that men and women experience similar incidences of mild depressive episodes but that their reactions to these may differ systematically. When women feel depressed, they tend to focus on their distress and ruminate about their problems. A later study showed that individuals who employ such a ruminative coping style suffer more prolonged and severe bouts of depression (Nolen-Hoeksema, 1995). There are echoes here of Gove and Tudor's (1973) suggestion that being a housewife allows time to brood over troubles.

Nolen-Hoeksema et al. (1999) tested a comprehensive theory that explains sex differences, and draws together the themes we have introduced in this section. The authors hypothesised that women's susceptibility to depressive symptoms reflects the facts that:

- their lives are more stressful than are those of men
- they have a lower sense of self-mastery than do men
- they employ more ruminative coping strategies than do men.

Nolen-Hoeksema and colleagues' two-wave study of 1,100 adults ranging in age from 25 to 75 years supported these predictions. The findings suggest that a comprehensive explanation of sex differences in depression has to involve different external events in the lives of men and women, different intrapsychic responses to such events, and different ways of dealing with mild depressive episodes once these occur.

Such complexities are a far cry from some of the older one-dimensional attempts to explain differences in mental health, for example by linking these to physiology and/or some basic psychological difference between the sexes. The psychoanalyst Helene Deutsch (1945) explained what were labelled the passive and masochistic tendencies of women as adaptations to their reproductive functions in menstruation and childbirth. Her account is typical of theories that Osofsky and Seidenberg (1970) described as confused, fuzzy, and prejudiced, in that they link female psychology to female biology yet manage to separate male psychology from male biology. The review of sex differences from a psychiatric perspective by Weissman and Klerman (1977) examined the evidence available at the time for hormonal influences on depression, and found this to be incomplete. They doubted whether these variables would explain the large difference between male and female incidence. Later research on the role of hormones in mood changes associated with the menstrual cycle, childbirth, and the menopause have supported this conclusion, as indicated earlier in this chapter. Parry (1994) suggested that a small group of women who experience both increased depressive symptoms premenstrually and who have also been diagnosed with major depressive episodes at other times have a general vulnerability to depression that is not specifically triggered by hormonal changes.

Most of the explanations we have considered so far are broadly compatible with a social role interpretation which views women's higher rates of depression as arising from problems associated with their social position and their powerlessness to influence that social position. An alternative account of the increased probability of depression among women has been developed from an evolutionary perspective (McGuire et al., 1997). In chapter 3 we considered sex differences in mate selection and reproductive strategies. McGuire and his colleagues argued that disorder prevalence and responses to environmental conditions are related to these differences. They suggested that sources of female vulnerability to depression include the following: men have a greater preference for short-term relationships contrasting with women's greater desire for enduring relationships; men show more possessiveness, guarding and restricting their women partners, thus restricting their usual social support systems; men also prefer submissive females. McGuire et al. concluded that such events, which contribute to women's depression, are more common than those that contribute to men's, such as loss of status in the male world or female threats of infidelity. In a way, this explanation implicitly acknowledges the exercise of power by men over women, emphasised by the social role view. Both sexes are viewed as having sources of depression that can be traced to reproductive conflicts of interest, but it is men's ability to control women in the pursuit of their own reproductive interests that is viewed as being crucial. One prediction from this theory is that when women are free from such controls, for example in long-term lesbian relationships, or when they have strong mutual support systems, their levels of depression should be reduced accordingly.

Conclusions

Differences between men and women in the expression of fear and anxiety, explored in the beginning of this chapter, suggest a link between the stereotypes of men and women such that women are allowed to display negative emotions while men are not. Evidence fails to support a straightforward biological explanation for greater mood swings in women than in men, sometimes associated with fluctuations in women's hormone levels, in particular during the premenstrual phase, postpartum, and following the menopause. Indeed, recent research has drawn attention to hormonal fluctuations in men. A new approach to the question of postpartum depression is an as yet unverified theory that suggests that it may be adaptive in reducing parental investment in circumstances where the infant may fail to thrive.

The DSM-IV provides a framework for evaluating sex differences in mental health even after consideration of the problems that diagnosis involves. Suicide is characterised by a male predominance, with data only from rural China challenging this conclusion. The evidence is clear that women are more likely to suffer bouts of major depression than are men. Interestingly, bipolar illnesses involving both depression and mania are not characterised by sex differences. Although there is a general predominance of women among sufferers of generalised anxiety, findings are more complex when other anxiety disorders are considered.

The objective criteria of DSM-IV have also yielded a more complex picture for sex differences in schizophrenia and other psychotic disorders. One clear difference is age of onset. Men present more commonly between the ages of 14 to 24 while women are usually diagnosed in the decade beginning at 24 years. Antisocial PD is diagnosed primarily among men.

Evidence supports popular stereotypes, with eating disorders more common among women, and men more often abusing various substances. It is predictable that this leads to male violence as well. Social role theory in terms of both role expectations and stereotypes plays an important part in explanations of sex differences in mental health, but does not provide a complete account. Intrapsychic processes, such as rumination, as well as biological factors, will contribute to more complete explanations of reliable sex differences in mental health.

Further reading

Fischer, A. H. (ed.) (2000) *Gender and Emotion*. Cambridge University Press.
> This set of chapters by a distinguished collection of social psychologists takes the issue of gender differences in emotions well beyond the summary account available in this chapter.

Nolen-Hoeksema, S. (2001). *Abnormal Psychology, second edition*. Boston et al.: McGraw Hill.
> This updated textbook offers a clear review of the entire field of psychopathology and includes targeted reading on sex differences though use of the index entry, gender.

8   The domestic sphere

Introduction

In this chapter and the next, we consider the worlds of home and work, the private and public spheres of social life. Record numbers of women in Western industrial societies are now in employment, and work from home is becoming ever more commonplace. Though for much of the twentieth century it was widely held that a woman's place was in the home and a man's in the world of work, outside the home, that distinction is rapidly breaking down. In these linked chapters we challenge such beliefs by asking whether men can keep house and provide satisfactory care for young children, and whether women have the abilities and motivation to fill skilled jobs and meet professional demands.

In considering the domestic sphere, it is useful to bear in mind a distinction between households and families. Recent research examining time spent doing housework clarifies this distinction. Sometimes a household is composed of a 'traditional family' consisting of a married couple and their dependent children; but families today include single parents and two parents of the same sex and their children. Recent changes in the structure of families challenges the assumption that children are generally cared for by their cohabiting, married, biological parents.

In chapter 7, we examined the argument advanced by some feminist sociologists and anthropologists that it is male power which keeps women in their place – the home. Even when women are engaged in full-time employment, they are expected to clean, cook, and shop – to keep house for their families. Time-budget studies undertaken in the 1970s showed that the amount of time husbands spent doing housework, including taking out the rubbish and keeping the grounds, was not influenced by wives' employment outside the home (Feldman, 1982). From a broader perspective – one that reflects the changing composition of households – South and Spitze (1994) examined the amount of time women and men spent doing housework. They identified six household arrangements:

- married couples
- cohabiting (heterosexual) couples
- never-married individuals living with their parents
- never-married individuals living independently
- divorced persons
- widowed persons.

Although women do more housework than men across all six domestic arrangements, South and Spitze reported significant differences, with women in both married and cohabiting couples doing more housework than women in other domestic living arrangements. They proposed that women and men living together differentiate their gender-appropriate statuses through differences in domestic labour. South and Spitze describe the process of establishing a gender identity as 'doing gender'. Among gay and lesbian couples, where gender identities are defined differently, domestic labour is also performed differently. Kurdek (1995) reports, both from his own and others' research, that gay and lesbian partners do not undertake the large amount of housework characteristic of wives in married couples. Although housework provides an opportunity for individuals to enact their gender identities, both social and economic factors such as children in the home, unemployment, educational limits, and job requirements also influence individual choices about how much time to spend doing housework (cf. Kroska, 1997).

The gap between the contributions of men and women to housework is greatest in married couples, where it is 19 hours. Even among unmarried individuals, living in their parental home, women spend 4 hours a week more than men engaged in household labour. All unmarrieds living independently do more housework than do those living with parents, but the increase for women is greater, and the gap between the time spent by women and men grows to 6 hours. However, among the divorced and widowed, women do less housework and men more.

Study of the domestic division of labour is typical of a social science approach to understanding the domestic sphere. An examination of the influences of psychological, social, and economic processes upon each other provides explanation of the *proximate* causes of satisfaction and unhappiness within the family. Evolutionary psychology supplements this knowledge by investigating the impact of heritable predispositions, and poses questions about the likely occurrence of particular behaviours in specific situations. Such examination of *ultimate* causes (see chapter 3) seeks to explain why certain behaviours occur frequently, and draws upon an understanding of adaptations that aided the survival of the multi-generational human family groups in pre-industrial, pre-agricultural times (cf. Emlen, 1997).

We begin our discussion of the domestic sphere by considering the impact of the changing nature of the family and of marriage on men and women. Marriage remains a major institution in most societies, despite significant changes in familial values and functions. None the less, with more frequent divorce, marriage at later ages, and widowhood, a significant part of adult life may well be spent living alone or in relationships outside legally sanctioned marriage.

In 1995–6, a married couple headed 4 out of 5 families with children in the United Kingdom (*Social Focus on Families*, 1997). The next most common family arrangement was that of a lone parent, rather than a cohabiting couple. Among the under sixties, 25 per cent of households were comprised of lone parents or cohabiting couples. Among the over sixties, 90 per cent of living units were composed of married couples whose children had usually left home. Ethnic variations emerged when 'traditional families', that is, a couple with children under the age of 16, or unmarried 16- to 18-year-olds in full-time education living at home, were examined. In the white group, almost 80 per cent of families with dependent children were couples, and this proportion rose to almost 90 per cent among families from the Indian sub-continent, but fell to less than 50 per cent in black families with dependent children. Most recent surveys indicate that the number of one-parent families has trebled since 1971, bringing their number to almost 25 per cent of all families with dependent children. As men remarry more quickly after divorce, and children usually live with their mothers, the majority of one-parent families are headed by women. These variations demonstrate that caution and attention to particular circumstances are necessary before generalising about the impact of the family on women and men.

Early results from the 2000 year census in the United States also record rapid change in family structures (*New York Times*, 2001). A third of all households were reported to be composed of non-family members, either people living on their own or with others to whom they were not related. Of these households, 5.5 million were unmarried couples, up from 3.2 million in 1990. Only 23.5 per cent of all households in 2000 were married couples living with children under 18 years of age, compared with 25.6 per cent in 1990 and 45 per cent in 1960. Perhaps even more strikingly, there was a 25 per cent growth in the number of single mother–child families, but only a 6 per cent growth across the 1990s in the number of children in married-couple households.

We begin our examination of the domestic sphere by considering the impact of marriage on men and women, despite recent statistics, and then examine domestic roles. In the 1960s and 1970s, female sociologists sought to balance the greater attention that had earlier been given to work roles (Gavron, 1966; Oakley, 1974). After reviewing the changing nature of families, their structure and social functions, we focus on one major familial function, that of child-rearing. Psychologists, often men, have sought to describe in detail the contribution of fathers to child care (Lamb, 1997; Lewis, 1997). We first consider early attachment and the importance of the mother. After questioning whether women have a unique contribution to make to early development, we compare the roles of mother and father in the care of young children.

The family and marriage

An emphasis on the family should not be interpreted to mean that we believe that a 'traditional family' formed by a man and a woman in a legally sanctioned relationship is the only legitimate domestic setting within which to live and to raise children. In the second half of the twentieth century, both the nature of marriage and membership in a family have undergone major changes. The gay and lesbian communities are currently challenging the definition of marriage. There is demand for reforms that would permit permanent, same-sex relationships to be legally recognised, and claims that this step would allow gay persons, in stable relationships, the same social benefits as those enjoyed by heterosexual couples. The question is yet to be settled, and there are strong views on either side. Knight (1997) has argued that 'to place domestic-partner relationships on a par with marriage denigrates the marital imperative. But to describe such relationships as "marriage" destroys the definition of marriage altogether' (p. 297).

The changing family

The institution of heterosexual marriage itself has undergone significant change in the 1970s and 1980s. Elliot (1996) noted four significant changes in marriage that have occurred in Anglo-Saxon and north-Western European societies. These are:

- separation of sex from marriage
- separation of childbearing and child-rearing from marriage
- reconstruction of marriage as a terminable arrangement
- reworking of the sexual division of labour.

Elliot drew her conclusions from a survey of recent social science research. Even though sex is no longer deemed appropriate only within marriage, she noted that cohabiting was expected eventually to result in marriage. In addition, extramarital and even extra-relationship sex was frowned upon and faithfulness was expected both in marriage and in cohabiting relationships. Although older research indicated that women had been more faithful than men in marriage, in current cohabiting relationships there was no difference in the infidelity rates of women and men (Wellings et al., 1994). What has changed profoundly is that women now seek pleasure in sex and, consequently, are no longer virgins at marriage, have had a number of partners before they marry, and may engage in adulterous relationships within it.

Alongside the separation of sex and marriage there has also been a separation of parenting from marriage. Biological paternity no longer leads inevitably to fatherhood within marriage. In Sweden, cohabiting couples register half of first births, while in Britain the figure is roughly 1 in 3. Cohabiting couples split up more readily and relationships are of shorter duration than in marriage. Consequently, the bond between biological fathers and their children has grown weaker. According to 1992 statistics, the highest proportion of single parenthood in a developed country occurs in the USA (23%) and the lowest in Japan (6%) (Bronfenbrenner et al., 1996). Evidence that mother-headed families in the USA are most frequently black and least commonly white, with Hispanic mothers in between, is similar to British data discussed earlier. Socio-economic factors produce consistent effects with mother-headed families least common among the middle classes and most common among those living in poverty. In Britain in 1992, divorced or separated mothers headed 11 per cent of families and never-married mothers headed a further 7 per cent.

Fathers, predominantly unmarried, cared for children under 6 years of age in 10 per cent of single-parent families in the USA in 1994 (Bronfenbrenner et al., 1996). In Britain, lone fathers headed only 2 per cent of single-parent families; 98 per cent of all dependent children in Britain lived with their mother. The mother–child relationship remains intact despite increasing separation of child-rearing from marriage and of biological fathers from their children.

The weakening of the father–child bond is also a consequence of the liberalisation of divorce law in the 1960s and 1970s. Although the rate of marriage is declining, divorce rates are increasing. Again the USA has the highest rate with 4.6 per 1,000 population, and Japan the lowest, at 1.4 per 1,000 population (Bronfenbrenner et al., 1996). Extrapolation from current trends suggests that, of first marriages, 3 out of 5 marriages in the USA and 4 out of 10 in England will end in divorce. Despite measurable changes in rate and length of marriage, a positive belief in marriage and two-person child-rearing persists.

Evolutionary psychology can be invoked to examine phenomena such as the belief in faithfulness in cohabiting and marital relationships, the predominance of one-parent families headed by mothers, and the persistence of a belief in marriage and shared child-rearing. Emlen (1997) argued that an appreciation of heritable predispositions would assist in dealing with the impact of the changes in family life that have occurred in the past few decades by sensitising professionals to issues that are likely to be difficult for reconstituted family units.

Turning now to domestic roles, we have already noted that women do more household labour than do men, whatever the domestic arrangements. Women have come into the workforce in increasing numbers, but again this has not led to greater participation by men in routine household work. Rather it has, as Hochschild (1989) has vividly described, resulted in women working two shifts, one in the domestic sphere, the other in the public sphere. Child care is the domestic area that has seen greater male participation. Men 'help out' with children and value fatherhood. In other areas of domestic life, attitudes may have changed, but women are still left with the majority of the domestic work.

Women and marriage

Traditionally marriage has brought greater change for women, but it has been found to be more beneficial for men (Bernard, 1972). Wives are likely to modify their personalities and their values in line with their husbands' expectations and, in the past, their marital happiness was related to their husbands' success both economically and at an interpersonal level (Barry, 1970). Fowers (1991) reported that men rated greater satisfaction with their marriages than did women. In chapter 7, we noted that a loss of self-esteem and control in marriage entails psychological costs for women. These are reflected in a higher incidence of mental illness, particularly depression, among married rather than single, divorced, or widowed women. Being at work protects women from the full impact of marriage. In Western society, men thrive on the care they receive in marriage, whereas women are healthier living on their own. So, too, when a marriage partner dies, bereavement brings greater suffering in terms of depression and loss of a sense of well-being to surviving husbands than to surviving wives (Archer, 1999; Stroebe and Stroebe, 1983).

Among the changes that marriage brings for women have been changes of name and residence, and sometimes job as well. With cohabiting an accepted step on the way to marriage, issues surrounding residence and occupation may have been resolved before a legal union is established. The practice of married women adopting their husbands' surnames has come to the fore and psychologists have begun to examine the issues that this practice raises. Alongside the traditional procedure whereby a wife takes her husband's surname, Masche (1995) identified four other possibilities. These are:

- husband takes his wife's surname
- husband keeps his name but his wife hyphenates her name to include that of her husband
- wife keeps her surname but the husband hyphenates his name to include that of his wife
- husband and wife both keep their own names.

Two American studies have focused on women and their marital name practices. Kline et al. (1996) suggested that relational qualities, that is, marital satisfaction, love, commitment, and intimacy, did not distinguish among women who changed, kept, or combined names on marriage. However, their combined, quantitative – qualitative questionnaire study of over 100 married women showed that women's choice of marital name was related to different views about the nature of marriage. Long, almost 5-hour interviews revealed that five American women who kept their own names upon marriage shared a need to be an equal partner in their marriage and a need to maintain a separate identity (Fowler and Fuehrer, 1997).

In theory at least, marriage brings changes for both sexes. A woman becomes a wife and usually a mother, while a man becomes a husband and usually a father. Reflecting earlier marriage and family patterns, Stoll (1978) claimed that only as men reached retirement did their primary concerns shift from work to the family (see Table 8.1). In her five-stage model of female development, the primary focus for women was other people – their husbands, their children, their grandchildren, and, finally, in widowhood, another partner. As Nancy Chodorow (1978) noted, the modern family, stripped of almost all the functions it had in earlier times, became 'a quintessentially relational and personal institution, *the* personal sphere of society'.

Perhaps the most profound change in marriage and the family is that described by Lionel Tiger (1999). He argues that the development of female contraception and the assertion of female social equality are responsible for the decline of marriage and, with it, the decline of men. In the past, premarital pregnancy, described colloquially as 'getting a woman in the family way', usually led to marriage, but it no longer does. Indeed, it had been unusual for a man to assume the role of father

Table 8.1 Roles of men and women in a traditional family household

	Men	Women

1 *Entry* Marriage or living together status	Becoming a husband or mate:
	    Change to responsibility status
	    Redefine self as 'mature'
		Becoming a housewife:
		    Changing to dependent
		    Acquire domestic skills
		    Redefine self as 'mature'

2 *Expanding circle* Childbirth	Becoming a father:
	    Increased support
	        responsibilities
	
	    Change in self-definition
	    Readjustments in spouse role
		Becoming a mother:
		    Acquire child-care skills
		    Restrictions on many
		        activities
		    Major self-redefinition
		    Change in spouse role

3 *Full-house plateau* Completed family	Self resignation:
	    Major redefinition of self
	    Acquire fathering skills
		Self-development:
		    Increased community
		        involvement
		    Return to work part time
		    Acquire child-rearing skills

4 *Shrinking circle* Departure of children	Self-change
	    Change in self regarding
	        sexuality and 'masculinity'
	    Disengagement from work
	    Acquire leisure pursuits
		Search for new roles:
		    Becoming a grandmother
		
		    Return to work or
		        education full time
		    Reorient to spouse
		    Change in self regarding
		        sexuality and 'femininity'

5 *Disengagement*	Widowed, divorced:
	    Becoming a potential spouse
	    Change to independent status
	    Acquiring domestic skills
		Widowed, divorced:
		    Becoming a potential spouse
		    Change to independent
		        status
		    Increased economic
		        responsibility

Remarriage	Becoming a husband, step-father:
	    Change to responsibility status
		Becoming a wife, step-
		    mother
		Change to dependency
		    status

Source: Adapted from Stoll (1978).

outside marriage. Tiger's (1999) theory, that the decline in marriage and weakening in paternal participation link to a more general decline in male power and occupational success, will be considered after discussing earlier models of marriage.

If we were to accept Tiger's argument, we would conclude that women have broken free of the constraints of marriage. They may find financial independence while living within marriage, or they may ignore the legal conventions of marriage while cohabiting, or they may raise their children on their own or with a female partner.

The family in history

Sociological accounts, intent upon showing that family roles are socially constructed, point out the time-boundedness of views of family roles and functions
that have been based upon Western, middle-class life (e.g., Walum, 1977). The
complete separation of production and reproduction – of the economy and of
child-rearing – is only a few centuries old. Before the advent of industrial society, the family was often a social and commercial centre. In rural areas, women
worked the land, tended livestock and poultry, made clothes, and processed and
stored food, as well as bearing children and rearing them. In cities, the homes of the
mercantile class were centres of trade and production. Merchant travellers along
with apprentices were housed and fed; children were trained; food, clothing, and
household articles were made in the home. In the poorest families, female labour
extending beyond child care was necessary for survival. Early in the Industrial
Revolution, women and even young children worked in mines and mills.

Baking bread and cultivating a garden may today represent a nostalgic quest
for meaning and purpose in the life of married middle-class women, alongside the
remaining functions of childbirth and child-rearing (French, 1978). This idealisation of housework is not restricted to women. One male author wrote: 'Household
work is the last area of preindustrial craft work that we have left . . . [It] should
be held up and praised as a way of escaping the estrangement to which many are
subject in modern life' (Beer, 1983). Neither the author nor the 56 men he surveyed
were full-time househusbands; this may explain the pleasure they found in tasks
that are obligatory for many women.

In so far as the modern family has been stripped of most functions other than
that of reproduction, it is tempting to seek biological explanations for its continued
existence. Alice Rossi, an avowedly feminist sociologist, adopted such a position
(1977, 1984) despite having earlier argued that women become mothers as the
result of their socialisation (1964). Although she proposed similar education for
boys and girls, she queried the wisdom of striving for equal participation by men
and women in the public sector and in the home. She questioned the quality of
child care that can be provided by men or even by those women whose lives are
committed equally to their families and to their work outside the home. Rossi
asserted that sociological theories that ignored 'the central biological fact that the
core function of any family system is human continuity through reproduction and
care-rearing' (p. 2) were bound to be inadequate. She held no brief for the older
view of the isolated nuclear family as the sole normal institution for reproduction and child care, nor was she sympathetic to the egalitarian approach, which
attempted to deny or obliterate all differences between the sexes.

In the 1970s, Rossi elaborated theories drawing on human evolutionary history
in hunter–gatherer societies. She claimed that women's manual dexterity, persistence, and physical and emotional endurance reflected the reproductive success
of those females capable of combining the bearing and care of their young with
gathering and small-game hunting. Rossi was careful to disclaim strict genetic

determinism, but argued instead that men and women learn particular skills with differential ease. Consequently, men would require greater training to be as good parents as women because their interests in reproduction are primarily sexual and lack the female's strong relational bond to the young. Similarly, she claimed that female cosmonauts and soldiers required special training to compensate for the absence of male musculature. Rossi saw *fathering* as being socially learned, whereas successful mothering, she posited, evolved over millions of years.

Rossi concluded that from the genetic code that organises male and female physiology, to hormones that regulate behaviour, the message is that each sex more easily acquires behaviour appropriate to its role in society. In spelling out the consequences of considering biological factors in role learning, Rossi was careful to distinguish rare from common roles. For example, to become a neurosurgeon requires delicate manual dexterity, and this is more common in women. Rossi noted that very few people become neurosurgeons, and, although social pressure has barred women – who are most likely to have the requisite aptitudes – there are still a few men with sufficient manual dexterity. When large numbers of manually dextrous workers are required, as in the electronics industry, women are in the majority (see chapter 9). So, too, with parenting; here Rossi believes that nature gives women the edge. She characterised men as essentially less interested in the young and hence, efforts to train male nurturing as unlikely to be successful.

Nancy Chodorow (1978) criticised Rossi's biosocial model not only on biological grounds but also in the context of her own account of mothering. Rather than ascribing women's mothering to genes, hormones, or socialisation, Chodorow claimed that the question 'Why do women mother?' remains to be answered. Along with Rossi, she found a simple socialisation explanation inadequate and so looked to modern psychoanalytic accounts, particularly those known as object relations theory, to explain the role of the mother in men's and women's inner worlds. Chodorow shifted theoretical attention from the interpersonal to the intrapersonal level (see chapter 1).

Chodorow's arguments take us back to the psychoanalytic concept of the Oedipal conflict, which we first encountered in chapter 5. Post-Freudian theorists stress the importance of pre-Oedipal relationships in the development of adult sexual aims and love objects choices. Differences in male and female development become clearer when the first year of life and an infant's relationship to the primary mothering agent is considered. In the process of growing up, a boy need not relinquish his feelings for mothers, though he must renounce his desires for his own mother. A girl must turn away from her mother only to compete with her or other women for the love and attention of her father and men in general. Adult heterosexuality for men includes the qualities of their first love, but adult heterosexuality for girls involves loss of the mother to some extent and feelings of jealousy and competition with the mother as well as love in relation to the father. These differences not only influence adult relationships between men and women, but also mothers' responses to their male and female infants.

The account Chodorow presents is considerably richer than this summary indicates. It offers detailed explanations of each sex's struggle for freedom from primary love and dependence as well as of the fantasies each entertains about its recapture. Yet the essential point is that the struggle is different for men and women. For the male it may result in hostility towards women, while for the female it can lead to idealisation of the male. At the risk of oversimplification, we can say that men potentially regain the mother through heterosexuality, whereas for women the consequences of post-Oedipal heterosexuality, tempered as it is by pre-Oedipal wishes, are that they can regain the mother only by becoming mothers themselves. Thus, according to Chodorow, men and women have very different needs and feelings about bearing and looking after children.

Contemporary evolutionary psychology offers a different perspective on family relationships particularly about the care of children. Attention is drawn to the heritable adaptations that have persisted because of the selective advantage they provided our ancestors, and hypotheses are tested by examining the contemporary social life of species whose social lives are structured in ways similar to those of our pre-agricultural forebears. Emlen (1997) has elaborated this approach in order to increase our understanding and improve interventions designed to compensate for the consequences of the disappearance of the extended family and, indeed, the disintegration of the two-parent nuclear family. In particular, he considers these changes in family life in terms of increasing child delinquency, school truancy and exclusion, and child abuse. All of these problems are more frequent in one-parent and step-parent families.

Fundamental to Emlen's analysis is his focus on family genetics. He describes the traditional family of two biological parents and their children, that we have already identified, as a 'simple' family and an 'intact' family, and differentiates it from 'reconstituted' or 'step' families in which an original biological parent has been replaced by an unrelated adult. Intact families are held to function co-operatively and amicably because individuals increase their inclusive fitness through investing in their own offspring or those of closely related relatives (see chapter 3). Inclusive fitness leads to four predictions about social relations in reconstituted families. Emlen provides evidence from humans in support of each of these.

First, in a reconstituted family, the step-parent gains little fitness through caring for unrelated young; hence Emlen predicts that stepparents will offer only minimal care of their new unrelated stepchildren. Second, since there is no biological link, step-parents are more likely than natural parents to be sexually attracted to stepchildren and, indeed, stepdaughters are at five times the risk of sexual abuse as are biological daughters. Third, among the children themselves there will be less co-operation among half-siblings than among full siblings with whom they share half their genes. Stepsiblings are not related genetically and gain no fitness through co-operation. Finally, reconstituted families will be less stable both through children leaving home earlier than in intact families and through the step-parents themselves divorcing. Emlen uses this evidence of stress in reconstituted families to propose five methods to counteract the effects of predispositions that lead to undesirable outcomes:

- increased awareness of the risks of conflict in reconstituted families
- appreciation of emotional issues such as guilt
- recognition of the types of issues that produce conflict
- greater awareness of family-oriented traits in choosing replacement mates
- formal recognition of risks to offspring through a stepfamily arrangement.

Our attention in this analysis of sex differences in the family has centred primarily on adults. We have presented Chodorow's psychodynamic theory not as an account of development, but as an explanation of the willingness of men and women to accept the traditional roles of husband and wife, father and mother. Even Emlen's proposals to improve the rearing of children in reconstituted families derive from the breakdown of marriage and traditional family life. In the section that follows, our primary focus is the growth and well-being of the infant and child per se.

Mothering and attachment

We follow conventional terminology in labelling this section 'Mothering and attachment' and in so doing draw attention to the pervasive stereotype of women as mothers. Many psychologists, as well as laypersons, believe that it is natural for women to mother and that women are better able to care for children (cf. Tiger, 1999). We will explore the extent to which psychological theory and research supports this view.

Developmental psychology has undergone dramatic changes in the past three decades. These changes reflect shifts in the theoretical outlook of psychologists generally and are not confined exclusively to theories of child development. In line with an attack on behaviourism, the view that the infant is a passive lump of clay to be moulded according to the needs of society has also been abandoned. Evolutionary psychology has emerged to offer an account of the history of the human species and its socio-biological trajectory.

Fagot (1995) suggested that the past 30 years have seen an initial lack of interest in the differential socialisation of girls and boys, then a middle period in which gender became an important issue, and currently a lack of attention to sex-differentiated child care. Her observation is relevant to our concerns, but there is also a need for psychological theory and research to move beyond the study of families composed of children living with two parents.

Attachment theory

John Bowlby was highly influential in altering the public's view of the nature of infant development. An expert in adolescent and child psychiatry, he undertook a study of homeless children for the United Nations shortly after World War II. His report, which has been the focus of much research and controversy, contains the widely quoted conclusion that 'mother-love in infancy and childhood is as important for mental health as are vitamins and proteins for physical health' (Bowlby, 1951:158). His report had an immediate impact, including major improvements in the institutional care of children. It also led mothers to a concern with their children's attachment bonds to them. Critics have held Bowlby responsible for speeding the return of women to the home after demobilisation, and for encouraging the social seclusion of mothers with their young children (Morgan and Ricciuti, 1969).

Bowlby's original report identified a problem – that of psychological and developmental impairment in children – and sought an explanation for it in the mother–child relationship. Research that followed, including much of Bowlby's own research, sought to understand this relationship, especially the processes of affiliation and attachment. Although trained as a psychoanalyst, Bowlby was dissatisfied with contemporary psychoanalytic accounts of the growth of mother-love. Freud held that the choice of the mother as the baby's first love object developed from the feeding relationship – from the breast that initially satisfied a physical need. Academic psychologists of a learning theory persuasion offered an account similar in its emphasis on the satisfaction of physical needs.

An early and major challenge to these 'cupboard-love' theories had come from Harry Harlow's experiments with infant monkeys (Harlow, 1958). He substituted inanimate objects for mothers and observed the development of baby monkeys. Harlow devised two sorts of surrogate mothers, each with a face and each able to provide milk. One was simply a wire frame, the other a frame covered with terry cloth. Offered the choice of the two, each of which provided milk, infant monkeys preferred the terry-cloth mother. When offered both the wire mother with milk and the terry-cloth surrogate without milk, the infant monkeys fed from the wire mother but spent much time clinging to the terry-cloth surrogate. The experience of feeding had not enhanced the attractiveness of the wire mother.

In a classic work published in 1969, Bowlby presented a comprehensive theory of attachment, drawing heavily on ethological studies of animals in natural surroundings as well as on the experimental work of Harlow. First, Bowlby proposed that the human infant is essentially social and predisposed by a number of instinctual response systems, which are primarily non-oral, to form an affective tie to its primary caregiver. Second, the affective tie develops in a regular manner and is usually well established by the second half of the first year. Third, in the normal course of development, the mother is both the primary caregiver and the attachment figure to whom the infant is bonded. Finally, once an attachment bond is well established, separation from the mother results in anxiety and protest. Prolonged separation results in an orderly sequence of protest, despair, and finally apparent detachment from the mother, so that upon her return the child may show no enthusiasm or interest. Total loss of the mother in the early years has a variety of long-lasting detrimental consequences.

Bowlby replaced orthodox psychoanalytic and learning theory explanations with an evolutionary account of the origins of attachment. The contemporary formulation of attachment theory views infants as being predisposed to emit signals such as crying, smiling, and visual tracking which elicit attention and nurturance from their caregivers. Consistent, prompt responding allows infants to develop trust and secure attachment bonds. When the response to infant signals is neither consistent nor predictable attachment may develop differently; the child may show avoidance or conflict in the presence of an attachment figure rather than a secure bond (cf. Chisholm, 1996, for a discussion of the evolutionary significance of different attachment relationships). Different styles of responding are also associated with different groups of caretakers such as mothers and fathers, and have consequences for infants' perceptions, affiliation, and attachment (Bridges et al., 1988).

Although there have been many challenges to the precise details of Bowlby's theoretical formulations, recognition of the importance of mothers' bonding to their infants and of infants' attachment to their mothers has led to major innovations in infant care (Klaus and Kennell, 1976; Rutter, 1981; Sluckin et al., 1983). Hospital deliveries in Europe and the USA increasingly include a period just after birth during which mothers and fathers are encouraged to look at their babies and to begin to get to know them. The care of premature and ill babies has been modified; mothers are now invited to stay in the hospital and take part in nursing their children.

Developmental psychologists have undertaken extensive research to establish the sequence and objects in the development of infant attachment. They have explored the consequences of individual differences in the strength of the attachment bond for other aspects of development, and sought the long-term consequences of maternal deprivation. We have selected issues that are relevant when considering the impact of gender in terms both of the providers of care for the young and for the infants receiving that care.

In the context of an examination of sex differences, the most obvious question is whether a father can function as an infant's and young child's primary attachment figure. A second issue relevant to our concerns is that of *monotropism* – the term used to indicate that attachment occurs to only one person at a time and ideally to the infant's natural mother. Finally, attachment theorists have held that under the stress of separation there is a hierarchical organisation such that infants prefer their mothers to their fathers.

Gender-related issues in the development of attachment bonds: caregivers

The issue of a single object of attachment is often confounded with that of the biological mother as a privileged object of attachment. In a sense, we are back to the original question – the deleterious effects of the failure to receive sufficient mother-love, or maternal deprivation. Schaffer and Emerson (1964) investigated the process of attachment and the objects of this attachment in a pioneering longitudinal study of 60 infants observed during each month in their first year. Although their study provided evidence of the development of attachment, Schaffer and Emerson showed that specific attachment need not be exclusively directed towards a single person. In the very first month in which a specific attachment was identified, 29 per cent of the babies developed such a tie with more than one other person; indeed, 10 per cent had ties with five or more other people. Even when the attachment object was a single person, the bond was not necessarily to the infant's mother. For a few infants, the sole bond was formed with a father or grandparent.

In 1996, Geiger published a monograph entitled *Fathers as Primary Caregivers* in which she sought to establish whether fathers who provided the majority of infant care, became primary attachment figures. She reported findings that echo those of Harlow. Although fathers who were primary care providers were unable to nurse their infants, these fathers became greater sources of comfort to their infants than their secondary caregiving mothers. Geiger explained this result by noting that she had observed that an infant's primary caretaker displayed more affection towards the infant than did the secondary caretaker, regardless of their biological sex.

The kibbutzim of Israel have often been cited in arguments about the nature of child care in our own society, as they provide unique data on the issue of attachment. In a kibbutz, the care of infants is shared between parents and *metaplot* (plural), trained caregivers who live with the children in special 'infant houses'. Fox (1977) studied the reactions of infants to separation and reunion with their mothers and their *metaplot* using a variety of measures. In the seven kibbutzim in which he worked, primary care of the infant usually passed to a *metapelet* (singular) when the infant was 3 to 4 months old. By the time the child was one and a half years old, the parents would visit once a day for 3 hours in the afternoon. Fox argued that, as attachment figures, mothers and *metaplot* were interchangeable and that each provided the infant with a secure base from which to explore the world. The only measures that did discriminate between mother and *metapelet* were those based upon reunion, but the results were heavily influenced by the greater anxiety of first-born children on being separated from their mothers. In the kibbutzim study, infants were observed to form attachments to more than one person at a time, although in each case these attachments were to women.

The third question we raised concerned a possible hierarchy of attachment such that an infant might only show a preference for its mother when extremely stressed. Geiger (1996), in her study of fathers as primary caregivers, also examined this issue. She reported that when babies experienced an adult stranger, or stress, they showed an even stronger preference for their primary caregiver, regardless of the caregiver's biological sex. Geiger's research provides a clear answer to the question as to whether an infant's mother is a privileged object of attachment, and establishes that an infant's response is not determined by the sex of its primary caregiver. In the work of Schaffer and Emerson we noted that, in addition to forming multiple attachments, a small proportion of infants became primarily attached to their fathers. The clear conclusion is that the object of initial attachment need not be the natural mother or even female.

Gender issues in the development of attachment bonds: infants and children

In this section we consider differences in the ways in which boy and girl infants establish affective and attachment ties with their primary caregivers and the consequences for other aspects of development. Information on this topic is scant. Fear of strangers is the behaviour usually employed to measure the strength of an attachment bond. Decarie et al. (1974) reported a clear difference between baby boys and girls, with females exhibiting a stronger negative reaction to being touched by a stranger than did males. Studies employing different measures of fear of strangers have confirmed a trend in the same direction, but have not yielded reliable results (Morgan and Ricciuti, 1969; Schaffer and Emerson, 1964; Tennes and Lampl, 1964).

Decarie and her students have suggested that the sex difference in fear reactions reflects a difference in the kind of understanding of the situation rather than the kinds of differences in fear discussed in chapter 7. Comparing infants of the same age and using the results of tests of intellectual development, object permanence, and the understanding of causality, they suggested that the negative response to being touched by strangers reflects the intellectual precocity of girls. They noted that when infants of both sex are a few months older all generally show a negative reaction to being touched by strangers.

Developmental hazards

Peter Smith (1980) challenged the conclusion that infants require an *exclusive*, warm, continuous relationship with a single person to develop emotional security. He speculated that there may be an upper limit on the number of caregivers that a child can encounter and still develop satisfactorily. Smith used data from a study of children who lived for at least 4 years from the age of 4 months in residential nurseries in London (Tizard and Hodges, 1978). He estimated that the children in that study had encountered 50 or more different caregivers in their 4 years' residence in nurseries. When assessed at 8 years of age, the majority of these children, whether they had returned to their natural parents, had been placed in foster homes, been adopted, or remained in care, posed problems in school. Although their intellectual development appeared normal, teachers described them as anti-social, attention seeking, and restless.

Although there probably is an optimal upper limit on the number of caregivers in the early years, problems in emotional development may result not from the number of caregivers per se, but from the nature of the interaction between the infant and the changing caregivers. Smith suggested that the transient caregiver typically had difficulty understanding and predicting the behaviour of the infant and hence failed to achieve a synchronous and mutually rewarding relationship. This, in turn, may have adversely influenced the caregiver's already fragile commitment to the infant, which may explain why it appears inevitable that the quality of infant care suffers when the number of caregivers is great.

In a review of the effects of maternal deprivation, Rutter (1981) noted that little effort had been directed towards assessing any differential effects on girls and boys. In his own research on the Isle of Wight, he had shown that short-term deprivation as the result of maternal illness or confinement is related to greater behavioural disturbance in boys than in girls (Wolkind and Rutter, 1973). However, when children were in the care of another person for a long time, as a result of prolonged maternal difficulties, there was as much disturbance among girls as among boys. Rutter (1981) concluded that there was evidence of differences in mother–infant interaction and in boys' and girls' reactions to stress, but that we cannot yet explain the nature of these differences and their long-term consequences. A study of older adults, women and men with an average age of 70 years, found that almost 40 per cent of both physical and mental illness in men could be accounted for by early life events. There were no significant relationships between early life events and health outcomes for women (Patterson et al., 1992). The authors concluded that: 'Women may be less vulnerable than men both to the adverse health consequences of childhood deprivation and other misfortunes' (p. 113).

It is a short step from consideration of the consequences of maternal deprivation to consideration of sex differences in the prevalence of mental illness in childhood. Although the diagnosis of psychopathology in children is even more problematic than it is in adults, mental illness in childhood raises a number of important questions (Earls, 1987; Eme, 1979). From 4 years of age, boys experience more problems than girls, more learning difficulties, more psychosexual disorders, and greater severity of anti-social behaviour, as well as more neurosis and psychosis. Girls begin to show problems increasingly in adolescence (McGee et al., 1990). More recently McDermott (1996) reported similar results derived from standardised observation by their teachers of 1,400 children aged 5 to 17 years. He found that boys outnumbered girls in most categories of problem behaviour. Confidence in this childhood sex difference in mental health is reinforced by a study of 6- to 13-year-old Chinese and American children (Weine et al., 1995). Data provided both by teachers and by parents showed that boys once again scored higher in attention problems, and on both delinquent and aggressive behaviour.

These results are puzzling in the light of the adult prevalences that we considered in chapter 7. There we saw that, with the exception of alcoholic psychosis, alcoholism, drug dependence, and personality and behavioural disorders, more women than men appeared in all categories on first admission to mental hospitals, and that there is a higher prevalence of mental illness among women generally. The discontinuity between childhood and adult psychopathology is striking and puzzling.

Gender role pressure has been invoked to explain the higher prevalence of mental illness in women. An analysis of the strains of the boy's gender role – growing up both in the family and in early formal education in an essentially female world, but one with emphases on masculinity and achievements – may not be sufficient to account for the higher prevalence of behavioural disturbance in boys. Biological factors as well as social mediators of stress reaction in boys need to be examined. It is tempting to imagine that the greater vulnerability of the male from conception and his developmental immaturity can explain the differential male reaction to psychological stress and deprivation.

Attachment and social development

The consequences of mothering and attachment that we have just considered are of a pathological nature. It is useful to ask whether in the normal course of development boys and girls acquire similar needs for other people and whether the strength of their attachment and dependence is generally the same. In narrative summaries, Maccoby and Jacklin (1974) examined research on dependence by grouping together reports of behaviour oriented towards the maintenance of closeness – proximity seeking, touching, and resistance to separation – and behaviour oriented towards eliciting social contact attention-seeking, social skills, and social responsiveness. Maintenance and eliciting contact directed both at adults and at other children were each examined. The general picture that emerged was one of little differentiation by sex.

The prevalence of divorce provides another setting within which to consider sex differences in dependence. Amato and Keith (1991) carried out an extensive meta-analysis that examined the effects of parental divorce on the well-being of children. Their seven dependent variables included academic achievement, conduct, both psychological and social adjustment, self-concept, and both mother–child and father–child relations. They concluded their analysis of sex differences by stating: 'when a large number of studies are considered, including studies that are infrequently cited, sex differences are not as pronounced as one might expect' (p. 33).

However, sex differences have been observed in the social behaviour of boys and girls described as having similar attachment bonds. Pre-school boys whose attachment was classified as insecure were described as aggressive and disruptive, while insecurely attached girls displayed greater dependence (Turner, 1991).

Mothering and attachment in the normal course of development appear to result in no major differences in girls' and boys' capacities for social responsiveness or dependence. The greater male vulnerability to stress may mean that boys find some situations more damaging than do girls, but knowledge about the caregiving process does not yet allow us to identity these situations with precision. Although Amato and Keith (1991) reported that boys showed poorer social adjustment following divorce, they could find no explanation for the sex difference on this variable, nor on any of the other six. At best, we conclude that most infants and young children develop satisfactorily when cared for by a few concerned people. These adults need not be female, but they must be sensitive to, and responsive to, the infant's needs.

Fathers and mothers

In this section we consider further the contribution of men to the care of children. Our discussion of mothering and attachment has included Geiger's (1996) thorough study of the affiliative and attachment behaviours of fathers who provide their infant's primary care. The past 25 years have seen the process of fathering become an important area for developmental psychological study (Biller, 1981; Lamb, 1976, 1997), and for evolutionary psychology (Draper and Harpending, 1988; Geary, 2000). The role of father has become an emerging issue within anthropology and sociology (Burgess, 1997; Coltrane, 1996; Hawkins and Dollahite, 1997; Marsiglio, 1995).

At one time, psychologists studied the effects of father absence, believing that, by comparing the intellectual, emotional, and social development of children growing up with and without fathers, they would learn about the contribution of fathers to those developments. Rather than focusing on fatherless families in order to understand the role of the father, we first consider the general impact on children of growing up in one-parent families. These constitute a frequent alternative to two-parent families in modern Britain and in many other Western countries. Second, we examine men's contributions to child care as described by their wives. Third, we compare the behaviour of fathers and mothers, having already noted that infants form attachments to fathers as well as to mothers. We begin our comparison by examining the nature of the infant's bond with its father and mother and then look briefly at each parent's share in play and in routine infant care. Finally, we examine the effects of fathers' personality on the development of their children.

One-parent families

We have already noted that children in the USA live increasingly in single-parent families. Michael Lamb stated in 1997 that approximately 50 per cent of American children spend some time in a single-parent family. Only 10 per cent of single-parent families are headed by fathers and they are usually unmarried (Bronfenbrenner et al., 1996). In Britain, 18 per cent of all one-parent families were headed by women who had divorced or never married the fathers of their children, but lone fathers headed only 2 per cent of single-parent families.

Before examining the effects on children of living in a single-parent family, it is useful to consider the transition process through divorce from life in a two-parent family to living with a single parent. For some children this is a brief phase, as remarriage and a two-parent reconstituted family follow quickly, and, sometimes, repeatedly. Results of the meta-analysis already considered (Amato and Keith, 1991) show that the well-being of children who experience family breakdown is compromised, but that the effects are small (median 0.14 standard deviation) and vary with the sophistication and era in which the research was undertaken. The report also emphasises the deleterious effects of parental conflict both before and following separation.

A serendipitous result of the increase in divorce in which one partner leaves a heterosexual marriage to become part of a gay or lesbian couple has been research designed to measure the impact on children of growing up in non-traditional families. The scientific evidence that these studies have produced has been used in courts to establish custody rights (Goode, 2001). The general tenor of this research has been to assert that the variety of family relationships has little consequence for child development. Stacey and Biblarz (2001) re-examined 21 such studies and argued that political correctness has led to a tendency to overlook differences in development, some of which may well be positive.

Despite the evidence of moderate negative effects of divorce, there is a long and sad litany that describes the effects of growing up in a single-parent family (Bronfenbrenner et al., 1996). It includes children from one-parent families more frequently truanting from school, performing less well at school, using drugs, cigarette smoking, and abusing alcohol more frequently than their peers from two-parent families, and, in the next generation, more frequently becoming one-parent families themselves.

These findings could reflect either the psychological effects of growing up in a one-parent family or general social differences between one- and two-parent families. The National Child Development Study showed that differences in the reading levels of 7- and 11-year-olds from one- and two-parent families were greatly reduced when socio-economic factors were taken into consideration (Ferri, 1976). However, arithmetic ability still remained low among children from fatherless families. This particular effect has also been reported in a number of other studies of father absence (Lamb, 1976).

Teachers rate children from one-parent families as less well adjusted (Mack, 1976). Mothers who raise children on their own claim that they have more problems with their children, especially with their daughters. These findings, based on adult ratings of children's behaviour, may be influenced by teachers' and mothers' negative stereotypes about growing up in one-parent families or 'broken homes' (Mack, 1976) and need to be treated with caution.

A study by Golombok and her colleagues provides clarification on this issue (Golombok et al., 1997). They compared children from intact heterosexual families with children raised in both heterosexual and lesbian single-mother families. Children rated themselves on cognitive and physical competencies, and maternal and peer acceptance. Despite being more securely attached to their mothers, children in single-parent families had a less positive perception of their cognitive and physical skills than did those children who grew up in two-parent families.

We cannot ignore the financial hardships experienced in one-parent families, particularly when that parent is the child's mother. Although two-parent families show important differences related to the father's occupation or social class, these are further accentuated in one-parent families (Ferri, 1976). When in the 1970s in Britain 6 per cent of two-parent families of manual workers received government assistance to bring their income up to a specified minimal level, the figure was 18 per cent in motherless families of manual workers, and reached 52 per cent in fatherless families. In the USA, socio-economic and ethnic factors interact to bring hardship for children in single-parent families. Among white and middle-class women with children, only 3 per cent are unmarried, but 42 per cent of black and poor women with children are unmarried (Bronfenbrenner, 1996). Some financial hardship may be ameliorated for children living with their lone fathers in the USA. There, both never-married and divorced fathers earned, on average, almost twice as much as never-married or divorced mothers (Bronfenbrenner et al., 1996).

There are difficulties other than those directly related to finances, but these vary little according to the biological sex of the single parent. For instance, 2 per cent of children in two-parent families spend some time in the care of the state; when divorced or separated men and women raise children on their own, the proportion rises to 12 per cent. The difficult life conditions of the one-parent family are further reflected in the greater number of schools these children attend. Both care and schooling are also influenced indirectly by economic factors.

Mothers' reports of fathers' caregiving

In mothers' reports of their husbands' contribution to child care we again see the influence of financial factors, even in two-parent families. The National Child Development Study provided information about fathers' contributions to child-rearing. When the children were 7 years old, and again when they were 11, their mothers were asked to estimate the amount of help they received from their husbands in looking after the children. More than half of mothers described fathers as taking an equal or a large share of responsibility for their children's care (Lambert and Hart, 1976). Of fathers, 10 per cent were described as leaving everything to the mother – these men tended to be the fathers of younger children in larger families or to have experienced financial difficulties in the year preceding the data collection.

Since these findings are based on wives' accounts of their husbands' behaviour, we may be tempted to dismiss them as subjective and biased. Hence it is important to find further evidence of the impact of fathers on their children's development. The National Child Development Study provided additional data linking parental interest and performance at school (Lambert and Hart, 1976). When both parents visited school to discuss their child's progress with teachers, their children's performance on both reading and arithmetic tests was 7 months ahead of that of children whose mothers alone visited the school. When neither parent took an interest in schooling, children were, on average, 13 months behind on both tests. Parental interest is important, and fathers can make a sizeable contribution to their children's school performance. These findings suggest that, from the viewpoint of a child, it is best to be one of few siblings and/or an older child in a family without financial problems in which the father takes an active interest in his children's development.

From the evidence that comes from the National Child Development Study, there can be little doubt that an actively involved father benefits his children.

Lamb (1997) also asserts that some of the most consistent findings from studies of increased father participation in child care since the 1980s have been their children's increased intellectual skills, their greater empathy, greater internal locus of control, and less gender stereotypic view of the social world.

Personality differences among fathers

The final issue that we consider is the impact on children of personality differences among fathers. We begin by returning once more to the study of attachment and then consider the influence of fathers' masculinity on that of their sons. Belsky (1996) has reported that fathers of securely attached sons tend to be both more agreeable and extroverted than are fathers of insecure or avoidantly attached sons. In addition, fathers of securely attached sons have more positive marriages and emotional satisfaction in work and in their families.

Both psychoanalytic and social learning theories agree that the model of masculine behaviour that the father provides is important for his son's gender development. Methodological problems encountered in the measurement of masculinity and femininity in chapter 2 reappear when studying the impact of the father on his children's development. If boys are first asked to rate themselves on a scale of masculinity and then asked to describe their fathers using the same scale, it is hardly surprising a similarity is found as the same person is making both ratings. A way around this problem has been to construct an artificial situation in which observers rate fathers' masculinity and mothers' femininity in terms of dominance. This technique has been used in studies in which parental dominance was related to pre-school and school-age children's gender-role preference (Hetherington, 1965). The child's gender-role preference was measured using a gender-neutral stick figure called IT, and children were asked to choose from masculine and feminine objects those they thought IT would like. Sons of dominant fathers tend to choose masculine objects.

Although the picture that at first emerged appeared straightforward, research has shown the process to be more complex (Biller, 1981). Boys' perceptions of their fathers' dominance have proved to be better predictors of their own gender preference and orientation than a psychological assessment of parental dominance. In addition, when fathers, who were rated high in dominance on the basis of their interactions with their wives, behave in a restrictive and controlling fashion towards their sons, the boys tend to be less masculine. Furthermore, unless the father is dominant and active in the family, his masculine behaviour in the world of work or leisure has little impact on his sons. Speaking again from the child's viewpoint, for a strong masculine identity to emerge in boys it is important to have a father who is actively involved in the home and takes a major role in family decision-making. Fathers who seek achievement primarily in the world of work and who leave the home to their wives may find their sons do not share their masculine preferences.

Parental participation is important for masculine development in boys and also in shaping a daughter's feminine gender identity (Biller, 1976). Biller viewed femininity positively: women were seen to be both independent and assertive, as well as nurturant and sensitive. A masculine father was believed to facilitate his daughter's feminine development. Indeed, some psychologists have argued that fathers have the potential to play a more important part than mothers in their children's gender differentiation (Biller, 1981; Heilbrun, 1965). Fathers make an important contribution to gender-differentiation – but within the limits of their children's dispositions and their own natures and positions in the wider society.

Conclusions

Our examination of the domestic sphere has raised many issues at various theoretical levels. It has led us to consider the changing nature of domestic life and the variety of family forms that are emerging. Roles within families are changing, and this has led us to frame questions such as: can women's domestic and workplace roles be combined satisfactorily? Can men become primary caregivers of infants? What are the particular hazards for children of reconstituted families? These topics raise issues primarily at the level of interpersonal interactions. We have also examined the effects of family life on intrapersonal processes, particularly on the attachment bonds that are formed within the family. An evolutionary psychological perspective supplements both psychoanalytic and social learning accounts throughout the chapter.

Further reading

Brody, L (1999). *Gender, Emotion and the Family*. Cambridge, MA and London: Harvard University Press.
    In this clearly presented text the material covered in chapter 8 is extended. In addition there is an innovative exploration of the influence of different family contexts upon sex differences in the development of emotional expression.
Hochschild, A. (1990) *The Second Shift: Working Parents and the Revolution at Home*. New York: Viking.
    This highly successful and widely read book by an American sociologist offers a vivid picture of the stresses of contemporary family life.
Lamb, M. E. (ed.) (1997). *The Role of the Father in Child Development* (3rd edn). New York: Wiley.
    This latest edition of a classic text provides a diverse examination of the role of fathers in child development.
Tiger, L. (1999). *The Decline of Males*. New York: Golden Books.
    Tiger's account of waning male power presents an apocalyptic vision of future family life.

9 Work, education, and occupational achievement

Introduction

In chapter 8 we discussed the family, traditionally regarded as a woman's sphere of influence and responsibility, and considered why it is that women look after children. Here we examine the world of work, viewed stereotypically as a man's sphere of influence, and ask why it is that men still occupy the most prestigious and highly valued positions.

The first explanation we consider is that men and women possess different abilities and skills. These might suit them for the world of family or work, or perhaps for different occupations within the world of work. It is often claimed in addition that sex differences in ability arise from biological differences. After examining the possibility that different abilities may underlie sex differences in work and achievement, we consider other explanations and discuss a number of related influences – principally the impact of gender stereotypes in the world of work, and motives for occupational choice.

Before discussing reasons for differences in occupational patterns, we must consider whether it is true that men achieve greater prestige and status in the world of work. We therefore begin by examining some statistics on career choices and earning potential.

Do men get better jobs and earn more money than women?

The short answer to this question is YES. Men still fill more top jobs and women are paid consistently less than their male counterparts, although one caveat is the considerable number of low-prestige manual jobs occupied by men (Glick et al., 1995). The preponderance of men in high-prestige occupations continues despite many changes in the Western world over the past 20 years in the proportion of women in the workforce, and in the occupations that employ them. Women have made progress in some respects, for example in the proportion training for professions such as medicine and the law in the USA (Hyde, 1999). Yet in other high-status professions, and particularly for leadership positions within these, the proportion of women is still very low, and many low-status occupations consist mainly of women.

Table 9.1 Participation in Modern Apprenticeships by sex

Type of apprenticeship	Girls %	Boys %
Electrical installation, plumbing, and construction	1	99
Motor industry	3	97
Engineering	3	97
Child care	97	3
Hairdressing	92	8
Travel services	86	14
Business administration	80	20
Information technology (IT)	33	67

Based on: DfEE Quality and Performance Improvement Division (1999).

We trace the development of the sex differences in occupational choice in three ways: by examining the career choices of English secondary-school students who do not go on to further education; by considering the age at which the pay differential first appears and charting its history; and by examining statistics from the USA illustrating the educational achievements and income of men and women.

English students who wish to leave secondary school at age 16 without pursuing further education are often encouraged by career advisors to take up a Modern Apprenticeship. Table 9.1 shows figures for the late 1990s, indicating that girls and boys begin to follow gender-stereotyped careers when they choose Modern Apprenticeships. As a consequence, the pay of girls begins to fall behind that of boys. When these data were collected, the average weekly wage of a person in engineering was £115, whereas in hairdressing it was £62. IT apprenticeships attracted the highest income at £140 per week, but only a third of entrants were female (Equal Opportunities Commission, 1999).

The British Government's Women's Unit (2000) reported on the income differential of men and women throughout their lifetimes. The definition of income included earnings, self-employment income, investments, pensions, and benefits. They reported that, on average, women earned £307 per week while men earned £423. This pay gap compared unfavourably with that in all European Union countries where, on average, women earned 76 per cent of the male average wage. At 73 per cent, Britain was among the least equal countries; the greatest gap occurred in Greece where the average pay of women was only 68 per cent of average male pay.

The study also found that, by the age of 20, women in the UK had, on average, £40 less income per week than their male counterparts. Pay discrimination also affected university graduates such that women with qualifications equal to those of men still earned less. Women's earnings peaked between 25 to 29 years of age, but they were then £100 per week less well off than men of the same age. The average income of women showed a dip throughout their 30s, recovered somewhat in their early 40s only to show even larger differences in retirement.

Table 9.2 Proportion of men and women gaining professional degrees in 1970 and 1995 (USA)

| | Total | | Percentage | | | |
| | | | Men | | Women | |
Professional degree	1970	1995	1970	1995	1970	1995
Medicine (MD)	8,314	15,537	91.6	61.2	8.4	38.8
Dentistry (DDS/DMD)	3,718	3,897	99.1	63.6	0.9	36.4
Law (LLB/JD)	14,916	39,349	94.6	57.4	5.4	42.6
Theology (BD/MDiv/MHL)	5,296	5,978	97.7	74.3	2.3	25.7

Based upon: US Bureau of the Census (1998), Table 327, p. 202.

A curious twist in the British statistics is the rise, over the past 20 years, of employment among women in their 50s and the decline among men of this age. A report from the Office for National Statistics (1999) showed that between 1986 and 1998 the proportion of women in work increased from 55 to 62 per cent. However, over the longer period from 1979 to 1998, the proportion of employed men in their 50s declined from 84 to 69 per cent. In part, this change can be explained by shifting occupational opportunities. In Britain, there has been a substantial decline in manufacturing, and many jobs in heavy industry have disappeared, while the service sector, including tourism, catering, and cleaning, which are stereotypically female occupations, has grown.

There have been dramatic changes in the educational and occupational achievements of women in the USA over the past 25 years, but women's income still lags behind that of men. Table 9.2 shows that the proportion of women attaining professional qualifications has grown rapidly. Even in dentistry and theology, fields that have seen little increase in the total numbers qualifying over the past 25 years, the proportion of women has increased substantially.

The award of Ph.D.s between 1971 and 1995 also demonstrates a dramatic increase in the proportion of women (US Bureau of the Census, 1998, Table 326). Even traditionally female domains have seen increases: education from 21 per cent in 1971 to 62 per cent in 1995, home economics from 61 to 74.5 per cent, and library sciences from 28.2 to 63.6 per cent Perhaps more interesting in terms of sex differences in abilities is the increase in the proportion of women gaining Ph.D.s in engineering and engineering technology. This rose from 0.6 per cent in 1971 to 11.9 per cent in 1995, and a similar rise was apparent for mathematics, from 7.6 to 22.1 per cent. We return to the question of the specific intellectual abilities of men and women in the next section.

Given the great improvement in women's education, we would expect changes in earned income. Statistics are available showing the median incomes of men and women in the USA from 1980 to 1996 in constant 1996 dollars, and their mean incomes by educational attainment in 1996. Table 9.3 shows that there has been an improvement in the median incomes of women, while that of men has scarcely

Table 9.3 Median incomes by sex in constant 1996 dollars from 1980 to 1996 (USA)

	1980	1990	1995	1996
Men	23,888	24,361	23,228	23,834
Women	9,380	12,089	12,488	12,815
Percentage of women's income as a proportion of men's income	39.3	49.6	53.8	53.8

Based upon: US Bureau of the Census (1998), Table 753, p. 476.

Table 9.4 Men's and women's mean income in 1996 dollars by educational attainment (USA)

	Men	Women	Women's income as a percentage of men's
Elementary school	20,153	15,150	75.2
High school 1–3 years	25,283	17,313	68.5
High school graduate	32,521	21,893	67.2
Some college	38,491	25,889	67.3
Bachelor's degree or more	63,127	41,339	65.5

Based upon: US Bureau of the Census (1998), Table 754, p. 476.

changed over the 16-year period. However, women still have a long way to go to achieve equal pay.

Inspection of Table 9.4 suggests that greater educational attainment had little influence in providing women with more equal pay. Examining mean income by age, within the group showing the greatest disparity – university graduates – might indicate that younger women are catching up their male peers. However, the data in Table 9.5 appear to echo the decline in income of English women in their 30s described above. An increasing differential with age suggests that abilities alone do not account for sex differences in pay. In the next section, we examine whether there are measurable differences in the abilities of men and women. We begin by examining the hypothesis that men's abilities are more variable than women's. In the absence of appreciable differences in the average performance of men and women, this hypothesis has been invoked to explain the greater occupational achievement of men, but has been attacked as 'pernicious" by Noddings (1992) and by other feminists.

Are there more men with high intellectual ability?

As we have just observed, contemporary statistics still show a male superiority in occupations and income. In the sections that follow, we consider the intellectual and social factors which may account for these inequalities. Here

Table 9.5 Mean income of college graduates in 1996 dollars by age and sex (USA)

	Men	Women	Women's income as a percentage of men's
18 to 24 years old	27,257	24,980	91.6
25 to 34 years old	44,355	34,132	77.0
35 to 44 years old	70,035	46,923	67.0
45 to 54 years old	72,461	45,012	62.1
55 to 64 years old	71,070	41,342	58.2

Based upon: US Bureau of the Census (1998), Table 754, p. 476.

we survey the evidence and theory concerning differences in intellectual ability. We first examine the variability hypothesis and then explore evidence of differences in specific abilities.

The hypothesis that men have a wider range of talents than women has a history that predates the development of intelligence tests. In 1885, Nordau wrote 'Woman is as a rule, typical; man, is individual. The former has average, the latter exceptional features' (Noddings, 1992, p. 85). Later, IQ tests were constructed so that, on average, men and women would score similarly (Archer and Lloyd, 1985; Halpern and LaMay, 2000). None the less, the overall distribution of IQ scores has been presented in support of the variability hypothesis. More men were reported at both the lower and higher ends, and more women in the middle. Occasionally this has been referred to as the mediocrity-of-women hypothesis (Heim, 1970). This evidence has been invoked to explain sex differences in exceptional occupational attainment. The presence of more men at the lower end of the distribution has been conveniently overlooked in most discussions.

The variability hypothesis still evokes controversy, but recent data and analyses may bring some closure to the debate (Feingold, 1992b, 1994b; Hedges and Nowell, 1995). Feingold's 1992b paper offers a thorough historical review of research on variability. He noted that in the 1930s an assumption of equal variability replaced that of a hypothesised greater male variability. The classic review of Maccoby and Jacklin (1974) established the superiority of average male performance on tests of mathematical and spatial abilities and higher female performance on verbal tests (chapter 1). Their findings were based largely on results describing means or averages. Their evidence concerning variability was much more limited.

Feingold (1992b, 1995) illustrated the differences between analyses that examine mean differences and those that consider variability. He provided distributions showing that the slightly higher male average on tests of mathematical reasoning could derive from similar distributions of male and female scores, greater male variability, or even from smaller male variability. Knowing the average differences per se tells us nothing about the distribution of scores. As we noted in chapter 1, relatively small sex differences in means and variability in abilities may have important implications for the observed differences in success at work and income. Hedges and Nowell (1995) provided a numerical example:

> a mean difference of 0.3 standard deviations, which would be judged 'small' by the convention of effect size introduced by Cohen (1977), coupled with a variance difference of 15%, could lead to 2.5 times as many males as females in the top 5% of the test score distribution and more than 6 times as many males in the top 0.1%. (p. 42)

Thus, in occupations requiring exceptional skills and abilities, male eminence might be accounted for by small mean differences combined with greater male variability.

An argument about the combined effects of mean and variability differences may be statistically compelling, but there are still questions about the quality of the data to which statistics are applied. Data used in the past to support the variability hypothesis have been notoriously controversial and biased. Not only were there only 19 women included among the 1,000 individuals in the first edition of *American Men of Science* (1906), but it was 1971 before the title was changed (Nodding, 1992). More than 80 years ago, Hollingworth (1914, 1922) argued that social factors accounted for the greater numbers of men in institutions for the mentally retarded, as well as their overrepresentation among the eminent. She contended that women of equally low ability could be cared for at home, while such men were exposed by the demands of earning a living and that this led to their institutionalisation in greater numbers. Furthermore, she asserted that women were excluded from careers in which they might gain distinction, and hence had failed to appear among the eminent.

More relevant to our concerns are sources of bias in data from tests of mental abilities. For example, Terman's (1925) study of gifted individuals, which reported more boys than girls with IQs over 140, suffered from bias in recruitment procedures; it was teachers who identified the children originally selected for inclusion in the study. In a thorough review of test performance data, McNemar and Terman (1936) concluded that the variability hypothesis could not be accepted or refuted on the basis of then available evidence. Their finding, that the performance of male university students was indeed more variable than that of female university students, underlines the importance of the samples chosen to test the hypothesis.

Data from a number of representative mental test surveys, involving samples drawn from the national population, have become available in the past twenty years in the USA. These have finally provided consistent results. Both Feingold (1992b) and Hedges and Nowell (1995) have reported that, despite average sex differences being small and relatively stable over time, test score variances of males were generally larger than those of females. Feingold found that males were more variable than females on tests of quantitative reasoning, spatial visualisation, spelling, and general knowledge. From this evidence of greater male variability, Feingold has argued that both measures of central tendency, averages, and variability need to be considered when describing sex differences in mental abilities. Hedges and Nowell go one step further and demonstrate that, with the exception of performance on tests of reading comprehension, perceptual speed, and associative memory, more males than females were observed among high-scoring individuals.

The question these results raise is whether differences at extremes can explain occupational segregation. While a greater concentration of males in science and technology might have resulted from their higher overall spatial and mathematical abilities, little has been said about the lower end of the distribution. As jobs in heavy industry have disappeared, perhaps it is men with lower mental abilities who are increasingly being left behind and rendered unemployable. If this is combined with a young age and little stake in mainstream society, it is likely to be associated with many other personal and social problems, notably mental illness, drug taking, and crime. Whatever the impact of ability differences, these have to be weighed alongside the influence of social expectations and stereotypes, about which there is considerable research, which we consider after examining evidence about differences in intellectual skills.

Specific cognitive abilities

In chapter 1, we mentioned briefly sex differences in specific mental abilities described in Maccoby and Jacklin's (1974) review. They concluded that, on average, men perform better than women on tests of spatial and mathematical ability, although women may perform better than men on tests of verbal ability. These and other results from psychometric tests are often used to explain and justify occupational sex differences. It is usually implied that the psychological ability is stable through time and is biologically based. Thus, occupational recruitment patterns are explained in terms of differences in psychological traits, and, in turn, these traits are explained in terms of biological differences between men and women.

Explanations of this type were offered to account for the predominance of women in clerical occupations and of men in scientific and technological occupations. The characteristics of perceptual speed and verbal fluency were said to suit women rather than men for secretarial work (Broverman et al., 1968; Garai and Scheinfeld, 1968). The higher spatial and mathematical abilities of the male population were said to fit men for scientific and technological professions (Garai and Scheinfeld, 1968; Heim, 1970). Here, we restrict our detailed discussion of differences in mental abilities and their explanations to spatial ability. This well-established sex difference has been used as an explanation for scientific and technological occupations being predominantly male, and there is research showing that it is indeed influenced by hormonal fluctuations.

Spatial ability may be viewed as an organism's capacity to navigate in a three-dimensional space and to succeed in locating its goals. This ability is assessed differently in different species: rodents are tested running mazes, and humans, while sometimes assessed in mazes, are more usually presented with batteries of other tests. These include paper-and-pencil tasks which require mental rotation, transformation and manipulation of visually presented stimuli, estimation of water levels, and, more recently, spatial memory tasks that demand the recall of objects, locations, or both together.

In chapter 1, we referred to Hyde's (1981) meta-analysis of sex differences in spatial ability, which concluded that the overall difference was around half a standard deviation. However, when spatial tasks involving mental rotation in three-dimensional space were analysed, the difference was found to be greater (Masters and Sanders, 1993; Voyer et al., 1995; Willingham and Cole, 1997).

Both maze learning ability and performance on a traditional battery of paper-and-pencil tests were measured among male and female university students in Canada (Moffat et al., 1998). All students undertook five learning trials on each of two computer generated mazes as well as completing a verbal and spatial test battery. Once again, a male superiority was reported on the paper-and-pencil tests of spatial ability, and male students also made fewer errors and required less time to learn the mazes. The effect sizes were very large for both measures of maze learning (errors, d = 1.40; time, 1.59). A strong positive correlation was found between maze and test-task performance.

A study carried out in Japan and Canada has added to the growing cross-cultural evidence demonstrating a consistent male superiority in spatial ability (Silverman et al., 1996). Two spatial tasks were used. The male advantage on the mental rotation task showed the predicted very large effect size in both samples (d = 1.36 and 1.19 in Japan and Canada respectively). The effect sizes on tests of space relations was smaller (d = 0.31 and 0.46, respectively). Two aspects of this study are of interest. First, it strengthens the hypothesis that there is a biological component to the male superiority in spatial processing, as it provides additional cross-cultural data alongside that drawn from studies in England (Lynn, 1992), India, South Africa, and Australia (Porteus, 1965), Scotland and Sierra Leone (Berry, 1966). Despite different cultural contexts and socialisation, male performance on these spatial tasks is superior to that of females. Second, the difference in the size of effects suggests that different tests may be assessing different aspects of spatial processing and that the male superiority varies in magnitude across different types of spatial processing.

The male superiority in spatial processing across cultures and tasks has led to an exploration of possible biological influences. In particular, there have been investigations of sex differences in spatial ability among other species, and studies of hormonal influences on spatial ability. It is known that similar sex differences occur in some rodent species (see below) and in rhesus monkeys, at least at young ages (Lacreuse et al., 1999). A number of studies have provided evidence for hormonal influences (Geary, 1999; Janowsky et al., 1998; O'Connor et al., 2001b, c). There is an apparently paradoxical relationship between spatial ability and circulating testosterone in adulthood. Women's performance improves as their level of testosterone increases, whereas men with moderate testosterone levels are better than those with lower or higher levels. The most likely interpretation is that moderate levels of the hormone improve spatial performance, but higher levels make it worse. Other studies (e.g., Phillips and Silverman, 1997) show changes in spatial performance across the menstrual cycle, higher scores being found around the menstrual phase when oestrogen levels are low.

In pursuit of a complete evolutionary explanation of the pattern of sex differences in human spatial abilities, Silverman and Eals (1992) drew attention to forms of spatial processing where a female superiority might be expected. We referred to their hypothesis in chapter 3, in relation to the origins of psychological sex differences. Looking to early hominid societies that were assumed to be based upon hunting and gathering, they pointed out that, while men hunted and required navigational skills related to tracking, women foraged and needed to remember the location of plant resources. The spatial specialisation associated with foraging has been identified as spatial memory, and there is now extensive evidence for a female superiority in this type of spatial task (Silverman and Phillips, 1998), which involves different areas of the brain to those involved in tasks showing male superiority (Geary, 1999). Women outperform men in memory for both frequencies and locations of objects, whether this learning is incidental or directed. For the incidental learning of locations in a naturalistic setting, females' mean scores exceeded males' by 60 to 70 per cent for measures of both recognition and recall.

Although the evidence is clear, it is by no means certain that the contrasting spatial abilities of men and women did arise from their hunter–gatherer past, since it appears not to be restricted to the human species. As indicated in chapter 3, Gaulin and Fitzgerald (1989) proposed the competing evolutionary explanation for the ubiquitous male superiority in spatial ability, that it was characteristic of species with a polygynous mating system. The relevance of this to humans is that the sex difference in body size is similar to that found in other species whose mating system is mildly polygynous. Gaulin and Fitzgerald argued that, in polygynous species, spatially adept males would have a reproductive advantage as it would enable them to control large territories. Females, on the other hand, in both monogamous and polygynous species, inhabit small territories. Hence, they predicted and then observed a male superiority only in polygynous species of mammals (Gaulin et al., 1990).

In a recent study designed to clarify inconsistencies from published studies of spatial memory, Gaulin and colleagues collected new data from humans (McBurney et al., 1997). They employed a commercial game called Memory™ and a mental rotation task. American male university students performed better than female students on the mental rotation task ($d = 0.67$) but in the game, Memory™, it was women who performed better ($d = -0.87$). Performance on the two tasks was correlated for women but not for men. This suggested that spatial ability is a multidimensional trait involving different kinds of processing. These, in turn, may have provided different selective advantages to males and females in ancestral environments. Furthermore, the authors concluded that the commercial game provided a valid analogue of foraging, and that their results supported Silverman's foraging hypothesis (although again we should note the misgivings outlined in chapter 3).

This exploration of spatial memory raises once again the issue of bias in research on sex differences (chapter 1). It was only when Silverman considered the activities of female hominids that the possibility of a female advantage in spatial memory was even raised as a possible line of investigation. We are left to speculate whether in this domain, in which a male superiority has long been accepted, there are other processes in which females excel – processes that have been overlooked because they have never been placed on the research agenda.

Our brief examination of spatial skills has provided some convincing evidence that there are sex differences in these skills, and that, contrary to what was believed for a long time, these occur in both directions. But the exploration of spatial skills – or any other ability differences for that matter – can only explain very specific patterns of work skills. It still leaves us a long way from explaining why it is that men still occupy a wide range of the most prestigious and highly valued positions in the world of work, notably those involving leadership roles. If we were to consider the full extent of sex differences in skills, including female superiority in short-term memory, verbal fluency, and non-verbal skills such as judging emotional cues from facial expressions (Geary, 1999), there is little fit between these and the numbers of men and women in particular occupations. If there were, we should expect more women in managerial positions that require considerable ability in what used to be called 'man management'. An overall view of men's and women's skills, both cognitive and social, indicates that they are indeed different, but not in a way that could easily explain occupational differences.

Gender stereotypes in occupations and training

In chapter 2 we considered gender stereotypes in some detail, and described research by Orlofsky and his colleagues on activities and interests that were stereotyped according to the sex with which they were typically associated, or seen as desirable for (e.g., Orlofsky, 1981). Occupations, in the form of vocational interests, formed an important component of Orlofsky's analysis of gender-stereotyped activities. The list he obtained conforms to the traditional commonsense notion of 'men's work' and 'women's work'. Although there has been some loosening of the structural and psychological barriers that maintain this distinction over the years since the 1960s, there are still many occupations whose composition reflects traditional stereotypic beliefs.

Beliefs about what is appropriate for men and women in the occupational sphere do not form a simple cause and effect relationship with the pattern of occupations taken up by men and women. They form part of an interrelated system which includes, in the earlier years, interests, aspirations, and opportunities in particular types of school subjects, which form the basis for later occupational decisions. Later, men and women may have different training opportunities that are reflected in apprenticeships, professional training, and higher education.

Educational interests are just as subject to gender stereotyping as are vocational and other interests. The way these gender stereotypes have been investigated is slightly different from the method used for other stereotypic interests. Instead of asking which of a list of activities are typical of, and desirable for, a woman and a man, particular school subjects have been individually presented to children or young adults for them to assess along a number of descriptive dimensions, including masculine–feminine. This is based on the traditional method of measuring attitudes, the semantic differential (Osgood et al., 1957), and it was first used by Weinreich-Haste (1979, 1981) to examine the extent to which common school subjects were viewed as masculine or feminine by British college students and schoolchildren in the 1970s.

The British school curriculum was changed in the late 1980s, so that many of the subjects examined in the original study of schoolchildren are no longer relevant. In addition, there is evidence that the gender associations of common subjects, such as Mathematics and English, have changed so that they are no longer seen as gender stereotyped (Archer, 1992d). An examination of 17 subjects that were on the revised UK secondary-school curriculum (Archer and Macrae, 1991) found that subjects such as personal and social education, religious education, and home economics were perceived as feminine, whereas craft, design and technology, information technology, and physics were viewed as masculine. Another study at around the same time (Archer and Freedman, 1989) involved British further-education college students taking Advanced level[1] courses. As expected, engineering, physics, chemistry, and mathematics were viewed as masculine, with sociology, psychology, French, biology, and English being seen as feminine.

Male chauvinism or masculine chauvinism?

In chapter 2, we discussed two views of stereotypes: the first that they are predictive devices, and the second that they represent justifications for the existing social arrangements. Applying these different views to the gender stereotyping of occupations produces two alternative perspectives: either that these follow from the numbers of men and women in them, or that they follow from the implied traits associated with them. Glick (1991) referred to these two alternatives respectively as 'male chauvinism' and 'masculine chauvinism'. For many occupations, the two features will be present together. For example, nursing is viewed as being predominately a female occupation, and also a *feminine* occupation in that it requires a caring disposition.

These two features have been separated in studies designed to assess which one is more important in determining how people judge the gender connotations of occupations. Krefting et al. (1978) presented US business students with a packet

[1] British 'A-levels' are immediately pre-undergraduate level.

of 96 cards, each describing a job in terms of its occupational classification, the proportion of men and women in it, and its required characteristics. In one study, the students were asked to classify each job in terms of whether it was more suitable for a man or a woman, and in a second they were asked to rate them in terms of perceived masculinity or femininity. In both cases, the proportion of the men and women already in the occupation was the primary feature used for assigning its suitability or gender category. Similarly, for the masculine–feminine ratings of school subjects described in the previous section, there is a correspondence with boys' and girls' preferences for the subjects (Ormerod, 1981), and with the sex ratio of examination passes (Central Statistics Office, 1985; Murphey, 1979).

Male-dominated occupations are seen not only as more masculine, but also as having higher status. Research from the 1970s showed that manipulating information about the supposed proportion of women in an occupation influenced its perceived occupational prestige: the larger the proportion of women, the lower the prestige (Touhey, 1974). These findings were consistent with observations that certain occupations had declined in status over the years as the numbers of women had increased, and with cross-national comparisons of the status of occupations which differ in their sex ratio in different countries (Archer and Lloyd, 1985). However, we should also caution that several subsequent studies have not replicated Touhey's results (Glick, 1991).

It would be surprising if characteristics assumed to be required for particular occupations played no part in determining whether they are viewed as masculine or feminine. There are everyday examples of traits associated with an activity or object being used to infer its masculinity or femininity. A British advertisement for language-teaching software referred to the programmes as the 'French mistress' and the 'German master'. Pet food products are labelled 'good girl cat treats' and 'good boy dog treats'. It is clear to everyone that both German speakers and cats come in roughly equal numbers of both sexes. Therefore the gender connotations must have been derived from implied associations between German and masculinity, and cats and femininity (presumably because German is viewed as an instrumental language and cats are viewed as nurturant animals).

Glick (1991) found evidence that a similar process applied to occupational prestige. People were asked to rate 46 jobs in terms of their association with gender-traits from Bem's BSRI (chapter 2), their proportion of men and women, prestige, and salaries. The jobs were divided into those rated as having over 60 per cent women, those with over 60 per cent men, and those that were in between. They were classified as masculine, feminine, androgynous, and undifferentiated (chapter 2) on the basis of the BSRI ratings. Overall, the assigned trait categories were broadly associated with the sex-ratio classifications, but there was also some significant dissociation between the two. Examining the influence of masculine and feminine traits showed that both were viewed as being required for gender-neutral and women's jobs. The prestige of a job was associated with its perceived masculinity, but not with its perceived sex ratio. Masculinity also provided the best predictor of salary, although the proportion of women in a job was additionally (negatively) related to this. We should note that, in Glick's study, salaries and sex ratios were estimated by the study participants, but they were very close to real figures obtained from other sources.

Based on the view that stereotypes serve to justify inequalities in a social system (chapter 2), Cejka and Eagly (1999) obtained ratings of a large number of familiar occupations along 56 attributes that might be viewed as necessary for success in each occupation. The attributes were simplified into six gender stereotyped dimensions, consisting of appearance, personality, and cognitive skills, each with a masculine and feminine version. They also obtained a number of other ratings of each occupation, including how attractive it was to men and women, and its sex ratio. The main finding was that the real and perceived sex segregation in an occupation was associated with the stereotypic attributes regarded as necessary for it. If an occupation was male dominated, masculine personality and physical attributes were viewed as essential, whereas, if it was female dominated, feminine personality or physical attributes were seen as essential for it. Occupations also gained prestige according to the extent to which they were viewed as requiring masculine personality or cognitive attributes, but only the personality attributes were associated with higher earnings.

We should note that, contrary to Touhey's well-known earlier study, both Glick (1991) and Cejka and Eagly (1999) found that people associated the prestige of an occupation with the attributes associated with it. Overall, the evidence supports a link between stereotypic attributes associated with an occupation, its sex ratio, prestige, and rate of pay. Needless to say, male occupations have the advantage in terms of pay and prestige.

Does sex bias operate in occupational decisions?

These studies show that gender stereotypes are connected with the distribution of men and women in occupations. How this pattern has arisen is another matter. It could arise from personal preferences, women preferring occupations requiring feminine qualities and men preferring those requiring masculine ones. Or it could arise from other people choosing women for feminine occupations and men for masculine ones because of their perceived qualities. In other words, the assumed general characteristics of men and women, generated by gender stereotypes, might affect judgements made about their work performance or potential, or indeed their suitability for particular occupations. The main issue concerns judgements about women's achievements when they seek to enter occupations that are traditionally the domain of men, whose assumed characteristics tend to be those that are seen as fitting them for higher-status masculine occupations. Women have traditionally been associated with the domestic sphere, and their assumed characteristics tend to be those that fit them for this rather than the world of work, or for occupations that are seen as requiring domestic skills, such as child care, cooking, or cleaning. Specific stereotypic traits associated with women might, if applied to a woman in a masculine occupation, count against her. For example, there are beliefs that women are not expected to achieve as highly as men, and that they are not expected to achieve in particular domains which are viewed as more difficult and to be the province of men. This type of stereotypic reasoning would apply particularly strongly to leadership roles, which are viewed as requiring agentic, masculine, characteristics (Eagly and Karau, in press).

Research has investigated the extent to which gender stereotypes are used to judge an individual in preference to specific and relevant information about that individual's performance. Studies on the impact of stereotypes (e.g., Locksley and Colten, 1979) show that they are most readily activated under the following conditions: when judgements are being made about another person rather than oneself; when other information about the person is lacking; and when category membership (in this case sex) is viewed as salient. If all you know is that there is a woman applicant for a vacancy in an engineering company, stereotypes are more likely to be activated than if a woman who is personally known to you applies for a position as a child-care worker.

Deaux (1976) found that people use gender stereotypes to make attributions about the reasons why men and women do well or poorly at specific tasks. For masculine tasks, good performance by a man is generally attributed to ability (a stable cause) to a greater extent than is good performance by a woman. Unstable causes such as effort or luck are more likely to be used to explain good performance by a woman. Failure is also judged differently in that it is more likely to be attributed to a stable cause such as lack of ability in the case of a woman and an unstable cause in the case of a man.

A more recent meta-analysis (Swim and Sanna, 1996) of over 50 studies has largely confirmed the overall interpretation in terms of stable versus unstable causal attributions identified by Deaux, but with a number of caveats. Effect sizes for the different attributions applied to men and women are generally small, and they apply more to masculine tasks, where the observer has an expectation that men will perform better than women. Thus, if the actual performance is in line with this, it is attributed to a stable trait, ability, in the case of a man, or lack of ability in the case of a woman. If the actual performance is inconsistent with the expectation, it is attributed to a more temporary or unstable cause, such as luck or effort, or the nature of the specific task. Swim and Sanna also found that the attributions are applied to a greater extent when explaining failure than when explaining success.

Swim and Sanna (1996) identified an additional problem with the studies they reviewed, which was that the measurements of the different sorts of attributions all tended to be related to one another: in opting for one sort of attribution, the participant would automatically rule out others, so that it was difficult to tell which of the different options was the important one. The only attribution that was shown to differ using independent measures was that based on effort, women seen as making more effort than men when successful on masculine tasks, and men seen as making less effort than women when unsuccessful on masculine tasks.

These studies concern the explanations people use to explain the performance of men and women. More attention has been paid to the way in which stereotypes about men and women might affect how people judge their level of performance. The two main areas on which this research has been conducted are job-selection interviews and assessment of students' work.

First we consider a study on possible bias in occupational selection decisions. Based on earlier studies, Glick et al. (1988) reasoned that a person would have a greater chance of being offered a position if the stereotype about people in that occupation and the characteristics of the applicant were congruent. For example, if the occupation were child care – associated with nurturance – a person is more likely to be hired if their application indicates that they are a nurturant person, or if it can be assumed that they are nurturant. This 'goodness of fit' view of occupational selection would account for sex bias as follows. Most desirable, high-paying, high-status, occupations are stereotypically masculine, and are associated with masculine instrumental traits. Men are more likely than women to possess instrumental traits, and therefore men's characteristics will be more congruent with the occupational requirements of these positions than will those of women. Men are therefore more likely to be hired.

This view of sex bias concentrates on the presumed traits of men and women, and their match or mismatch with occupational requirements. It can be contrasted with the simple sex-bias hypothesis, where the assumption is that, for a masculine occupation, women will be discriminated against simply because they are women, irrespective of the traits they possess or are presumed to possess.

Glick et al. (1988) set about testing which might be correct, by designing a study to determine whether the effects of sex bias in selection could be overcome by providing counter-stereotypic information. If a woman applies for a vacancy in a masculine occupation, is she as likely as a man to be offered the position if her background indicates that she has masculine instrumental traits and interests? They asked 212 business professionals (mostly men) to read 6 different résumés where the names indicated a man or a woman, and the information indicated past experience with masculine occupations, hobbies, and interests, or feminine ones, or gender-neutral ones.

Each participant rated the target individuals' chances of being interviewed for three occupations, which were either masculine (sales manager in a heavy machine firm), or feminine (dental receptionist and secretary), or neutral (administrative assistant in a bank). Participants also rated the target people on masculine and feminine traits.

The findings supported, in part, both of the original hypotheses. Men were favoured for the masculine occupation, women for the feminine one, and neither sex for the neutral occupation. Women were discriminated against just because they were women in the case of the masculine occupation. However, if their résumé indicated that they had instrumental characteristics, they were discriminated against much less. On the other hand, providing male applicants for the dental-receptionist post with expressive characteristics did not increase their chances of being interviewed.

The trait ratings of these individuals indicated that supplying gender-stereotypic information about their activities led to them being rated accordingly on the traits: for example, a woman who had masculine leisure interests would be rated as instrumental. Despite the effectiveness of opposite gender-stereotypic information in influencing the stereotypic traits that were ascribed to a person, when a woman was applying for a masculine occupation, there still remained a degree of sex bias that was independent of her presumed characteristics.

In a similar study involving 35 occupations, Glick (1991) again found that applicants were matched to jobs on the basis of information about both their personality traits and their sex. In this study they also investigated the impact of the proportion of women to men in the occupations. After controlling for the influence of personality traits, a linear trend was found in the preference for women over men according to the percentage of women in the jobs. Thus, for hiring decisions, a high proportion of women in an occupation would lead to more women being appointed, and a high proportion of men would lead to more men being appointed.

A further study (Hartman et al., 1991) was concerned with promotion rather than hiring decisions. Students of business studies were asked to make decisions about two comparable masculine and feminine occupations, an installation supervisor and a word processing supervisor. It was mainly the person's personal characteristics that influenced the promotion decision, regardless of the gender association of the job, the sex of the employee, or the sex of the person making the decision. In particular, women employees with masculine characteristics were viewed as most promotable.

These experimental studies were designed to separate the influence of different variables associated with sex and gender on hiring and promotional decisions. They form part of a wider range of studies on what is termed 'sex bias', which usually means discrimination against women. These also include studies of possible bias in the judgements of students' work. Of course, if this could be clearly demonstrated, it would be a cause of concern for students and lecturers alike. There have been several claims of such bias based on analyses of the numbers of men and women obtaining particular degree classes in the UK (Kiley, 1988; Weedon, 1982), but these are unsound statistically and in other ways (Archer, 1992e). Likewise, comparisons of students' degree marks before and after the introduction of anonymous marking (which would largely eliminate sex bias) generally indicate little evidence of sex bias (Bradley, 1984; Hartley, 1992; Newstead and Dennis, 1990; Warren, 1997).

North American psychologists have adopted an experimental approach, of the type used by Glick and his colleagues for hiring decisions, to examine possible bias in educational decisions. Instead of a middle-aged male lecturer marking real students' work, introductory psychology students are asked to rate a piece of work supposedly written by a male or a female student. Although such studies manage to introduce experimental control, they are artificial. Yet the artificiality is likely to err in the direction of reducing bias.

The first study of this type was by Goldberg (1968). He presented participants with six articles differing in subject matter, assigned to either a male or female author, by using the names John T. Mackay or Joan T. Mackay. The articles were rated on a number of evaluative dimensions, and evidence of bias against women authors was found for 3 of the 6 articles, involving law and city planning – which were chosen as masculine topics – and for linguistics – which was chosen as one of two neutral topics. There was no evidence of bias in the other gender-neutral topic, and in two feminine stereotypic topics.

Goldberg's study has entered psychological folklore, and has been frequently (and incorrectly) cited in texts as having shown overwhelming evidence for sex bias in all of the topics investigated. Many similar studies have been carried out since, with variable findings. Swim et al. (1989) reported a meta-analysis of studies available at the time, together with those involving occupational choice (like that of Glick and his colleagues). Aggregating all studies together indicated a small degree of pro-male bias[2] in evaluations.

To obtain an idea of the extent of the overall or average bias, imagine that there are 200 marked students' essays, half with a woman's name and half with a man's name. The male-authored essays are placed in one pile, and the female-authored ones in another pile. Each successive pair of male and female-authored essays is taken off the respective piles, and the marks compared. If we assume that there is no real difference in the standard of the male and female essays, and that there are no tied marks, the overall bias found by Swim and her colleagues is such that there will be 56 pairs where the male author has been given the higher mark, and 44 where the female author has been given the higher mark.[3] A similar calculation for studies involving simulated job applications, like that of Glick et al. (1988), revealed a higher pro-male bias, with 60 pairs showing the male applicant preferred over the female one.

Put in these terms, there is some reason to be concerned about the extent of the bias against women shown by these studies. If the size of the bias is expressed in terms of the conventional psychological statistic of the proportion of the variance in marks accounted for by bias, it does not seem large (it is less than 5%), and it is relatively small when compared to other psychological effects. This could lead to the conclusion that there is hardly evidence of a great injustice, which would be premature because it omits several other important considerations.

The first is that an apparently low level of bias can assume practical importance at high levels of performance, for example where we are dealing with selection for a high-status occupation. We have already described Feingold's explanation of how a small *average* sex difference in an ability can be transformed into one that

---

[2] The mean weighted effect size was d = 0.05 to 0.08; for masculine stereotypic topics it was 0.10.
[3] These calculations were made by the first author, using the Binomial Effect Size Display of Rosenthal (1990, 1991).

is much larger, and matters in practical terms, at the top end of the distribution. Although this was applied to ability differences, the same statistical principle will apply irrespective of the source of the difference, whether it arises from within (ability differences) or from without (sex bias).

Career success is a well-studied topic, and Rosenbaum (1979, 1984) has characterised an individual's progress through an organisation as involving a series of implicit tournaments, with success at early stages influencing subsequent career progression. Martell et al. (1996) were concerned with how sex bias could affect one aspect of this process, the impact of the repeated selection processes that lead to promotion in an organisation. This form of tournament could magnify the influence of a series of small biases operating at each stage, so that they culminate in a large overall effect. How this would operate was demonstrated by a computer simulation which showed that, with a pro-male bias involving 5 per cent of the variance, and eight promotion steps, the percentage of women at top levels would be 29. With a figure of 1 per cent, there would be 35 per cent women at top levels. Again, we have a process that will magnify small biases, in this case through the impact of cumulative selection.

A third consideration is that, although the overall effect found by Swim et al. (1989) was relatively small, this figure hides considerable variation between different conditions, some of which may produce no sex bias, and others a much larger degree of bias. An analysis of the conditions under which higher levels of bias are likely to operate (Archer, 1992e) led to the following conclusions. Sex bias was strongest when only the sex of the applicant, or writer of an essay, is known, which is consistent with what is known about when stereotypes affect people's judgements. Even a paragraph of information about someone decreases the magnitude of bias 10- to 12-fold in experimental studies. However, this information must be relevant to the task being judged (Heilman, 1984; Locksley et al., 1980).

If the criteria for judging a person are completely clear-cut, there will be little scope for bias. The less clear are the criteria, and the more ambiguous the written work or application is in relation to these criteria, the more likely it is that stereotypic beliefs will enter into the evaluation process.

We have already encountered the important influence of whether an occupation is perceived as predominantly masculine or feminine. Experimental studies also indicate that, following Goldberg's original study, stereotypically masculine domains attract the most frequent and pronounced bias against women. A more recent meta-analysis of 49 studies using the Goldberg method (Davison and Burke, 2000) found that men were preferred over women to a considerable extent (d = 0.34) for stereotypically masculine topics, but that women were preferred over men (d = −0.26) for stereotypically feminine ones. Bias is less or absent for gender-neutral topics. These findings are broadly similar to those found for job applications by Glick and his colleagues.

Even if the experimental research suggests that there is bias against men entering stereotypically feminine occupations, this will be of lesser practical importance than bias against women for masculine occupations. The reason is that few men seek to enter feminine occupations, in contrast to the many women who seek to enter the higher-status, better-paid, masculine occupations. Eagly and Karau (in press) have considered the particular case of bias against women entering elite leadership positions. They set out a comprehensive theory of prejudice towards women who either aspire to or attain such positions. Their theory is an extension of the more general social role theory we have encountered in various chapters of this book. Like the analysis of occupational bias, it involves role congruity, in that managerial leadership roles are viewed as requiring masculine agentic characteristics (chapter 2), whereas women as a category are viewed as not possessing these characteristics. There is, therefore, a mismatch between the perceived requirements of their gender role, and the leadership role, which leads to less favourable evaluations of their potential as leaders. Furthermore, if a woman does attain a position of leadership, she may be evaluated less favourably than a male leader because of her perceived feminine attributes. Alternatively, if she is seen as a successful leader, operating in a masculine agentic manner, she may be perceived as lacking femininity, and be unfavourably evaluated for this reason (Rudman and Glick, 1999).

While the particular type of occupation is the most important variable accounting for the direction and extent of sex bias, there are others that may moderate the extent of such bias. One is physical attractiveness. There are conflicting findings regarding its impact on judgements of competence. Some studies have found bias against an attractive woman, thus conforming to the stereotype that, for women, beauty and brains seldom mix, epitomised by terms such as 'dumb blonde' and 'bimbo'. Other studies find an attractive woman to be rated more favourably, conforming to what social psychologists refer to as 'the physical attractiveness stereotype', a positive bias towards physically attractive people (Kaplan, 1978; Landy and Sigall, 1974). Eagly and Karau (in press) suggested that a woman's physical attractiveness can operate to make her gender role, and hence her presumed stereotypic attributes, more salient. The impact of this will depend on the type of job for which the woman is applying, with physical attractiveness being particularly disadvantageous for masculine high-status managerial positions.

We would expect some people to be more biased than others. In chapter 2, we discussed rating scales measuring negative attitudes towards women's rights, including the world of work, and also individual differences in gender-stereotypic traits and activities. Although we would expect such personal attributes to predict the degree of bias, there is little research evidence available; what there is indicates that traditional attitudes and traits predict greater sex bias (Frable, 1989; Swim et al., 1989; Top, 1991).

We can conclude that there is evidence from the experimental studies that bias operates, but that it is affected by a number of variables, which have been outlined in this section. What is not clear at present is how these variables interact to attenuate or exaggerate bias. From the present knowledge, we should expect bias to be strongest when a person with traditional gender-attitudes judges a good application or piece of written work on a masculine topic area, attributed to a woman, with no additional information about her, or information indicating that she is feminine in personality and interests.

Self-stereotyping

Stereotypes may be used by one individual when judging another, but they may also influence how a member of a stereotyped group sees her- or himself. A general finding from a series of studies of self-judgements undertaken in the early 1970s (Deaux, 1976) was that women hold lower expectations for their performance than men do. This was found across a variety of tasks and age ranges. Deaux referred to this process as self-stereotyping, since it involved the application to the self of judgements based on the gender stereotype of lower female competence.

Deaux cited a study of her own in which men and women worked at an anagram task and then were asked to account for their performance. The task was either easy or difficult, and labelled as masculine or feminine by saying that either women or men typically performed well at it. For the masculine task, when successful, men were more likely to claim that their ability was the cause of their success, whereas women tended to say that luck was the most likely cause. When unsuccessful, men were more likely to attribute their failure to task difficulty, whereas women tended to say that their lack of ability was the reason. The results for the feminine task were less clear.

A number of similar studies were carried out after Deaux's article was written, and from these Frieze et al. (1982) concluded that there are no general differences over a range of different tasks, but that the different self-attributions were restricted to tasks on which women had little or no experience. We should note that in Deaux's study the findings were restricted to the masculine task. They did, nevertheless, indicate that a gender stereotype is capable of being activated under some conditions, possibly when the person is unsure of his or her own ability.

Whitley et al. (1986) followed up this review with a meta-analysis of such studies, finding that overall men were slightly (d = 0.13) more likely than women to attribute their success to ability, and were also slightly more likely to attribute their failures to lack of ability. There was, however, only a very slight difference in attributions involving luck. More recent studies (e.g., Russo et al., 1991) have indicated that the notion that women attribute their success to luck and men attribute theirs to ability (which had been widely publicised as a result of the earlier studies) does not apply to women who are successful in occupations.

These studies all involve attributions people make for their successes or failures. Self-stereotyping may also influence the level of performance. In chapter 2, we described studies of children showing that whether the same task was presented to them as being appropriate for their own or the opposite sex influenced their performance on it. Thus, girls' performance on a task could be depressed simply by telling them that this was a task more appropriate for boys.

Such studies provide clear evidence that viewing a task as gender-appropriate or gender-inappropriate can influence performance among children up to the age of 16 years. There is now evidence of much more subtle influences on a person's performance in one specific gender-stereotyped domain, mathematics. In a series of studies, Steele (1997) selected a group of college students, male and female, who were good at maths and identified with it, and gave them difficult maths tests one at a time. Under these conditions, the women underperformed relative to the men. When the maths test was easier, women and men performed at a comparable level. A similar exercise involving students with high literature skills also produced comparable performance by men and women. Thus high ability women underperformed when the domain was mathematics and the material was hard. Steele explained these findings in terms of 'stereotype threat' – a state induced by the thought that a negative stereotype about a group that one belongs to could apply to current performance.

These results might alternatively be attributed to a specific sex difference in mathematical performance only manifesting itself at the higher end of the distribution (as indicated in the section on specific abilities). A subsequent study ruled out this possibility, by showing that high-ability women did not underperform relative to men when the tasks were introduced as ones which typically yielded no sex differences, but they did when the tasks were introduced as ones on which men performed better than women. Women's performance was also lowered by anxiety associated with presentation of the procedures rather than expectations about poorer performance.

A study by Brown and Josephs (1999) again demonstrated the influence of gender-stereotypic expectations on performance in a task involving mathematical ability. College students were presented with a maths test, introduced as either indicating whether they were exceptionally strong at maths or exceptionally weak. These instructions influenced performance along gender-stereotypic lines: men performed poorly if they believed that the task was designed to identify strength, whereas women performed poorly if they believed that the test was designed to identify weakness in maths. The researchers concluded that the mere suggestion of group differences can evoke expectations influenced by the gender stereotype, which subsequently influences performance through inducing a threat of failure.

These studies indicate that gender stereotypes can have influences on how people perform on certain tasks, and that these go beyond the general lowering or raising of performance as a result of labelling it as a man's or woman's domain. They suggest that, when such tasks are presented in an educational setting, the way in which they are introduced has to be chosen with care so as to avoid unwitting influences on performance.

Social dominance orientation

So far we have been concerned with the impact of ability differences and gender stereotypes in occupational and educational settings. A very different approach to explaining the occupational patterns of men and women has been proposed and studied by Felicia Pratto and her colleagues (e.g., Pratto, 1996; Pratto et al., 1994). It involves the concept of *social dominance orientation* (SDO), which is the extent to which people favour inequality in social arrangements, and support belief systems that justify inequalities between groups and individuals. It is unrelated to *dominance*, used in the sense of a personality characteristic. A range of studies have found a consistent sex difference, with men being more likely than women to favour inequitable social arrangements.[4]

Pratto et al. (1994) classified occupations as hierarchy-enhancing (HE) or hierarchy-attenuating (HA). The former involve higher-status occupations whose net effect is to maintain and accentuate the power differentials between people. HA occupations are those whose effect is to mitigate social divisions and power differentials, for example social worker or charity worker. Pratto et al. (1994) argued that there is occupational segregation of men and women in most societies, so that men tend to be concentrated in HE occupations and women in HA occupations. Their own studies (Pratto et al., 1994) indicated that American men's and women's choices of occupations conformed to this distinction. They depart from those who argue for gender-stereotypic attributes of occupations accounting for these choices (e.g., Konrad et al., 2000). Instead, they attribute occupational choice to men's and women's different beliefs about social dominance, their SDO. Within the sexes, an individual's score on measures of SDO is associated with his or her liking for HE and HA occupations.

Pratto et al. (1997) again found that women tended to choose HA occupational descriptions and men HE descriptions, and that these choices were related to the individual's SDO. Controlling for men's and women's SDO reduced the sex difference in occupational choice to a statistically insignificant level. SDO was also associated with a person's expected work values, such as gaining status or personal power. We can therefore conclude that it is the sex difference in SDO that accounts for the occupational preferences of men and women. A further study selected men and women who were either high or low in SDO and examined their occupational preferences. In this case, there was no sex difference, since the important difference between the sexes had been selected out. It was also found that the important feature associated with the choice was the hierarchy-enhancing or attenuating aspect of the occupation, rather than its other attributes.

These studies were all concerned with people's occupational preferences and how these are driven by individual differences in beliefs about social dominance. This is not the whole story. A further study (Pratto et al., 1997) examined people's selection biases, in a similar way to Glick et al. (1988). Recollect that Glick and

[4] The magnitude of the sex difference is about half a standard deviation (d = 0.54).

his colleagues were concerned with the extent to which job-relevant individual information about a person could overcome sex bias in occupational decisions. Pratto and her colleagues were concerned with the extent to which information about a person's previous experience with HE or HA occupations could override their sex when people assigned them in terms of occupational suitability. Students were asked to imagine that they were working for an employment agency and to rate people's suitability for various occupations. They were presented with information about the person's prior occupational experience (either HE or HA) and their sex. Consistent with Glick et al.'s findings, the raters were influenced both by the person's previous experience, and independently by their sex, when making occupational choices. These findings were also found when the raters were a sample of business people.

Pratto et al. (1997) concluded that there were three processes contributing to men's and women's different distributions in occupations: first, self-selection of occupational preferences, arising from the sex difference in social dominance orientation; second, bias arising from the perceived association of men with HE occupations and women with HA ones; and third, an additional bias which assigns men to HE and women to HA occupations irrespective of their individual characteristics.

One important implication of the social dominance approach is that it is not the instrumental or expressive characteristics of men and women that are the essential variable underlying sex bias and selection, but their relative SDO. We might expect the two to be closely associated, since a high belief in social dominance would involve some of the same features as an instrumental view of the world. However, only agency or expressiveness was found to correlate with SDO at an individual level (Pratto et al., 1994). It remains for future studies to assess whether SDO or the instrumental–expressive distinction provides a better prediction of sex bias and of sex differences in preference for different occupations. Pratto (personal communication, 1999) suggests that SDO can explain a wider range of attributes, including sex differences in occupations, than the agency–communion distinction.

In contrast to Eagly's (1987) view that sex differences in social behaviour, and gender stereotypes, have their origins in historically located social roles (chapters 2 and 3), Pratto (1996) described an indirect route from sexual selection to the sex differences in SDO. This route starts with female choice, which produces male competition, and males coming to monopolise resources to attract females. In humans, this process is associated with a set of beliefs, involving those with the resources seeking to convince those without that this position is a legitimate and fair one. This is where social dominance orientation comes in, since it legitimises all sorts of social beliefs that justify inequality and in-group favouritism. Pratto (1996) has argued that such beliefs serve the interests of high-status males in a polygynous society,[5] and that it leads not only to men exerting sexual and political control over women, but also to the oppression of lower-status men. In such a society, higher-status women collude with higher-status men to maintain

---

[5] As indicated in chapter 3, societies can be effectively polygynous if there are liberal divorce laws, and higher-status men marry a series of progressively younger women.

the status quo, since it is also in their interests to do so (among women, SDO is associated with a desire for a higher-status mate).

Pratto and Hegarty (2000) have extended this view, by examining the association between SDO and the reproductive strategies of men and women. In this study, they were concerned with the extent to which SDO was associated with an endorsement of aspects of reproductive behaviour that were predicted by sexual selection theory for that sex. For example, was SDO strongest in those men who were more likely to be unfaithful to their long-term partner and who were most sexually jealous? Was SDO strongest among those women who attached more importance to status and money when choosing a mate? The answer in both cases was that SDO is associated with these characteristics. This finding not only strengthens the link between occupational preference, SDO, and sexual selection, but it also highlights variations within each sex. Most research has emphasised the ways in which men and women differ in their approach to the opposite sex, whereas this study complements the emphasis on within-sex variation found in the evolutionary based account of reproductive strategies by Gangestad and Simpson (2000), noted in chapter 1.

Conclusions

In chapter 1, we introduced the concept of levels of explanation in the social sciences. In seeking to explain the pattern of occupational choice in this chapter, we have concentrated on psychological processes, what Doise (1986) referred to as the *intrapersonal* level. This took the form of people's stereotypes of occupations, their attitudes towards men and women in particular occupations, and the manner in which differences in social dominance orientation influenced occupational choice. We also considered the *interpersonal* and *situational* level in the form of the influence of beliefs about men and women on occupational decisions, such as hiring and promotion. We indirectly considered the *positional* and *ideological* levels, in acknowledging that stereotypic beliefs about men and women in relation to occupations were associated with the traditional societal roles of men and women, and their unequal power relations.

Although it was acknowledged that processes such as stereotypes operating at an interpersonal level reflect wider societal structures, this analysis is primarily restricted to the psychological or individual level. It is therefore important to note that there will also be wider social processes influencing – or, rather, hindering – the occupational advancement of women (Hyde, 1999). Foremost among these is women's child care and domestic responsibilities, which for working women constitute what has been called 'the second shift' (Hochschild, 1989). Associated with this is the interruption of women's careers through caring full time or part time for infants and children, and the lack of geographical mobility that is associated with having children (Hyde, 1999).

Many traditionally male occupations involve a masculine subculture that excludes women from sources of informal networking that promote occupational advancement. In addition, women are more likely than men to be subjected to sexual harassment at work, and they are more likely to suffer damaging consequences as a result (Gutek, 1985). In some occupations, sexual harassment is part of an overtly sexist and 'barrack-room' masculine culture that also serves to marginalise women who do venture into such occupations. Examples of this process in operation find their way into the pages of the more enlightened Western newspapers. They include, in the UK, reports by two women journalists who worked as 'brickies' (bricklayers) and, according to their account, challenged the entrenched attitudes of their male comrades by showing that they could physically manage all that the job required them to do. At the other end of the spectrum, in terms of occupational status, a case for sexual discrimination was brought against the Deutsche Bank UK by a well-paid City banker (Gregoriadis, 1999). She claimed that her manager openly used terms such as 'hot totty' and 'a bit of all right' when referring to women colleagues, and harassed her with more specific and continued sexual innuendo, until she eventually resigned. According to Gutek's (1985) study, this is the typical consequence of such harassment for women, although in this case it was not left to rest.

There are, therefore, a wider range of social influences operating against women's occupational advancement that go beyond the more subtle and often unconscious biases and beliefs studied by social psychologists. They constitute the overt and visible face of discrimination against women which is gradually being challenged in courtrooms and tribunals throughout the modern Western world.

Further reading

Eagly, A. H and Karau, S. J. (in press). Role congruity theory of prejudice towards female leaders. *Psychological Review*.
A theory of prejudice towards women leaders, based on social role theory. Women are viewed as having a lesser potential for undertaking the managerial role, on account of their stereotype as being nurturant and caring. Women who do become managers are evaluated more negatively, since the requirements for this role are viewed as being at odds with the stereotype of femininity.

Halpern, D. F. (2000). *Sex Differences in Cognitive Abilities. 3rd edn*. Mahwah, NJ: Erlbaum.
A thorough and comprehensive discussion of contemporary research on sex differences in cognition, in relation to theories about their causes. Halpern adopts an approach that encompasses biological, psychological, and social influences on these differences, to provide an integration that goes beyond simple explanations in terms of nature or nurture.

Pratto, F. (1996). Sexual politics: the gender gap in the bedroom, the cupboard, and the cabinet. In D. M. Buss and N. Malamuth (eds.), *Sex, Power and Conflict: Evolutionary and Feminist Perspectives* (pp. 179–230). New York: Oxford University Press.
A summary of the theory that sex differences in occupational choices derive from different beliefs men and women hold about about social inequality.

10 Looking back and looking ahead

Introduction

The reader who has followed our current account of *Sex and Gender* and is also familiar with our previous edition is probably struck by a number of changes that have occurred in the past 15 years. In particular, the piecemeal and generally atheoretical approaches of earlier research have given way to coherent statistical investigations and ambitious conceptual models. In this final chapter, we comment upon these changes and suggest the direction studies of sex differences may take in the future.

In the first section, we explore the limitations of meta-analysis, the technique that we described in chapter 1, and which is currently used to summarise systematically a body of research evidence. Throughout the following chapters, we drew upon meta-analyses to provide summaries of sex differences in behaviour such as sexuality, mental health, parenting, and cognitive capacities. Here we consider the problems that may be encountered by even the most thorough meta-analysts. Our focus is on the databases that have been used for the meta-analyses, rather than the statistical techniques. In particular, the databases are restricted in terms of age-range, cultural identity, and historical time.

In the second part of the chapter, we consider two theoretical developments that have changed the way we view sex and gender and how it is studied. These are evolutionary psychology and social role theory. Both represent broad pictures of the origins and immediate causes of sex differences in social behaviour and cognition. In preceding chapters, we highlighted the theoretical impact of evolutionary psychology on the study of sex differences, and, in particular, the novel hypotheses it generated. Its impact on research about sex differences led some prominent social science researchers to re-examine their accounts and considerably extend them. In particular, social role theory, which was built upon the efforts of earlier researchers to link social psychology with sociology and anthropology, has been broadened and developed in recent accounts.

We conclude the chapter by examining the implications of these two broad frameworks for differences within as well as between the sexes, and introduce a third type of explanation that concentrates on national differences, in the form of Hofstede's (1980) notion of masculinity and femininity as societal variables.

The limitations of existing meta-analyses

In chapter 1 we introduced meta-analysis, a technique for systematically summarising a body of research evidence. This is particularly suitable for comparing categories such as men and women along consistent psychological measures, for example aggression and spatial ability. The meta-analyses that we reported throughout this book have improved upon the classic narrative summary of Maccoby and Jacklin published in the mid-1970s by providing a precise measure of differences, and have enabled assessments of how these differences are moderated by other variables.

Although the technique of meta-analysis is well suited for comparing men and women, its application to psychological measures has a number of limitations which restrict the conclusions that can be drawn. The major meta-analyses of sex differences in behaviour, that began with Hall's analysis of the decoding of non-verbal cues in 1978, typically involve a restricted age-range of individuals, from a restricted range of societies, and from relatively recent times. These limitations are largely inherent in the available databases that typically involve young adults (many of whom are students), from North America, in studies undertaken relatively recently. One of the drawbacks of meta-analysis is that it requires similar methods to have been used, which mitigates against inclusion of studies undertaken at earlier historical periods, and in cultures whose psychology has developed in different ways to that of the USA.

The reliance on laboratory research in North American cognitive and social psychology has further tended to restrict the majority of investigations to the populations most readily at hand, that is undergraduates. There is also a tendency for North American researchers to inhabit a North American academic world, so that the database may be deliberately confined to that found in journals published in the USA. In what has now become a classic review of sex differences found in experimental studies of aggression (Eagly and Steffen, 1986), the database for the meta-analysis was restricted in advance to participants who were from the USA or Canada (ibid., p. 313). Admittedly, the particular tradition of research being investigated in this case was a North American one, so that there would have been relatively little information from elsewhere.

In the following three sections, we explore how restrictions in the evidence base may have influenced the conclusions that can be drawn from the available research evidence. We consider, first, the restricted age-range, second, cultural and national representation, and, third, the historical context.

Age-range

As we have indicated, there is an emphasis in North American psychological research on studying young people. To a considerable extent this is probably due to the convenience of undergraduates as available participants, but it may also be a reflection of a wider culture that emphasises the achievements of youth. Among psychological studies of sex differences, and of stereotypes and attitudes, there are relatively few involving people outside this age-range, apart from those on children and adolescents. For example, an ongoing meta-analysis of sex differences in aggression (Archer, 2001a) revealed 128 samples providing useable self-report data. Of these, 5 were based upon people aged between 30 and 40 years of age, 2 involved people between 41 and 49, and 1 had studied people over 70 years of age. Of the remaining 120, around 40 were of young adults of college age and about 50 were of children and adolescents.

These figures are typical of other areas. For example, among the older studies (from Maccoby and Jacklin, 1974) used in Feingold's (1994a) meta-analyses of sex differences in personality, there were 34 of self-esteem, 49 of internal *locus* of control, and 22 of assertiveness. Apart from 2 that did not specify age, and 1 small-scale study of assertiveness among older adults, all the participants in these studies were under 20 years of age. Among 27 samples from the early 1970s onwards measuring self-esteem, one involved old-aged adults, another 50-year-olds, and a third 34-year-olds: the remaining 24 samples consisted of young adults (16 to 25 years). Of 18 samples measuring anxiety, the oldest mean age was 24 years, and in 15 studies of assertiveness, only 1 included people over 30 years of age. In a meta-analysis of sex differences in risk-taking (Byrnes et al., 1999), age categories were analysed by comparing four age groups, 3 to 9 years, 10 to 13, 14 to 17 and 'over 21', again indicating the lack of information on middle- and old-aged adults.

These statistics raise the question of whether the restricted age-range has influenced the conclusions that are drawn. The answer from the rather fragmentary evidence for older-age categories indicates that it does matter for a number of areas that we have covered in this book. Consider people's self-ratings of their gender-linked personality attributes (discussed in chapter 2). Typically, the bulk of the evidence comes from college-age young adults, with some from younger ages. Yet one study comparing middle-aged with younger people found higher instrumental ('masculine') personality ratings for middle-aged than for college-aged men (Spence and Helmreich, 1979). The same study found that the gender-related attitudes of the middle-aged men and women – parents of college students – were significantly more traditional than those of their offspring.

Turning again to aggression research, there is consistent evidence that even across a few years in the young-adult range, measures of aggression tend to decrease from around 17 years of age (e.g., Archer and Haigh, 1997a,b; Broadbent, 1999; Harris, 1996). If we look further afield to evidence from violent and other crime statistics (chapter 6), there are very pronounced changes with age, both for all crimes (Campbell, 1995; Courtwright, 1996) and for homicides (Daly and Wilson, 1990). Both increase dramatically among males after puberty, reaching a peak at around 20 years of age for all arrests and around 27 years for homicides. For females, the absolute levels are much less in both cases, with the peak for arrests coming a few years earlier than is the case for males. Among the male population, there is a steep decline across the adult lifespan from the earlier peak, so that the levels at round 50 years of age for all crimes are around a quarter (UK figures) to an eighth (US figures) of those at the peak years. For homicides, the level at 50 to 54 years is about a sixth of that at peak ages.

The age and sex distribution of people committing violent crimes has been attributed to heightened male competition (as a consequence of sexual selection) at younger ages among males (Campbell, 1995, 1999; Daly and Wilson, 1990), associated with a greater willingness to take risks and disregard the future at these ages. Because the studies seldom extend beyond young adulthood, this hypothesis remains essentially untested in psychological studies of physical aggression or risk-taking.

One exception is a study of aggression among older adults by Walker et al. (2000) which set out to test the hypothesis that older adults would be more likely to use safer, more indirect, forms of aggression (Walker and Richardson, 1998). They recruited 110 people aged from 55 to 89 years from Boca Raton in southern Florida and asked them to complete several self-report measures. Even at these ages, the mean being 71 years, they still found evidence of greater male than female involvement in direct aggression, although there was no appreciable sex difference for indirect aggression. Consistent with their hypothesis, they did find that indirect forms of aggression were reported more at older ages.

These findings raise the general question of what happens to sex differences during middle- and old-age. In the case of aggression, both sexes seem to show a decline in overt confrontational forms, probably replacing these with indirect aggression; thus the incidence of aggression among older men becomes similar to that of women of a younger age. Yet the relative sex difference in direct aggression is still maintained. However, there is practically no evidence for older ages available for other characteristics, such as self-esteem, assertiveness, and impulsiveness (see above). We cannot therefore answer the general question of whether their absolute values, and the sex differences, decline during middle- and old-age, as would be predicted by sexual selection theory.

National and cultural representation

As indicated earlier, the USA dominates the databases of the major meta-analyses. We have already mentioned one major review of aggression that sampled only North American research. Here, we discuss the national representation of the databases used in other analyses. In the ongoing meta-analysis of sex differences in questionnaire measures of aggression (Archer, 2001a), 128 samples were derived from 18 countries. However, 87 of the samples were from the USA. The others were mainly European (covering 12 countries), with a minority from Asia (China, India, and Japan), and none from Africa.

Feingold's (1994a) meta-analyses of personality traits also included samples from a variety of countries, although again the USA dominated. Although the 27 samples measuring self-esteem included entries from Australia, Ireland, the Netherlands, and Hong Kong, there were still 16 US and 5 Canadian data-sets.

Of the 18 samples measuring anxiety, 12 were from the USA, and a further 2 from Canada. Although slightly more diverse, with samples from India, Norway, and Thailand, 12 out of the 15 studies of assertiveness were located in the USA. In the meta-analysis of risk-taking by Byrnes et al. (1999), the nationality of each study was not mentioned nor was it included in the analysis.

These examples suggest that even when we are dealing with general attributes that are presumed to have a measure of cross-national consistency, such as aggressiveness and particular personality traits, there are still relatively few studies from nations other than the USA. We are left with the question of whether the conclusions on sex differences in psychological attributes from US-dominated databases generalise to other nations.

In contrast, there is a large-scale, cross-national study of gender stereotypes (but again among college students), carried out by Williams and Best (1982, 1990). They sampled 27 countries, from Europe, Asia, Africa, Oceania, and the Americas, using a standard measure, the Adjective Check List, which they had used in their earlier North American study (chapter 2). Although there were some interesting variations associated with cultural differences, the main finding from their study was the degree of similarity in the characteristics that people associated with men and women in the 27 countries.

Williams et al. (1999) extended the cross-national analysis of stereotypes to assess how they relate to the Big Five Model of personality structure (McCrae and Costa, 1990), which consists of Extraversion, Conscientiousness, Emotional Stability, Openness to Experience, and Agreeableness. Across the 25 nations included in the first survey (Williams and Best, 1982), the masculine stereotype showed higher ratings for all the factors except Agreeableness, which was higher for the feminine stereotype. A subsequent study (Williams et al., in press) investigated the degree of consistency in these ratings across all the nations included in the later version of the survey (Williams and Best, 1990), finding that all four factors that generally applied more to men than to women showed considerable cross-national agreement. In each case, the overall finding applied to 24 or more of the 27 nations. Agreeableness was viewed as applying more to women than to men in 22 nations.

Williams et al., also calculated the sum of the five difference scores, to produce an overall index of gender stereotyping. They then assessed how this overall index was related to cultural-level values. There were no significant correlations with Hofstede's (1980) work-related values (see below): individualism, power distance, uncertainty avoidance, and masculinity. Swartz's (1994) cultural dimensions: harmony, conservatism, hierarchy, mastery, affective autonomy, intellectual autonomy, and egalitarian commitment fared little better, only the last of these being significantly correlated[1] with the index of gender stereotyping; stereotyping was more pronounced in nations with less egalitarian commitment. Two demographic variables showed larger associations, stereotyping being higher when fewer of the

---

[1] $r = -0.42$.

population showed Christian affiliation[2] and when there were fewer women at university.[3] Both these variables seem to reflect traditional cultures where the economic and social freedoms of women are curtailed compared to Western standards.

So far in this section we have referred to nations, since most comparisons are between samples representing dominant groups within particular nations. The overlapping concept of culture can be studied within national boundaries, by comparing different ethnic groups within a multicultural society, or comparing nations that do truly represent different cultures, for example when comparing India and the USA. One example of a different pattern of sex differences found for different ethnic groups within a single nation can be found in data for partner assaults based on the 1998 British Crime Survey (Mirrlees-Black et al., 1998). All the reports in the survey were derived from a computer-assisted anonymous method of data collection. The proportion of women among all individuals who said their partner had assaulted them over the previous year was 0.59. This figure indicates that a considerable number of men reported that their female partner had assaulted them (chapter 6).

A breakdown of the figures according to ethnic group revealed an interesting pattern: among those identifying themselves as white, the proportion of men and women assaulted was more or less equal. Among Afro-Caribbean people, there were slightly more women than men who had been assaulted by a partner. For the two groups from the Indian subcontinent (India and Pakistan–Bangladesh analysed separately) the proportion of male victims was considerably reduced, although the proportion of women victims was similar to that found in the other ethnic groups. These findings indicate either a much lower rate of assault by wives on their husbands in the Asian samples, or that these men were less willing than white or Afro-Caribbean men to acknowledge assault by a wife. Whichever of these is the case, the subject deserves further study in relation to the cultural beliefs that might account for the differences (Archer, 2000a).

Some researchers have sought to sidestep limitations inherent in the available psychological database by using archival data on different cultures located in the Human Relations Area Files (HRAFs). Rosenblatt et al. (1976) used this source to examine accounts of the expression of grief in a wide variety of cultures. For our purposes, the most noteworthy aspect of the study was that women were generally more likely to cry than were men, and men were more likely to act out their anger against others. Women, however, were more likely to injure themselves than were men. Rosenblatt and Cunningham (1976) speculated that these differences may be the consequence of both hormonal and socialisation influences that accentuate men's proneness to anger and aggression (chapter 6). Sanday (1981) also used a standard sample of cultures to test hypotheses about rape (chapter 6). Wood and Eagly (in press) used the HRAFs to undertake a cross-cultural analysis of men's and women's roles, in order to assess social role theory explanations in relation to the alternatives – evolutionary psychology and social constructivism.

[2] $r = -0.58$.   [3] $r = -0.41$.

Finally, we should note that there are cultures and subcultures whose views about gender roles are radically different from those of modern Western states. Whatever the limits to the rights of women operating in Western societies, the position of women in such societies contrasts greatly with that in states whose law and customs are dictated by political interpretations of Islamic doctrine. The extreme versions of this in Afghanistan under the Taliban were widely publicised in the 1990s, including (by Western standards) pronounced oppression of women.

Historical context

The rate with which new research findings appear in the natural and social sciences of the Western world is associated with a perceived need to keep up-to-date and an emphasis on findings that are recent. We reflect this trend in rewriting our book in the light of findings appearing since the mid-1980s. Although we have sought to balance this by not losing sight of older contributions, we have largely been concerned with sources published in the last 40 years. Apart from some classic studies, it is now unusual to cite investigations of sex and gender published before the 1970s. There are some good reasons for this, since much of the modern research has been stimulated by feminist or evolutionary writings dating from the 1960s. The contents of many meta-analyses of sex differences again reflect this historical trend (e.g., Archer, 2000a; Byrnes et al., 1999), depending on the particular measure involved. Some analyses of sex differences in classic individual difference measures (associated with intelligence and personality tests) draw upon much earlier research. Thus Feingold's (1994) meta-analysis of personality traits contains two studies from the 1930s and three from the 1950s (derived from Maccoby and Jacklin's (1974) narrative review), although most are from 1960 onwards.

The relatively short historical time period during which most studies on sex and gender have been published does raise the question of whether their findings would generalise to other historical times. In his classic paper entitled 'Social psychology as history', Gergen (1973) argued that late twentieth-century social psychology was an endeavour located in history, and therefore findings do not necessarily have the historical durability they are assumed to have. Certain classic findings such as those relating to obedience to authority, or group conformity, will be heavily dependent on the socio-political climate of the time. Gergen outlined a continuum of historical durability, in order to locate findings in terms of their stability over time.

Gergen's analysis can be applied to research on sex and gender by examining changes over the historical period since the first studies were undertaken. Scales measuring attitudes to equality for women were first constructed in the early 1970s (chapter 2). A meta-analysis of scores from US college students on the most widely used scale, the AWS (Attitude Toward Women Scale), revealed a very large shift towards endorsing equality in both men's and women's attitudes over the years from 1970 to 1995 (Twenge, 1997a). This occurred despite the political attitudes of US college students becoming generally more conservative in the 1970s and

1980s. In a separate analysis, Lueptow et al. (1995) identified both large changes in attitudes to men's and women's roles, and in the roles themselves, over the previous 20 to 25 years in the USA. Yet their analysis of the gender stereotyping of traits showed that these remained fairly stable over this period, which led Lueptow et al. to argue against the social role interpretation of gender stereotypes (chapter 2).

Although adopting a very different theoretical framework from Gergen, some evolutionary psychologists have also been sensitive to the overreliance upon findings from a particular time in history (and from a particular restricted culture). Their standpoint is generally one that involves looking for findings and explanations that are stable at different times and in different places. The pioneering evolutionary study of homicide by Daly and Wilson (1988) used mainly a combination of North American crime statistics and cross-national data, to assess how a variety of evolutionary principles might apply to the pattern of human killings. They also used some historical sources, for example, information on collaborative killing in England during the thirteenth century, recorded in the Norman courts or *eyres* of the time. In this case they showed a pattern of kinship ties between the (male) killers which is consistent with the evolutionary principle of inclusive fitness (chapter 3). Dunbar et al. (1995) applied the same principle to an analysis of two Viking sagas, to assess the degree to which kinship and perceived costs influenced alliances, the willingness to murder and to demand vengeance for a murder. Again they found that the degree of kinship predicted murderous alliances, and also a reluctance to murder related individuals, but they found that this could be overridden when the benefits of so doing were likely to be high. When Betzig (1992) analysed accounts of polygyny in the ancient civilisations, it was to assess a view derived from sexual selection (chapter 3), that political power would enable men to have the widest possible sexual access. Her analysis of the Roman emperors was certainly consistent with this view.

These evolutionary analyses of historical sources were undertaken to assess whether hypotheses derived from evolutionary principles would apply to cultures very different from ours, using evidence recorded a long time before such principles were established. In an earlier section, we indicated that young males consistently showed high levels of crime. We can use some limited historical sources to assess the generality of this pattern. The Belgian sociologist Adolphe Quetelet (1833/1984) noted age and sex differences in the propensity to crime in general, and to violent crime and theft in particular. He identified men of around 25 years of age as committing the maximum numbers of crimes. A slightly earlier peak is found in crime figures from England in the early 1840s, which is also consistent with data from the USA for the second half of the twentieth century (Courtwright, 1996). There is therefore evidence for consistency in the pattern of crimes committed by men and women at different ages across different historical periods.

Major theoretical developments

There are several theoretical perspectives that have been applied to research on sex differences. In understanding such explanations, it is useful to combine Tinbergen's (1963) distinction between the different time-scales involved in different types of explanations of behaviour with Doise's (1986) distinction between different levels of explanation, introduced in chapter 1. Tinbergen distinguished between explanations that concerned ultimate origins, evolutionary history or survival value in ancestral environments, and those that concerned causes operating within an individual's lifespan, during their development or over shorter time spans. Doise distinguished between explanations of social behaviour that concerned events within the individual or operating between individuals, from those that considered the social positions of the people involved or of ideological beliefs that are shared by many individuals.

In this book, we have examined explanations that seek to explain the immediate causes of sex differences, for example when individuals' beliefs about the gender-appropriateness of a task influence their performance (chapter 9); or when the perception that a man's honour has been insulted leads to violent retaliation (chapter 6). We have also described explanations that involve the longer-term origins of adult sex differences in terms of developmental processes (chapter 4). The perspectives that have been applied to the development of sex differences represent the different theoretical approaches that psychologists have adopted to understand social development – social cognitive, cognitive developmental, biological (chapter 4), and psychoanalytical (chapter 5).

As we have indicated throughout the book, research undertaken from within these perspectives has resulted in many continued and varied contributions to the understanding of the immediate causes and developmental origins of sex differences. However, there are two approaches that have emerged over the last 15 years or so that have the potential to advance our understanding of sex and gender to a greater extent than theoretical frameworks that are restricted to developmental antecedents or immediate causes. Both these approaches, in different ways, seek to understand the wider picture: the origins of sex differences, and how processes at an individual level relate to those at the higher or ideological level of widespread beliefs.

The evolutionary perspective (chapter 3) views differences between women and men as having originated from the process of sexual selection. Certain general principles, operating throughout those parts of the animal kingdom where there are males and females, lead to the two sexes showing different dispositions. These dispositions are not necessarily inflexible and may – according to some accounts – be very sensitive to events in the developmental and immediate environments (Crawford and Anderson, 1989; Smith et al., 2000). Sexual selection theory has primarily been concerned with explaining differences in reproductive behaviour, and in aggression and violence, but it can be extended to the explanation of other forms of social behaviour (Archer, 1996) and to differences in cognitive abilities (Geary, 1999). From this viewpoint, widespread beliefs about sex and gender – Doise's positional level – represent the ideological articulation of different dispositions shown by men and women and the conflicts of interests that their different reproductive roles inevitably produce.

In contrast, the social role perspective views differences between women and men as arising from their respective societal roles, which, in turn, have their origins in history and biology (chapter 3). Initially, the division of labour into homemakers and full-time employees was emphasised, along with the unequal status of these roles (Eagly, 1987). More recent accounts (Eagly and Wood, 1999; Eagly et al., 2000; Wood and Eagly, in press) have greatly extended the theory in terms of the origins of various forms of division of labour based on biological sex, throughout human history and pre-history. In its current version, social role theory seeks to explain how certain recurrent ways of organising the labour of women and men arose as a consequence of the mammalian method of reproduction and the need for prolonged offspring care, together with the greater size and strength of men. Wood and Eagly refer to this as a biosocial theory, to distinguish it from viewpoints that emphasise the social construction of men's and women's roles without recognising the constraints and influences of a method of reproduction inherited from the biological past of the human species.

Nevertheless, this is a biosocial theory that some evolutionary theorists tend not to recognise as such. The central reason was put forcefully by a group of critics of Eagly and Wood's (1999) article. Although Wood and Eagly (in press) recognise biological influences in the form of evolved physical sex differences that must have arisen before the division of labour, they do not recognise any associated evolved psychological sex differences. Their position is essentially that the physical sex differences are pre-adaptations that make certain activities easier to undertake, and that this has led to different gender roles and associated sex differences in social behaviour. Friedman et al. (2000) described this position as involving a form of Cartesian dualism, in that it recognises the evolution of the body but not of the mind. The answer to this is that female reproductive behaviour has had a much more profound influence on human behaviour than evolved dispositions, by constraining the sorts of role specialisations that are likely to arise in most circumstances (Eagly, personal communication).

Nevertheless, recognition of evolved physical differences, but not evolved mental differences, is likely to remain a telling criticism of social role theory. Awkward questions can also be asked about certain aspects of the evolutionary position. Consider paternity uncertainty (chapter 4) which – along with paternal care – is regarded as the source of male sexual jealousy. Studies by Buss and his colleagues have shown that men are more likely to react strongly to sexual infidelity, whereas women are more likely to react strongly to emotional infidelity (chapter 3). However, the studies only show a difference in the relative proportions of each sex that are more upset by sexual rather than emotional infidelity. If paternity certainty were so overwhelmingly important as the evolutionary reason for this sex difference, we should expect that 90–100 per cent of men (rather than the 60 per cent consistently found in the studies) would be more upset by sexual infidelity. This is because paternity uncertainty is always there for men, but maternity uncertainty is never there for women. Rearing another man's child will always result in a catastrophic loss of fitness, and therefore we should expect it always to be guarded against.

The social role and evolutionary perspectives both involve analyses of origins and of immediate causes. The evolutionary account involves events that have taken place in an evolutionary time-span. The social role view is primarily concerned with events that have occurred in human history and prehistory. It is therefore essentially a human-centred theory. Both approaches are also theories of immediate causes, evolutionary emphasising evolved dispositions and how they interact with various environments, and the social role with the impact of gender stereotypes derived from social roles on the behaviour of women and men (chapters 2 and 8).

Evolutionary critics of the social role position (e.g., Kenrick and Li, 2000; Kleyman, 2000) have focused on its neglect of the important and well-established process of sexual selection that must, they argue, have impacted on the human species. The social role position set out by Wood and Eagly (in press) would not seem to require much alteration to acknowledge that either or both reproductive, and size and strength differences could be associated with different dispositions to act. This, in conjunction with an emphasis on behaviour developing so as to be adapted to suit local conditions, would go some way towards a position that recognised both the importance of sexual selection, and the subsequent development of social roles.

One very useful addition that would also bring the two approaches together is an emphasis on the variability in sex differences in behaviour as a consequence of adaptations to local conditions. This variability is recognised by Wood and Eagly's analyses, but not in terms of an adaptive framework, as it is in the writings of behavioural ecologists (e.g., Smith et al., 2000) and of some evolutionary psychologists who refer to 'context-dependent shifts' (Buss et al., 2000). Yet Eagly and Wood (1999) do recognise that behaviour is subject to change as a consequence of people maximising individual benefits and minimising costs. This is a very short distance from the evolutionary theorising of behavioural ecologists who emphasise flexible decision-making based on implicit cost–benefit analyses of environmental cues, which are ultimately related to reproductive fitness. Yet, in making such a seemingly small change, a shift in mind-set is involved – from viewing historically developed roles as the driving force for sex differences, with biology a secondary consideration, to viewing sexual selection as the driving force for human sex differences, with social roles arising from these. Whatever the theoretical developments in the future, the willingness of social role theorists to understand the evolutionary psychologists position and to engage in critical dialogue with them has paved the way to one of the most intellectually stimulating and forward-looking exchanges in scientific writings about sex and gender. It has also led to clarification and modification of positions on both sides.

Beyond sex differences

Both social role theory and evolutionary psychology hold that sex differences arise from broader features that differ between the sexes. Their identification of what these broader features are does, of course, differ markedly. In the first case, it is the societal roles of men and women that are the reason people attribute different characteristics to them, and the reason that their behaviour has come to differ. In the case of evolutionary psychology, it is the minimum level of parental investment associated with the two sexes that has produced widespread sex differences. The time frame of the two theories is, of course, very different, social role theory being concerned with human history and pre-history, and evolutionary theory with the much longer evolutionary time. In both cases their proponents can point out ways in which sex differences come to vary as a consequence of changing the crucial variable. In chapter 2 we presented studies that convincingly demonstrated that directly manipulating the occupational role and sex of a target person changed the psychological characteristics individuals assigned to them. In the case of evolutionary approaches, reversals of the usual sex difference occur in the animal world when the level of parental investment is the reverse of the usual pattern of a higher level in females than males.

Although very different in their details and their orientation, both major theories are claiming that to really understand how the sexes differ we need to look beyond sex as a category and examine other features that are generally associated with sex. In their different ways, they are saying that there is nothing inherent in producing a particular type of gamete or germ cell (the way that biologists define sex) that is linked to behaving in a particular way. There may be usual patterns associated with each sex that have tended to develop throughout the animal kingdom, and there may be social roles that have tended to develop from the reproductive differences characteristic of male and female mammals. But neither is *always* associated with being male or female.

Viewing sex differences as arising from attributes associated with each sex can lead to new ways of investigating how the sexes differ, ones which are more rooted in theory than those of earlier times. It can also enable the emphasis to be shifted away from sex as a category to important variables generally associated with one or other sex, but varying considerably within each sex. Some examples of this approach have been described in this book. In chapter 9, sex differences in occupational choice were found to disappear once people's social dominance orientation had been controlled. Parental investment – the variable linked with sexual selection in evolutionary theorising about sex differences – may differ between individual men and may be associated with characteristics that differ between the sexes, such as direct aggression (chapter 6).

The debate (chapter 1) about whether researchers should concentrate on sex differences or on our common humanity, irrespective of a person's sex, can be informed and moved forward, by a shift of emphasis, to considering certain types of individual differences between individuals of the same sex. Gangestad and Simpson (2000) have set out this debate in relation to a framework used by evolutionary biologists for understanding certain consistent behavioural differences within members of the same sex (usually males). Different individuals of one sex may adopt alternative reproductive strategies: different ways of achieving mating and reproductive success (Gross, 1996). The most common example, which occurs in many animal species, is the existence of 'fighter' and 'sneaker' males; the former compete actively with other males for access to females, and the latter achieve their mating success by stealth and subterfuge. These strategies are usually identifiable in terms of the larger size of the fighters. In some species, the two forms may differ in other ways, for example their colour.

Gangestad and Simpson are not the first to argue that individual differences between males can be understood in such terms, but they have presented a comprehensive account of some of the features that may provide markers of different reproductive strategies among men. In particular, they have linked different strategies to their own research on bodily symmetry. In this case, the distinction seems to be between men who show a greater or lesser tendency towards parental investment and fidelity, rather than the more usual fighter–sneaker distinction.

These evolutionary-based analyses concentrate on differences between individual men. Social role analyses and feminist-based analyses in general have tended to concentrate on variations between women, as a consequence of changes in societal roles. In particular, the more instrumental traits associated with masculine occupations are viewed as being adopted by women who enter masculine occupations (chapter 9). More generally, younger women in the Western world show the 'laddish' behaviour of their male counterparts, including heavy drinking and casual sex, again as a consequence of adopting aspects of the masculine role.

Therefore, both the evolutionary and social role positions can in their different ways provide frameworks for understanding the great variation between the behaviour of particular men and women. One other framework can also provide a way of doing so, but in the context of differences between different cultures. *Masculinity and Femininity: The Taboo Dimension of National Cultures* (Hofstede et al., 1998) can be read as a radical re-presentation of two terms we have so far used only in relation to the attributes typically associated with men or women, and how these operate at the individual level of analysis. Hofstede theorises 'masculinity' and 'femininity' at an ideological or societal level. As an evolutionary social psychologist and a psychoanalytically oriented psychologist, we are more familiar with Doise's (1986) interpersonal, situational, and intrapersonal levels. Hofstede's project is based upon a comparison of societies; he uses the terms 'masculinity' and 'femininity', along with other dimensions, to characterise and to contrast different societies.

As we have already noted, psychologists usually measure sex differences in terms of individual differences. Hofstede included in *Masculinity and Femininity* some of the cross-national research of Williams and Best (1982, 1990) that we considered in an earlier section . Their investigation of masculinity and femininity, as gender stereotypes and self and ideal-self descriptions, is typical of an individual differences approach. Their formulation rests on two propositions. One is that certain characteristics are more typical of one sex group than of the other; and the second is that within each group there is variability among individuals in the incidence of these characteristics.

Hofstede described Masculinity/Femininity (M/F) in his earlier book *Culture's Consequences* (1980) as one of four independent cultural dimensions. The others are Power Distance (unequal versus equal), Uncertainty Avoidance (rigid versus flexible), and Individualism/Collectivism. These four, plus Long- or Short-Term Orientation, which he added later (Hofstede, 1991), are intended to capture cultural differences among nation-states. Hofstede has described these dimensions as 'anthropological distinctions'. They were derived from questionnaire responses collected in large-scale surveys, in which nations form the units of comparison. Hofstede and his colleagues (1998) explored the validity and cultural consequences of these national differences. They also considered the influence of national differences on psychological and sociological processes. In addition, they examined the influences of culture on the sexes and the combined influences of culture, sexuality, and religion.

Hofstede et al. (1998) suggested that there are close theoretical similarities between their dimensions, and Inkeles and Levinson's (1969) functional analyses of national character, which identified three analytic issues held to be derived from basic, world-wide, human problems. They proposed that the culture-specific solutions to these problems have had major consequences for societies, groups in societies, and individuals within groups. Hofstede and his colleagues (1998) linked their Power Distance dimension to the earlier 'relation to authority' issue, and Uncertainty Avoidance to 'primary dilemmas/conflicts and ways of dealing with them'. Inkeles and Levinson split their third analytic issue, 'conception of self', into values relating to position in society and masculinity–femininity (M/F). These distinctions are echoed in Hofstede's dimensions: Individualism/Collectivism and M/F.

Both Individualism/Collectivism and M/F were originally derived empirically from ratings of the importance of 14 work goals in an ideal job. These were: challenge, living in a desirable area, earnings, co-operation with colleagues, training, benefits, recognition, physical working conditions, freedom, job security, career advancement, use of skills, relationship with manager, and time for personal or family life. Two independent dimensions were identified from the responses of matched samples of IBM employees in 40 countries. Hofstede's 1980 book inspired much research in cross-cultural psychology, but the main focus has been on the Individualism/Collectivism dimension. The political climate has been such that the M/F dimension has been considered politically incorrect and even omitted from some large studies (e.g., Zandpour and Harich, 1996).

A masculine society is characterised as one in which value is placed upon men who are assertive, tough, and focused on material success, and on women who are modest, tender, and concerned with the quality of life. In masculine societies, both men and women espouse these values. A feminine society is one in which modesty, tenderness, and concern with the quality of life are highly valued by both men and women. High scores on the M/F or MAS scale indicate masculine societies, and low scores feminine societies. Ego-goals are opposed to social-goals along this dimension. Importantly, it is not to be confused with the Individualism/Collectivism dimension, nor with individual differences in personality. Japan gained 95, the highest MAS score Hofstede recorded, and was followed by Austria on 79 and Venezuela on 70. Great Britain and Germany tied for tenth place with scores of 66, while a score of 62 placed the USA in fifteenth place. The Scandinavian countries were the lowest and hence described as feminine societies, with Sweden and Norway scoring 5 and 8 respectively. The Netherlands was third from the bottom at 14, then Denmark with 16.

The M/F dimension has a number of interesting properties. It is the only one of the dimensions identified by Hofstede and colleagues that is *not* correlated with national wealth. M/F is also the only one of the five dimensions along which men and women favour different values, hence yielding differences both at the levels of national and individual difference. Generally, men rate ego-goals higher, whereas women value social-goals more. The only exception to this pattern is found in feminine cultures where both men and women are supposed to be modest, tender, and concerned with the quality of life. The presence of individual differences along a dimension that also measures national differences introduces further conceptual complexity to the broad picture provided by evolutionary and social role theory. An example of this complexity is the finding that M/F 'is the only dimension associated with the values that play a role in the differentiation of gender cultures' (1998:11). Thus the values which define the cultural difference between masculine and feminine societies are also the values that structure gender relations within a culture.

A number of cultural correlates of national differences in M/F were also presented. Hoppe (in Hofstede et al., 1998) suggested that in masculine countries individuals live in order to work, while in feminine countries work is viewed differently – people work in order to live. Arrindell (also in Hofstede et al., 1998) argued that relative wealth is necessary for a country to live up to the societal norms and political priorities dictated by feminine values, and hence the picture concerning subjective well-being is complex. National wealth and a certain resource level are implicated, in addition to MAS. De Mooij (in Hofstede et al., 1998) demonstrated a link between MAS and consumer behaviour, as the latter reflects both ego- and social-goals. For example, in a feminine culture, individuals read more fiction than do people in a masculine culture, where reading is generally oriented towards the learning of facts. To maintain conceptual clarity, it is necessary to remember that these national comparisons are based upon proportions of people within a country, engaging in particular behaviour.

In his long chapter, 'Culture of Gender', Hofstede (Hofstede et al., 1998) illustrated the influence of national-level differentiation of M/F upon the typical behaviour and values of groups in society. In masculine countries, men's values differ more from those of women, and the values of older people differ more from those of younger people. A table of 19 gender-related values summarised this discussion. A sample of these values includes the contrast between modesty and tenderness values in feminine cultures with assertiveness and toughness values typical of masculine cultures. There is less sex segregation in higher education in feminine than in masculine countries, particularly when they are affluent. In developed feminine nations, more women serve in parliament and in government offices than in developed masculine countries. However, economic possibilities and necessities, rather than a country's position on the MAS scale, play a major part in determining women's activities outside the family sphere. Perhaps the most challenging and innovative idea to emerge from this analysis is the proposition that national values, masculine or feminine, influence the construction of gender differences between the two groups. Thus, feminist ideology takes different forms in masculine and feminine societies.

The conceptual difficulties of this discourse are illustrated by Best and Williams' presentation of their research on gender stereotypes and self and ideal self descriptions in Hofstede's book, and his summary of it in the preceding chapter. Best and Williams found that the traits differentially assigned men and women in feminine cultures were more universal – those assigned in masculine countries were more country-specific. Hofstede concluded that men's and women's use of the same terms for their self-concepts is positive within a masculine culture but viewed as a failure of women to express their own nature within a feminine society.

As we noted earlier in this chapter, Williams and Best (1982, 1990) find little convergent validity for Hofstede's (1980) concept of M/F, in that a country's MAS score was unrelated to its measure of gender stereotyping based on individual ratings. In seeking to reconcile this disparity, we are again confronted with the issue of levels of discourse. It could be argued that Williams and Best focus on the individual level, and their cross-cultural data collection is designed to ensure the validity of measures of stereotyping within particular societies, that is, to develop appropriate emic instruments. Such instruments would employ measures that members of a particular society found meaningful and important, but these are evidently different from the terms 'masculinity' and 'femininity' as used by Hofstede to characterise national and cultural differences. However, one of the main concerns of Williams and Best's research has been shared beliefs about men and women held by particular cultures and how these differ from one another. In this sense, they are measuring shared cultural values, not individual-level phenomena (which are better characterised as schema: chapter 2).

Hofstede et al. also invoked national values to explain patterns of mate selection, a subject already addressed in different ways by social role and evolutionary theory (Buss, 1989; Eagly and Wood, 1999). They linked men's preference for industrious, wealthy, and chaste brides to collectivist values. The role of inclusive fitness was brushed aside by the suggestion that theory building in masculine Anglo-American science biologises sexuality and fails to take account of cultural values. With this aspect of Hofstede's work, we have returned to a Standard Social Science Model (chapter 1) which holds that explanations at a cultural level are sufficient, and that evolutionary considerations are unnecessary. The challenge still remains to integrate a concern with differences between whole societies, with the social role and sexual selection frameworks, both of which provide broad frameworks for understanding sex and gender. Whatever their limitations, Hofstede's concepts represent an attempt to characterise something that neither the social role nor the evolutionary framework tackles – national differences. We anticipate future attempts to synthesise all three viewpoints into a coherent overall model of sex and gender.

Postscript

One notable feature of the 20 years since we began reviewing studies concerned with sex and gender for the first edition of this book is the volume of empirical research that has been undertaken. Fortunately this growth in information has been associated with both the development of the techniques for integrating research findings, and the growth of wider-ranging theories, both discussed in this chapter. These enable larger bodies of research to be described more parsimoniously and to be understood within a wider theoretical framework. We hope the reader will agree with us that this represents a considerable advance over a time when researchers used simple narrative reviews of research, and were guided by limited explanations conceived in terms of socialisation or specific biological influences (chapter 4).

At the beginning of the twentieth century, Helen Thompson Woolley commented on nineteenth- and early twentieth-century psychologists' and physiologists' efforts to understand sex differences. She wrote: 'There is perhaps no field aspiring to be scientific where flagrant personal bias, logic martyred in the cause of supporting prejudice, unfounded assertions, and even sentimental rot and drivel, have run riot to such an extent as here' (Woolley, 1910:340). We are confident, nearly a hundred years later, that, although it is easy to find particular examples that fit her characterisation, these are far outweighed by the substantial developments in research, synthesis, and theory that we have sought to describe in this book.

Further reading

Gangestad, S. W. and Simpson, J. A. (2000). The evolution of mating: trade-offs and strategic pluralism. *Behavioral and Brain Sciences*, 23: 573–644.
     The theory is that there are different reproductive strategies within the male sex that cause them to behave differently. If confirmed, it could provide a new way of looking at sex differences in behaviour. The article is followed by extensive commentaries written by psychologists, biologists, and social scientists.
Hofstede, G., Arrindell, W. A., and Best, D. L. et al. (1998). *Masculinity and Femininity: The Taboo Dimension of National Cultures*. Thousand Oaks, CA: Sage Publications.

In this book Hofstede elaborates his dimension Masculinity/Femininity that he first identified in *Culture's Consequences* (1980) alongside Power Distance (unequal versus equal), Uncertainty Avoidance (rigid versus flexible) and Individualism/Collectivism. These dimensions, derived from questionnaire surveys comparing national samples, provide a novel perspective.

Smith, E. A., Borgerhoff Mulder, M., and Hill, K. (2001). Controversies in the evolutionary social sciences: a guide for the perplexed. *Trends in Ecology and Evolution*, 16: 128–35.

An outline of different evolutionary approaches to human behaviour, with particular emphasis on the ways in which human behavioural ecology differs from the better-known evolutionary psychology.

Williams, J. E., and Best, D. L. (1990). *Measuring Sex Stereotypes: A Multination Study* (rev. edn). Beverly Hills, CA: Sage.

This book provides an updated account of the authors' extensive cross-cultural comparisons of gender stereotypes across a range of nations.

References

Abramson, L. Y., Metalsky, G. I., and Alloy, L. B. (1989). Hopelessness depression: a theory-based subtype of depression. *Psychological Review*, 96: 358–72.

Adams, H. E., Wright, L. W., and Lohr, B. A. (1996). Is homophobia associated with homosexual arousal? *Journal of Abnormal Psychology*, 105: 440–5.

Adelmann, P. K., Antonucci, T. C., Crohan, E. E., and Coleman, L. M. (1989). Empty nest, cohort, and employment in the well-being of midlife women. *Sex Roles*, 20: 173–89.

Ainsworth, M. D. S. (1965). Further research into the adverse effects of maternal deprivation. In J. Bowlby (ed.), *Child Care and the Growth of Love* (2nd edn, pp. 191–241). Harmondsworth: Penguin.

Alcock, J. (1975). *Animal Behavior: An Evolutionary Approach*. Sunderland, MA: Sinauer.

Alexander, G. M. and Hines, M. (1994). Gender labels and play styles: their relative contribution to children's selection of playmates. *Child Development*, 65: 869–79.

Allen, B. P. (1995). Gender stereotypes are not accurate: a replication of Martin (1987) using diagnostic vs. self-report and behavioral criteria. *Sex Roles*, 32: 583–600.

Allport, G. W. (1954). *The Nature of Prejudice*. Cambridge, MA: Addison-Wesley.

Amato, P. R. and Keith, B. (1991). Parental divorce and well-being of child: a meta-analysis. *Psychological Bulletin*, 110: 26–46.

Anastasi, A. (1958). *Differential Psychology* (3rd edn). New York: Macmillan.

Anderson, B. L., Cyranowski, J. M., and Aarestad, S. (2000). Beyond artificial, sex-linked distinctions to conceptualise female sexuality: comment on Baumeister (2000). *Psychological Bulletin*, 126: 380–4.

Anderson, E. (1994). The code of the streets. *Atlantic Monthly*, 273: 81–94.

Archer, J. (1971). Sex differences in emotional behaviour: a reply to Gray and Buffery. *Acta Psychologica*, 35: 415–29.

(1975). Rodent sex differences in emotional and related behavior. *Behavioral Biology*, 14: 451–79.

(1976). Biological explanations of psychological sex differences. In B. B. Lloyd and J. Archer (eds.), *Exploring Sex Differences* (pp. 241–66). New York: Academic Press.

(1984). Gender roles as developmental pathways. *British Journal of Social Psychology*, 23: 245–56.

(1986). Adolescent gender stereotypes: a comment on Keyes. *British Journal of Social Psychology*, 25: 71–2.

(1987). Beyond sex differences: comments on Borrill and Reid. *Bulletin of the British Psychological Society*, 40: 88–90.

(1988). *The Behavioural Biology of Aggression*. Cambridge University Press.

(1989a) The relationship between gender role measures: a review. *British Journal of Social Psychology*, 28: 173–84.

(1989b). Childhood gender roles: structure and development. *The Psychologist*, 2: 367–70.

(1991). The influence of testosterone on human aggression. *British Journal of Psychology*, 82: 1–28.

(1992a). *Ethology and Human Development*. Hemel Hempsted, UK: Harvester-Wheatsheaf.

(1992b). Childhood gender roles: social context and organization. In H. McGurk (ed.), *Childhood Social Development: Contemporary Perspectives* (pp. 31–61). Hove, UK and Hillsdale, NJ: Lawrence Erlbaum.

(1992c). Mating tactics are complex and involve females too. *Behavioral and Brain Sciences*, 15: 379–80 (commentary on Thornhill and Thornhill, 1992).

(1992d). Gender stereotyping of school subjects. *The Psychologist*, 5: 66–9.

(1992e). Sex bias in evaluations at college and work. *The Psychologist*, 5: 200–4.

(1994a). Introduction: male violence in perspective. In J. Archer (ed.), *Male Violence* (pp. 1–20). London and New York: Routledge.

(1994b). Violence between men. In J. Archer (ed.), *Male Violence* (pp. 121–40). London and New York: Routledge.

(1994c). Power and male violence. In J. Archer (ed.), *Male Violence* (pp. 310–31). London and New York: Routledge.

(1994d). Testosterone and aggression. *Journal of Offender Rehabilitation*, 21: 3–25.

(1995). What can ethology offer the social psychological study of human aggression? *Aggressive Behavior*, 21: 243–55.

(1996). Sex differences in social behavior: are the social role and evolutionary explanations compatible? *American Psychologist*, 51: 909–17.

(1997). On the origin of sex differences in social behavior: Darwinian and non-Darwinian accounts. *American Psychologist*, 52: 1383–4.

(1999). *The Nature of Grief: The Evolution and Psychology of Reactions to Loss*. London and New York: Routledge.

(2000a). Sex differences in aggression between heterosexual partners: a meta-analytic review. *Psychological Bulletin*, 126: 651–80.

(2000b). Sex differences in partner aggression: a reply to Frieze (2000), O'Leary (2000), and White, Smith, Koss and Figueredo (2000). *Psychological Bulletin*, 126: 697–702.

(2001a). Sex differences in aggression: a meta-analysis. Unpublished manuscript, Department of Psychology, University of Central Lancashire, Preston, UK.

(2001b). Evolving theories of behaviour. *The Psychologist*, 14: 414–19.

(2001c). Evolutionary social psychology. In W. Stroebe and M. Hewstone (eds.), *Introduction to Social Psychology: A European Perspective* (3rd edn, pp. 23–46). Oxford, UK: Blackwell.

(In press). Sex differences in physically aggressive acts between heterosexual partners: a meta-analytic review. *Aggressive and Violent Behavior: A Review Journal*.

Archer, J., Birring, S. S., and Wu, F. C. W. (1998). The association between testosterone and aggression among young men: empirical findings and a meta-analysis. *Aggressive Behavior*, 24: 411–20.

Archer, J. and Browne, K. (1989). Concepts and approaches to the study of aggression. In J. Archer and K. Browne (eds.), *Human Aggression: Naturalistic Approaches* (pp. 3–24). London and New York: Routledge.

Archer, J. and Freedman, S. (1989). Gender stereotypic perceptions of academic disciplines. *British Journal of Educational Psychology*, 59: 306–13.

Archer, J. and Haigh, A. (1997a). Do beliefs about aggression predict self-reported levels of aggression? *British Journal of Social Psychology*, 36: 83–105.

(1997b). Beliefs about aggression among male and female prisoners. *Aggressive Behavior*, 23: 405–15.

Archer, J., Holloway, R., and McLaughlin, K. (1995a). Self-reported physical aggression among young men. *Aggressive Behavior*, 21: 325–42.

Archer, J. and Huntingford, F. A. (1994). Game theory models and escalation of animal fights. In M. Potegal and J. F. Knutson (eds.), *The Dynamics of Aggression: Biological and Social Processes* (pp. 3–31). London and Hillsdale, NJ: Lawrence Erlbaum.

Archer, J. and Lloyd, B. B. (1985). *Sex and Gender*. New York: Cambridge, University Press.

Archer, J. and Macrae, M. (1991). Gender-perceptions of school subjects among 10–11 year olds. *British Journal of Educational Psychology*, 61: 99–103.

Archer, J., Monks, S., and Connors, E. (1997). Comments on SP0409: A. Campbell, M. Sapochnik and S. Muncer: Sex differences in aggression: does social representation mediate forms? *BJSP*, 1997, 36, 161–171. *British Journal of Social Psychology*, 36: 603–6.

Archer, J., Smith, J., and Kilpatrick, G. (1995b). The association between gender scale measures and gender clustering in recall. *Sex Roles*, 33: 299–308.

Archer, J. and Vaughan, A. E. (2001). Evolutionary theories of rape. *Psychology, Evolution and Gender*, 3: 95–101.

Arias, I. and Johnson, P. (1989). Evaluations of physical aggression among intimate dyads. *Journal of Interpersonal Violence*, 4: 298–307.

Arnold, A. P. (1996). Genetically triggered sexual differentiation of brain and behavior. *Hormones and Behavior*, 30: 495–505.

Aube, J., Norcliffe, H., Craig, J. A., and Koestner, R. (1995). Gender characteristics and adjustment-related outcomes: questioning the masculinity model. *Personality and Social Psychology Bulletin*, 21: 284–95.

Baker, S. (1980). Biological influences on human sex and gender. *Signs*, 6: 80–96.

Baker, R. R. and Bellis, M. A. (1995). *Human Sperm Competition*. London: Chapman and Hall.

Baldwin, A. C., Critelli, J. W., Stevens, L. C., and Russell, S. (1986). Androgyny and sex role measurement: a personal construct approach. *Journal of Personality and Social Psychology*, 51: 1081–8.

Bandura, A. (1989). Social cognitive theory. In R. Vasta (ed.), *Annals of Child Development: Vol. 6. Six Theories of Child Development* (pp. 1–60). Greenwich, CT: JAI.

Bandura, A., Ross, D., and Ross, S. A. (1961). Transmission of aggression through imitation of aggressive models. *Journal of Abnormal and Social Psychology*, 63: 575–82.

Bandura, A. and Walters, R. H. (1963). *Social Learning and Personality Development*. New York: Holt, Rinehart and Winston.

Barkley, R. A., Ullman, D. G., Otto, L., and Brecht, J. M. (1977). The effects of sex-typing and sex-appropriateness of modelled behavior on children's imitation. *Child Development*, 48: 721–5.

Barlow, D. H., Brown, T. A., and Craske, M. G. (1994). Definitions of panic attacks and panic disorder in the DSM-IV: implications for research. *Journal of Abnormal Psychology*, 103: 553–64.

Baron-Cohen, S., (ed.) (1997). *The Maladapted Mind: Classic Readings in Evolutionary Psychopathology*. Hove, East Sussex: Psychology Press.

Baron-Cohen, S. and Hammer, J. (1997). Is autism an extreme form of the 'male brain'? *Advances in Infancy Research*, 11: 193–217.

Barry, W. A. (1970). Marriage research and conflict: an integrative review. *Psychological Bulletin*, 73: 41–54.

Bart, P. B. (1971). Depression in middle-aged women. In V. Cornick and B. K. Maran (eds.), *Women in Sexist Society* (pp. 99–117). New York: Basic Books.

Bauer, P. J. (1993). Memory for gender-consistent and gender-inconsistent event sequences by twenty-five-month old children. *Child Development*, 64: 285–97.

Baumeister, R. F. (1988). Should we stop studying sex differences altogether? *American Psychologist*, 43: 1092–5.

  (2000). Gender differences in erotic plasticity: the female sex-drive as socially flexible and responsive. *Psychological Bulletin*, 126: 347–74.

Baumeister, R. F., Catanese, K. R., Campbell, W. K., and Tice, D. M. (2000). Nature, culture and explanations for erotic plasticity: reply to Anderson, Cyranowski and Aarestad (2000) and Hyde and Durik (2000). *Psychological Bulletin*, 126: 385–9.

Baumeister, R. F., Smart, L., and Boden, J. M. (1996). Relation of threatened egotism to violence and aggression: the dark side of high self-esteem. *Psychological Review*, 103: 5–33.

Beasley, C. (1999). *What is Feminism? An Introduction to Feminist Theory*. London, Thousand Oaks, New Delhi: Sage Publications.

Beckwith, J. B. (1993). Gender stereotypes and mental health revisited. *Social Behavior and Personality*, 21: 85–8.

Beer, W. R. (1983). *Househusband: Men and Housework in American Families*. New York: Praeger/Bergin.

Beere, C. A., King, D. W., Beere, D. B., and King, L. A. (1984). The Sex Role Egalitarianism Scale: a measure of attitudes towards equality between the sexes. *Sex Roles*, 10: 563–76.

Belsky, J. (1996). Parent, infant, and social-contextual antecedents of father–son attachment security. *Developmental Psychology*, 32: 905–13.

Bem, D. (1996). Exotic becomes erotic: a developmental theory of sexual orientation. *Psychological Review*, 103: 320–35.

Bem, S. L. (1974). The measurement of psychological androgyny. *Journal of Consulting and Clinical Psychology*, 42: 155–62.

  (1975). Sex role adaptability: one consequence of psychological androgyny. *Journal of Personality and Social Psychology*, 31: 634–43.

  (1977). On the utility of alternative procedures for assessing psychological androgyny. *Journal of Consulting and Clinical Psychology*, 45: 196–205.

(1981). Gender schema theory: a cognitive account of sex-typing. *Psychological Review*, 88: 354–64.

(1985). Androgyny and gender schema theory: a conceptual and empirical integration. In T. B. Sondereggar (ed.), *Nebraska Symposium on Motivation No. 32* (pp. 179–226). Lincoln: University of Nebraska Press.

(1989). Genital knowledge and gender constancy in pre-school children. *Child Development*, 60: 649–62.

(1993). *The Lenses of Gender: Transforming the Debate on Sexual Inequality*. New Haven, CT: Yale University Press.

(1995). Dismantling gender polarization and compulsory heterosexuality: should we turn the volume down or up? *The Journal of Sex Research*, 32: 329–34.

Benenson, J. F. (1993). Greater preference among females than males for dyadic interaction in early childhood. *Child Development*, 64: 544–55.

(1994). Ages four to six years: changes in the structures of play networks of boys and girls. *Merrill Palmer Quarterly*, 40: 478–87.

Benenson, J. F., Liroff, E. R., Pascal, S. J., and Cioppa, G. D. (1997). Propulsion: a behavioural expression of masculinity. *British Journal of Psychology*, 15: 37–50.

Benson, P. L. and Vincent, S. (1980). Development and validation of the Sexist Attitudes Towards Women Scale (SATWS). *Psychology of Women Quarterly*, 5: 276–91.

Berenbaum, S. A. (1998). How hormones affect behavioral and neural development: introduction to the special issue on 'Gonadal hormones and sex differences in behavior'. *Developmental Neuropsychology*, 14: 175–96.

(1999). Effects of early androgens on sex-typed activities and interests in adolescents with congenital adrenal hyperplasia. *Hormones and Behavior*, 35: 102–10.

Berenbaum, S. A. and Hines, M. (1992). Early androgens are related to childhood sex-typed toy preferences. *Psychological Science*, 3: 203–6.

Berenbaum, S. A. and Resnick, S. M. (1997). Early androgen effects on aggression in children and adults with congenital adrenal hyperplasia. *Psychoneuroendocrinology*, 22: 505–15.

Berkowitz, L. (1962). *Aggression: A Social Psychological Analysis*. New York: McGraw-Hill.

Bernard, J. (1972). *The Future of Marriage*. New York: Bantam Books.

Bernard, M. E. (1979). Does sex role behavior influence the way teachers evaluate students? *Journal of Educational Psychology*, 71: 553–62.

Berrill, M. and Arsenault, M. (1982). Mating behavior of the green shore crab *Carcinus maenas*. *Bulletin of Marine Science*, 32: 632–8.

Berry, J. W. (1966). Temme and Eskimo perceptual skills. *International Journal of Psychology*, 1: 207–29.

Bertram, B. C. R. (1975). Social factors influencing reproduction in wild lions. *Journal of Zoology*, 177: 463–82.

Betzig, L. (1992). Roman polygyny. *Ethology and Sociobiology*, 13: 309–49.

Bibring, E. (1953). The mechanism of depression. In P. Greenacre (ed.), *Affective Disorders* (pp. 13–48). New York: International Universities Press.

Bifulco, A. and Moran, P. (1998) *Wednesday's Child Research into Women's Experience of Neglect and Abuse in Childhood, and Adult Depression*. London and New York: Routledge.

Biller, H. B. (1981). The father and sex role development. In M. E. Lamb (ed.), *The Role of the Father in Child Development* (pp. 319–58), New York: Wiley.

Birkhead, T. and Moller, A. P. (1992). *Sperm Competition in Birds*. London: Academic Press.

Bjorkqvist, K., Lagerspetz, K. M. J., and Kaukiainen, A. (1992a). Do girls manipulate and boys fight? Developmental trends in regard to direct and indirect aggression. *Aggressive Behavior* 18: 117–27.

Bjorkqvist, K., Osterman, K., and Kaukiainen, A. (1992b). The development of direct and indirect aggressive strategies in males and females. In K. Bjorkqvist and P. Niemela (eds.), *Of Mice and Women: Aspects of Female Aggression* (pp. 51–64). San Diego, CA: Academic Press.

Bjorkqvist, K., Osterman, K., and Lagerspetz, K. M. J. (1994). Sex differences in covert aggression among adults. *Aggressive Behavior*, 20: 27–33.

Blazer, D. G., Kessler, R. C., McGonagle, K. A., and Swartz, M. S. (1994). The prevalence and distribution of major depression in a national community sample: the National Comorbidity Study. *American Journal of Psychiatry*, 151: 979–86.

Block, J. H. (1978). Another look at sex differentiation in the socialization behaviors of mothers and daughters. In J. Sherman and F. Denmark (eds.), *Psychology of Women: Future Directions of Research* (pp. 29–87). New York: Psychological Dimensions.

Blurton Jones, N. G. (1967). An ethological study of some aspects of social behaviour of children in nursery school. In D. Morris (ed.), *Primate Ethology* (pp. 347–68). London: Weidenfeld and Nicholson.

   (1972). Categories of child–child interaction. In N. G. Blurton Jones (ed.), *Ethological Studies of Child Behaviour* (pp. 97–127). London: Cambridge University Press.

Blurton Jones, N. G. and Konner, M. J. (1973). Sex differences in the behaviour of London and Bushman children. In R. P. Michael and J. H. Crook (eds.), *Comparative Ecology and Behaviour of Primates* (pp. 689–750). London and New York: Academic Press.

Boissy, A. and Bouissou, M. F. (1994). Effects of androgen treatment on behavioral and physiological responses of heifers to fear-eliciting situations. *Hormones and Behavior*, 28: 66–83.

Borland, D. C. (1982). A cohort analysis approach to the empty-nest syndrome among three ethnic groups of women: a theoretical position. *Journal of Marriage and the Family*, 44: 117–29.

Boulton, M. J. (1991). Children's abilities to distinguish between playful and aggressive fighting: a developmental perspective. *British Journal of Developmental Psychology*, 11: 249–63.

Bower, T. (1989). *The Rational Infant: Learning and Infancy*. New York: Freeman.

Bowlby, J. (1951). *Maternal Care and Mental Health*. Geneva: World Health Organisation.
   (1965). *Child Care and the Growth of Love*. (2nd edn). Harmondsworth: Penguin.
   (1969). *Attachment and Loss. Vol. 1: Attachment*. London: Hogarth Press.

Boyle, J. (1977). *A Sense of Freedom*. London: Pan Books.

Bradley, C. (1984). Sex bias in the evaluation of students. *British Journal of Social Psychology*, 23: 147–53.

Breed, M. D. and Bell, W. J. (1983). Hormonal influences on invertebrate aggressive behavior. In B. B. Svare (ed.), *Hormones and Aggressive Behavior* (pp. 577–90). New York: Plenum.

Bridges, L. J., Connell, J. P., and Belsky, J. (1988). Similarities and differences in infant–mother and infant–father interaction in the Strange Situation: a component process analysis. *Developmental Psychology*, 24: 92–100.

British Crime Survey (2000). Website address: (www.homeoffice.gov.uk/rds/pdfs/hosb 1801.pdf).

British Government's Women's Unit (2000). Young people and gender: a review of research. A report submitted to the Women's Unit, Cabinet Office, and the Family Policy Unit, Home office. Crown copyright.

Broadbent, J. (1999). Age differences in aggression. Unpublished B.Sc. dissertation, Department of Psychology, University of Central Lancashire, Preston, UK.

Bronfenbrenner, U., McClelland, P., Wethington, E., Moen, P., and Ceci, S. J. (1996). *The State of Americans.* New York: Free Press.

Broverman, I. K., Broverman, D. M., Clarkson, F. E., Rosenkrantz, P. S., and Vogel, S. R. (1970). Sex role stereotypes and clinical judgements in mental health. *Journal of Consulting and Clinical Psychology*, 34: 1–7.

Broverman, D. M., Klaiber, E. L., Kobayashi, Y., and Yogel, W. (1968). Roles of activation and inhibition in sex differences in cognitive abilities. *Psychological Review*, 75: 23–50.

Brown, D. E. and Hotra, D. (1988). Are prescriptively monogamous societies effectively monogamous? In L. Betzig, M. Borgerhoff Mulder, and P. Turke (eds.), *Human Reproductive Behaviour: A Darwinian Perspective* (pp. 153–9). Cambridge and New York: Cambridge University Press.

Brown, G. W. and Harris, T. O. (1978). *Social Origins of Depression: A Study In Psychiatric Disorder in Women.* London: Tavistock.

Brown, G. W., Harris, T. O., and Bifulco, A. (1985) Long term effects of early loss of parent. In M. Rutter, C. Izard, and P. Read (eds.), *Depression in Young People: Developmental and Clinical Perspectives* (pp. 251–96). New York: Guilford Press.

Brown, J. H. and Lasiewski, R. C. (1972). Metabolism of weasels: the cost of being long and thin. *Ecology*, 53: 939–43.

Brown, R. (1988). *Group Processes: Dynamics Within and Between Groups.* Oxford and New York: Blackwell.

Brown, R. P. and Josephs, R. A. (1999). A burden of proof: stereotype relevance and gender differences in math performance. *Journal of Personality and Social Psychology*, 76: 247–57.

Browne, B. A. (1998). Gender stereotypes in advertising on children's television in the 1990s: a cross-national analysis. *Journal of Advertising*, 27: 83–96.

Brownmiller, S. (1975). *Against Our Will: Men, Women and Rape.* New York: Simon and Schuster.

Budaev, S. V. (1999). Sex differences in the Big Five personality factors: testing an evolutionary hypothesis. *Personality and Individual Differences*, 26: 801–13.

Bullough, V. L. (1974). Transvestites in the Middle Ages. *American Journal of Sociology*, 79: 1381–94.

Burgess, A. (1997). *Fatherhood Reclaimed: The Making of the Modern Father.* London: Vermilion.

Burke, J. (1999). Teenage rape victim shot for bringing 'shame' to her tribe. *The Observer*, London, 18 April, p. 19.

Burn, S. M., O'Neil, A. K., and Nederend, S. (1996). Childhood tomboyism and adult androgyny. *Sex Roles*, 34: 419–28.

Burt, M. (1980). Cultural myths and support for rape. *Journal of Personality and Social Psychology*, 38: 217–30.

Buss, D. M. (1989). Sex differences in human mate preferences: evolutionary hypotheses tested in 37 cultures. *Behavioral and Brain Sciences*, 12: 1–49.

(1994). *The Evolution of Desire: Strategies of Human Mating*. New York: Basic Books.

(1999). *Evolutionary Psychology: The New Science of the Mind*. Boston, MA and London: Allyn and Bacon.

Buss, D. M., Larsen, R. J., Westen, D., and Semmelroth, J. (1992). Sex differences in jealousy: evolution, physiology, and psychology. *Psychological Science*, 3: 251–5.

Buss, D. M. and Schmitt, D. P. (1993). Sexual strategies theory: an evolutionary perspective of human mating. *Psychological Review*, 100: 204–32.

Buss, D. M., Shackelford, T. K., and Kirkpatrick, L. A., et al. (1999). Jealousy and the nature of beliefs about infidelity: tests of competing hypotheses about sex differences in the United States, Korea, and Japan. *Personal Relationships*, 6: 125–50.

Buss, D. M., Shackelford, T. K., and LeBlanc, G. J. (2000). Number of children desired and preferred spousal age difference: context-specific mate preference patterns across 37 cultures. *Evolution and Social Behavior*, 21: 323–31.

Bussey, K. and Bandura, A. (1992). Self-regulatory mechanisms governing gender development. *Child Development*, 63: 1236–50.

(1999). Social cognitive theory of gender development and differentiation. *Psychological Review*, 106: 676–713.

Buunk, B. P., Angleitner, A., Oubaid, V., and Buss, D. M. (1996). Sex differences in jealousy in evolutionary and cultural perspective. *Psychological Science*, 7: 359–63.

Byrnes, J. P., Miller, D. C., and Schafer, W. D. (1999). Gender differences in risk-taking: a meta-analysis. *Psychological Bulletin*, 125: 367–83.

Cairns, E. (1980). The development of ethnic discrimination in young children in Northern Ireland. In J. Harbison and J. Harbison (eds.), *Children and Young People in Northern Ireland: A Society under Stress* (pp. 115–27). Somerset, UK: Open Books.

Campbell, A. (1986). The streets and violence. In A. Campbell and J. J. Gibbs (eds.), *Violent Transactions: The Limits of Personality* (pp. 115–32). Oxford, UK: Blackwell.

(1995). A few good men: evolutionary psychology and female adolescent aggression. *Ethology and Sociobiology*, 16: 99–123.

(1999). Staying alive: evolution, culture and women's intra-sexual aggression. *Behavioral and Brain Sciences*, 22: 203–52 (including commentaries).

(1997). Aggression and testosterone: testing a bio-social model. *Aggressive Behavior*, 23: 229–38.

(1998). Primacy of organising effects of testosterone. *Behavioral and Brain Sciences*, 21: 365 (commentary).

Campbell, A., Sapochnik, M., and Muncer, S. (1997). Sex differences in aggression: Does social representation mediate form of aggression? *British Journal of Social Psychology*, 36: 161–71.

Campbell, D. W. and Eaton, W. O. (1999). Sex differences in the activity level of infants. *Infant and Child Development*, 8: 1–17.

Cancian, F. M. (1987). *Love in America: Gender and Self Development*. Cambridge and New York: Cambridge University Press.

Cantor, C. H. (2000). Suicide in the Western world. In K. Hawton and C. Van Heeringtgen (eds.), *The International Handbook of Suicide and Attempted Suicide* (pp. 9–28). Chichester: John Wiley and Sons.

Carroll, R. (1998). Gangs put the boot into old ideas of femininity. *The Guardian*, London, 22 July.

Carruthers, M. (1996). *The Male Menopause: Restoring Vitality and Virility*. Wellingborough, Northants.: Thorsons.

Cashmore, E. (1999). Women's greatest handicaps: sex, medicine, and men. *British Journal of Sports Medicine*, 33: 76–7.

Cavalli-Sforza, L. L. and Feldman, N. W. (1981). *Cultural Transmission and Evolution: A Quantitative Approach*. Princeton University Press.

Cejka, M. A. and Eagly, A. H. (1999). Gender-stereotypic images of occupations correspond to the sex segregation of employment. *Personality and Social Psychology Bulletin*, 25: 413–23.

Central Statistics Office (1985). *Social Trends 1984*. London: HMSO.

Chang, J. (1977). *The Tao of Love and Sex: The Ancient Chinese Way to Ecstasy*. London: Wildwood House.

Check, J. V. and Malamuth, N. M. (1983). Sex role stereotyping and reactions to depictions of stranger versus acquaintance rape. *Journal of Personality and Social Psychology*, 45: 344–56.

Cheng, A. T. A. and Lee, C.-S. (2000) Suicide in Asia and the Far East. In K. Hawton and C. Van Heeringtgen (eds.), *The International Handbook of Suicide and Attempted Suicide* (pp. 121–35). Chichester: John Wiley and Sons.

Chesler, P. (1972). *Women and Madness*. New York: Doubleday.

Chisholm, J. S. (1996). The evolutionary ecology of attachment organisation. *Human Nature*, 7: 1–38.

Chodorow, N. (1978). *The Reproduction of Mothering*. Berkeley, CA: University of California Press.

Clark, D. C. and Fawsett, J. (1992). Review of empirical risk factors for evaluation of suicidal patients. In B. Bongar (ed.), *Suicide: Guidelines for Assessment, Management and Treatment* (pp. 16–48). New York: Oxford University Press.

Clark, R. D. III and Hatfield, E. (1989). Gender differences in receptivity to sexual offers. *Journal of Psychology and Human Sexuality*, 2: 39–55.

Clegg, S. R. (1989). *Frameworks of Power*. Newbury Park, CA and London: Sage.

Clifton, A. K., McGrath, D., and Wick, B. (1976). Stereotypes of woman: a single category? *Sex Roles*, 2: 135–48.

Clutton-Brock, T. H. and Parker, G. A. (1995). Sexual coercion in animal societies. *Animal Behaviour*, 49: 1345–65.

Cohen, H., Rosen, R. C., and Goldstein, L. (1976). Electroencephalographic laterality changes during human sexual orgasm. *Archives of Sexual Behavior*, 5: 189–99.

Cohen, J. (1988). *Statistical Power Analysis for the Behavioral Sciences* (2nd edn). Hillsdale, NJ: Lawrence Erlbaum.

Collaer, M. L. and Hines, M. (1995). Human behavioral sex differences: a role for gonadal hormones during early development. *Psychological Bulletin*, 118: 55–107.

Coltrane, S. (1996). *Family Man: Fatherhood, Housework and Gender Equity*. New York: Oxford University Press.

Constantinople, A. (1973). Masculinity–femininity: an exception to a famous dictum. *Psychological Bulletin*, 80: 389–407.

Conway, M., Pizzamiglio, M. T., and Mount, L. (1996). Status, communality, and agency: implications for stereotypes of gender and other groups. *Journal of Personality and Social Psychology*, 71: 25–38.

Cook, E. P. (1985). *Psychological Androgyny*. New York: Pergamon.

Cooper, H. (1979). Statistically combining independent studies: a meta-analysis of sex differences in conformity research. *Journal of Personality and Social Psychology*, 37: 131–46.

Corbitt, E. M. and Widiger, T. A. (1995). Sex differences among the personality disorders: an exploration of the data. *Clinical Psychology: Science and Practice*, 2: 225–38.

Cosmides, L. M. and Tooby, J. (1981). Cytoplasmic inheritance and intragenomic conflict. *Journal of Theoretical Biology*, 89: 83–129.

Costa, P. T. and McCrae, R. R. (1992). *NEO-PI-R Professional Manual*. PAR Inc.

Courtwright, D. T. (1996). *Violent Land: Single Men and Social Disorder, From the Frontier to the Inner City*. Cambridge, MA: Harvard University Press.

Crawford, C. B. and Anderson, J. L. (1989). Sociobiology: an environmentalist discipline? *American Psychologist*, 44: 1449–59.

Cronin, H. (1991). *The Ant and the Peacock*. Cambridge and New York: Cambridge University Press.

Cunningham, E. J. A. and Birkhead, T. R. (1998). Sex roles and sexual selection. *Animal Behaviour*, 56: 1311–21.

Dalgleish, T., Rosen, K., and Marks, M. (1996). Rhythm and blues: the theory and treatment of seasonal affective disorder. *British Journal of Clinical Psychology*, 35: 163–82.

Dalton, K. (1969). *The Menstrual Cycle*. Harmondsworth, UK: Penguin.
  (1994). *Once a Month* (revised edn). Glasgow: Fontana.

Daly, M. and Wilson, M. (1988). *Homicide*. New York: Aldine de Gruyter.
  (1990). Killing the competition: Female/female and male/male homicide. *Human Nature*, 1: 81–107.

Daly, M., Wilson, M., and Weghurst, S. J. (1982). Male sexual jealousy. *Ethology and Sociobiology*, 3: 11–27.

Darwin, C. (1871). *The Descent of Man and Selection in Relation to Sex*. London: Murray.

Davies, D. R. (1982). The effects of sex-typed labelling on the performance of boys and girls. Unpublished doctoral dissertation, University of London, UK.
  (1986). Children's performance and sex-typed labels. *British Journal of Social Psychology*, 25: 173–5.

Davies, M. (in press). Male sexual assault victims: a selective review of the literature and implications for support services. *Aggression and Violent Behavior. A Review Journal*.

Davies, M., Pollard, P., and Archer, J. (in press). The influence of victim gender and sexual orientation on blame towards the victim in a depicted stranger rape. *Violence and Victims*.

Davison, H. K. and Burke, M. J. (2000). Sex discrimination in simulated employment contexts: a meta-analytic investigation. *Journal of Vocational Behavior*, 56: 225–48.

Dean, K. E. and Malamuth, N. M. (1997). Characteristics of men who aggress sexually and of men who imagine aggressing: risk and moderator variables. *Journal of Personality and Social Psychology*, 72: 449–55.

Deaux, K. (1976). Sex: A perspective on the attribution process. In J. H. Harvey, W. J. Eckes, and R. F. Kidd (eds.), *New Directions in Attribution Research, Volume 1* (pp. 335–52). Hillsdale, NJ: Erlbaum.

(1984). From individual differences to social categories: analysis of a decade's research on gender. *American Psychologist*, 39: 105–16.

Deaux, K., Kite, M. E., and Lewis, L. L. (1985a). Clustering and gender schemata: an uncertain link. *Personality and Social Psychology Bulletin*, 11: 387–97.

Deaux, K. and Lewis, L. L. (1984). Structure of gender stereotypes: interrelationships among components and gender label. *Journal of Personality and Social Psychology*, 46: 991–1004.

Deaux, K., Winton, W., Crowley, M., and Lewis, L. (1985b). Level of categorization and content of gender stereotypes. *Social Cognition*, 3: 145–67.

de Beauvoir, S. (1953). *The Second Sex*. London: Jonathan Cape.

Decarie, T. G., Goulet, J., Brossard, M. D., Rafman, S., and Shaffran, R. (1974). *The Infant's Reaction to Strangers*. New York: International Universities Press.

Deleuze, G. and Guattari, F. (1977). *Anti-Oedipus: Capitalism and Schizophrenia*. Trans. R. Hunley, M. Seem, and H. R. Lane. New York: Viking.

Deutsch, H. (1945). *The Psychology of Women*. New York: Grune and Stratton.

DeVries, R. (1969). Constancy of generic identity in the years three to six. *Monographs of Society for Research in Child Development*, no. 127 34 (3).

DfEE Quality and Performance Improvement Divison (1999). *Modern Apprenticeships and Gender Stereotyping*, QPID Study Report no. 71. Sheffield: QPID/D/DfEE <http://www.dfee.gov.uk/skillnet_old/Q-7htm>.

Diekman, A. B. and Eagly, A. H. (2000). Stereotypes as dynamic constructs: women and men of the past, present and future. *Personality and Social Psychology Bulletin*, 26: 1171–8.

Diekstra, R. and Garnefski, N. (1995). On the nature, magnitude and causality of suicidal behavior: an international perspective. *Suicide and Life Threatening Behavior*, 25: 36–57.

DiPietro, J. A. (1981). Rough-and-tumble play: a function of gender. *Developmental Psychology*, 17: 50–8.

Dittmann, R. W. (1992). Body positions of movement patterns in female patients with congenital adrenal hyperplasia. *Hormones and Behavior*, 26: 441–56.

Dobash, R. E. and Dobash, R. P. (1977–8). Wives: the 'appropriate' victims of marital violence. *Victimology: An International Journal*, 2: 426–42.

(1980). *Violence Against Wives: A Case Against the Patriarchy*. London: Open Books.

Dobash, R. P., Dobash, R. E., Wilson, M., and Daly, M. (1992). The myth of sexual symmetry in marital violence. *Social Problems*, 39: 71–91.

Doise, W. (1986). *Levels of Explanation in Social Psychology*. London and New York: Cambridge University Press.

Dollard, J. and Miller, N. E. (1950). *Personality and Psychotherapy: An Analysis in Terms of Learning, Thinking and Culture*. New York: McGraw-Hill.

Drabman, R. S., Robertson, S. J., Patterson, J. N., Jarvie, G. J., Hammer, D., and Cordua, G. (1981). Children's perceptions of media-portrayed sex roles. *Sex Roles*, 7: 379–89.

Draper, P. (1975). !Kung women: contrasts in sexual egalitarianism in foraging and sedentary contexts. In R. Reiter (ed.), *Towards an Anthropology of Women* (pp. 77–109). New York and London: Monthly Review Press.

Draper, P. and Harpending, H. (1982). Father absence and reproductive strategy: an evolutionary perspective. *Journal of Anthropology Research*, 38: 255–73.

(1988). A sociobiological perspective on the development of human reproductive strategies. In K. B. MacDonald (ed.), *Sociobiological Perspectives on Human Development* (pp. 340–72). New York and Berlin: Springer-Verlag.

Dunbar, R. I. M., Clark, A., and Hurst, N. L. (1995). Conflict and cooperation among the Vikings: contingent behavioral decisions. *Ethology and Sociobiology*, 16: 233–46.

Duncan, J. (1998). Breasts, PMT and the pill bar women from boxing. *The Guardian*, London, p. 4.

Durham, W. C. (1991). *Co-evolution: Genes, Culture and Human Diversity*. Stanford University Press.

Durkin, K. (1985a). Television and sex role acquisition 1: Content. *British Journal of Social Psychology*, 24: 101–13.

(1985b). Television and sex role acquisition 2: Effects. *British Journal of Social Psychology*, 24: 191–210.

(1985c). Television and sex role acquisition 3: Counterstereotyping. *British Journal of Social Psychology*, 24: 211–22.

Durkin, K. and Nugent, B. (1998). Kindergarten children's gender-role expectations for television actors. *Sex Roles*, 38: 387–402.

Dutton, D. G. (1994). Patriarchy and wife assault: the ecological fallacy. *Violence and Victims*, 9: 167–82.

Eagly, A. H. (1983). Gender and social influence: a social psychological analysis. *American Psychologist*, 38: 971–81.

(1987). *Sex Differences in Social Behavior: A Social Role Interpretation*. Hillsdale, NJ: Lawrence Erlbaum.

(1995a). The science and politics of comparing women and men. *American Psychologist*, 50: 145–58.

(1995b). Reflections on the commenters' views. *American Psychologist*, 50: 69–171.

(1997). Sex differences in social behavior: comparing social role theory and evolutionary psychology. *American Psychologist*, 52: 1380–3.

Eagly, A. H. and Chaiken, S. (1993). *The Psychology of Attitudes*. Orlando, FL: Harcourt, Brace and Jovanovich.

Eagly, A. H. and Karau, S. J. (1991). Gender and the emergence of leaders: a meta-analysis. *Journal of Personality and Social Psychology*, 60: 685–710.

(in press). Role congruity theory of prejudice towards female leaders. *Psychological Review*.

Eagly, A. H. and Mladinic, A. (1989). Gender stereotypes and attitudes towards women and men. *Personality and Social Psychology Bulletin*, 15: 543–58.

Eagly, A. H., Mladinic, A., and Otto, S. (1991). Are women evaluated more favorably than men? An analysis of attitudes, beliefs, and emotions. *Psychology of Women Quarterly*, 15: 203–16.

Eagly, A. H. and Steffen, V. J. (1984). Gender stereotypes stem from the distribution of women and men into social roles. *Journal of Personality and Social Psychology*, 46: 735–54.

(1986). Gender and aggressive behavior: a meta-analytic review of the social psychological literature. *Psychological Bulletin*, 100: 309–30.

Eagly, A. H. and Wood, W. (1991). Explaining sex differences in social behavior: a meta-analytic perspective. *Personality and Social Psychology Bulletin*, 17: 306–15.

(1999). The origins of sex differences in human behavior: evolved dispositions versus social rules. *American Psychologist*, 54: 408–23.

Eagly, A. H., Wood, W., and Diekman, A. B. (2000). Social role theory of sex differences and similarities: a current appraisal. In T. Eckes and H. M. Trautner (eds.), *The Developmental Social Psychology of Gender* (pp. 123–74). Mahwah, NJ: Erlbaum.

Earls, F. (1987). Sex differences in psychiatric disorders: origins and developmental influences. *Psychiatric Developments*, 1: 1–23.

Eaton, W. O. and Enns, L. R. (1986). Sex differences in human motor activity level. *Psychological Bulletin*, 100: 19–28.

Eckes, T. (1994). Features of men, features of women: assessing stereotypic beliefs about gender subtypes. *British Journal of Social Psychology*, 33: 107–23.

Edwards, G. H. (1992). The structure and content of the male gender role stereotype: an exploration of subtypes. *Sex Roles*, 27: 533–51.

Edwards, V. J. and Spence, J. T. (1987). Gender-related traits, stereotypes, and schemata. *Journal of Personality and Social Psychology*, 53: 146–54.

Efoghe, G. B. (1989). Are extraverts more conjugally aggressive than introverts? A study of Nigerian couples. *Indian Journal of Behaviour*, 13 (4): 1–9.

Ehrhardt, A. A. and Baker, S. W. (1974). Fetal androgens, human central nervous system differentiation, and behavior sex differences. In R. C. Friedman, R. M. Richart, and R. L. van de Wiele (eds.), *Sex Differences in Behavior* (pp. 33–51). New York: Wiley.

Ehrhardt, A. A., Epstein, R., and Money, J. (1968). Fetal androgens and female gender identity in the early-treated adrenogenital syndrome. *Johns Hopkins Medical Journal*, 122: 160–7.

Ehrhardt, A. A., Ince, S. E., and Meyer-Bahlberg, H. F. L. (1981). Career aspiration and gender role development in young girls. *Archives of Sexual Behavior*, 10: 281–99.

Ehrhardt, A. A., Meyer-Bahlberg, H. F. L., and Rosen, L. R. et al. (1989). The development of gender-related behavior in females following prenatal exposure to diethylstilbestrol (DES). *Hormones and Behavior*, 23: 526–41.

Einon, D. (1998). How many children can one man have? *Evolution and Human Behavior*, 19: 413–26.

Elliott, A. (1998). *Freud 2000*. Cambridge: Polity Press.

Elliot, F. R. (1996). *Gender, Family and Society*. Baskingstoke and London: Macmillan, Press, Ltd.

Ellis, L. J. and Bentler, P. M. (1973). Traditional sex-determined role standards and sex stereotypes. *Journal of Personality and Social Psychology*, 25: 28–34.

Eme, R. F. (1979). Sex differences in childhood psychopathology: a review. *Psychological Bulletin*, 86: 574–95.

Emlen, S. T. (1997). The evolutionary study of human family systems. *Social Science Information*, 36: 563–89.

Emmerich, W., Goldman, K. S., Kirsch, B., and Sharabany, R. (1977). Evidence for a transitional phase in the development of gender constancy. *Child Development*, 48: 930–6.

England, E. M. (1988). College student stereotypes of female behavior: maternal professional women and assertive housewives. *Sex Roles*, 19, 365–85.

England, E. M. and Hyland, D. T. (1987). The content and structure of stereotypic subcategories of females and males. *Social and Behavioral Sciences Documents*, 17: 2.

Equal Opportunities Commission (1999). *Key Gender Issues in Education and Training*. Manchester: Equal Opportunities Commission.

Fagot, B. I. (1977). Consequences of moderate cross-gender behavior in pre-school children. *Child Development*, 48: 902–7.

(1995). Parenting boys and girls. In M. H. Bornstein (ed.) *Handbook of Parenting, Vol. 1.* (pp. 163–83) Hillsdale, NJ: Erlbaum.

Fagot, B. I. and Leinbach, M. D. (1993). Gender-role development in young children: from discrimination to labelling. *Developmental Review*, 13: 205–24.

Fagot, B. I., Leinbach, M. D., and Hagan, R. (1986). Gender labelling and adoption of sex-typed behaviors. *Developmental Psychology*, 22: 440–3.

Feingold, A. (1992a). Gender differences in mate selection preferences: a test of the parental investment model. *Psychological Bulletin*, 112: 125–39.

(1992b). Sex differences in variability in intellectual abilities: a new look at an old controversy. *Review of Educational Research*, 62: 61–84.

(1994a). Sex differences in personality: a meta-analysis. *Psychological Bulletin*, 116: 429–56.

(1994b). Gender differences in variability in intellectual abilities: a cross-cultural perspective. *Sex Roles*, 30: 81–92.

(1995). The additive effects of differences in central tendency and variability are important in comparisons between groups. *American Psychologist*, 50: 5–13.

Feinman, S. (1981). Why is cross-sex-role behavior more approved for girls than boys? A status characteristic approach. *Sex Roles*, 7: 289–300.

(1984). A status theory of the evaluation of sex-role and age-role behavior. *Sex Roles*, 10: 445–6.

Feldman, L. B. (1982). Sex roles and family dynamics. In F. Walsh (ed.), *Normal Family Processes* (pp. 354–79). New York: Guildford.

Felson, R. B. (1984). Patterns of aggressive social interactions. In A. Mummendey (ed.), *Social Psychology of Aggression: From Individual Behavior to Social Interaction* (pp. 107–26). Berlin: Springer-Verlag.

Felson, R. B., Baccaglini, W., and Gmelch, G. (1986). Bar-room brawls: aggression and violence in Irish and American bars. In A. Campbell and J. J. Gibbs (eds.), *Violent Transactions: The Limits of Personality* (pp. 153–66). Oxford, UK: Blackwell.

Ferri, E. (1976). *Growing Up in a One-Parent Family.* Windsor, UK: National Foundation for Educational Research.

Feshbach, N. (1969). Sex differences in children's modes of aggressive responses towards outsiders. *Merrill Palmer Quarterly*, 15: 249–58.

Fiebert, M. S. and Gonzalez, D. M. (1997). College women who initiate assaults on their male partners and the reasons offered for such behavior. *Psychological Reports*, 80: 583–90.

Fillion, K. (1997). *Lip Service: The Myth of Female Virtue in Love, Sex and Friendship.* New York: HarperCollins.

Fitch, R. H., Cowell, P. E., and Denenberg, V. H. (1998). The female phenotype: nature's default? *Developmental Neuropsychology*, 14: 213–31.

Fitch, R. H. and Denenberg, V. H. (1998). A role for ovarian hormones in sexual differentiation of the brain. *Behavioral and Brain Sciences*, 21: 311–52 (including commentaries).

Forest, M. G., Sizonenko, P. C., Caithiard, A. M., and Bertrand, J. (1974). Hypophyso-gonadal function in humans during the first year of life. 1. Evidence for testicular activity in early infancy. *Journal of Clinical Investigation*, 53: 819–28.

Foucault, M. (1979). *The History of Sexuality*. London: Allen Lane.

Fowers, B. J. (1991). His and her marriage: a multivariate study of gender and marital satisfaction. *Sex Roles*, 24: 209–21.

Fowler, R. (1999). When girl power packs a punch. *The Guardian*, London, 12 July, G2, pp. 6–7.

Fowler, R. I. and Fuehrer, A. (1997). Women's marital names: an interpretative study of name retainers' concepts of marriage. *Feminism and Psychology*, 7: 315–20.

Fox, N. (1977). Attachment of kibbutz infants to mother and metapelet. *Child Development*, 48: 1228–39.

Frable, D. E. S. (1989). Sex typing and gender ideology: two facets of the individual's gender psychology that go together. *Journal of Personality and Social Psychology*, 56: 95–108.

Frable, D. E. S. and Bem, S. L. (1985). If you are gender schematic, all members of the opposite sex look alike. *Journal of Personality and Social Psychology*, 49: 459–68.

Frank, L. G. (1994). Animal models of aggression: mice are nice but a hyaena is meaner. Paper presented at XIth World Meeting of International Society for Research on Aggression, Delray Beach, Florida, July. (Abstract published in *Aggressive Behavior*, 1995, 21: 171–2.)

Frank, L. G., Glickman, S. E., and Licht, P. (1991). Fetal sibling aggression, precocial development, and androgens in neonatal spotted hyenas. *Science*, 252: 702–4.

(1997). Evolution of genital masculinization: Why do female hyaenas have such a large 'penis'? *Trends in Ecology and Evolution*, 12: 58–62.

Frazier, S. H. and Carr, A. C. (1967). Phobic reactions. In A. M. Freedman and H. I. Kaplan (eds.), *Comprehensive Textbook of Psychiatry* (pp. 899–911). Baltimore: Williams and Wilkins.

Freedman, D. G. (1980). Sexual dimorphism and status hierarchy. In D. R. Omark, F. F. Strayer, and D. G. Freedman (eds.), *Dominance Relations: An Ethological View of Human Conflict and Social Interaction* (pp. 261–71). New York and London: Garland STPM Press.

French, M. (1978). *The Woman's Room*. London: Deutsch.

Frenkiel, O. (1999). *Murder in Purdah*. Programme broadcast by BBC2, 23 January (also report in *The Guardian*, London, 30 January, entitled 'If our women are unfaithful – we kill them').

Freud, S. (1905). *Three Essays on the Theory of Sexuality*, vol. 7 (std edn). London: Hogarth Press, 1953.

(1917/1915). *Mourning and Melancholia*, vol.14 (std edn). London: Hogarth Press, 1957.

(1920). *Beyond the Pleasure Principle*, vol.18 (std edn). London: Hogarth Press, 1955.

(1923). *The Ego and The Id*, vol. 19 (std edn). London: Hogarth Press, 1961

(1924). *The Dissolution of the Oedipus Complex*, vol. 19 (std edn). London: Hogarth Press, 1961.

(1925). *Some Psychical Consequences of the Anatomical Distinction between the Sexes*, vol. 19 (std edn). London: Hogarth Press, 1961.

(1931). *Female Sexuality*, vol. 21 (std edn). London: Hogarth Press, 1961.

(1940). *An Outline of Psychoanalysis*, vol. 23, (std edn). London: Hogarth Press, 1964.

Frey, K. S. and Ruble, D. N. (1992). Gender constancy and the "cost" of sex-typed behavior: a test of the conflict hypothesis. *Developmental Psychology*, 28: 714–21.

Friedman, B. X., Bleske, A. L., and Scheyd, G. J. (2000). Incompatible with evolutionary theorizing. *American Psychologist*, 55: 1059–60.

Frieze, I. H., Whitley, B. E. Jr., Hanusa, B. H., and McHugh, M. C. (1982). Assessing the theoretical models for sex differences in causal attributions for success and failure. *Sex Roles*, 8: 333–43.

Furnham, A., Lavancy, M., and McClelland, A. (2001). Waist to hip ratio and facial attractiveness: a pilot study. *Personality and Individual differences*, 30: 491–502.

Galen, B. R. and Underwood, M. K. (1997). A developmental investigation of social aggression among children. *Developmental Psychology*, 33: 589–600.

Galenson, E. and Roiphe, H. (1977). Some suggested revisions concerning early infant development. In H. P. Blum (ed.), *Female Psychology: Contemporary Psychoanalytic Views*. New York: International Universities Press.

Gangestad, S. W. and Simpson, J. A. (2000). The evolution of mating: trade-offs and strategic pluralism. *Behavioral and Brain Sciences*, 23: 573–644.

Gangestad, S. W. and Thornhill, R. (1997). Human sexual selection and developmental stability. In J. A. Simpson, and D. T. Kenrick (eds.), *Evolutionary Social Psychology* (pp. 169–95). Mahwah, NJ: Erlbaum.

Garai, J. E. and Scheinfeld, A. (1968). Sex differences in mental and behavioral traits. *Genetic Psychology Monographs*, 77: 169–299.

Gaulin, S. J. C. and Fitzgerald, R. W. (1986). Sexual selection for spatial learning ability. *American Naturalist*, 127: 74–88.

 (1989). Sexual selection for spatial-learning ability. *Animal Behaviour*, 37: 322–31.

Gaulin, S. J. C., Fitzgerald, R. W., and Wartell, M. S. (1990). Sex differences in spatial ability and activity in two vole species (*Microtus ochrogaster and M. pennsylvannicus*). *Journal of Comparative Psychology*, 108: 88–93.

Gavron, H. (1966). *The Captive Housewife: Conflict of Housebound Mothers*. London: Routledge and Kegan Paul.

Geary, D. C. (1995a). Reflections of evolution and culture in children's cognition: Implications for mathematical development and instruction. *American Psychologist*, 50: 24–37.

 (1995b). Sexual selection and sex differences in spatial cognition. *Learning and Individual Differences*, 7: 289–301.

 (1996). Sexual selection and sex differences in mathematical abilities. *Behavioral and Brain Sciences*, 19: 229–84 (including commentaries).

 (1999). *Male, Female: The Evolution of Human Sex differences*. Washington, DC: American Psychological Association.

 (2000). Evolution and proximate expression of human paternal investment. *Psychological Bulletin*, 126: 55–77.

Geiger, B. (1996). *Fathers as Primary Caregivers. Contributions in Family Studies, No. 17*. Westport, CT and London: Greenwood Press.

George, M. J. (1994). Riding the donkey backwards: men as the unacceptable victims of marital violence. *The Journal of Men's Studies*, 3: 137–59.

Gergen, K. J. (1973). Social psychology as history. *Journal of Personality and Social Psychology*, 26: 309–20.

Gergen, M. (1990). Beyond the evil empire: horseplay and aggression. *Aggressive Behavior*, 16: 381–98.

Gibbs, J. J. (1986). Alcohol consumption, cognition and context: examining tavern violence. In A. Campbell and J. J. Gibbs (eds.), *Violent Transactions: The Limits of Personality* (pp. 121–40). Oxford, UK: Blackwell.

Gilligan, C. (1982). *In a Different Voice*. Cambridge, MA: Harvard University Press.

Gilmore, D. D. (1990). *Manhood in the Making: Cultural Concepts of Masculinity*. New Haven, CT, and London: Yale University Press.

Glick, P. (1991). Trait-based and sex-based discrimination in occupational prestige, occupational salary, and hiring. *Sex Roles*, 25: 351–78.

Glick, P. and Fiske, S. T. (1996). The ambivalent sexism inventory: differentiating hostile and benevolent sexism. *Journal of Personality and Social Psychology*, 70: 491–52.

(1997). Hostile and benevolent sexism: measuring ambivalent sexist attitudes towards women. *Psychology of Women Quarterly*, 21: 119–35.

(2001). An ambivalent alliance: hostile and benevolent sexism as complementary justifications for gender inequality. *American Psychologist*, 56: 109–18.

Glick, P., Wilk, K., and Perreault, M. (1995). Images of occupations: components of gender and status in occupational stereotypes. *Sex Roles*, 32: 565–82.

Glick, P, Diebold, J., Bailey-Werner, B., and Zhu, L. (1997). The two faces of Adam: ambivalent sexism and polarized attitudes towards women. *Personality and Social Psychology Bulletin*, 23: 1333–44.

Glick, P., Zion, C., and Nelson, C. (1988). What mediates sex discrimination in hiring decisions? *Journal of Personality and Social Psychology*, 55: 178–86.

Glickman, S. E., Frank, L. G., Holekamp, K. E., Smale L., and Licht, P. (1993). Costs and benefits of "androgenization" in the female spotted hyena: the natural selection of physiological mechanisms. In P. P. G. Bateson, P. H. Klopfer, and N. S. Thompson (eds.), *Perspectives in Ethology, Volume 10: Behavior and Evolution* (pp. 87–117). New York and London: Plenum.

Gold, J. H. and Severino, S. K. (1994). *Premenstrual Dysphoria Myths and Realities*. Washington, DC: American Psychiatric Press, Inc.

Goldberg, P. (1968). Are women prejudiced against women? *Transaction*, 5: 28–30.

Goldberg, S. and Lewis, M. (1969). Play behavior in the year-old infant: early sex difference. *Child Development*, 40: 21–31.

Golombok, S., Tasker, F., and Murray, C. (1997). Children raised in fatherless families from infancy: family relationships and the socioemotional development of children of Lesbian and single heterosexual mothers. *Journal of Child Psychology and Psychiatry*, 38: 783–91.

Goode, E. (2001) A rainbow of differences in Gays' children. *The New York Times*, 17 July.

Gough, H. G. and Heilbrun, A. B. (1965). *Adjective Checklist Manual*. Palo Alton, CA: Consulting Psychologists' Press.

Gould, D. C., Petty, R., and Jacobs, H. S. (2000). Education debate. For and Against. The male menopause – does it exist? *British Medical Journal*, 320: 858–61 (25 March).

Gould, S. J. (1978). Women's brains. *New Scientist*, 80: 364–6.

Gouze, K. R. and Nadelman, L. (1980). Constancy of gender identity for self and others in children between the ages of three and seven. *Child Development*, 51: 275–8.

Gove, W. R. and Tudor, J. F. (1973). Adult sex roles and mental illness. *American Journal of Sociology*, 78: 812–25.

Gowaty, P. A. and Bridges, W. C. (1991). Behavioral, demographic, and environmental correlates of extrapair fertilizations in eastern bluebirds, *Sialia sialis*. *Behavioral Ecology*, 2: 339–50.

Goy, R. W. (1968). Organizing effects of androgen on the behavior of rhesus monkeys. In R. P. Michael (ed.), *Endocrinology and Human Behaviour* (pp. 12–13). Oxford University Press.

Goy, R. W. and McEwan, B. S. (1980). *Sexual Differentiation in the Brain*. Cambridge, MA: MIT Press.

Graber, B. (ed.) (1982). *Circumvaginal Musculature and Sexual Function*. Basle: Karger.

Graham-Kevan, N. and Archer, J. (2001a). Physical aggression and control in heterosexual relationahips: the effect of sampling procedure. Unpublished manuscript, Department of Psychology, University of Central Lancashire, Preston, UK.

(2001b). Patriarchal terrorism and common couple violence: a test of Johnson's predictions in four British samples. Unpublished manuscript, Department of Psychology, University of Central Lancashire, Preston, UK.

Gray, J. A. (1971). Sex differences in emotional behaviour in mammals including man: endocrine bases. *Acta Psychologica*, 35: 29–46.

Gray, J. A. and Buffery, A. W. H. (1971). Sex differences in emotional and cognitive behaviour in mammals including man: adaptive and neural bases. *Acta Psychologica*, 35: 89–111.

Green, A. (1997). Sexuality in contemporary psychoanalysis. *International Journal of Psychoanalysis*, 78: 345–50.

Green, R., Roberts, C. W., Williams, K., Goodman, M., and Mixon, A. (1987). Specific cross-gender behaviour in boyhood and later homosexual orientation. *British Journal of Psychiatry*, 151: 84–8.

Gregoriadis, L. (1999). Banker 'victim of hot totty jibes'. *The Guardian*, London, 23 December, p. 6.

Griffin, C. (1986). Qualitative methods and female experience. Young women from school to the job market. In S. Wilkinson (ed.), *Feminist Social Psychology* (pp. 173–91). Milton Keynes and Philadelphia, PA: Open University Press.

Griggs, C. (1998). *S/he Changing Sex and Changing Clothes*. Oxford and New York: Berg.

Gross, M. R. (1996). Alternative reproductive strategies and tactics: diversity within sexes. *Trends in Ecology and Evolution*, 11: 92–8.

Grossman, M. and Wood, W. (1993). Sex differences in intensity of emotional experience: a social role interpretation. *Journal of Personality and Social Psychology*, 65: 1010–22.

Gutek, B. A. (1985). *Sex and the Workplace*. San Francisco: Jossey-Bass.

Hagen, E. H. (1999). The functions of postpartum depression. *Evolution and Human Behavior*, 20: 325–59.

Halasa, M. (1991). Killer queen. *The Guardian*, London, 7 February.

Halberstadt-Freud, H. C. (1998). Electra versus Oedipus: femininity reconsidered. *International Journal of Psycho-Analysis*, 79: 41–56.

Hall, J. A. (1978). Gender effects in decoding nonverbal cues. *Psychological Bulletin*, 85: 845–57.

(1984). *Non-verbal Sex Differences*. Baltimore, MD: Johns Hopkins University Press.

Hall, J. A. and Carter, J. D. (1999). Gender-stereotype accuracy as an individual difference. *Journal of Personality and Social Psychology*, 77: 350–9.

Halperin, D. M. (1990). *One Hundred Years of Homosexuality and Other Essays on Homosexual Love*. New York: Routledge.

Halpern, C. T., Udry, J. R., Campbell, B., and Suchindran, C. (1994a). Relationships between aggression and pubertal increases in testosterone: a panel analysis of adolescent males. *Social Biology*, 40: 8–24.

Halpern, C. T., Udry, J. R., Campbell, B., Suchindran, C., and Mason, G. A. (1994b). Testosterone and religiosity as predictors of sexual attitudes and activity among adolescent males: a biosocial model. *Journal of Biosocial Science*, 26: 217–34.

Halpern, D. F. (2000). *Sex Differences in Cognitive Abilities* (3rd edn). Mahwah, NJ: Erlbaum.

Halpern, D. F. and LaMay, M. L. (2000). The smarter sex: a critical review of sex differences in intelligence. *Educational Psychology Review*, 12: 229–46.

Hamilton, W. D. (1964) The genetical evolution of social behavior, I and II. *Journal of Theoretical Biology*, 7: 1–52.

Hamilton, W. D., Axelrod, R., and Tanese, R. (1990). Sexual reproduction as an adaptation to resist parasites (A review). *Proceedings of the National Academy of Sciences USA*, 87: 3566–73.

Hammock, G. S. and Richardson, D. R. (1997). Perceptions of rape: the influence of closeness of relationship, intoxication, and sex of participant. *Violence and Victims*, 12: 237–46.

Hargreaves, D. R. (1976). What are little boys and girls made of? *New Society*, 37: 542–4. (1977). Sex roles in divergent thinking. *British Journal of Social Psychology*, 47: 25–32.

Hargreaves, D. J., Bates, H. M., and Foot, J. M. C. (1985). Sex typed labelling affects task performance. *British Journal of Social Psychology*, 24: 153–5.

Harkness, S. and Super, C. M. (1985). The cultural context of gender segregation in children's peer groups. *Child Development*, 56: 219–24.

Harlow, H. (1958). The nature of love. *American Psychologist*, 13: 673–85.

Harper, L. V. and Sanders, K. M. (1978). Sex differences in preschool children's social interactions and use of space: an evolutionary perspective. In T. E. McGill, D. A. Dewsbury, and B. D. Sachs (eds.), *Sex and Behavior: Status and Prospects* (pp. 61–81). New York and London: Plenum Press.

Harries, K. (1974). *The Geography of Crime and Justice*. New York: McGraw-Hill.

Harris, B. (1996a). Hormonal aspects of postnatal depression. *International Review of Psychiatry*, 8: 27–38.

Harris, J. A., Rushton, J. P., Hampson, E., and Jackson, D. N. (1996). Salivary testosterone and self-report aggressive and pro-social personality characteristics in men and women. *Aggressive Behavior*, 22: 321–31.

Harris, J. R. (1995). Where is the child's environment? A group socialization theory of development. *Psychological Review*, 102: 458–89. (1998). *The Nurture Assumption: Why Children Turn Out the Way They Do*. London: Bloomsbury.

Harris, M. B. (1992). Sex and ethnic differences in past aggressive behaviors. *Journal of Family Violence*, 7: 85–102. (1994). Gender of subject and target as mediators of aggression. *Journal of Applied Social Psychology*, 24: 453–71.

(1996). Aggressive experiences and aggressiveness: relationship to ethnicity, gender, and age. *Journal of Applied Social Psychology*, 26: 843–70.

Harris, R. J. and Cook, C. A. (1994). Attributions about spouse abuse: It matters who batterers and victims are. *Sex Roles*, 30: 553–65.

Hartley, J. (1992). Sex bias, blind marking and assessing students. *Psychological Teaching Review*, 1: 66–75.

Hartman, S. J., Griffith, R. W., Crino, M. D., and Harris, O. J. (1991). Gender-based influences: the promotion recommendation. *Sex Roles*, 25: 285–300.

Hawkins, A. J. and Dollahite, D. C. (eds.) (1997). *Generative Fathering Beyond Deficit Perspectives.* London and New York: Sage.

Hawton, K. (2000) Sex and suicide: gender differences in suicidal behaviour. *British Journal of Psychiatry*, 177: 484–5.

Hedges, L. V. and Nowell, A. (1995). Sex differences in mental test scores, variability, and numbers of high scoring individuals. *Science*, 269: 41–5.

Heesacker, M., Wester, S. R., and Vogel, D. L. et al. (1999). Gender-based emotional stereotyping. *Journal of Counselling Psychology*, 46: 483–95.

Heilbrun, A. B. (1965). An empirical test of the modelling theory of sex-role learning. *Child Development*, 36: 789–99.

Heilman, M. E. (1984). Information as a deterrent against sex discrimination: the effects of applicant sex and information type on preliminary employment decisions. *Organizational Behavior and Human Performance*, 33: 174–86.

Heim, A. (1970). *Intelligence and Personality.* Harmondsworth: Penguin.

Heiman, J. R. (1975). The physiology of erotica: women's sexual arousal. *Psychology Today*, April: 90–4.

Heise, D. R. (1965). Semantic differential profiles for 1,000 most frequent English words. *Psychological Monographs: General and Applied*, 79 (8): whole no. 601, 1–31.

Helmreich, R. L., Spence, J. T., and Holahan, C. K. (1979). Psychological androgyny and sex role flexibility: a test of two hypotheses. *Journal of Personality and Social Psychology*, 37: 1631–44.

Helzer, J. E. and Canino, G. J. (1992). *Alcoholism in North America, Europe and Asia.* Oxford University Press.

Henley, N. M., Meng, K., O'Brien, D., McCarthy, W. J., and Sockloskie, R. J. (1998). Developing a scale to measure the diversity of feminist attitudes. *Psychology of Women Quarterly*, 22: 317–48.

Henss, R. (2000). Waist-to-hip ratio and female attractiveness. Evidence from photographic stimuli and methodological considerations. *Personality and Individual Differences*, 28: 501–13.

Herdt, G. (ed.) (1994). *Third Sex, Third Gender: Beyond Sexual Dimorphism in Culture and History.* New York: Zone Books.

Hetherington, E. M. (1965). A developmental study of the effects of the sex of the dominant parent on sex-role preferences, identification and imitation in children. *Journal of Personality and Social Psychology*, 2: 188–94.

Hines, M., and Kaufman, F. R. (1994). Androgen and the development of human sex-typical behavior: Rough-and-tumble play and sex of preferred playmates in children with congenital adrenal hyperplasia (CAH). *Child Development*, 65: 1042–53.

Hite, S. (1976). *The Hite Report.* New York: Macmillan.

(1981). *The Hite Report on Male Sexuality.* New York: Knopf.

Hochschild, A. (1989). *The Second Shift: Working Parents and the Revolution at Home.* New York: Viking.

Hocquenghem. G. (1978). *Homosexual Desire.* Trans. D. Dangoor. London: Allison and Busby.

Hoffman, C., and Hurst, N. (1990). Gender stereotypes: perception or rationalization? *Journal of Personality and Social Psychology*, 58: 197–208.

Hofstede, G. (1980). *Culture's Consequences: International Differences in Work-related Values.* Beverly Hills, CA: Sage.

(1991). *Cultures and Organisations: Software for the Mind.* London: McGraw-Hill.

Hofstede, G., Arrindell, W. A., and Best, D. L. et al. (1998). *Masculinity and Femininity: The Taboo Dimension of National Cultures.* Thousand Oaks, CA: Sage Publications.

Hollingworth, L. S. (1914). Variability as related to sex differences in achievement: a critique. *American Journal of Sociology*, 19: 510–30.

(1922). Differential action upon the sexes of forces which tend to segregate the feeble-minded. *Journal of Abnormal and Social Psychology*, 17: 35–57.

Horney, K. (1924). On the genesis of the castration complex in women. *International Journal of Psychoanalysis*, 5: 50–65.

Horrocks, R. (1997). *An Introduction to the Study of Sexuality.* London: Macmillan.

Houston, J. E., Crozier, W. R., and Walker, P. (1990). The assessment of ethnic sensitivity among Northern Ireland schoolchildren. *British Journal of Developmental Psychology*, 8: 419–22.

Howes, C. and Phillipsen, L. (1992). Gender and friendship: relationship within peer groups of young children. *Social Development*, 1: 230–42.

Hrdy, S. B. (1981). *The Woman That Never Evolved.* Cambridge, MA: Harvard University Press.

(1997). Raising Darwin's consciousness: female sexuality and the prehominid origins of patriarchy. *Human Nature*, 8: 1–49.

Hunt, M. G. (1993). Expressiveness does predict well-being. *Sex Roles*, 29: 147–69.

Huston, A. C. (1985). The development of sex typing: themes from current research. *Developmental Review*, 5: 1–17.

Hutt, C. (1972). *Males and Females.* Harmondsworth, UK: Penguin.

Hyde, J. S. (1981). How large are cognitive gender differences? A meta-analysis using ω^2 and d. *American Psychologist*, 36: 892–901.

(1994). Can meta-analysis make feminist transformations in psychology? *Psychology of Women Quarterly*, 18: 451–62.

(1999). Women's slow progress up the professional ladder: just one big schema? *Contemporary Psychology: APA Review of Books*, 44: 31–3.

Hyde, J. S. and DeLamater, J. D. (1996). *Understanding Human Sexuality, Sixth Edition.* London: McGraw-Hill.

Hyde, J. S. and Durik, A. M. (2000). Gender differences in erotic plasticity – evolutionary or sociocultural forces? Comment on Baumeiseter (2000). *Psychological Bulletin*, 126: 375–9.

Hyde, J. S. and Plant, E. A. (1995). Magnitude of psychological gender differences: another side to the story. *American Psychologist*, 50: 159–61.

Hyde, J. S., Rosenberg, B. G., and Behrman, J. A. (1977). Tomboyism. *Psychology of Women Quarterly*, 2: 73–5.

Iacono, W. G. and Beiser, M. (1992). Where are the women in first episode studies of schizophrenia? *Schizophrenia Bulletin*, 18: 471–80.

Ingrams, R. (1999). Diary. *The Observer*, London, 19 December, p. 30.

Inkeles, A. and Levinson, D. J. (1969) National character: the study of modal character and sociocultural systems. In G. Lindzey and E. Aronson (eds.), *The Handbook of Social Psychology*. 2nd edn., vol. 4 (pp. 418–506). Reading, MA: Addison-Wesley.

Jacklin, C. N. (1979). Epilogue. In M. A. Wittig and A. C. Peterson (eds.), *Sex Related Difference in Cognitive Functioning: Developmental Issues* (pp. 357–71). New York: Academic Press.

Jacklin, C. N., Maccoby, E. E., and Dick, A. E. (1973). Barrier behavior and toy preference: sex differences (and their absence) in the year-old child. *Child Development*, 44: 196–200.

Janowsky, J. S., Chavez, B., Zamboni, B. D., and Orwoll, E. (1998). The cognitive neuropsychology of sex hormones in men and women. *Developmental Neuropsychology*, 14: 421–40.

Jenni, D. A. (1974). Evolution of polyandry in birds. *American Zoologist*, 14: 129–44.

Johnson, A. (1994). Rude girls rule – but only on the periphery. *The Guardian*, London, 25 November.

Johnson, A. M., Wadsworth, J., Welling, J., and Field, J. (1994). *Sexual Attitudes and Lifestyles*. Oxford: Blackwell Scientific Publications.

Johnson, M. P. (1995). Patriarchal terrorism and common couple violence: two forms of violence against women. *Journal of Marriage and the Family*, 57: 283–94.

(1999). Two types of violence against women in the American family: identifying patriarchal terrorism and common couple violence. Paper presented at the Annual Meeting of the National Council on Family Relations, Irvine, CA, November.

Josephs, R. J., Markus, H. R., and Tafarodi, R. W. (1992). Gender and self-esteem. *Journal of Personality and Social Psychology*, 63: 391–402.

Jost, A. (1972). A new look at the mechanisms controlling sex differentiations in mammals. *Johns Hopkins Medical Journal*, 130: 38–53.

Jost, J. T. and Banaji, M. R. (1994). The role of stereotyping in system-justification and the production of false consciousness. *British Journal of Social Psychology*, 33: 1–27.

Judd, C. M. and Park, B. (1993). Definition and accuracy in social stereotypes. *Psychological Review*, 100: 109–28.

Kahn, M. W. and The Behavioral Health Technician Staff (1980). Wife beating and cultural context: prevalence in an Aboriginal and Islander community in northern Australia. *American Journal of Community Psychology*, 8: 727–31.

Kaplan, M. (1983). A woman's view of the DSM-III. *American Psychologist*, 38: 786–92.

Kaplan, R. M. (1978). Is beauty talent? Sex interaction in the attractiveness halo effect. *Sex Roles*, 4: 195–204.

Kass, F., Spritzer, R. L., and Williams, J. B. W. (1983). An empirical study of the issue of sex bias in the diagnostic criteria of DSM-III axis II Personality disorder. *American Psychologist*, 38: 799–801.

Kasser, T. and Sharma, Y. S. (1999). Reproductive freedom, educational equality, and females' preference for resource-acquisition characteristics in mates. *Psychological Science*, 10: 374–7.

Katchadourian, H. A. (1985). *Fundamentals of Human Sexuality, Fourth Edition*. New York: Holt.

Katchadourian, H. A. and Lunde, D. T. (1980). *Fundamentals of Human Sexuality (3rd Edition)*. New York: Holt, Rinehart and Winston.

Katz, D. and Braly, K. W. (1935). Racial prejudice and racial stereotypes. *Journal of Abnormal and Social Psychology*, 30: 175–93.

Kendall, P. C. and Hammen, C. (1998). *Abnormal Psychology: Understanding Human Problems*. Boston: Houghton Mifflin.

Kennedy, I. (1980). 'Great caution must be exercised in visiting the status of mentally ill on anyone'. The Reith Lectures, 'Unmasking medicine'. *The Listener*, 4 December, pp. 745–8.

Kenrick, D. T. and Li, N. (2000). The Darwin is in the detail. *American Psychologist*, 55: 1060–1.

Kessler, R. C., McGonagle, K. A., and Zhao, S. et al. (1994). Lifetime and 12 month prevalence of DSM-III-R psychiatric disorders in the United States. *Archives of General Psychiatry*, 5: 8–19.

Kessler, S. J. and McKenna, W. (1978). *Gender: An Ethnomethodological Approach*. New York: Wiley.

Kettle, M. (1999). Gun control to be key election issue. *The Guardian*, London, 24 April, p. 3.

Key Gender Issues in Education and Training. (1999). Equal Opportunities Commission, Manchester.

Kiley, S. (1988). Sexism shown in university exams. *The Times, Student Special*, Autumn, p. 1.

Kim, K-i and Cho, Y-g (1992). Epidemiological survey of spousal abuse in Korea. In E. C. Viano (ed.), *Intimate Violence: Interdisciplinary Perspectives* (pp. 277–82). Washington, DC: Hemisphere.

Kimura, D. (1999). *Sex and Cognition*. Cambridge, MA: MIT Press.

Kinsey, A. C., Pomeroy, W. B., and Martin, C. E. (1948). *Sexual Behavior in the Human Male*. Philadelphia: Saunders.

Kinsey, A. C., Pomeroy, W. B., Martin, C. E., and Gebhard, P. H. (1953). *Sexual Behavior in the Human Female*. Philadelphia: Saunders.

Klaus, M. H. and Kennell, J. H. (1976). *Maternal–Infant Bonding*. Saint Louis: Mosby.

Kleyman, E. (2000). From allies to adversaries? *American Psychologist*, 55: 1061–2.

Kline, S. L., Stafford, L., and Miklosovic, J. C. (1996). Women's surnames: decisions, interpretations and associations with relational qualities. *Journal of Social and Personal Relationships*, 13, 593–617.

Knight, R. H. (1997). How domestic partnerships and 'Gay marriage' threaten the family. In J. Corvino (ed.), *Same Sex: Debating the Ethics, Science and Culture of Homosexuality* (pp. 289–303). Lanham, MD: Rowman and Littlefield.

Kohlberg, L. (1966). A cognitive developmental analysis of children's sex role concepts and attitudes. In E. E. Maccoby (ed.), *The Development of Sex Differences* (pp. 82–173). Stanford University Press.

Kolakowski, D. and Malina, R. M. (1974). Spatial ability, throwing accuracy and man's hunting heritage. *Nature*, 251: 410–12.

Kolb, B. and Whishaw, I. Q. (1996). *Fundamentals of Human Neuropsychology* (4th edn). New York: W. H. Freeman.

Komarovsky, M. (1950). Functional analyses of sex roles. *American Sociological Review*, 15: 508–16.

Konrad, A. M., Ritchie, Jr., J. E., Lieb, P., and Corrigall, E. (2000). Sex differences and similarities in job attribute preferences: a meta-analysis. *Psychological Bulletin*, 126: 593–641.

Koski, P. R. and Mangold, W. D. (1988). Gender effects in attitudes about family violence. *Journal of Family Violence*, 3: 225–37.

Koss, M. P., Gidycz, C. A., and Wisniewski, N. (1987). The scope of rape: incidence and prevalence of sexual aggression and victimization in a national sample of higher education students. *Journal of Consulting and Clinical Psychology*, 55: 162–70.

Krahé, B., Schutze, S., Fritsche, I., and Waizenhofer, E. (2000). The prevalence of sexual aggression and victimization among homosexual men. *Journal of Sex Research*, 37: 142–50.

Krefting, L. A., Berger, P. K., and Wallace, M. J. Jr. (1978). The contribution of sex discrimination, job content, and occupational classification to job sex typing: two studies. *Journal of Vocational Behavior*, 13: 181–91.

Kroska, A. (1997). The division of labor in the home: a review and reconceptualization. *Social Psychology Quarterly*, 60: 304–22.

Kuhn, D., Nash, S. C., and Bruchan, L. (1978). Sex role concepts of two and three year olds. *Child Development*, 49: 445–51.

Kujawski, J. H. and Bower, T. G. R. (1993). Same-sex preferential looking during infancy as a function of abstract representation. *British Journal of Developmental Psychology*, 11: 201–9.

Kumagai, F. and Straus, M. A. (1983). Conflict resolution tactics in Japan, India, and the USA. *Journal of Comparative Family Studies*, 14: 377–92.

Kurdek, L. A. (1995) Lesbian and gay couples. In A. R. D'Augelli and C. J. Patterson (eds.), *Lesbian, Gay and Bisexual Identities in Families: Psychological Perspectives* (pp. 243–61). Oxford University Press.

Lacan, J. (1966). The significance of the phallus. In *Ecrits*. Paris: Editions de Seuil (reprinted *Ecrits: A Selection*. Trans. A. Sheridan. London: Tavistock, 1977).

Lacreuse, A., Herndon, J. G., Killiany, R. J., Rosene, D. L., and Moss, M. B. (1999). Spatial cognition in rhesus monkeys: male superiority declines with age. *Hormones and Behavior*, 36, 70–6.

LaFreniere, P., Strayer, F. F., and Gaulthier, R. (1984). The emergence of same-sex affiliative preferences among preschool peers: a developmental ethological perspective. *Child Development*, 46: 19–26.

Laing, R. D. (1967). *The Politics of Experience*. Harmondsworth: Penguin.

Lamb, M. E. (ed.) (1976). *The Role of the Father in Child Development*. New York: Wiley.
  (1981). *The Role of the Father in Child Development* (2nd edn). New York: Wiley.
  (1997). *The Role of the Father in Child Development* (3rd edn). New York: Wiley.

Lambert, L. and Hart, S. (1976). Who needs a family? *New Society*, 37: 80.

Landy, D. and Sigall, H. (1974). Beauty is talent. Task evaluation as a function of the performer's physical attractiveness. *Journal of Personality and Social Psychology*, 29: 299–304.

Laqueur, T. (1990). *Making Sex: Body and Gender from the Greeks to Freud*. Cambridge, MA: Harvard University Press.

Larimer, T. (1997). Picking up the pieces. *Time*, 7 July, p. 33.

Lazarus, J. (1990). The logic of mate desertion. *Animal Behaviour*, 39: 672–84.

Leakey, R. and Lewin, R. (1979). *People of the Lake*. London: Collins.

Leaper, C., Anderson, K. J., and Sanders, P. (1998). Moderators of gender effects on parents talk to their children: a meta-analysis. *Developmental Psychology*, 34: 3–27.

Le Boeuf, B. J. (1974). Male–male competition and reproductive success in elephant seals. *American Zoologist*, 14: 163–76.

Leinbach, M. D. and Fagot, B. I. (1986). Acquisition of gender labelling: a test for toddlers. *Sex Roles*, 15: 655–66.

Leonard, S. P. and Archer, J. (1989). A naturalistic investigation of gender constancy in three- to four-year-old children. *British Journal of Developmental Psychology*, 7: 341–6.

Lerner, R. M. (1976). *Concepts and Theories of Human Development*. Reading, MA: Addison-Wesley.

Levinson, D. (1989). *Family Violence in Cross-Cultural Perspective*. Newbury Park, CA: Sage.

Levy, G. D. and Fivush, R. (1993). Scripts and gender: a new approach for examining gender-role development. *Developmental Review*, 13: 126–46.

Lewis, C. (1997). Fathers and preschoolers. In M. E. Lamb (ed.), *The Role of the Father in Child Development* (3rd edn, pp. 121–42). New York: Wiley.

Lewis, M. and Brooks-Gunn, J. (1979). *Social Cognition and the Acquisition of Self*. New York: Plenum.

Liben, L. S. and Signorella, M. L. (1993). Gender-schematic processing in children: the role of initial interpretations of stimuli. *Developmental Psychology*, 29: 141–9.

Lippman, W. (1922). *Public Opinion*. New York: Harcourt Brace.

Lipshitz, S. (1978). Women and psychiatry. In J. Chetwynd and O. Hartnett (eds.), *The Sex Role System* (pp. 93–108). London: Routledge and Kegan Paul.

Litman, G. K. (1978). Clinical aspects of sex role stereotyping. In J. J. Chetwynd and O. Hartnett (eds.), *The Sex Role System* (pp. 109–26). London: Routledge and Kegan Paul.

Lloyd, B. B. (1976). Social responsibility and research on sex differences. In B. B. Lloyd and J. Archer (eds.), *Exploring Sex Differences* (pp. 1–23). New York: Academic Press.

Lloyd, B. B. and Smith, C. (1985). The social representation of gender and young children's play. *British Journal of Developmental Psychology*, 3: 65–73.

Lloyd, B. B. and Stroyan, J. (1994). Preschool children's genital knowledge: does Bem's report of a male deficit survive replication? *British Journal of Developmental Psychology*, 12: 251–8.

Lobel, T. E. and Menashri, J. (1993). Relations of conceptions of gender-role transgressions and gender constancy to gender-typed toy preferences. *Developmental Psychology*, 29: 150–5.

Locksley, A., Borgida, E., Brekke, N., and Hepburn, C. (1980). Sex stereotypes and social judgements. *Journal of Personality and Social Psychology*, 39: 821–31.

Locksley, A. and Colten, M. E. (1979). Psychological androgyny: a case of mistaken identity. *Journal of Personality and Social Psychology*, 37: 1017–31.

Lowe, M. (1982). Social bodies: the interaction of culture and women's biology. In R. Hubbard, M. S. Henifin, and B. Fried (eds.), *Biological Woman – The Convenient Myth* (pp. 91–116). Cambridge, MA: Schenkman.

Lubinski, D., Tellegen, A., and Butcher, J. N. (1981). The relationship between androgyny and subjective indicators of emotional well-being. *Journal of Personality and Social Psychology*, 40: 722–30.

(1983). Masculinity, femininity and androgyny viewed and assessed as distinct concepts. *Journal of Personality and Social Psychology*, 44: 428–39.

Lueptow, L. B., Garovich, L., and Lueptow, M. B. (1995). The persistence of gender stereotypes in the face of changing sex roles: evidence contrary to the socialization model. *Ethology and Sociobiology*, 16: 509–30.

Lukes, S. (1974). *Power: A Radical View*. London: Macmillan.

Lynn, R. (1992). Sex differences on the differential aptitude test in British and American students. *Educational Psychology*, 12: 101–6.

Lyons, J. (1968). *Introduction to Theoretical Linguistics*. Cambridge University Press.

Lytton, H. and Romney, D. M. (1991). Parents' differential socialization of boys and girls: a meta-analysis. *Psychological Bulletin*, 109: 267–96.

McBurney, D. H., Gaulin, S. J. C., Devineni, T., and Adams, C. (1997). Superior spatial memory of women: stronger evidence for the gathering hypothesis. *Evolution and Human Behavior*, 18: 165–74.

McCaul, K. D., Gladue, B. A., and Joppa, M. (1992). Winning, losing, mood, and testosterone. *Hormones and Behavior*, 26: 486–504.

McCauley, C. and Stitt, C. L. (1978). An individual and quantitative measure of stereotypes. *Journal of Personality and Social Psychology*, 36: 929–40.

McCauley, C., Stitt, C. L., and Segal, M. (1980). Stereotyping: from prejudice to prediction. *Psychological Bulletin*, 87: 195–208.

Maccoby, E. E. (1986). Social groupings in childhood: their relationship to prosocial and anti-social behavior in boys and girls. In D. Olweus, J. Block and M. Radke-Yarrow (eds.), *Development of Anti-social and Prosocial Behavior: Research, Theories and Issues* (pp. 263–84). New York and London: Academic Press.

(1988). Gender as a social category. *Developmental Psychology*, 24: 755–65.

(1990). Gender and relationships: a developmental account. *American Psychologist*, 45: 513–20.

(1998). *The Two Sexes: Growing Up Apart, Coming Together*. Cambridge, MA and London: Belknap Press of Harvard University Press.

Maccoby, E. E. and Jacklin, C. N. (1974). *The Psychology of Sex Differences*. Stanford University Press.

(1980). Sex differences in aggression: a rejoinder and reprise. *Child Development*, 51: 964–80.

(1987). Gender segregation in childhood. In H. W. Reese (ed.), *Advances in Child Development and Behavior*, vol. 20 (pp. 239–87). New York and London: Academic Press.

McCrae, R. R. and Costa, P. T. (1990). *Personality in Adulthood*. New York: Guilford.

McDermott, P. A. (1996). A nation-wide study of developmental and gender prevalence for psychopathology in childhood and adolescence. *Journal of Abnormal Child Psychology*, 24: 53–66.

McEwan, I. (1978). *The Cement Garden*. London: Jonathan Cape.

McGee, R., Feehan, M., Williams. S., Partridge, F., Silva, P. A., and Kelly, J. (1990). DSM-III Disorders in a large sample of adolescents. *Journal of the American Academy of Child and Adolescent Psychopathology*, 29: 611–19.

McGuire, M. T., Troisi, A., and Raleigh, M. M. (1997). Depression in evolutionary context. In S. Baron-Cohen (ed.), *The Maladapted Mind Classic Readings in Evolutionary Psychopathology*. Hove, East Sussex: Psychology Press.

Mack, J. (1976). Children half alone. *New Society*, 38: 6–8.

McNemar, Q. and Terman, L. M. (1936). Sex differences in variational tendency. *Genetic Psychology Monographs*, 18: 1–65.

Magee, W. J., Eaton, W., Wittchen, B., Hans-Ulrich, C., McGonagle, K. A., and Kessler, R. C. (1996). Agoraphobia, simple phobia, and social phobia in the national comorbidity survey. *Archives of General Psychiatry*, 53: 159–68.

Maggio, R. (1998). *The Nonsexist Word Finder: A Dictionary of Gender-Free Usage.* Boston, MA: Beacon Press.

Malamuth, N. M. (1996). The confluence model of sexual aggression: feminist and evolutionary perspectives. In D. M. Buss and N. M. Malamuth (eds.), *Sex, Power, Conflict: Evolutionary and Feminist Perspectives* (pp. 269–95). New York and Oxford: Oxford University Press.

Malamuth, N. M., Linz, D., Heavey, C. L., Barnes, G., and Acker, M. (1995). Using the confluence model of sexual aggression to predict men's conflict with women: a 10-year follow-up study. *Journal of Personality and Social Psychology*, 69: 353–69.

Malamuth, N. M., Sockloskie, R. J., Koss, M. P., and Tanaka, J. S. (1991). Characteristics of aggressors against women: testing a model using a national sample of college students. *Journal of Consulting and Clinical Psychology*, 59: 670–81.

Malamuth, N. M. and Thornhill, N. H. (1994). Hostile masculinity, sexual aggression and gender-biased domineeringness in conversation. *Aggressive Behavior*, 20: 185–93.

Matlin, M. W. (1987). *The Psychology of Women* (2nd edn). Fort Worth, TX: Harcourt Brace Jovanovich.

Maltz, D. N. and Borker, R. A. (1982). A cultural approach to male–female miscommunication. In J. J. Gumperz (ed.), *Language and Social Identity* (pp. 196–216). New York: Cambridge University Press.

Manning, J. T., Baron-Cohen, S., Wheelwright, S., and Sanders, G. (2001). The 2nd to 4th digit ratio and autism. *Developmental Medicine and Child Neurology*, 43: 60–4.

Marcus, D. E. and Overton, W. F. (1978). The development of cognitive gender constancy and sex role preferences. *Child Development*, 49: 434–44.

Marecek, J. (1995). Gender, politics, and psychology's ways of knowing. *American Psychologist*, 50: 162–3.

Marks, I. M. (1987). *Fears, Phobias, and Rituals*. Oxford University Press.

Marlowe, F. and Wetsman, A. (2001). Preferred waist-to-hip ratio and ecology. *Personality and Individual differences*, 30: 481–9.

Marsh, H. W., Antill, J. K., and Cunningham, J. D. (1987). Masculinity, femininity and androgyny: relations to self-esteem and social desirability. *Journal of Personality and Social Psychology*, 55: 661–83.

Marsh, H. W. and Byrne, B. M. (1991). Differentiated additive androgyny model: relations between masculinity, femininity and multiple dimensions of self-concept. *Journal of Personality and Social Psychology*, 61: 811–28.

Marsh, P. (1980). Violence at the pub. *New Society*, 52: 210–12.

Marsiglio, M. A. (ed.) (1995). *Fatherhood: Contemporary Theory, Research and Social Policy*. London and New York: Sage.

Martell, R. F., Lane, D. M., and Willis, C. E. (1996). Male–female differences: a computer simulation. *American Psychologist*, 51: 157–8.

Martin, C. L. (1987). A ratio measure of sex stereotyping. *Journal of Personality and Social Psychology*, 52: 489–99.

(1993). New directions for investigating children's gender knowledge. *Developmental Review*, 13: 184–204.

Martin, C. L. and Halverson, C. F. Jr. (1981). A schematic processing model of sex typing and stereotyping in children. *Child Development*, 52: 1119–34.

(1983). Gender constancy: a methodological and theoretical analysis. *Sex Roles*, 9: 775–90.

Martin, C. L., and Little, J. K. (1990). The relation of gender understanding to children's sex-typed preference and gender stereotypes. *Child Development*, 61: 1427–39.

Martin, M. K. and Voorhies, B. (1975). *The Female of the Species*. New York: Macmillan.

Martin, C. L., Wood, C. H., and Little, J. K. (1990). The development of gender stereotype components. *Child Development*, 61: 1891–904.

Masche, G. (1995). Geschlechts- und geschlechtsrollenspezifische Praferenzen zur Wahl des Ehenamens. (Gender-specific and sex-role-specific preferences regarding the choice of married surname.) *Zeitschrift für Differentielle und Diagnostische Psychologie*, 16: 113–24.

Masters, W. H. and Johnson, V. E. (1966). *Human Sexual Response*. Boston: Little Brown.

(1970). *Human Sexual Inadequacy*. Boston: Little Brown.

(1979). *Homosexuality in Perspective*. Boston: Little Brown.

Masters, W. H., Johnson, V. E., and Kolodny, R. C. (1992). *Human Sexuality, Fourth Edition*. New York: HarperCollins.

Masters, M. S. and Sanders, B. (1993). Is the gender difference in mental rotation disappearing? *Behavior Genetics*, 23: 337–41.

Matteo, S. (1988). The effect of gender-schematic processing on decisions about sex inappropriate sport behavior. *Sex Roles*, 18: 41–58.

Maynard Smith, J. (1977). Parental investment: a prospective analysis. *Animal Behaviour*, 29: 1–9.

(1978). *The Evolution of Sex*. Cambridge University Press.

Mazur, A. and Lamb, T. A. (1980). Testosterone, status, and mood in human males. *Hormones and Behavior*, 14: 236–46.

Meehl, P. E. (1962). Schizotaxia, schizotypy, schizophrenia. *American Psychologist*, 17: 827–38.

Melzack, R. and Wall, P. (1982). *The Challenge of Pain*. Harmondsworth, UK: Penguin.

Mental Health, United States 1996 (1997). Washington, DC: Substance Abuse and Mental Health Services Administration.

Mihalic, S. W. and Elliott, D. (1997). If violence is domestic, does it really count? *Journal of Family Violence*, 12: 293–311.

Miles, A. (1996). *Integrative Feminisms: Building Global Visions 1960–1990s*. New York and London: Routledge.

Miller, G. F. (1998). How mate choice shaped human nature: a review of sexual selection and human evolution. In C. Crawford and D. L. Krebs (eds.), *Handbook of Evolutionary Psychology: Ideas, Issues and Applications* (pp. 87–129). Mahwah, NJ: Erlbaum.

(2000). *The Mating Mind: How Sexual Choice Shaped the Evolution of Human Nature*. London: Heinemann.

Miller, N. E. and Dollard, J. (1941). *Social Learning and Imitation*. New Haven, CT: Yale University Press.

Mills, C. J. and Tyrell D. J. (1983). Sex-stereotypic encoding and release from proactive interference. *Journal of Personality and Social Psychology*, 45: 772–81.

Milovchevich, D., Howells, K., Drew, N., and Day, A. (2001). Sex and gender role differences in anger: an Australian community study. *Personality and Individual Differences*, 31: 117–27.

Mirrlees-Black, C., Budd, T., Partridge, S., and Mayhew, P. (1998). *Domestic violence: Findings from a new British Crime Survey Self-Completion Questionnaire*. Home Office Research Study 191. London: Home Office.

Mischel, W. (1966). A social learning view of sex differences. In E. E. Maccoby (ed.), *The Development of Sex Differences* (pp. 56–81). Stanford University Press.

(1970). Sex-typing and socialization. In P. H. Mussen (ed.), *Carmichael's Manual of Child Psychology*, vol. 2 (3rd edn, pp. 1–72). New York: Wiley.

Mitchell, J. (1966). Women: the longest revolution. *New Left Review*, 40: 11–37.

(1974). *Psychoanalysis and Feminism*. London: Allen Lane.

MMWR Weekly (1994). Current trends: homicides among 15–19-year-olds – United States, 1963–1991. *MMWR Weekly*, 43 (40): 725–7.

Moffat, S. D., Hampson, E., and Hatzipantelis, M. (1998). Navigation in a 'virtual' maze: sex differences and correlation with psychometric measures of spatial ability in humans. *Evolution and Human Behavior*, 19: 73–87.

Moin, B. (1994). *Khomeini: Life of the Ayatollah*. Tauris.

Money, J. and Ehrhardt, A. A. (1972). *Man and Woman, Boy and Girl*. Baltimore, MD: Johns Hopkins University Press.

Montemayor, R. (1974). Children's performances in a game and their attraction to it as a function of sex-typed labels. *Child Development*, 45: 152–6.

Morgan, G. A. and Ricciuti, H. N. (1969). Infant's response to strangers during the first year. In B. Foss (ed.), *Determinants of Infant Behaviour*, vol. 4 (pp. 253–72). London: Methuen.

Morgan, M. (1996). Qualitative research: a package deal. *The Psychologist*, 9: 31–2.

Morley, R. (1994). Wife beating and modernization: the case of Papua New Guinea. *Journal of Comparative Family Studies*, 25: 35–52.

Morris, J. (1974). *Conundrum*. London: Faber and Faber.

Moscicki, E. K. (1995). Epidemiology of suicide behaviour. In M. M. Silverman and R. W. Maris (eds.), *Suicide Prevention: Towards the Year 2,000*. New York: Guildford, 22–35.

Mosley, N. (1990). *Hopeful Monsters*. London: Secker and Warburg (quotation from 1991 Minerva edition).

Murnen, S. K. and Stockton, M. (1997). Gender and self-reported sexual arousal in response to sexual stimuli: a meta-analytic review. *Sex Roles*, 37: 135–53.

Murphey, R. J. L. (1979). Sex differences in examination performance: do these reflect differences in ability or sex-role stereotypes? In O. Hartnett, G. Boden, and M. Fuller (eds.), *Women: Sex Role Stereotyping* (pp. 159–67). London: Tavistock.

Mushanga, T. M. (1977–78). Wife victimization in East and Central Africa. *Victimology*, 2: 479–85.

National Center for Injury Prevention and Control (1998). Violence: firearm injuries and fatalities. <http://www.cdc.gov/ncipc/dvp/fafacts.htm>.

National Commission on Marijuana and Drug Abuse (1973). *Drug Use in America*. Washington, DC: US Government Printing Office.

Neppl, T. K. and Murray, A. D. (1997). Social dominance and play patterns among preschoolers: gender comparisons. *Sex Roles*, 36: 381–93.

Nesse, R. M. (1991). What good is feeling bad – the evolutionary benefits of psychic pain. *Sciences*, 31: 30–7.

(2000). Is grief really maladaptive? Book review of John Archer, *The Nature of Grief: The Evolution and Psychology of Reactions to Loss. Evolution and Human Behavior*, 21: 59–61.

New York Times (2001) Nuclear families drop below 25% of households for the first time. 15 May.

Newsham, G. (1994). *In a League of Their Own. Dick Kerr Ladies Football Club 1917–1965*. Chorley, UK: Pride of Publishing.

Newstead, S. E. and Dennis, I. (1990). Blind marking and sex bias in student assessment. *Assessment and Evaluation in Higher Education*, 15: 132–9.

Nicolson, P. (1990). Understanding post-natal depression: a mother-centred approach. *Journal of Advanced Nursing*, 15: 689–95.

(1998) *Post-natal Depression Psychology, Science and the Transition to Motherhood*. London and New York: Routledge.

Nisbett, R. E. (1998). Everyman his own sheriff: violence and the culture of honor in the south. Presented at the 10th Annual Meeting of the Human Behavior and Evolution Society, University of Davis, California, July 8–12.

Nisbett, R. E. and Cohen, D. (1996). *Culture of Honor: The Psychology of Violence in the South*. Boulder, CO: Westview Press.

Noddings, N. (1992). Variability: a pernicious hypothesis. *Review of Educational Research*, 62: 85–8.

Nolen-Hoeksema, S. (1987). Sex differences in unipolar depression: evidence and theory. *Psychological Bulletin*, 101: 259–82.

(1990). *Sex Differences in Depression*. Stanford University Press.

(1995). Gender differences in coping with depression across the lifespan. *Depression*, 3: 81–90.

(1998). *Abnormal Psychology*. Boston, MA: McGraw Hill.

Nolen-Hoeksema, S. and Girgus, J. S. (1994). The emergence of gender differences in depression during adolescence. *Psychological Bulletin*, 115: 424–43.

Nolen-Hoeksema, S., Larson, J., and Grayson, C. (1999). Explaining the gender difference in depressive symptoms. *Journal of Personality and Social Psychology*, 77: 1061–72.

Noseworthy, C. M. and Lott, A. J. (1984). The cognitive organization of gender-stereotypic categories. *Personality and Social Psychology Bulletin*, 10: 474–81.

Oakley, A. (1974). *Housewife*. London: Allen Lane.

O'Brien, M. and Huston, A. C. (1985). Activity level and sex stereotyped toy choice in toddler boys and girls. *Journal of Genetic Psychology*, 146: 527–34.

O'Connell, H. E., Hutson, J. M., Anderson, C. R., and Plenter, R. J. (1998). Anatomical relationship between urethra and clitoris. *Journal of Urology*, 159: 1892–7.

O'Connor, D. B., Archer, J., and Wu, F. W. C. (2001a). Androgens and cognitive function in men. In B. Robaire, H. Chemes, and C. Mordes (eds.), *Andrology in the 21st Century* (pp. 113–22). Englewood, NJ: Medimond Publishing Co.

(2001b). Measuring aggression: self-reports, partner reports and responses to provoking scenarios. *Aggressive Behavior*, 27: 73–101.

O'Connor, D. B., Archer, J., Hair, W. M., and Wu, F. C. W. (2001c). Activational effects of testosterone on cognitive function in men. *Neuropsychologia*, 39: 1385–94.

Office for National Statistics (1999). *Annual Abstract of Statistics*. Edition 135. London: The Stationery Office.

Olioff, M. and Stewart, J. (1978). Sex differences in the play behavior of prepubescent rats. *Physiology and Behavior*, 20: 113–15.

Olivardia, R., Pope, H. G., Mangweth, B., and Hudson, J. I. (1995). Eating disorders in college men. *American Journal of Psychiatry*, 152: 1279–85.

Oliver, M. B. and Hyde, J. S. (1993). Gender differences in sexuality: a meta-analysis. *Psychological Bulletin*, 114: 29–51.

Orlofsky, J. L. (1981). Relationships between sex role attitudes and personality traits and the sex role behavior scale – 1: a new measure of masculine and feminine role behaviors and interests. *Journal of Personality and Social Psychology*, 40: 927–40.

Orlofsky, J. L. and O'Heron, C. A. (1987a). Stereotypic and nonstereotypic sex role trait and behavior orientations: implications for personal adjustment. *Journal of Personality and Social Psychology*, 52: 1034–42.

(1987b). Development of a short form sex role behavior scale. *Journal of Personality Assessment*, 51: 267–77.

Orlofsky, J. L., Cohen, R. S., and Ramsden, M. W. (1985). Relationship between sex-role attitudes and personality traits and the revised sex-role behavior scale. *Sex Roles*, 12: 377–91.

Orlofsky, J. L., Ramsden, M. W., and Cohen, R. S. (1982). Development of the revised sex-role behavior scale. *Journal of Personality Assessment*, 46: 632–8.

Ormerod, M. B. (1981). Factors differentially affecting the science subject preferences, choices and attitudes of boys and girls. In A. Kelly (ed.), *The Missing Half: Girls and Science Education* (pp. 100–12). Manchester University Press.

Osgood, C. E., Succi, G. J., and Tannenbaum, P. H. (1957). *The Measurement of Meaning*. Urbana, IL: University of Illinois Press.

Osofsky, J. and Seidenberg, R. (1970). Is female menopausal depression inevitable? *American Journal of Obstetrics and Gynecology*, 36: 611–15.

Owens, L. D. (1996). Sticks and stones and sugar and spice: girls' and boys' aggression in schools. *Australian Journal of Guidance and Counselling*, 6: 45–55.

Pagelow, M. D. (1984). *Family Violence*. New York: Praeger.

Parker, G. A. (1974). Courtship persistence and female-guarding as male time investment strategies. *Behaviour*, 48: 157–84.

Parlee, R. M. (1982). The psychology of the menstrual cycle: biological and physiological perspectives. In R. C. Friedman (ed.), *Behavior and the Menstrual Cycle* (pp. 77–99). New York: Dekker.

Parry, B. L. (1994). Biological correlates of premenstrual complaints. In J. H. Gold and S. K. Severino (eds.), *Premenstrual Dysphoria Myths and Realities* (pp. 47–66). Washington, D.C.: American Psychiatric Press.

Parry, G. (1983). A British version of the Attitudes towards Women Scale (AWS-B). *British Journal of Social Psychology*, 22: 261–3.

Parsons, M. (2000). Sexuality and perversion a hundred years on: discovering what Freud discovered. *International Journal of Psychoanalysis*, 81: 37–51.

Parsons, T. and Bales, R. F. (1955). *Family, Socialization, and Interaction Processes*. Glencoe, IL: Free Press.

Patterson, T. L., Smith, L. W., and Smith, T. L. et al. (1992). Symptoms in late adulthood are related to childhood social deprivation and misfortune in men but not in women. *Journal of Behavioral Medicine*, 15: 113–25.

Payne, T. J., Connor, J. M., and Colletti, G. (1987). Gender-based schematic processing: an empirical investigation and reevaluation. *Journal of Personality and Social Psychology*, 52: 937–45.

Pennington, V. (1957). Meprobamate (Miltown) in premenstrual tension. *Journal of the American Medical Association*, 164: 638–41.

Peplau, L. A. and Conrad, E. (1989). Beyond nonsexist research: the perils of feminist methods in psychology. *Pychology of Women Quarterly*, 13: 379–400.

Perry, K. (2000). Secret aid for forced marriage victims. *The Guardian*, London: 5 August, p. 9.

Peterson, M. K. and Smith, P. B. (1997) Does national culture or ambient temperature explain cross-national differences in role stress? No sweat! *Academy of Management Journal*, 40: 930–46.

Phillips, K. and Silverman, L. K. (1997). Differences in relationship of menstrual cycle phase to spatial performance on two- and three-dimensional tasks. *Hormones and Behavior*, 32: 167–75.

Phoenix, C. H. (1974). Prenatal testosterone in the nonhuman primate and its consequences for behavior. In R. C. Friedman, R. M. Richart, and R. L. van de Wiele (eds.), *Sex Differences in Behavior* (pp. 19–32). New York: Wiley.

Phoenix, C. H., Goy, R. W., Gerall, A. A., and Young, W. C. (1959). Organizing action of prenatally administered testosterone propionate on the tissues mediating mating behavior in the female guinea pig. *Endocrinology*, 71: 231–8.

Piccinelli, M. and Wilkinson, G. (2000). Gender differences in depression: critical review. *British Journal of Psychiatry*, 177: 486–92.

Pitcher, E. G. and Schultz, L. H. (1983). *Boys and Girls at Play: The Development of Sex Roles*. New York: Praeger.

Plavcan, J. M. and van Schaik, C. P. (1997). Intrasexual competition and body weight dimorphism in anthropoid primates. *American Journal of Physical Anthropology*, 103, 27–68.

Plumb, P. and Cowan, G. (1984). A developmental study of desterotyping and androgynous activity preferences of tomboys, nontomboys, and males. *Sex Roles*, 10, 703–12.

Pollard, P. (1992). Judgements about victims and attackers in depicted rapes: A review. *British Journal of Social Psychology*, 31: 309–26.

  (1994). Sexual violence against women: characteristics of typical perpetrators. In J. Archer (ed.), *Male Violence* (pp. 170–94). London and New York: Routledge.

Pomerleau, A., Bolduc, D., Malcuit, G., and Cossette, L. (1990). Pink or blue: environmental gender stereotypes in the first two years of life. *Sex Roles*, 22: 359–67.

Porteus, S. D. (1965). *Porteus Maze Test: Fifty Years Application*. Palo Alto, CA: Pacific Books.

Powlishta, K. K. (1995). Intergroup processes in childhood: social categorization and sex role development. *Developmental Psychology*, 31: 781–8.

Powlishta, K. K. and Maccoby, E. E. (1990). Resource utilization in mixed-sex dyads: the influence of adult presence and task type. *Sex Roles*, 23: 223–40.

Pratto, F. (1996). Sexual politics: the gender gap in the bedroom, the cupboard, and the cabinet. In D. M. Buss and N. Malamuth (eds.), *Sex, Power and Conflict: Evolutionary and Feminist Perspectives* (pp. 179–230). New York: Oxford University Press.

Pratto, F. and Hegarty, P. (2000). The political psychology of reproductive strategies. *Psychological Sciences*, 11: 57–62.

Pratto, F., Sidanius, J., Stallworth, L. M., and Malle, B. F. (1994). Social dominance orientation: a personality variable relevant to social roles and intergroup relations. *Journal of Personality and Social Psychology*, 67: 741–63.

Pratto, F., Stallworth, L. M., Sidanius, J., and Siers, B. (1997). The gender gap in occupational role attainment: a social dominance approach. *Journal of Personality and Social Psychology*, 72: 37–53.

Quadagno, D. M., Briscoe, R., and Quadagno, J. S. (1977). Effect of perinatal gonadal hormones on selected nonsexual behavior patterns: a critical assessment of the human and nonhuman literature. *Psychological Bulletin*, 84: 62–80.

Quetelet, A. (1833/1984). *Recherches sur le penchant au crime aux différents âges.* Bruxelles: M. Hayez. [Trans. S. F Sylvester, as "Research on the propensity for crime at different ages." Cincinnati, Ohio: Anderson.]

Quillin, Vio. (1984). *Women's Work.* London: Elm Tree Books/Hamish Hamilton.

Radloff, L. S. (1980). Depression and the empty nest. *Sex Roles*, 6: 775–81.

Raine, A., Brennan, P. (A.), and Farrington, D. P. (1997). Biosocial bases of violence: conceptual and theoretical issues. In A. Raine, P. A. Brennan, D. P. Farrington, and A. A. Mednick (eds.), *Biosocial Bases of Violence* (pp. 1–20). New York: Plenum.

Ramcharan, S., Love, E., Fick, G., and Goldfien, A. (1992). The epidemiology of premenstrual symptoms in a population-based sample of 2650 urban women: attributable risk and risk factors. *Journal of Clinical Epidemiology*, 45: 377–92.

Rapee, R. M. (1991). Generalized anxiety disorder: a review of clinical features and theoretical concepts. *Clinical Psychology Review*, 11: 419–40.

Reinsch, J. M. (1981). Prenatal exposure to synthetic progestins increases potential for aggression in humans. *Science*, 211: 1171–3.

Rekers, G. A. and Yates, C. E. (1976). Sex-typed play in feminoid boys versus normal boys and girls. *Journal of Abnormal Child Psychology*, 4: 1–8.

Rheingold, H. and Cook, K. (1975). The context of boys' and girls' rooms as an index of parents' behavior. *Child Development*, 46: 459–63.

Ridley, M. (1993). *The Red Queen: Sex and the Evolution of Human Nature.* London: Viking.

Riley, H. T., Bryant, D. M., Carter, R. E., and Parkin, D. T. (1995). Extra-pair fertilizations and paternity defence in house martins, *Delichon urbica. Animal Behaviour*, 49: 495–509.

Robinson, S. J. and Manning, J. T. (2000). The ratio of 2nd to 4th digit length and male homosexuality. *Evolution and Human Behavior*, 21: 333–45.

Roscoe, W. (1994). How to become a berdache: towards a unified analysis of gender diversity. In G. Herdt (ed.), *Third Sex, Third Gender Beyond Sexual Dimorphism in Culture and History* (pp. 329–72). New York: Zone Books.

(1998). *Changing Ones: Third and Fourth Genders in Native North America.* Houndmills, Basingstoke, UK: Macmillan.

Rosenbaum, J. E. (1979). Tournament mobility: career patterns in a corporation. *Administrative Science Quarterly*, 24: 220–41.

(1984). *Career Mobility in a Corporate Hierarchy.* San Diego, CA: Academic Press.

Rosenblatt, P. C. and Cunningham, M. R. (1976). Sex differences in cross-cultural perspective. In B. B. Lloyd and J. Archer (eds.), *Exploring Sex Differences* (pp. 71–94). London and New York: Academic Press.

Rosenblatt, P. C., Walsh, R., and Jackson, D. A. (1976). *Grief and Mourning in Cross-cultural Perspective.* Human Relations Area File Press.

Rosenkrantz, P. S., Vogel, S. R., Bee, H., Broverman, I. K., and Broverman, D. M. (1968). Sex role stereotypes and self-concepts in college students. *Journal of Consulting and Clinical Psychology*, 32: 287–95.

Rosenthal, R. (1984). *Meta-analytic Procedures for Social Research*. Beverly Hills, CA: Sage.

(1990). How are we doing in soft psychology? *American Psychologist*, 45: 775–7.

(1991). Meta-analysis: a review. *Psychosomatic Medicine*, 53: 247–71.

Rossi, A. S. (1964). Equality between the sexes: an immodest proposal. *Daedalus*, 93: 607–52.

(1973). Maternalism, sexuality and the new feminism. In J. Zubin and J. Money (eds.) *Contemporary Sexual Behavior: Critical Issues for the 1970s* (pp. 145–73). Baltimore: Johns Hopkins University Press.

(1977). A biosocial perspective on parenting. *Daedalus*, 106: 1–31.

(1984). Gender and parenthood. *American Sociological Review*, 49: 1–19.

Rubin, L. (1985). *Just Friends: The Role of Friendship in our Lives*. New York and London: Harper and Row.

Rubin, J. Z., Provenzano, F. J., and Luria, Z. (1974). The eye of the beholder: parents' views on the sex of newborns. *American Journal of Orthopsychiatry*, 44: 512–19.

Ruble, D. N. and Brooks-Gunn, J. (1979). Menstrual symptoms: a social recognition analysis. *Journal of Behavioral Medicine*, 2: 171–94.

Ruble, D. N. and Stangor, C. (1987). Stalking the elusive gender schema: insights from developmental and social psychological analyses of gender schemas. *Social Cognition*, 4: 227–61.

Rudman, L. A. and Glick, P. (1999). Feminized management and backlash towards agentic women: the hidden costs to women of a kinder, gentler image of middle managers. *Journal of Personality and Social Psychology*, 77: 1004–10.

Russo, N. F., Kelly, R. M., and Deacon, M. (1991). Gender and success-related attributions: beyond individualistic conceptions of achievement. *Sex Roles*, 25: 331–50.

Rutter, M. (1981). *Maternal Deprivation Reassessed* (2nd edn). Harmondsworth: Penguin.

(1999). Review of "The nurture assumption: why children turn out the way they do" by J. R. Harris. *The Times Higher Educational Supplement*, 22 January, p. 29.

Ryan, K. M. (1998). The relationship between courtship violence and sexual aggression in college students. *Journal of Family Violence*, 13: 377–94.

Sanday, P. R. (1981). The socio-cultural context of rape: a cross-cultural study. *Journal of Social Issues*, 37: 5–27.

Sankis, L. M., Corbitt. E. M., and Widiger, T. A. (1999). Gender bias in the English language? *Journal of Personality and Social Psychology*, 77: 1289–95.

Sarason, I. G. and Sarason, B. R. (1999). *Abnormal Psychology The Problem of Maladaptive Behavior 9th Edition*. Upper Saddle River, NJ: Prentice Hall.

Sarbin, T. R. (1954). Role theory. In G. Lindzey (ed.), *Handbook of Social Psycholoogy, Volume 1: Theory and Method* (pp. 223–258). Cambridge, MA: Addison-Wesley Publishing Co.

Sayers, J. (1982). *Biological Politics: Feminist and Anti-Feminist Perspectives*. London: Tavistock.

Schachter, S. and Singer, J. (1962). Cognitive, social and psychological determinants of emotional state. *Psychological Review*, 69: 379–99.

Schaffer, D., Garland, A., Gould, M., Fisher, P., and Trautman, P. (1988). Preventing teenage suicide: a critical review. *Journal of the American Academy of Child and Adolescent Psychiatry*, 27: 275–91.

Schaffer, H. R. and Emerson, P. (1964). The development of attachments in infancy. *Monographs of the Society for Research in Child Development*, 29, Serial no. 94, no. 3.

Schafer, R. (1977). Problems in Freud's psychology of women. In H. P. Blum (ed.), *Female Psychology: Contemporary Psychoanalytic Views*. New York: International Universities Press.

Schaller, M. and Latané, B. (1996). Dynamic social impact and the evolution of social representations: a natural history of stereotypes. *Journal of Communication*, 46: 64–71.

Scheper-Hughes, N. (1992). *Death Without Weeping: The Violence of Everyday Life in Brazil*. Berkeley, CA: University of California Press.

Schlegal, A. (1972). *Male Dominance and Female Autonomy*. New Haven, CT: Human Relations Area File Press.

Schneider, J. A., O'Leary, A., and Jenkins, S. R. (1995). Gender, sexual orientation and disordered eating. *Psychology and Health*, 10: 113–28.

Schuler, S. R., Hashemi, S. M., Riley, A. P., and Akhter, S. (1996). Credit programs, patriarchy and men's violence in rural Bangladesh. *Social Science and Medicine*, 43: 1729–42.

Schwartz, S. H. (1994). Beyond individualism/collectivism. New cultural dimensions of values. In U. Kim, H. C. Triandis, C. Kagitcibasi, S. Choi, and G. Yoon (eds.), *Individualism and Collectivism: Theory, Method and Applications* (pp. 85–119). Thousand Oaks, CA: Sage.

Selander, R. K. (1972). Sexual selection and dimorphism in birds. In B. B. Campbell (ed.), *Sexual Selection and the Descent of Man* (pp. 180–230). Chicago: Aldine.

Seligman, M. E. P. (1975). *Helplessness: On Depression, Development and Death*. San Francisco: Freeman.

Serbin, L. A., O'Leary, K. D., Kent, R. N., and Tonick, I. J. (1973). A comparison of teacher response to preacademic problems and problem behavior of boys and girls. *Child Development*, 44: 796–804.

Shapiro, D. Y. (1979). Social behaviour, group structure, and the control of sex reversal in hermaphroditic fish. In J. S. Rosenblatt, R. A. Hinde, C. Beer, and M. C. Busnel (eds.), *Advances in the Study of Behavior*, vol. 10. New York: Academic Press.

Sherfey, M. J. (1973). *The Nature and Evolution of Female Sexuality*. New York: Vintage.

Shields, M. and Duveen, G. (1982). Animism and gender concepts in young children's representations of persons. Paper presented at British Psychological Society London Conference, December.

  (1986). The young child's image of the person and the social world: some aspects of the child's representations of persons. In J. Cook-Gumperz, W. A. Corsaro, and J. Streeck (eds.), *Children's Worlds and Children's Language* (pp. 173–203). Berlin and New York: Mouton de Gruyter.

Shirley, L. (2000). The development of sex-congruent preference in infancy – a longitudinal study. Unpublished Doctoral dissertation, University of Durham, UK.

Shirley, L. and Campbell, A. (2000). Same-sex preference in infancy: visual preference for sex-congruent stimuli at three months. *Psychology, Evolution and Gender*, 2: 1–18.

Short, R. V. (1980). The origins of sexuality. In C. R. Austin and R. V. Short (eds.), *Reproduction in Mammals, Vol. 8: Human Sexuality* (pp. 1–33). Cambridge University Press.

Siegal, M. (1987). Are sons and daughters treated more differently by fathers than by mothers? *Developmental Review*, 7: 183–209.

Silverman, I. and Eals, M. (1992). Sex differences in spatial abilities: evolutionary theory and data. In J. H. Barkow, L. Cosmides, and J. Tooby (eds.) *The Adapted Mind Evolutionary Psychology and the Generation of Culture*. New York and Oxford: Oxford University Press.

Silverman, I. and Phillips, K. (1998). The evolutionary psychology of spatial sex differences. In C. Crawford and D. L. Krebs (eds.), *Handbook of Evolutionary Psychology: Ideas, Issues and Applications* (pp. 595–612). Mahwah, NJ: Erlbaum.

Silverman, I., Phillips, K., and Silverman, L. K. (1996). Homogeneity of effect sizes for sex across spatial tests and cultures: implications for hormonal theories. *Brain and Cognition*, 31: 90–4.

Singh, D. (1993). Adaptive significance of female physical attractiveness: role of waist-to-hip ratio. *Journal of Personality and Social Psychology*, 65: 293–307.

(1995). Female judgements of male attractiveness and desirability for relationships: role of waist-to-hip ratio and financial status. *Journal of Personality and Social Psychology*, 69: 1089–101.

(2001). Cross cultural data validates waist–hip ratio and female attractiveness hypothesis. Paper presented at the Human Behavior and Evolution Society meeting, University College London, 13–17 June.

Singh, D. and Luis, S. (1995). Ethnic and gender consensus for the effect of waist-to-hip ratio on judgement of women's attractiveness. *Human Nature*, 6: 51–65.

Slaby, R. G. and Frey, K. S. (1975). Development of gender constancy and selective attention to same-sex models. *Child Development*, 46: 849–56.

Slocum, S. (1975). Woman the gatherer: male bias in anthropology. In R. Reiter (ed.), *Towards an Anthropology of Women* (pp. 36–50). New York: Monthly Review Press.

Sluckin, W., Herbert, M., and Sluckin, A. (1983). *Maternal Bonding*. Oxford: Basil Blackwell.

Smith, C. and Lloyd, B. B. (1978). Maternal behavior and perceived sex of infant. *Child Development*, 49: 1263–5.

Smith, E. A., Borgerhoff Mulder, M., and Hill, K. (2000). Evolutionary analysis of human behaviour: a commentary on Daly and Wilson. *Animal Behaviour*, 60: F21–F26 <http://www.idealibrary.com>.

Smith, P. K. (1980). Shared care of young children: alternative models to monotropism. *Merrill Palmer Quarterly*, 26: 371–90.

(1982). Does play matter: functional and evolutionary costs of animal and human play. *Behavioral and Brain Sciences*, 5: 139–84 (including commentaries).

(1986). Exploration, play and social development in boys and girls. In D. Hargreaves and A. Colley (eds.), *The Psychology of Sex Roles* (pp. 118–41). London and New York: Harper and Row.

(1989). Ethological approaches to the study of aggression in children. In J. Archer and K. Browne (eds.) *Human Aggression: Naturalistic Approaches* (pp. 65–93). London and New York: Routledge.

Smith, P. K. and Boulton, M. J. (1990). Rough-and-tumble play, aggression and dominance: perception and behavior in children's encounters. *Human Development*, 33: 271–82.

Smith, P. K. and Daglish, L. (1977). Sex differences in parent and infant behavior in the home. *Child Development*, 48: 1250–4.

Smith, P. K. and Lewis, K. (1985). Rough-and-tumble play, fighting, and chasing in nursery school children. *Ethology and Sociobiology*, 6: 175–81.

Smith-Rosenberg, C. (1975). The female world of love and ritual: relations between women in nineteenth-century America. *Signs*, 1: 1–29.

Smuts, B. (1992). Male aggression against women: an evolutionary perspective. *Human Nature* 3: 1–44.

(1995). The evolutionary origins of patriarchy. *Human Nature*, 6: 1–32.

Social Focus on Families (1997). London: Crown publication.

Solloway, F. J. (1995). Birth order and evolutionary psychology: a meta-analysis. *Psychological Inquiry*, 6: 75–80.

Sommer, B. (1982). Cognitive behavior and the menstrual cycle. In R. C. Friedman (ed.), *Behavior and the Menstrual Cycle* (pp. 101–27). New York: Dekker.

South, S. J. and Spitze, G. (1994). Housework in marital and nonmarital households. *American Sociological Review*, 59: 327–47.

Spence, J. T. (1984). Masculinity, femininity and gender related traits: a conceptual analysis and critique of current research. In B. A. Maher and W. B. Maher (eds.), *Progress in Experimental Personality Research*, vol. 13 (pp. 2–97). New York: Academic Press.

(1985). Gender identity and its implications for the concepts of masculinity and femininity. In T. B. Sondereggar (ed.), *Nebraska Symposium on Motivation No. 32* (pp. 59–95). Lincoln: University of Nebraska Press.

(1993). Gender-related traits and gender ideology: evidence for a multifactorial theory. *Journal of Personality and Social Psychology*, 64: 624–35.

Spence, J. T. and Buckner, C. E. (2000). Instrumental and expressive traits, trait stereotypes, and sexist attitudes: What do they signify? *Psychology of Women Quarterly*, 24: 44–62.

Spence, J. T. and Helmreich, R. L (1972). The Attitudes Towards Women Scale. *JSAS Catalog of Selected Documents in Psychology*, 2: MS 153.

(1978). *Masculinity and Femininity: Their Psychological Dimensions, Correlates and Antecedents.* Austin: University of Texas Press.

(1979). Comparison of masculine and feminine personality attributes and sex role attitudes across age groups. *Developmental Psychology*, 15: 583–4.

(1981). Androgyny versus gender schema: a comment on Bem's gender schema theory. *Psychological Review*, 88: 365–8.

Spence, J. T., Helmreich, R., and Stapp, J. (1973). A short version of the Attitudes Towards Women Scale (AWS). *Bulletin of the Psychonomic Society*, 2: 219–20.

(1974). The Personal Attributes questionnaire: a measure of sex role stereotypes and masculinity–femininity. *JSAS Catalog of Selected Documents in Psychology*, 4: 43 (MS 617).

(1975). Ratings of self and peers on sex role attributes and their relation to self-esteem and conceptions of masculinity and femininity. *Journal of Personality and Social Psychology*, 32: 29–39.

Srole, L. and Fisher, A. K. (1980). The Midtown Manhattan longitudinal studies "the mental Paradise Lost" doctrine. *Archives of General Psychiatry*, 37: 209–21.

Stacey, J. and Biblarz, T. J. (2001). (How) does the sexual orientation of parents matter? *American Sociological Review*, 66: 159–83.

Stangor, C. and Ruble, D. N. (1987). Development of gender role knowledge and gender constancy. In L. S. Liben and M. L. Signorella (eds.), *Children's Gender Schemata* (pp. 5–22). San Francisco: Jossey-Bass.

Steele, C. M. (1997). A threat in the air: how stereotypes shape intellectual identity and performance. *American Psychologist*, 52: 613–29.

Steinhausen, H. C. (1994). Anorexia and bulimia nervosa. In M. M. Rutter, E. Taylor, and L. Hersov (eds.), *Child and Adolescent Psychiatry* (pp. 425–40). Oxford: Blackwell Scientific Publications.

Steinman, D. L., Wincze, J. P., Sakheim, K., Barlow D. H., and Mavissakalian, M. (1981). A comparison of male and female patterns of sexual arousal. *Archives of Sexual Behavior*, 10: 529–47.

Steinmetz, S. (1977). Wifebeating, husbandbeating: a comparison of the use of physical violence between spouses to resolve marital fights. In M. Roy (ed.), *Battered Women: A Psychosociological Study of Domestic Violence* (pp. 63–72). New York: Van Nostrand.

Stern, M. and Karraker, K. H. (1989). Sex stereotyping of infants: a review of gender labelling studies. *Sex Roles*, 20: 501–22.

Sternglanz, S. and Serbin, L. A. (1974). Sex-role stereotyping in children's television programmes. *Developmental Psychology*, 10: 710–15.

Stockard, J. and Johnson, M. M. (1979). The social origins of male dominance. *Sex Roles*, 5: 199–218.

Stoll, C. S. (1978). *Female and Male: Socialization, Social Roles and Social Structure*. Dubuque, IA: William C. Brown.

Straus, M. A. (1990). The Conflict Tactics Scales and its critics: an evaluation and new data on validity and reliability. In M. A. Straus and R. J. Gelles (eds.), *Physical Violence in American Societies: Risk Factors and Adaptations to Violence in 8,145 Families* (pp. 49–73). New Brunswick: Transaction Publications.

    (1997). Physical assaults by women partners: a major social problem. In M. R. Walsh (ed.), *Women, Men and Gender: Ongoing Debates* (pp. 210–21). New Haven, CT: Yale University Press.

Straus, M., Gelles, R., and Steinmetz, S. (1980). *Behind Closed Doors: Violence in the American Family*. New York: Anchor Press.

Straus, M. A., Hamby, S. L., Boney-McCoy, S., and Sugarman, D. B. (1996). The revised Conflict Tactics Scales (CTS2): Development and preliminary psychometric data. *Journal of Family Issues*, 17: 283–316.

Stroebe, M. S. and Stroebe, W. (1983). Who suffers more? Sex differences in health risks of the widowed. *Psychological Bulletin*, 93: 279–301.

Struckman-Johnson, C. (1988). Forced sex on dates: it happened to men too. *Journal of Sex Research*, 24, 234–41.

Sulloway, F. J. (1995). Birth order and evolutionary psychology: a meta-analytic overview. *Psychological Inquiry*, 6: 75–80.

Susser, S. A. and Keating, C. F. (1990). Adult sex role orientation and perceptions of aggressive interactions between girls and boys. *Sex Roles*, 23: 147–55.

Swim, J. K. and Cohen, L. L. (1997). Overt, covert, and subtle sexism: a comparison between the Attitudes Towards Women and Modern Sexism Scales. *Psychology of Women Quarterly*, 21: 103–18.

Swim, J., Borgida, E., Maruyama, G., and Myers, D. G. (1989). Joan McKay versus John McKay: do gender stereotypes bias evaluations? *Psychological Bulletin*, 105: 409–29.

Swim, J. K. and Sanna, L. J. (1996). He's skilled, she's lucky: a meta-analysis of observers' attributions for women's and men's success and failures. *Personality and Social Psychology Bulletin*, 22: 507–19.

Symonds, A. (1971). Phobias after marriage: women's declarations of independence. *American Journal of Psychoanalysis*, 31: 144–52.

Symons, D. (1979). *The Evolution of Human Sexuality*. New York: Oxford University Press.
   (1995). Beauty is in the adaptations of the beholder: the evolutionary psychology of female sexual attractiveness. In P. R. Abramson and S. D. Pinkerton (eds.), *Sexual Nature, Sexual Culture* (pp. 80–118). Chicago and London: University of Chicago Press.

Szasz, T. S. (1970). *The Manufacture of Madness*. New York: Harper and Row.

Szymanski, S. R., Lieberman, J. A. and Alvir, J. M. et al. (1995). Gender differences in the onset of illness, treatment response, course and biologic indexes in first-episode schizophrenia patients. *American Journal of Psychiatry*, 152: 519–25.

Tapper, K. and Boulton, M. (1998). Unpublished data, Department of Psychology, Keele University, Staffordshire, UK.

Tassinary, L. G. and Hansen, K. A. (1998). A crucial test of the waist-to-hip ratio hypothesis of female physical attractiveness. *Psychological Science*, 9: 150–5.

Tavris, C. (1992). *The Mismeasure of Woman*. New York: Simon and Schuster.

Taylor, M. C. and Hall, J. A. (1982). Psychological androgyny: theories, methods and conclusions. *Psychological Bulletin*, 92: 347–66.

Tennes, K. M. and Lampl, E. E. (1964). Stranger and separation anxiety. *Journal of Mental and Nervous Diseases*, 139: 247–54.

Terman, L. M. (1925). Mental and physical traits of a thousand gifted children. *Genetic Studies of Genius, vol. 1*. Stanford University Press.

Thompson, E. H. and Pleck, J. H. (1986). The structure of male role norms. *American Behavioral Scientist*, 29: 531–43.

Thompson, S. K. and Bentler, P. M. (1971). The priority of cues in sex discrimination by children and adults. *Developmental Psychology*, 5: 181–5.

Thompson, T. L. and Zerbinos, E. (1995). Gender roles in animated cartoons: has the picture changed in 20 years? *Sex Roles*, 32: 651–73.

Thorne, B. (1986). Boys and girls together . . . but mostly apart: gender arrangements in elementary schools. In W. W. Hartup and Z. Rubin (eds.), *Relationships and Development* (pp. 167–84). Hillsdale, NJ: Lawrence Erlbaum.
   (1993). *Gender Play: Girls and Boys in School*. Buckingham, UK: Open University Press.

Thornhill, R., Gangestad, S. W., and Comer, R. (1997). Human female orgasm and mate fluctuating asymmetry. *Animal Behaviour*, 50: 1601–15.

Thornhill, R. and Thornhill, N. W. (1992). The evolutionary psychology of men's coercive sexuality. *Behavioral and Brain Sciences*, 15: 363–421 (including commentaries).

Tiefer, L. (1978). The context and consequences of contemporary sex research: a feminist perspective. In T. E. McGill, D. A. Dewsbury, and B. D. Sachs (eds.), *Sex and Behavior: Status and Prospects*. New York: Plenum.

Tieger, T. (1980). On the biological basis of sex differences in aggression. *Child Development*, 51: 943–63.

Tiger, L. (1970). The possible biological origins of sexual discrimination. *Impact of Science on Society*, 20: 29–45.

(1999). *The Decline of Males*. New York: Golden Books.

Tinbergen, N. (1963). On the aims and methods of ethology. *Zeitschrift fur Tierpsychologie*, 20: 410–13.

Tizard, B. and Hodges, J. (1978). The effect of early institutional rearing on the development of eight-year-old children. *Journal of Child Psychology and Psychiatry*, 29: 99–118.

Tooby, J. (1999). The view from the president's window: the most testable concept in biology, Part 1. *Human Behavior and Evolution Society Newsletter*, 8 (2): 1–5.

Tooby, J. and Cosmides, L. (1992). The psychological foundations of culture. In J. H. Barkow, L. Cosmides, and J. Tooby (eds.), *The Adapted Mind: Evolutionary Psychology and the Evolution of Culture* (pp. 19–136). New York and Oxford: Oxford University Press.

Top, T. J. (1991). Sex bias in the evaluation of performance in the scientific, artistic, and literary professions: A review. *Sex Roles*, 24: 73–106.

Touhey, J. C. (1974). Effects of additional women professionals on ratings of occupational prestige and desirability. *Journal of Personality and Social Psychology*, 29: 86–9.

Tovee, M. J., Reinhardt, Emery, J. L., and Cornelissen, P. L. (1998). Optimum body-mass index and maximum sexual attractiveness. *Lancet*, 352: 548.

Trivers, R. (1972). Parental investment and sexual selection. In B. B. Campbell (ed.), *Sexual Selection and the Descent of Man* (pp. 136–79). Chicago: Aldine.

Turner, P. J. (1991). Relations between attachment, gender, and behavior with peers in preschool. *Child Development*, 63: 1475–88.

Twenge, J. M. (1997a). Attitudes towards women, 1970–1995. *Psychology of Women Quarterly*, 21: 35–51.

(1997b). Changes in masculine and feminine traits over time: a meta-analysis. *Sex Roles*, 36: 305–25.

Ullian, D. Z. (1976). The development of conceptions of masculinity and femininity. In B. B. Lloyd and J. Archer (eds.), *Exploring Sex Differences* (pp. 25–47). London and New York: Academic Press.

Ussher, J. M. (1991). *Women's Madness: Misogyny or Mental Illness*. New York: Harvester Wheatsheaf.

US Bureau of the Census (1998). *Statistical Abstract of the United States* (118th edition). Washington, D.C.

van Wyk, P. H. and Geist, C. S. (1984). Psychosocial development of heterosexual, bisexual, and homosexual behavior. *Archives of Sexual Behavior*, 13: 505–44.

Vandenheede, M. and Bouissou, M. F. (1993). Effects of androgen treatment on fear reactions in ewes. *Hormones and Behavior*, 27: 435–48.

Voyer, D., Voyer, S., and Bryden, M. P. (1995). Magnitude of sex differences in spatial abilities: a meta-analysis and consideration of critical variables. *Psychological Bulletin*, 117: 250–70.

Walker, A. E. (1997). *The Menstrual Cycle*. London and New York: Routledge.

Walker, L. E. A. (1989). Psychology and violence against women. *American Psychologist*, 44: 659–702.

(1990). Response to Mills and Mould. *American Psychologist*, 45: 676–7.

Walker, S. and Richardson, D. S. (1998). Aggression strategies among older adults: delivered but not seen. *Aggression and Violent Behavior: A Review Journal*, 3: 287–94.

Walker, S., Richardson, D. S., and Green, L. R. (2000). Aggression among older adults: the relationship of interaction networks and gender role to direct and indirect responses. *Aggressive Behavior*, 26: 145–54.

Wallen, K. W. (1996). Nature needs nature: the interaction of hormonal and social influences on the development of behavioral sex differences in rhesus monkeys. *Hormones and Behaviour*, 30: 364–78.

Walum, L. R. (1977). *The Dynamics of Sex and Gender: A Sociological Perspective.* Chicago, IL: Rand McNally.

Warren, E. (1997). Sex bias in student assessments. Unpublished M.Phil. dissertation, University of Central Lancashire, Preston, UK.

Washburn, S. L. and Lancaster, C. S. (1968). The evolution of hunting. In R. B. Lee and I. DeVore (eds.), *Man the Hunter* (pp. 293–303). Chicago, IL: Aldine.

Waterman, C. K. and Chiauzzi, E. J. (1982). The role of orgasm in male and female sexual satisfaction. *Journal of Sex Research*, 18: 146–59.

Watt, N. (1999). Terror of couple fleeing a forced marriage. *The Guardian*, London, 17 May, p. 9.

Weedon, C. (1982). Engendering stereotypes. *Journal of Literature, Teaching and Politics*, 1: 37–49.

Weeks, J. (1978). Movements of affirmation: sexual means and homosexual identities. Paper presented at British Sociological Association Conference, University of Sussex.
  (2000) (ed.). *Making Sexual History* (pp. 125–41). Cambridge: Polity Press.

Weine, A. M., Phillips, J. S., and Achenbach, T. M. (1995). Behavioral and emotional problems among Chinese and American children: parent and teacher reports for ages 6 to 13. *Journal of the American Academy of Child and Adolescent Psychology*, 34: 336–47.

Weinreich-Haste, H. (1979). What sex is science? In O. Hartnett, G. Boden, and M. Fuller (eds.), *Women: Sex Role Stereotyping* (pp. 168–81). London: Tavistock.
  (1981). The image of science. In A. Kelly (ed.), *The Missing Half: Girls and Science Education* (pp. 216–29). Manchester University Press.

Weisfeld, G. (1994). Aggression and dominance in the social world of boys and girls. In J. Archer (ed.), *Male Violence* (pp. 42–69). London and New York: Routledge.

Weissman, M. M. and Klerman, G. L. (1977). Sex differences and the epidemiology of depression. *Archives of General Psychiatry*, 34: 98–111.

Weissman, M. M., Bland, R. C., and Canino, G. J. et al. (1996). Cross-national epidemiology of major depression and bipolar disorder. *Journal of the American Medical Association*, 276: 293–9.

Wellings, K., Field, J., Johnson, A. M., and Wadsworth, J. (1994). *Sexual Behaviour in Britain*. Harmondsworth: Penguin.

Wheelright, J. (1989). *Amazons and Military Maids: Women who Dressed as Men in the Pursuit of Life, Liberty and Happiness*. Boston and London: Pandora.

Whiffen, V. E. (1992). Is postpartum depression a distinct diagnosis? *Clinical Psychology Review*, 12: 485–508.

White, J. W. and Kowalski, R. M. (1994). Deconstructing the myth of the nonaggressive woman: a feminist analysis. *Psychology of Women Quarterly*, 18: 487–508.

White, J. W., Smith, P. H., Koss, M. P., and Figueredo, A. J. (2000). Intimate partner aggression – what have we learned? Comment on Archer (2000). *Psychological Bulletin*, 126: 690–6.

Whiting, B. B. and Edwards, C. P. (1988). *Children of Different Worlds: The Formation of Social Behavior*. Cambridge, MA: Harvard University Press.

Whitley, B. E., McHugh, M. C., and Frieze, I. H. (1986). Assessing the theoretical models of sex differences in causal attributions of success and failure. In J. S. Hyde and M. C. Linn (eds.), *The Psychology of Gender: Advances through Meta-analysis* (pp. 102–35). Baltimore, MD: Johns Hopkins University Press.

Wiederman, M. W. and Kendall, E. (1999). Evolution, sex, and jealousy: investigation with a sample from Sweden. *Evolution and Human Behavior*, 20: 121–8.

Wikan, U. (1977). Man becomes woman: transsexualism in Oman as a key to gender roles. *Man*, 12: 304–19.

Wilkinson, S. (1986). *Feminist Social Psychology: Developing Theory and Practice*. Milton Keynes and Philadelphia: Open University Press.

Williams, J. B. W. and Spitzer, R. L. (1983). The issue of sex bias in DSM-III: "A woman's view of the DSM-III" by Marcie Kaplan. *American Psychologist*, 38: 793–8.

Williams, J. E. and Bennett, S. M. (1975). The definition of sex stereotypes via the adjective check list. *Sex Roles*, 1: 327–37.

Williams, J. E. and Best, D. L. (1982). *Measuring Sex Stereotypes: A Thirty-Nation Study*. Beverly Hills, CA: Sage.

(1990). *Measuring Sex Stereotypes: A Multination Study* (rev. edn). Beverly Hills, CA: Sage.

Williams, J. E., Satterwhite, R. C., and Best, D. L. (1999). Pancultural gender stereotypes revisited: the Five Factor Model. *Sex Roles*, 40: 513–25.

Williams, J. E., Satterwhite, R. C., Best, D. L., and Inman, G. L. (in press). Gender stereotypes in 27 countries examined via the Five Factor Model. *International Journal of Psychology*.

Williams, J. M. G., Watts, F. N., MacLeod, C., and Mathews, A. (1997). *Cognitive Psychology and Emotional Disorders*. Chichester: Wiley.

Williamson, S. and Nowak, R. (1998). The truth about women. *New Scientist*, 1 August, pp. 34–5.

Willingham, W. W. and Cole, N. S. (1997). *Gender and Fair Assessment*. Mahwah, NJ, and London: Lawrence Erlbaum.

Wilson, M. and Daly, M. (1992a). Who kills whom in spouse killings? On the exceptional sex ratio of spousal homicides in the United States. *Criminology*, 30: 189–215.

(1992b).The man who mistook his wife for a chattel. In J. H. Barkow, L. Cosmides, and J. Tooby (eds.), *The Adapted Mind* (pp. 289–321). New York: Oxford University Press.

(1993a). Lethal confrontational violence among young men. In N. J. Bell and R. W. Bell (eds.), *Adolescent Risk-Taking* (pp. 84–106). Newbury Park, CA: Sage.

(1993b). An evolutionary psychological perspective on male sexual proprietariness and violence against wives. *Violence and Victims*, 8: 271–94.

(1999). Human evolutionary psychology and animal behaviour. *Animal Behaviour*, 57: 509–19.

Winter, J. S. D., Hughes, I. A., Reyes, F. I., and Faiman, C. (1976). Pituitary–gonadal relations in infancy: 2. Patterns of serum gonadal steroid concentrations in man from birth to two years of age. *Journal of Clinical Endocrinology and Metabolism*, 42: 679–86.

Wolfgang, M. (1958). *Patterns of Criminal Homicide*. Philadelphia, PA: University of Pennsylvania Press.

Wolkind, S. and Rutter, M. (1973). Children who have been "in care": an epidemiological study. *Journal of Child Psychology and Psychiatry*, 14: 97–105.

Wood, W. and Eagly, A. (in press). A cross-cultural analysis of the behavior of women and men: implications for the origins of sex differences. *Psychological Bulletin*.

Woolley, H. T. (1910). A review of the recent literature on the psychology of sex. *Psychological Bulletin*, 7: 335–42.

Wrangham, R. W. (1980). An ecological model of female-bonded primate groups. *Behaviour*, 75: 262–300.

Wright, P. H. (1988). Interpreting research on gender differences in friendship: a case for moderation and a plea for caution. *Journal of Social and Personal Relationships*, 5: 367–73.

Wright, R. (1994). *The Moral Animal: Evolutionary Psychology and Everyday Life*. New York: Pantheon.

    (1996). The dissent of woman: what feminists can learn from Darwinism. *Demos*, 10: 18–24.

Wynn, T. G., Tierson, F. D., and Palmer, C. T. (1996). Evolution of sex differences in spatial cognition. *Yearbook of Physical Anthropology*, 39: 11–42.

Yonkers, K. A. and Gurgis, G. (1995). Gender differences in the prevalence and expression of anxiety disorders. In M. V. Seeman (ed.), *Gender and Psychopathology* (pp. 113–30). Washington, D.C.: American Psychiatric Press.

Yount, K. (1986). A theory of productive activity: the relationships among self-concept, gender, sex-role stereotypes, and work-emergent traits. *Psychology of Women Quarterly*, 10: 63–88.

Yu, D. W. and Shepard, G. H. (1998). Is beauty in the eye of the beholder? *Nature*, 396: 321–2.

Zandpour, F. and Harich, K. R. (1996) Think and feel country clusters: a new approach to international advertising standardization. *International Journal of Advertising*, 15: 325–3.

Index

NOTE: page numbers in *italics* refer to tables.

DSM-IV *see Diagnostic and Statistical
    Manual of Mental Disorder*
Dunbar, R. I. M., 214
Durkin, K., 64
Dutton, D. G., 133
Duveen, G., 69

Eagly, A. H.
    approach to analysis, 9, 212
    and attitudes to women, 29–30
    and male power, 50, 55–6
    and occupational achivement, 194, 200
    and social role theory, 13, 23–4, 53–4,
        153, 216, 217
    and status, 25, 40
    and stereotypic traits and roles, 23–5,
        194
Eals, M., 52, 190
earnings, 182, 183, 184–5
eating disorders, 151–2
Eaton, W. O., 74–5
educational achievements, 179, 184, 185
educational decisions, 197–8
educational subjects, 192
effect size, 10–11
ego, 94
Elliot, F. R., 163
Elliott, A., 93
Emerson, P., 172–3
Emlen, S. T., 164, 169
emotions
    fluctuation in women, 137–42
    sex differences, 2–3, 135–6
employment *see* occupations
'empty-nest' phenomenon, 141–2
Enns, L. R., 74
environmental approach, 13, 75–6
    see also biosocial approach; social
        learning theory; social role theory
environmental influences, 59, 62–3
equality, attitudes toward, 29, 213–14
ethnic groups, in meta-analyses, 212
ethnic variations in family structure,
        161–2, 163
evolutionary approach, 215–17
    to depression, 140, 158
    to family, 167–8, 169

to fear and anxiety, 136
historical context, 214
levels of analysis, 16
to patriarchy, 55
principles of, 13–14
rise of, 56
to sex differences, 12, 215–16, 218,
    219
sexual dimorphism and selection, 43–6
sexual reproduction, 40–1
to spatial abilities, 190–1
to two sexes, 42–3
to violence and aggression, 116–17,
    122–3, 128–9
excitement phase of orgasm, 86
explanations *see* psychological
        explanations
expressiveness
    link with women, 2, 22–3, 24, 25, 30, 31
    and occupational decisions, 196–7
    and sexual division of labour, 53
    and social dominance orientation, 204

Fagot, B. I., 67, 170
families
    changing nature of, 163–4
    compared with households, 160
    men's and women's roles in, 165, *166*
    single parent, 163–4, 177–9
    socialisation in, 60–3
    theories of, 167–70
    variations in, 161–2
    violence in, 123–6, 131–3, 212
    see also childcare and socialisation;
        parents
family researchers, 123–4, 131
fathers
    attachment to children, 173
    paternity uncertainty, 45, 49–50, 216–17
    personality differences among, 180–1
    role in childcare, 177, 179–80
    treatment of boys and girls, 61–2
    see also polygyny
fear, of strangers in infancy, 174
fearfulness, 135–6, 149–50
Feingold, A., 10, 11–12, 135, 186, 187,
    209, 210